PAVED WITH GOOD INTENTIONS

PAVED
WITH
GOOD INTENTIONS

The Failure of Race Relations in Contemporary America

Jared Taylor

Carroll & Graf Publishers, Inc.
New York

First Carroll & Graf Edition 1992

Carroll & Graf Publishers, Inc.
260 Fifth Avenue
New York, NY 10001

Library of Congress Cataloging-in-Publication Data

Manufactured in the United States of America

Acknowledgments

I am grateful to many people who gathered information for this book and who suggested improvements to the text. Byron Walker was an unfailing source of valuable material, and Thomas Jackson and Dr. Wayne Lutton supplied me with useful publications I would not normally have consulted. Carol Fusco tirelessly gathered newspaper clippings and read the manuscript with a critical eye. John Craig sent much useful material, and his comments greatly improved early versions of the text. Dr. Evelyn Rich found many invaluable references, and corrected later versions of the text with great patience and diligence. My editor, Kent Carroll, took a particular interest in the subject and devoted himself to an unusual degree to improving the manuscript.

Finally, I am in deepest debt to my agent, Theron Raines, who was my most generous source of current information and without whose dedication this book would not have been published.

Contents

Introduction

Race is the great American dilemma. This has always been so, and is likely to remain so. Race has marred our past and clouds our future. It is a particularly agonizing and even shameful dilemma because, in so many other ways, the United States has been a blessing to its people and a model for the world.

The very discovery by Europeans of a continent inhabited by Indians was an enormous crisis in race relations—a crisis that led to catastrophe and dispossession for the Indians. The arrival of the first black slaves to Virginia in 1619 set in motion a series of crises that persist to the present. Indirectly, it brought about the bloodiest war America has ever fought, Reconstruction, segregation, the civil rights movement, and the seemingly intractable problems of today's underclass.

Despite enormous effort, especially in the latter half of this century, those two ancient crises remain unresolved. Neither Indians nor blacks are full participants in America; in many ways they lead lives that lie apart from the mainstream.

After 1965, the United States began to add two more racial groups to the uneasy mix that, in the heady days of civil rights successes, seemed finally on the road to harmony. In that year, Congress passed a new immigration law that cut the flow of immigrants from Europe and dramatically increased the flow from Latin America and Asia. Now 90 percent of all legal immigrants are nonwhite, and Asians and Hispanics have joined the American mix in large numbers. The United States has embarked on a policy of multiracial nation-building that is without precedent in the history of the world.

Race is therefore a prominent fact of national life, and if our immigration policies remain unchanged, it will become an increasingly central fact. Race, in ever more complex combinations, will continue to be the great American dilemma.

Nevertheless, even as the nation becomes a mix of many races, the quintessential racial divide in America—the subject of this book—is between black and white. Blacks have been present in large numbers and have played an important part in American history ever since the nation began. Unlike recent immigrants, who are concentrated in Florida, California, New York, and the Southwest, blacks live in almost all parts of the country. Many of our major cities are now largely populated and even governed by blacks. Finally, for a host of reasons, black/white frictions are more obtrusive and damaging than any other racial cleavage in America.

In our multiracial society, race lurks just below the surface of much that is not explicitly racial. Newspaper stories about other things—housing patterns, local elections, crime, antipoverty programs, law-school admissions, mortgage lending, employment rates—are also, sometimes only by implication, about race. When race is not in the foreground of American life, it does not usually take much searching to find it in the background.

Race is a looming presence because it is a category that matters in nearly every way that we know how to measure. The statistical picture of black society, and the real world behind the statistics, are fundamentally different from the world in which whites live. From 1983 to 1988, the homicide rate for young black men increased by two thirds, while the rate for young white men scarcely budged. Black men between ages fifteen and twenty-four are now nearly nine times as likely to kill each other as are whites of the same ages,[1] and homicide has become the leading cause of death for all black men between ages fifteen and forty-four. Murder has become so common that it has dragged down the overall life expectancy for blacks for the fourth straight year, and that of black men for the fifth year in a row. Life expectancy for whites increased or held steady.[2] In Harlem, there are so many killings that a black man living there is less likely to reach age sixty-five than is a man living in Bangladesh.[3] One in four black men in their twenties is either in jail, on parole, or on probation.[4] This is approximately ten times the rate for whites of the same age.[5] Though they are only 12 percent of the population, blacks commit more than half of all rapes and robberies and 60 percent of the murders in America.[6]

Other measures are just as grim. From 1985 to 1990, while syphilis rates for whites continued their long-running decline, they rose 126 percent for black men and 231 percent for black women. Blacks are now fifty times more likely to have syphilis than whites.[7] Blacks have the highest infant mortality rates for any American racial group and are twice as likely as whites to die in their first year.[8] Black children are four times as likely as whites to be living in poverty,[9] and less than half as likely to be living with two parents.[10] Illegitimacy rates for blacks have climbed steadily, and now more than 66 percent of all black children are born out of wedlock. The rate for whites is 19 percent.[11]

Young blacks are half as likely to be working as young whites,[12] and at some urban high schools, nearly 70 percent fail to graduate.[13] The median net worth for a black family is only $3,397, less than one eleventh that of a white family.[14] Blacks are more than four and a half times more likely than whites to be on public assistance,[15] and even after welfare, food stamps, Medicaid, and subsidized housing, the median black household income is only 64 percent of the white median.[16]

Just one or two of these numbers would be evidence of a nation gone wrong. Taken together, they are a catastrophe—and in the time since they were collected, many have gotten worse.

If the races were statistically indistinguishable, or if the advantages were evenly distributed, race might be nothing more than an anthropological curiosity. Unfortunately, the differences are both stark and consistent. They explain why race is the fearful question that looms behind every social problem in America.

"Our nation is moving toward two societies, one black, one white—separate and unequal."[17] This is the most famous sentence in the six-hundred-page Kerner Commission report, published after the race riots of the 1960s. Despite the social programs that the report called for, and despite the progress that blacks have made in some areas, the numbers just cited suggest that our nation has been unable to halt the drift toward two societies.

Something has gone badly wrong. The civil rights movement, which seemed to point the way to unity, has become a divisive struggle for group rights rather than individual freedom. There is very little left of the confidence with which America marched toward the 1970s. Despite the best efforts of an admittedly imperfect society, many of the changes of the past quarter century have been for the worse.

What happened? One of the most important things that happened is that America's thinking about race hardened into doctrine.

On the surface, it might seem otherwise. America often gives the impression of tackling problems of race head on. No other nation in the world has such elaborate mechanisms for taking its own racial temperature or for dissecting the racial implications of every new policy or proposal. There are civil rights acts, equal housing acts, voting rights acts, and commissions and bureaucracies to enforce them. Minority groups have their own organizations that seek out discrimination and prod the nation toward ever-greater awareness of their needs. Local governments, universities, and businesses employ thousands of people to ensure equal opportunity in every area of American life. Our society is officially —and officiously—race-conscious.

At the same time, the race-relations industry operates according to assumptions that have not changed in thirty years. Official thinking about race is a closed book. Despite our obvious failure to reach the racial solutions that seemed within our grasp, any new thinking about race, any departure from the assumptions of the 1960s has become heresy. We have made race such a grim and serious thing that we may speak of it only in a handful of approved phrases. Our very thoughts have become as stilted as our speech.

Race is therefore not only the great dilemma, it is also the great paradox. It is in race relations that America has gone most obviously wrong, yet it is about race that we dare not think anything new or different. If there is a body of thought that shows all the signs of doctrinaire rigidity, willful ignorance, and even duplicity, it is what is thought and said about race. It is where we are failing the worst that honesty and clear thinking are least welcome. Because the field is so dominated by doctrine, public debate about race is as stylized and as predictable as the changing of the guard at Buckingham Palace. Stylized thinking does not solve problems. It makes them worse.

Orthodoxies do not survive unless they are shored up by the forces of authoritarian righteousness. And indeed, race relations give rise to beliefs that are virtually religious. It is one of the few subjects about which one may hold a considered position that others will say is not simply wrong but also *evil.* An imprudent word or ill-chosen phrase can ruin a career; an unguarded comment can make a man be considered unfit to hold public office. There is no other subject in America—not sex, not religion, not drugs, not abortion—about which the forces of orthodoxy are so monolithic and unforgiving.

Naturally, this gives rise to heresies, large and small. Sometimes they break out with a peculiar viciousness of their own, in acts of racial hatred. But more often they lead to cynicism and hypocrisy, to private exchanges of taboo opinions. Anyone who searches his memory—or his conscience—knows that there is no other subject about which public pronouncements diverge so sharply from private opinions.

This would be nothing more than a huge, ironic joke were the subject not one that is crucial to America's future. Lives, public policies, reputations, perhaps even the social order are at stake. We cannot afford to be limited by rigid thinking. An atmosphere of heresy-hunting is not one that leads to understanding. We must set forth the facts of our racial problems without forcing them to fit fruitless conventions.

In a metaphor that is both poetic and disturbing, the essayist Wendell Berry calls American race relations "the hidden wound."[18] A hidden wound *cannot be treated.* This one is festering so deeply that it threatens the health of the entire body politic.

People from every political perspective agree that race relations are a horrible wound crying out for healing. But there can be no cure without correct diagnosis. Correct diagnosis is impossible without honest, even fearless investigation. *At the very least, Ameri-*

cans must be able to talk about race without fear of retribution. If the notion of free speech has any meaning at all, it must apply to the oldest, greatest, most dangerous problem our nation faces. We must say in public what we think in private; we must throw off the shackles of orthodoxy.

Orthodoxy very nearly kept this book from being published. Two editors who rejected the manuscript put it as plainly as possible when they said that for a publisher to accept the book the author would have to be black. These men are prisoners of the mental habits of our time. Though black/white relations are, by definition, experienced by both races, blacks are thought to have the qualifications to write about them but whites are not. Some truths may be uttered by blacks but not by whites. Double standards like this are a sure sign that our thinking has fallen into rigid, even dangerous conventions.

What are these conventions? Although there are many, and much of this book is devoted to refuting them, there is one central doctrine on which they all depend: Whites are responsible for the problems blacks face. Black crime, black poverty, black illegitimacy, black difficulties of all kinds can be traced to a heritage of slavery and to inveterate white racism. In other words, it is the malevolence of whites that causes blacks to fail. Although the doctrine is not often stated as sweepingly or as bluntly as this, it underlies virtually every public pronouncement on race relations and virtually every public program designed to improve them.

One of the less famous sentences in the Kerner Commission report begins with the words, "White racism is essentially responsible for the explosive mixture which has been accumulating in our cities. . . ."[19] This sentence has gotten little attention because its truth was taken for granted.

It is still taken for granted. Yale president Benno Schmidt, devoting his commencement address to the subject of racism, told the Yale Class of 1989, "I hope that you will recognize that the problems of racial injustice in this society require the attention of this nation as urgently as at any time in our history."[20] Susan Estrich, who was Massachusetts governor Michael Dukakis's presidential campaign manager, explains what America should be doing to reduce crime: "fighting racism, in the criminal justice system, in our economic system, and, yes, in the political system, with as much fervor as we fight crime."[21] Not even Jesse Jackson goes much further when he says, "Racism is now so powerful again in our domestic and foreign policy that it threatens the soul of our nation and our status as leader of the free world."[22]

Rev. T. J. Jemison is president of the 7.8-million-member National Baptist Convention, which is the largest black denomination in America. In his 1990 presidential address, he told his church that racism in America "is worse now than it's ever been." The United Church of Christ echoes this view. In a pastoral letter to be read from every pulpit in the denomination, it blamed the "quiet riots" of unemployment, poverty, crime, and family disintegration squarely on racism.[23] A 1987 front-page article in *The Wall Street Journal* quotes a black spokesman who claims, "If you wiped out racism, 90 percent of black people's problems would disappear."[24] The white author of a recent well-received book on race relations agrees. His concluding view is that whites are responsible for the woes of blacks, even for the fact that so many young black men are killing each other that it "amounts to a self-inflicted genocide."[25]

Americans are so accustomed to hearing—and repeating—this view that they scarcely bother to think about what it means. It means, essentially, that white people, not blacks, are responsible for black behavior. It implies that blacks are helpless and cannot make progress unless whites transform themselves. This inverted version of the doctrine, with its unpleasant odor of paternalism, is almost never heard, but it finds expression in a host of race-based explanations that have sprung up to explain the failures of underclass blacks:

Do blacks drop out of school? Teachers are insensitive to their needs. Do black women have children out of wedlock? Slavery broke up the black family. Are blacks more likely than whites to commit crimes? Oppression and poverty explain it. Are ghetto blacks unemployed? White businesses are prejudiced against them. Do blacks have IQ scores fifteen points lower than whites? The tests are biased. Are blacks more likely to be drug addicts? They are frustrated by white society. Are half our convicts black? The police are racist.[26] There is scarcely any form of failure that cannot, in some way, be laid at the feet of racist white people.

This kind of thinking denies that blacks should be expected to take responsibility for their own actions. More subtly, it suggests that they cannot do so. When whites make excuses for the failures of blacks—excuses they would scorn for themselves or for their own children—they treat blacks as inferiors, whether they mean to or not.

Tentatively and hesitantly, a few people have begun to recognize the limits of conventional thinking. Even such pillars of the Democratic Party as Senators Bill Bradley of New Jersey and John Kerry of Massachusetts have begun to break the unwritten rules of public discussion about race. In the spring of 1992, both called on blacks to stop making groundless accusations of racism and to take responsibility for their lives.[27]

No one would argue that America is free of racism. A nation that enslaved blacks, freed them only after a terrible war, disfranchised them, segregated them, lynched them—such a nation cannot entirely free itself from its past. However, though America is by no means perfect, racism is no longer central to its national character.

Of course, it is possible to find instances of cruel and repulsive acts of racism committed against black people in America. Some blacks are no doubt held back by white racism, both subtle and unsubtle. However, white racism has receded dramatically in every area of American life. Wherever it comes to light, it is vigorously denounced by blacks and whites alike. Racism is now more popular as an excuse for black failure than it is plausible as an explanation for it. Often, where racism has not been found, it has been necessary to invent it.

For many people, both white and black, the notion that white racism explains black failure is the key to understanding American society. They are so convinced of the prevalence of white racism that they refuse even to consider the possibility that it may not be the sole obstacle to success for black Americans. For them, white racism is a brutal fact that seldom need be questioned—to question it may be immoral. Assumptions that are thought to be beyond examination often need it most.

This book examines assumptions about racism in several different ways. The first is simply to look for racism. The awful statistics about black crime, poverty, and illegitimacy are not, by themselves, proof of racism. Instead, there must be evidence that blacks are imprisoned, denied work, or impoverished simply because they are black. Many people, both black and white, have looked hard for this evidence but have been unable to find very much. When the circumstances of Americans differ only by race, society treats them much the same.

Second, if whites in America are inveterately bigoted, other nonwhite races should face obstacles similar to those faced by blacks. Yet Chinese, Japanese, Koreans, and even black West Indians have overcome America's storied racism and are often more successful than native-born whites. Instead of complaining about oppression and prejudice—of which there used to be plenty—they have taken responsibility for themselves and seized opportunities for a better life.

Third, America has made historically unprecedented efforts to correct the evils of the past. We have not only prohibited discrimination against blacks but have created preferential opportunities for them. Our crusade to undo the mischief of the past has done mischief of its own, and by formally discriminating against whites, it has stood both justice and the law on their heads.

Finally, America practices a host of double standards that permit much to blacks that is denied to whites. The doctrine of white racism excuses blacks even when they are guilty of what is least tolerated in whites: racism itself.

These are not popular positions to take in America today. Nor is there any joy in calling attention to failure, especially failure in race relations. One cannot express a divergent opinion about race without having one's motives scrutinized. Nevertheless, facts exist independently of motives. It is on a firm foundation of facts that the conclusions of this book, as well as the recommendations in its final chapter, are meant to rest.

Almost from its opening pages, this book casts doubt on the basic assumptions about race and society that have driven social policy for decades. In attempting to show how mistaken assumptions begot mistaken policy, it has been necessary to show just how miserably those policies have failed.

Hideous things are happening in our country. Millions of Americans—many of them black—live in conditions of violence and squalor that would shame the rulers of Third World nations. It takes a certain hardness of heart to live in the same society with such horror, much less to countenance policies that make it worse. The last two chapters of this book are an unblinking look at the misery in which too many black Americans live.

Nevertheless, it would be a mistake to think that this is a gloomy or pessimistic book. The opposite is true. If the policies that brought us this horror were founded on perfect understanding and were the wisest policies imaginable, then we would have reason to be distressed. In fact, though they were propounded with the best of intentions, our understanding and our policies were wrong— sometimes hopelessly wrong. A gloomy book would be one that cheerfully urged yet more measures of the kind that have failed.

Like that on race relations, the consensus that has developed around social programs can be so strident as to discourage debate. Although that consensus has begun to crack, it is still a delicate matter to ask seriously whether the government programs that are supposed to solve our social ills have not actually made them worse.

Single parenthood and illegitimacy, now largely destigmatized, appear again and again in studies of crime, poverty, welfare, and the failure to finish school. There is scarcely a social problem in this country that would not be well on its way toward solution if Americans adopted a rule their ancestors lived by and took for granted: They did not have children until they had a spouse and an income. The concluding chapters of this book seek to understand the connection between welfare and the disappearance of the obstacles—moral, social, and financial—that once prevented Americans from bearing children they could not support. More programs of the kind that were born in the 1960s, and that have continued to grow through every succeeding administration, will have little effect on the great unspoken problem that underlies all the others: Millions of Americans are bringing children into the world whom they cannot support or rear.

This is an especially great and urgent problem for black Americans, who have seen marriage practically disappear from many of their communities. Nevertheless, the same forces of dissolution that have left inner cities in ruins are at work in the larger society. Rates of illegitimacy and marriage breakup among whites are now approaching the rates among blacks that prompted the so-called Moynihan report of the mid-1960s (see Chapter Eight).

It is vital to consider the possibility that welfare has contributed to these problems, because if it has, solutions lie elsewhere. There are effective measures we can take—some simple and short-term, others more complex and far-reaching—once we conclude that our efforts have been misguided. There is bitterness in acknowledging mistakes, but to do so is our only salvation. For if our thinking was wrong, let us think again. If our policies were wrong, let us abandon them. It is *because* we have made such serious errors that this book can be hopeful. With correct diagnosis and proper cure, even the hidden wound can be healed.

1

Racism

O N DECEMBER 28, 1991, THOUSANDS OF BLACK RAP MUSIC FANS gathered in Harlem for what promised to be an especially entertaining performance. Some of the biggest names in "hip-hop"—LL Cool J, Heavy D, Run-D.M.C., and Bell Biv DeVoe—were to play basketball against each other. The event was heavily advertised, and soon there were far more fans than the gymnasium could hold. People without tickets decided to rush the doors and crowd into the gymnasium without paying. They started a stampede that bent the metal pole of a streetlight, broke through glass doors, and trampled ticketholders who were waiting to get in. Nine people were crushed to death.[28]

After rescue crews arrived and relieved the press of the crowd, fans stepped over bodies to get close to the rappers, and several robbed corpses. Rap stars who tried to help evacuate some of the dozens of injured were prevented by mobs of autograph-seekers.[29] Five emergency rescue men were also injured when they were attacked by the crowd.[30]

It was, in short, a sorry display of callousness. Journalists, however, could not bring themselves to say so. The Associated Press blamed the horror on "the beast": "The beast bent a lightpole in front of the gym building; it pestered rappers for photo ops and

21

autographs in the morgue of the gym floor, distracting those who were trying to help the injured; it laughed and joked outside amid the despair; it robbed the dead." "It" killed nine people.[31]

One white music critic went farther: "It's no secret that our society teaches minorities to hate themselves. If you are not white, male, straight, middle-class, well-educated or well-off, you are told . . . that you and others like you are disposable. . . . You self-destruct and aid in the destruction of others. You do as you are told. . . . Should it come as any surprise that people trapped like animals in cages are going to rip each other apart out of sheer frustration? Why should they value human life when society judges their lives as meaningless?"[32]

At a memorial service two weeks after the deaths, speakers blamed the tragedy on the police, city officials, the "white establishment," and "Uncle Tom blacks." Rev. Lawrence Lucas of the Resurrection Roman Catholic Church called the deaths an "orchestrated disaster" designed to give the police an excuse to attack young blacks and to take power from them. Rev. Timothy Mitchell of the Ebenezer Missionary Baptist Church said the deaths were a "painful reminder of the racist, capitalist, individualistic society in which we live." Thus exhorted, the crowd left the memorial service and promptly tried to storm a building as a protest.[33]

The way these deaths were reported and explained was not a departure from the way news about blacks is often handled. And yet many people must have found it strange. Why did the speakers at the memorial service seek excuses for inexcusable behavior? How did the "white establishment" start the stampede? How did racism cause young blacks to rob the corpses of other young blacks? Just who is it that is teaching minorities to hate themselves, and how do they manage it? No one asked those questions because no one ever asks those questions.

If racism can make blacks do such horrible things, it must be a fearfully powerful force, and there must be a great many white racists. And yet, who are these racists? How are they able to do all the things they are said to do? Most whites probably cannot find in themselves the desire to oppress or persecute blacks. Most probably do not even know anyone who wants to do that. Could they even confidently cite the name of someone they have heard of who actively seeks to oppress blacks? Do you, the reader, oppress black people? If you wanted to, how would you go about it?

It is unanswered questions like these—How did racism start that stampede in Harlem? Who teaches blacks to hate themselves?—that prompted the investigations in this chapter.

Looking for Racism

Many people think that to show that white racism causes black failure, all they must do is show that blacks fail. The *cause* falls into place by itself. This is a common but incorrect style of reasoning. People often collect symptoms and effects, and then attribute them to a cause that suits their own argument.

In fact, it is a style of thinking that has often characterized American political thinking in the past. At various periods, and on the flimsiest evidence, Jews, Catholics, blacks, immigrants, or Communists have been blamed for everything that was wrong with the country. The historian Richard Hofstadter calls this the paranoid style in American politics.[34] Today America is in the grip of yet another massive attack of paranoia, except that it is the majority white population that is automatically blamed for whatever goes wrong. Charges of racism can be made with the same reckless impunity as were charges of communism at the height of the McCarthy era. To ask for the facts that support the charge is only to prompt more accusations.

To make a convincing case for racism, it must be shown that America treats otherwise similar blacks differently from whites. Anecdotal evidence is insufficient. It is only in the larger sweep of society that we will find forces powerful enough to oppress an entire people. Those who look carefully for evidence of racism— and not just for evidence of black failure—are likely to come up short.

America often judges people by how much money they make. Although we assume that blacks want money as much as whites do, they make less. To show that this is the fault of racist employers, one must show that even if blacks are just as well qualified and hardworking as whites, they are still forced into bad jobs with low pay. Research by Richard Freeman, an economist at Harvard, shows that this rarely happens. Comparisons of blacks and whites who grew up in the same circumstances and went on to get similar educations show no differences in their average incomes. This was not always so. In the past, smart, qualified blacks could not get equivalent jobs. But by 1969—more than twenty years ago—blacks made just as much money as whites with the same backgrounds.[35] The trend toward parity was firmly established well before affirmative action and other special programs for minorities.

Mr. Freeman sees the big change as having taken place in the 1960s, during what he calls a "dramatic collapse" in patterns of discrimination.[36] He summarizes the situation a decade later:

> By the 1970s black women earned as much as or more than whites [women] with similar educational attainment; black female college graduates obtained a moderate premium over their white peers; young black male college graduates attained rough income parity with young white graduates, and all black male graduates had more rapid increases in income than whites. . . ."[37]

Women have made especially dramatic progress. In 1946, the median wage for black women was *only 36 percent* of that for white women. It has since climbed steadily, and by 1974 it was 98 percent.[38] Black women with a college education have actually outstripped whites. By 1950, black women college graduates already made 91 percent of the wages paid to white female college graduates. By 1960, they earned 2 percent *more* than whites, and by 1970, the difference had grown wider still.[39] By 1979, all black women, whatever their qualifications, earned 8 percent more than white women of equal qualifications.[40] The reason for this advantage is that they have been steadier workers than whites. When black and white women hold similar jobs, the black woman, on average, has been on the job 38 percent longer.[41] It is normal that she be paid more, because she has more experience.

This essential parity between the wages of equally qualified black and white women is well known in specialist circles but virtually unknown to the public at large. The economist Walter Williams, who is himself black, calls this comparative data on working women "one of the best-kept secrets of all times and virtually totally ignored in the literature on racial differences."[42] Why do the organs of public information fail to report this powerful argument against the existence of pervasive work place racism?

Today, 19 percent of black women in the work force hold professional and managerial jobs, whereas only 13 percent of black men do.[43] For whites, men are more likely to hold such higher-level jobs. Of all technical jobs held by whites, women hold 48 percent. By contrast, women hold 63 percent of the technical jobs held by blacks.[44] If desirable jobs that have traditionally been filled by men are open to black women, what is keeping black men out of them? It is difficult to explain how white racism shackles black men but not black women—women who presumably labor under the double disadvantage of both sex and race.

Another black author, Thomas Sowell, points out that some believers in racism do not merely ignore these data. "There is a positive hostility to analyses of black success," he writes, if they suggest that racism may not be the cause of black failure.[45]

This hostility has not stopped Mr. Sowell. He has shown that in 1969, while American-born blacks were making only 62 percent of the average income for all Americans, blacks from the West Indies made 94 percent. Second-generation immigrants from the West Indies made 15 percent *more* than the average American.[46] Although they are only 10 percent of the city's black population, foreign-born blacks—mostly from the West Indies—own half of the black-owned businesses in New York City.[47] Their unemployment rate is lower than the national average, and many times lower than that of American-born blacks.[48] West Indian blacks look no different from American blacks; white racists are not likely suddenly to set aside their prejudices when they meet one.

For nearly twenty years, young blacks who manage to stay married have had family incomes almost identical to those of young white couples. Until recently, the only exception had been the South, but even there the difference has vanished. Now, in families where both parents are college-educated and both work, black families make *more* money than white families. This is true in all parts of the United States and for families of all ages.[49] In some professions, where affirmative action programs have created an artificial demand for qualified minorities, blacks may earn more than whites simply because they are black. This is the case for college professors,[50] who can command stiff salary premiums because they help fulfill hiring goals.

Many blacks have not let talk of racism daunt them but have instead figured out that what counts in America are brains and hard work. The number of black families that are "affluent" (earning more than $50,000 in inflation-adjusted dollars) went from one in seventeen in 1967 to one in seven in 1989.[51] Such families increased, in actual numbers, from 323,000 to 1,509,000,[52] a 467 percent rise. From 1982 to 1987, the number of companies owned by blacks grew by a third, and their receipts more than doubled.[53] In 1991, the hundred biggest black-owned businesses in the country had revenues of $7.9 billion, a 10.4 percent increase over the previous year.[54]

Between 1972 and 1991, the number of black accountants shot up by 479 percent, the number of lawyers by 280 percent, and the number of professional computer programmers by 343 percent. Preachers are virtually the only white-collar group in which the number of blacks declined during that period.[55] From 1950 to 1990, the black population of America doubled but the number of blacks in white-collar jobs increased more than *ninefold*.[56] Blacks, as a proportion of managers in companies with more than a hundred employees, have gone from 0.9 percent in 1966 to 3.7 percent in 1978 and 5.2 percent in 1990.[57] If racism is such a force in our society, why did it not stop this progress?

It is true that blacks are still under-represented in management. H. F. Henderson Industries, a small defense contractor in West Caldwell, New Jersey, is not unusual in that the proportion of whites in professional and technical jobs (80 percent) is much higher than in the company as a whole (48 percent). The only unusual aspect is that Henry F. Henderson, the company's founder, is black. He would like to have more blacks in management, but since he hires by qualifications rather than by race, most of his skilled employees are white.

J. Bruce Llewellyn, chairman of the Philadelphia Coca-Cola Bottling Company is also black, and faces the same situation. "You have to look longer and harder to find these people [qualified minorities]," he says: "It's just obvious that the pool of talented white people is bigger than the one of talented black people."[58]

To draw useful conclusions about racial discrimination, it is necessary to compare like with like. When this is not done, the results can suggest racism where there may be none. For example, magazines and newspapers often report that black college graduates make less money than white college graduates. The difference is said to be due to employer discrimination. The trouble with this comparison is that it includes *all* black and white college graduates. Whites are more likely to attend top-ranked colleges than blacks and are more likely to major in well-paid fields such as business and engineering. A physics graduate from Yale is likely to earn more money than a sociology graduate from Foothills Community College, whatever their races. Careful comparisons of blacks and whites who have graduated from equivalent colleges with equivalent degrees show that the blacks earn *more* than the whites.[59]

"Racism" frequently dwindles away as analysis goes deeper. During the ten years from 1970 to 1980, the median household income for whites rose by 0.8 percent, while the median household income for blacks *fell* by 11 percent. What accounted for this? Did racism get worse? The problem in this analysis is that the income unit is households and not people. During the 1970s, many families, both black and white, broke up. Also, every time a young woman had a child and went on welfare, a new household was established.

The fact is that while individual blacks' incomes were actually rising more quickly than those of individual whites, blacks were splintering into new households at a much more rapid rate. According to one study, if black family composition had held steady during the decade, median black household income would have *risen* 5 percent. If white household composition had held steady, the white median household income would have risen by 3 percent (instead of its actual rise of 0.8 percent).

People of both races were actually making more money, but they were spreading it out over more households. In fact, the actual incomes of black husband-and-wife families rose four times as quickly as those of white families. In families in which both the husband and wife worked, the family income of blacks increased *five times* as quickly as that of whites.[60] Black family income fell during the 1970s, not because of "racist" employers but because of disintegrating families.

Conclusions like these are the results of taking the time to compare like with like. Whenever this is done, differences that can be attributed to racism are elusive. The trouble, of course, is that the black population is not identical to the white population. The black population is less well educated, less experienced, and less qualified. Believers in racism insist that these differences are due to past racism. To some extent they undoubtedly are. But our thinking must change as America changes. Whatever effects the past may have had on the present, employers who pay qualified blacks as much as or more than they pay qualified whites are not now practicing racism.

Moreover, the conviction that blacks are constantly held back because of white racism impugns not only the morals but also the intelligence of whites. If rampant prejudice were preventing thousands of talented blacks from getting jobs, they would presumably be willing to work for less than the prevailing wage—just as they were forty and fifty years ago, when they could not get jobs that matched their training. If that were still so, it would not take a few clever employers long to realize that they could hire able blacks at low wages, undercut their competitors, and make boom-time profits. Why is it that we have never heard of a single company doing something so obvious?

Even in the antebellum South, free black workers were a grave threat to white tradesmen, and could be kept out of professions only *by law*. A white employer was not going to pass up a hardworking black if he could hire him for less than the white wage. In 1857, *at the height of slavery*, white tradesmen petitioned the Atlanta city council for regulations to keep free blacks out of their professions:

We refer to Negro mechanics [who] . . . can afford to underbid the regular resident mechanics . . . to their great injury. . . . We most respectfully request [that the council] afford such protection to the resident mechanics.[61]

"Negro mechanics" were a problem because white employers could not be trusted to let racial prejudice stand in the way of getting a job done cheaply. One of the most important purposes of Jim Crow laws was to bar blacks from certain professions. Seventy years ago, those laws were on the books because whites were so quick to set aside prejudice if it might interfere with what really mattered: profits. What was true then is more true today. Employers are in business to make money, not to indulge prejudices. If they start indulging prejudices, they make less money.

In South Africa, where blacks were still excluded by law from certain jobs right into the 1990s, employers routinely broke the law, and the government *fined* them for it. There is no more effective weapon against discrimination than a free labor market, and not even Afrikaner employers could resist it.[62]

Hunting for Racism

However, looking at job patterns and average incomes may not be the best way to hunt for racism; it will show only the effects of racism. Many people hunt for it directly. For example, studies are sometimes conducted in which blacks and whites with the same qualifications are sent to interview for the same job. If only the white is offered the job, it was presumably because of racism. This sort of experiment is tricky, because it is nearly impossible to find two people, even of the same race, who are identical in intelligence, poise, and attractiveness, yet the results are supposed to show a reaction to one thing only: race.

The most recent such study of black/white pairs involved applications for 476 entry-level jobs, mostly in retail, restaurant, hotel, or other service jobs. In 67 percent of the cases, neither applicant was offered a job. In 13 percent, both applicants were offered the job; in 15 percent only the white got the job, and in 5 percent only the black was offered the job. It would be hard to argue that this is evidence of large-scale, antiblack bias. Moreover, as one scholar has pointed out, this was strictly a private-sector experiment. If the same applications were made for government or university jobs, it is entirely possible that affirmative action would have skewed the results in favor of the blacks.[63]

One unusual seeker of racism is Yelena Hanga, a visitor from Russia who happens to be black. Her father is a Tanzanian and her mother is the daughter of an American black who emigrated to the Soviet Union in the 1930s.

In 1988, Miss Hanga, a Moscow journalist, worked for a time in Boston as part of an exchange of journalists. When she first came to America, she looked hard for white racism but could not find any. Her black friends explained to her that "the time has passed when discrimination is visible to the naked eye." They taught her about "institutional racism," "something a foreigner does not understand during a short stay in the United States." In spite of these instructions, she concluded that whites were not responsible for all the troubles that befall blacks: "In my country we know about racism between black and white, and I thought this was the only evil preventing black progress." "What upsets me most," she writes, "is the racism among blacks."[64]

What, in fact, is "institutional racism"? It appears to be the villain believers in white racism are left with when they cannot find *people* who are actually racist. Here is one definition:

> Institutional racism can be defined as those established laws, customs, and practices which systematically reflect and produce racial inequities in American society. If racist consequences accrue to institutional laws, customs, or practices, the institution is racist *whether or not the individuals maintaining those practices have racist intentions.*[65]

This is an attempt to transfer responsibility to an entire society, even when there is no *intent* to discriminate. It does away with the idea of individual responsibility, while essentially declaring all whites guilty.[66] It is thinking like this, which attributes to whites at large the sins that cannot be found in individual whites, that leads to indiscriminate, societywide "remedies" such as affirmative action.

A foreign journalist's views, though interesting, are only informal observation. Scholars have devised various more objective ways to hunt for racism. The most straightforward thing they do is to ask people what they think. Answers change over time. In 1942, 58 percent of American whites thought that blacks were less intelligent than whites. By 1956 that number was already down to 23 percent, and in a 1991 Harris poll it had dropped to 11 percent.[67] In 1942 only 30 percent of whites thought whites and blacks should go to the same schools, but by 1985, 93 percent thought they should. In 1963, 45 percent of whites told a Gallup poll they would move out if they got a black neighbor; in 1978 only 13 percent said they would,[68] and by 1990 the figure had dropped to 4 percent.[69]

Those who believe in racism will argue that these numbers may not reflect genuine changes in attitude; instead, the data may simply show that whites have learned to give hypocritical answers. Even if that were so, it is still significant if that many whites feel they have to be hypocritical when they used to be brazen. Furthermore, the answer to a different question suggests that whites may well be telling the truth. In 1958, 96 percent disapproved of racially mixed marriages, while in 1983 60 percent still disapproved.[70] According to a 1991 survey, 66 percent of whites said they would disapprove if a close relative married a black.[71] If large numbers of whites are willing to express an illiberal view of mixed marriage, it suggests that if more than the reported 7 percent really did not approve of integrated schools, they would say so. In any case, white attitudes have changed a great deal.

Still, since people might not be willing to tell a pollster what they really think, scientists have devised other ingenious ways to test for racism. One old trick is to offer a child two dolls that are

[67] Arthur A. Fletcher, "Is Affirmative Action Necessary to level the Playing Field?," *Los Angeles Times* (September 8, 1991), p. M6. It is interesting to note that in a recent survey, more blacks than whites said they thought blacks were less intelligent than whites. Marcus Mabry, "Bias Begins at Home," *Newsweek* (August 5, 1991), p. 33.

identical, except that one is black and the other is white. White children usually pick the white doll. If black children pick the white doll it is supposed to mean that their self-image has been damaged by a racist culture. When this experiment was done in 1987, two thirds of the black children chose the white doll. America must still be damaging the minds of black children. The odd thing about these results is that they were exactly the same as results from the early 1950s—long before "affirmative action," black TV anchormen, and "black pride."

The results were even more unexpected when the experiment was done in Trinidad, where 85 percent of the people are black and the government is 100 percent black. There, *more* than two thirds of the children chose the white doll.[72] People have tried very hard to explain this, but what at first looked like white American racism might be something entirely different.

Academics have come up with other ways to measure racism. For example, they make special videos in which actors play identical parts—except that the roles of blacks and whites are exchanged in different versions. They then show the different versions to different groups and ask them to rate the characters. Differences in ratings are supposed to reflect the only differences in the videos, namely, race. Or they try something closer to real life. They take a white woman and a black woman to the supermarket and ask them to drop groceries deliberately. They then see if whites help the white woman but not the black woman.

It is true that *some* of the experiments show differences based on race. One researcher, for example, found that whites helped the black lady with her groceries as often as they helped the white lady, but they did not always pick up as many pieces for her.[73] Other studies, somewhat inconveniently, show that blacks are just as "racist" as whites.

The people who study this sort of thing agree that what they have found is not exactly the blinkered prejudice we presumably had in the past. One report puts it this way: "Precisely because of their subtlety and indirectness, these modern forms of prejudice and avoidance are hard to eradicate. . . . [T]he modern forms of prejudice frequently remain invisible even to their perpetrators."[74] Another report about "modern racial prejudice" says that it is "informal, subtle, and indirect, and most importantly, it is typically invisible to the perpetuator [*sic*]. However, it *can* be detected in laboratory experiments."[75]

The authors of one study then go on to propose ways for whites to make up for this. They should undergo "sensitivity training." They should videotape their conversations with blacks and whites and study how their own body language may differ. They should evaluate black employees as parts of black/white teams so that unconscious antiblack prejudice will not creep in. Whites with black subordinates should be paid more if the blacks do well, etc.[76] The reasoning behind all this is that even when whites think they are being fair, they are still unconsciously racist. They must make special efforts to root out unconscious bias.

This is undoubtedly well meant, but it is not the way to solve America's racial problems. If racism is a problem in America, it is surely not unconscious racism that is detectable only in the laboratory. It is debatable whether there can even be unconscious, unintended prejudice, much less whether it can be overcome. The authors probably would not consider giving advice to blacks. They seem to feel that since whites are responsible for what happens to blacks, it is whites who must change. That is, in fact, the general view. Employers, for example, must bend over backward to accommodate blacks—and not just those from the ghetto.

Leanita McLain was a talented black writer who, by age thirty-two, had won many journalism awards and had become the first black on the editorial board of the *Chicago Tribune*. In 1984, she killed herself. One writer attributes her suicide, in part, to this:

> She put on the clothes, language, and habits of the white professional world, giving up her own cultural heritage for long hours.
>
> This is a common problem for many contemporary black professionals who have had very serious difficulty in adjusting to the white employment world . . . one that expects the victim to fit the mold, but not the mold to adapt to the black victim.[77]

Victim? It is a terrible pity that this gifted woman killed herself, but of what, exactly, was she a victim? What was the rest of the editorial board supposed to do to change the mold to "adapt to the black victim"?

Black economist William J. Wilson is tired of hearing whites blamed for everything. "[T]alented and educated blacks are experiencing unprecedented job opportunities . . ." he writes, "opportunities that are at least comparable to those of whites with equivalent qualifications."[78] As George Lewis, a hardworking black man who is vice president and treasurer of Philip Morris, says, "If you can manage money effectively, people don't care what color you are."[79]

Reginald Lewis is a black lawyer and investment banker. In 1987 his company, TLC Group, raised $985 million to acquire BCI Holdings, an international food conglomerate with $2.5 billion in sales. Mr. Lewis, whose net worth is estimated to be $100 million, is not very concerned about race. "I don't really spend a lot of time thinking about that," he says. "[T]he TLC Group is in a very competitive business and I really try not to divert too much of my energy to considering the kind of issues [race] . . . raised."[80]

Police Racism

Of course, it may be that blacks are treated fairly only in the white-collar world, where whites have managed to curb their racism. Perhaps the racists that conventional theory requires all have blue-collar jobs.

Police work is thought by many to be the profession most likely to harbor racists. Police officers are an unblushingly blue-collar group that handles guns, rides motorcycles, and often must do violence to people for a living. Traditionally the policeman's workplace has seldom even had the sensitizing presence of women to restrain excess.

Many people assume that the criminal justice system is inveterately racist. One black writes, "For many, many blacks there is no system, there is no justice, and it is criminal."[81] A black Yale professor writes deliberately of the criminal *processing* system because he thinks that for blacks it metes out process, not justice.[82] One nonwhite author says simply and colorfully, "police have one trigger finger for whites and another for blacks."[83] When Arthur Eve, a black New York State assemblyman, learned that blacks in his state are more than ten times more likely than whites to be in prison or under court jurisdiction, he had one explanation: "New York is the most racist state in America."[84]

Some people write almost as if the justice system deliberately keeps a certain proportion of blacks behind bars, whether or not they commit crimes: "Despite constitutional safeguards, police and prosecutors and judges still find it relatively easy to ensure that one out of every five black men will spend some part of his life behind bars."[85]

Black newspapers regularly go even farther and explain why the system would do this. As the Catholic pastor Lawrence Lucas writes in the *Amsterdam News* of New York City, one of the main purposes of the criminal justice system is "putting young black males in jails by any means necessary so that lower class whites can exercise authority, supremacy, and make a nice living."[86] In other words, an important goal of the justice system is to round up enough nonwhites to keep whites busy with well-paid prison jobs.

The same sentiments are echoed in the *City Sun* of Brooklyn, New York, which writes, "The system of racial control is being tied more strongly to the economic welfare of ordinary whites than at any time since slavery. In farming communities and small towns across the land, the control of Black and Latino males is replacing the growing of food and manufacture of products as a way of economic life."[87]

Although few white observers express themselves quite so categorically, they generally assume that the police and the courts consistently stack the deck against blacks. But once again, charges of bigotry must rest on evidence, not on emotion. Unfortunately, this is such a charged issue that not even scholars always treat the evidence rationally. One man recently wrote a paper about unjustified, "racist" arrests of minorities. In it, he cited eight different studies, but not one of them found evidence for "racist" arrests. When criminals were classed by groups that differed only by race, researchers found that police treated them essentially the same. Nevertheless, this did not prevent the author from concluding that police racism is widespread, because certain "authorities" have told him so.[88]

Careful investigators have usually reached the opposite conclusion. For example, during the five years from 1971 to 1975, researchers in New York City found that 60.2 percent of the people police shot at were black, even though blacks were only 20.5 percent of the population. Although whites were 64.1 percent of the population, police shot at them only 17.5 percent of the time. Blacks were thus more than ten times as likely as whites to be shot at by police. This sounds like a sure case of the itchy trigger finger for blacks.

However, during the same five-year period, 62.4 percent of the arrests for violent crime in New York City were of blacks and only 20.5 percent were of whites. Thus, shootings by race were proportionate to arrests for violent crime. Also, it is significant to note how these New Yorkers whom the police shot at were armed. Only 7.8 percent of the blacks were unarmed, whereas 15.5 percent of the whites were. Blacks were carrying a firearm 60.5 percent of the time, but only 34.4 percent of the whites were. Whites who were unarmed or just carrying a stick or knife were much more likely to be shot at by police than blacks were.

Finally, more than half of the men of all races who had gunfights with the police were under 24 years old. The median age of black male New Yorkers was 23.1 years and the median age of whites males was 33.3 years. That is to say that a larger number of blacks were in the age group that gets in trouble with the law, and this reason alone would explain part of their overrepresentation in crime figures. In conclusion, the authors of the report found no evidence that police shot at blacks just because they were black.[89]

There is good reason to examine this study in some detail. The first set of numbers, the ones that show that black New Yorkers are ten times more likely than whites to be shot at by police, are about as far as most newspapers get. They are certainly as far as television reports get. It takes patience and an open mind to learn that what appears to be police racism may not be.

What is true for New York City is true for the nation. Sixty percent of the people killed by police are black, even though they are only 12 percent of the population. Is this because the police are racist? Maybe not. Nationwide, blacks account for 58 percent of all arrests for weapons violations, 64 percent of all arrests for violent crimes, and 71 percent of all robbery arrests. It is less well known that blacks are responsible for 73 percent of justified, self-defense killings by civilians, and the overwhelming majority of the people they kill are other blacks.[90] Are the police then gunning for blacks, or are they simply shooting the people who are the most dangerous? Are they racist or just doing their jobs?

Many people have argued that the high crime rates reported for blacks only reflect the fact that police concentrate on the kinds of street crime blacks commit. According to this theory, whites break the law just as often, but commit "white-collar" crimes rather than assaults and robberies. In fact, blacks commit a disproportionate number of white-collar offenses as well. In 1990, blacks were nearly three times as likely as whites to be arrested for forgery, counterfeiting, and embezzlement, and were 3.4 times more likely to be arrested for receiving stolen property. These disproportions have been known for decades.[91]

Believers in racism insist that blacks are arrested more often than whites not because blacks commit more crime but because racist police deliberately arrest them more often. However, there is a reliable way to test this theory. With crimes such as rape, mugging, or assault, the victim usually gets a good enough look at the criminal to see what race he is. People report these crimes to the police because they want the perpetrator arrested. They are not going to say a man was black when he was actually white.[92] Therefore, if the system were hopelessly racist, there would be more reports of white crimes than arrests of white criminals. This is not the case. The ones who get away are just as likely to be black as the ones who are caught.[93]

There is another way to check for police racism. Whether or not

[92] A spectacular exception to this rule was the case of Charles Stuart of Boston. In 1989 he murdered his own wife and tried to throw police off the trail by claiming to have seen a black man kill her. This was widely decried as "racism," but if Mr. Stuart had decided to claim that a violent stranger had killed his wife, it was plausible to claim that a black man had done it. Mr. Stuart later killed himself when the police seemed about to see through his deception.

the police have the leeway to make "racist" arrests depends on the type of crime. With violent crime, the police usually make arrests based on what they are told by victims and witnesses. If everybody tells them a white man did it, they are not going to get away with arresting a black, no matter how much they might want to. Furthermore, there is a great deal of pressure on police to catch violent criminals. They cannot just walk away when people are raped or maimed.

Police have much more leeway to be "racist" in the case of nonviolent thefts, such as burglary. Often there are no witnesses, so if the police wanted to indulge a racist taste for arresting blacks, this would be the opportunity. In fact, blacks are most strongly overrepresented in precisely the crimes of violence in which the police have the *least* leeway for racist arrests. In the case of property crimes with no witnesses, where police leeway to make "racist" arrests is greater, blacks are a good deal less overrepresented in arrest statistics.

For some crimes, arrests are almost entirely up to the policeman. Whether he arrests a drunken driver is up to him—a perfect opportunity to treat blacks unfairly, if that is what he wishes to do. In fact, drunken white drivers are disproportionately a good deal *more* likely to be arrested than are drunken blacks.[94] Studies of arrests for public drunkenness and traffic violations—other crimes that give the police great leeway as to whether they will make an arrest—show no difference in the arrest rates for whites and blacks.[95]

There is every reason for white policemen consciously to avoid getting into confrontations with blacks. Why should they risk the public outcry? If they shoot or beat up a black, they must face daunting criticism from the press, the mayor, the police chief, and civil rights organizations. In America today, only foolish policemen would deliberately mistreat blacks.[96]

In fact, whenever white policemen use justified, self-protective violence against blacks, their actions are commonly scrutinized for bias. In 1988, a white Toronto police officer shot a black man who

---

[96] Please see Chapter Six for a discussion of the Rodney King case. The national outcry it provoked is a good indication of how the nation reacts to mistreatment of blacks by white police officers.

was swinging a knife. The black community protested, and the officer was indicted for manslaughter. The police were so outraged that they demonstrated publicly against the indictment. A group called the Black Action Defense Committee said that blacks might have to start arming themselves to avoid being "murdered" by the police. The president of the police union said that if things continue this way, crime will increase because the police "are going to be reluctant to arrest black people."[97]

But to return to statistics, even those who are convinced that the criminal justice system is racist would probably concede that it must have been even more racist in the past. We would therefore expect to find that, proportionately, the number of black prison inmates has dropped. That is to say, a black's chances of being in prison, though higher than those of a white, should be lower than they used to be. This is not the case. In 1932, a black was four times as likely as a white to be in prison. By 1979 the odds had worsened to the point where he was eight times as likely to be in prison.[98] Is our society becoming more racist, or is it that a black's chances of being in prison do not have much to do with police racism?

Another puzzle: If the police and courts are locking up blacks because of prejudice, many people would expect to see the most grievous effects of this in the South. A black's relative chances of being in jail should be worse where racism is thought to be worse. However, none of the states in which a black has the best chance of being in jail is in the South. In Minnesota, a black is *twenty-three times* more likely to be in jail than a white; in Iowa, twenty-one times; and in Wisconsin, nineteen times. The two states with the lowest differentials are Mississippi (three times) and New Hampshire (about equal chances). It would be hard to argue that the police and the courts in Minnesota are radically more racist than those in Mississippi. Nor are these state differences just a fluke. By region, the Northeast jails blacks at fifteen times the rate it jails whites, the South at only five and a half times.[99] Once again, the racism that is supposed to explain so much does not appear to explain anything at all.

Many people have argued that if police forces are integrated we will see a drop in differential crime and arrest rates. In spite of this widespread belief, few people have seriously looked into whether anything changes when there are blacks on the force. In fact, black policemen are more likely to shoot blacks than white police are. Is this because they are ill-disciplined and trigger-happy? Probably not. It is because they are more likely to be put to work in black neighborhoods, where there is more killing of all kinds.[100] Blacks and whites who both work in black neighborhoods are equally likely to shoot at blacks.[101]

In normal police work, researchers find that blacks are "more active disciplinarians" and "more likely to make arrests." That is to say, they are tougher cops. Some studies have found that both black and white police officers are more likely to treat criminals of their *own* race more roughly than they treat other races.[102]

What about black judges? Do they sentence blacks differently from white judges? What evidence there is seems to show that, if anything, black judges give *harsher* sentences to black criminals.[103] Some black judges have explained the difference by saying that they feel no mercy for black criminals who prey on other blacks.[104]

Sentencing is another aspect of the criminal justice system that is routinely accused of racism: Black criminals are said to get stiffer sentences than white criminals for the same crime. The most exhaustive, best-designed study shows that this is not the case. In a three-year analysis of 11,533 people convicted of crimes in California in 1980, Joan Petersilia found that the length of a sentence depended on such things as prior record and whether the criminal used a gun. She found that race had no effect. Miss Petersilia has had the courage to admit that these findings refute her own earlier work, in which she did not take other factors into account, and had concluded that race made a difference in sentencing.[105]

The death penalty has often been cited as proof of racist justice. It is true that someone who kills a white is more likely to get the death penalty than someone who kills a black (11.1 percent vs. 4.5 percent). This figure is often cited as proof that American society values white lives more than black lives. In fact, other death penalty statistics do not suggest racism at all. For example, white murderers, no matter whom they kill, are more likely to get the death penalty than black murderers (11.1 percent to 7.3 percent). Furthermore, whites who kill whites are slightly more likely to be on death row than *blacks* who kill whites. Finally, whites who kill blacks are slightly more likely to be on death row than blacks who kill whites.[106]

Given a choice of death penalty statistics such as these, newspapers commonly headline those that suggest white racism while ignoring those that do not.[107] They also trumpet the results of even the most flawed studies, as long as they support the thesis of unequal justice for blacks. For example, in 1989 the *Atlanta Journal and Constitution* published a major, multipage story on criminal sentencing in the state of Georgia. It found that in nearly two thirds of the state's jurisdictions, blacks were twice as likely as whites to go to jail for the same crimes. A front-page map showed which parts of the state were the most biased. Only forty-six inches into the story did it become clear that the newspaper's data ignored prior convictions![108] Every legal system in the world is tougher on repeat offenders than on first-timers, and many blacks are repeat offenders. A comparative study of sentencing that ignores prior convictions is very nearly worthless, and to base a major, sensational story on such a study is thoroughly irresponsible.

Slanted reporting of this kind has convinced many Americans that their justice system is riddled with racism. A black law student attending a recent political convention in New York City put it as bluntly as anyone: "The criminal justice system is set up to incarcerate blacks and Latinos, particularly the males."[109] This illusion can have real, unfortunate consequences. The Kerner Commission found that, in the 1960s, many blacks justified looting and burning

---

[106] *Dallas Times Herald* (November 17, 1985), p. 1, cited in William Wilbanks, *The Myth of a Racist Criminal Justice System* (Monterey: Calif.; Brooks/Cole Publishing Company, 1987), pp. 17f. William Wilbanks, "Times Herald Misused Statistics in Death Penalty Study," unpublished, p. 1. The question of who gets the death penalty is complicated by several factors, one of which is money. Rich murderers, who are able to hire shrewd lawyers, are more likely to get a lesser sentence than poor people who must make do with court-appointed lawyers.

Furthermore, not all killings are equivalent. Murder committed while engaged in another crime, for example, is likely to get heavier punishment than one that results from a domestic quarrel. A study of race and the death penalty would have to control for such variables to determine whether sentencing was influenced by race.

on the grounds that "the system" was racist.[110] One black sociologist says, "There has been a growing belief among blacks and lower-class groups . . . that the criminal processing system has been an instrument of political repression . . . and that criminal behavior may be the only way to produce social change. . . ."[111]

The riots in Los Angeles in the spring of 1992 were triggered by the belief among blacks that a racist court system had unjustly exonerated white police officers who had beaten a black motorist. Nevertheless, without a decades-old sense of resentment against white society in general, a single court case would never have started riots. This sense of resentment is fed by the constant refrain that American society is inveterately racist. Blacks have heard this message so frequently they cannot help but absorb it.

The seventeen-year-old mastermind of an Omaha drug-dealing ring has already learned the sociological excuses for his crimes. "Society is set up so that black people can't get ahead," he says. "I'm not supposed to have the American dream and all that. I'm supposed to be in jail."[112]

If people believe that society is unjust, it lowers their internal resistance to crime. Rather than feeling that it is wrong, they may feel that, through crime, they are striking blows for justice.[113] One researcher who studied prison inmates found that for whites, the more they identified with the criminal class, the lower their opinions were of themselves. This was not the case for blacks.[114] This difference probably reflects different feelings about the fairness of society and the legitimacy of crime.

Attitudes toward crime can corrode the minds even of blacks who do not break the law. One columnist writes of stopping to watch a line of black men break dancing on a sidewalk in New York City. Two of the dancers soon drifted into the crowd to ask for money, and received a shower of dollar bills. They received another shower, when one pointedly reminded the mostly white crowd, "Keep in mind, folks, we could be doing something

[110] *Report of the National Advisory Commission on Civil Disorders* (New York: Bantam Books, 1968), pp. 203–6. Although the report repeatedly mentions the widespread belief among blacks that the criminal justice system treats blacks differently from whites, the authors could find practically no evidence of this. They nevertheless concluded that police forces should revamp their policy and personnel standards to eliminate even the *perception* of bias, pp. 302–9.

worse."[115] Is crime such a natural—even legitimate—option for blacks that whites should feel grateful when they abstain from it?

In the 1960s, the black poet Imamu Amiri Baraka (LeRoi Jones) put it this way:

> [Y]ou can't steal nothin from a white man, he's already
>   stole it he owes
> you anything you want, even his life. All the stores will
> open if you
> will say the magic words. The magic words are: Up against
> the wall mother
> fucker this is a stick up! Or: Smash the window at night
> (these are magic
> actions) smash the windows daytime, anytime, together,
> let's smash the
> window drag the shit from in there. No money down. No
> time to pay. Just
> take what you want.[116]

Although they may not express themselves as colorfully as Mr. Baraka, many blacks are equally convinced that they have every right to tamper with the white man's system. During a recent murder trial, a California Superior Court judge disqualified a black juror who was overheard saying that he would give the death penalty only to whites.[117]

Biases like this are not always detected in time. At a murder trial in Washington, D.C., in 1990, the verdict of not guilty was so unexpected that the prosecutor gaped as it was read and the defendant fell over in his chair backward in his jubilation. The defendant was black, and so were all the witnesses. Three weeks later, one of the jurors caused a sensation at the court when he mailed in an anonymous letter. It explained that most of the jurors had thought the man was guilty but that a black-activist foreman had browbeaten them into a verdict of not guilty. The letter concluded with these words: "I let a man go free for murder with my vote, I hope God will forgive me."

When the *Washington Post* interviewed ten of the twelve jurors, it found that the activist had distributed literature from Louis Farrakhan's Nation of Islam and had worn a button supporting a separate nation for blacks. She insisted that society was to blame for all the ills of blacks, and she persuaded the other jurors not to send another young black man to jail. The defendant has since been indicted on another first-degree murder charge. This murder victim, like the previous one, was black.[118]

In the Bronx, in New York City, defendants and jurors are over-whelmingly black and Hispanic. Prosecutors and police who appear as witnesses are overwhelmingly white. Bronx jurors now have a firm reputation for doubting the testimony of police and letting off black and Hispanic defendants. A Bronx district attorney remembers the way it used to be: "When I started in this office, twenty years ago, the strongest case you could have . . . was when all your witnesses were police officers. Now, sadly, it's the weakest." Says another prosecutor: "If you have a case involving cops, you are almost certain to lose."[119] If the situation were reversed, and white juries were routinely doubting black policemen and letting off white defendants, there would be a deafening outcry.

One of these Bronx cases was that of Larry Davis. He wounded six policemen in a shoot-out, but in 1988 a jury of ten blacks and two Hispanics acquitted him of attempted murder. He was nevertheless convicted of illegal weapons possession and sentenced to five to fifteen years in prison. When his sentence was announced, his supporters chanted, "Never give up. Free Larry Davis. We gotta right, black power, we gotta fight, black power." In a speech afterward, Mr. Davis said that the presiding judge had "violated the law countless times" during the trial, and proclaimed, "There is no justice for the African-Latino people." Mr. Davis, a convicted felon like all four of his brothers,[120] then went on to face different charges for two separate murders, a kidnapping, an assault, and a car theft.[121]

On almost the same day that Mr. Davis was sentenced, the first black to be appointed to the elite, ninety-four-man Texas Rangers police squad said he looked forward to the day when the press stopped paying attention to his race. A forty-one-year-old professional lawman, Lee Roy Young said that he had never suffered discrimination nor seen others discriminated against.[122]

Campus Racism

Why does America prefer to believe a convict, Larry Davis, rather than a Texas Ranger, Lee Roy Young? As we shall see, there are a number of reasons for this, but universities play an important role in establishing and spreading the view that white people are racist and that it is white racism that accounts for the failures of nonwhites. College professors and administrators tend to be far more politically liberal than the population at large, and at many universities the search for racism and the struggle to eliminate it are pushed to the point of ideological excess. Although a college education should encourage reflection and discourage hasty judgments, universities are even more closed-minded on the subject of race than the rest of society.

Academics have created an atmosphere in which the slightest statement or gesture is analyzed for potential "racism," and deviations from orthodoxy are swiftly punished. The new mood of heightened sensitivity has been accompanied by what is said to be a worrying "resurgence" of campus racism.

Media reports about race on campus hew to conventional doctrine and generally imply that racist incidents are all perpetrated by whites against blacks. This is, of course, not the case. For example, four black football players at the University of Arizona went to jail for hunting down solitary whites and beating them up. Three of the blacks were on scholarships, and the biggest was a 6-foot-4, 255-pound lineman.[123] Brown University was considering asking for help from the FBI when, in the opening weeks of the 1989 school year, whites were attacked by urban blacks on sixteen different occasions.[124]

Eugene McGahen, a white freshman attending the historically black Tennessee State University, was beaten in his room by a group of blacks with covered faces. Brian Wilder, another white freshman at the same university, took to carrying a knife and sleeping with a baseball bat after receiving death threats and being told by blacks that they would "get" him.[125]

By contrast, some of the "racism" attributed to white students sounds exceedingly tame. During a late-night bull session at Southern Methodist University in Dallas, a freshman reportedly said that Martin Luther King was a Communist and then proceeded to sing "We Shall Overcome" in a "sarcastic" manner. The university made him do thirty hours of community service at a local minority organization. A graduate student reportedly called a classmate a "Mexican" in a "derogatory" manner after an intramural football game. Presumably he could have called him any number of obscene names and not been punished, but "Mexican" got him thirty hours of service also.[126] At Harvard, insensitivity was nipped in the bud when the dean for minority affairs learned that dining hall workers were planning a "Back to the Fifties" party. The fifties were segregated, argued the dean, so such a party would smack of racism.[127]

At Tufts University, a student was put on academic probation for saying "Hey, Aunt Jemimah" to a friend who was wearing a bandanna. A bystander was offended and brought charges against the student for violating the college speech code. The university's reasons for punishing the student were murky at best: "We did not find evidence to support [the] accusation [of harassment], nevertheless we decided [the student] still had no right to make the remark."[128]

In 1989, thirty fraternity members from the University of San Diego were discovered by a park ranger as they were burning a cross in a nature preserve. They were quickly hauled before the college authorities, to whom they explained that this was part of their initiation ritual, which was based on Emperor Constantine's conversion to Christianity. Each pledge was to make a list of his faults and burn it in the cross's fire. The university was eventually made to understand that the ritual had no racial significance at all. Nevertheless, the fraternity was put on probation for three years, forced to abandon the ritual, and its members each made to do twenty-five hours of community service. Just for good measure, every member of every fraternity and sorority on campus was made to attend workshops on racism.[129] This is "tolerance" taken to an intolerant limit.

Most reports of campus racism are of this kind of thing or of racial graffiti. Anything more than verbal abuse is extremely rare. Furthermore, a number of university administrators wonder if some well-publicized cases of anonymous graffiti have not been the work of minority students who think they can profit from the white breast-beating that inevitably follows.[130]

Some cases of racial "harassment" are pure play-acting. Sabrina Collins, a black student at Emory University in Atlanta, gained national attention when she received death threats in the mail, her dormitory room was repeatedly ransacked, and racial insults were scrawled on the walls and floor. She was so traumatized that she curled up into a ball and refused to talk. An investigation showed that the episodes began just as Miss Collins came under investigation for violating the school's honor code and that she probably staged everything herself.

The head of the Atlanta chapter of the NAACP said that so long as the incident highlighted the pressures that blacks face on mainly white campuses, "it doesn't matter to me whether she did it or not." University officials, just as incoherently, agreed that worrisome questions about white racism had been raised, whoever was responsible.[131] Whites are so zealous in their search for bigotry that even a hoax is cause for anguished soul-searching.

In this atmosphere, colleges all over the country are rushing to combat racism, real or imagined. One of the most common steps has been to ban what is usually called "hate speech." According to one count, by 1990 there were 137 American campuses that banned certain kinds of speech.[132] Speech codes are essentially based on the assumption that whites are racist, nonwhites are not, and the latter must be protected from the former.

Some universities are explicit about this. At the University of Cincinnati, the student handbook states that blacks are incapable of racism. Thus when a mixed group of black and white students insulted some Arab students during the Persian Gulf War, the whites were quickly convicted of racism by the student senate. The blacks were above the law.[133]

Most speech bans are written so as to apply to everyone, but most people understand that they will usually be invoked only against white students. Some are so broad and so vague that they have been struck down by the courts. At the University of Michigan, a rule was passed that prohibited students from, for example, venturing the opinion that women may be inherently better than men at understanding the needs of infants, or that blacks may be naturally better at basketball than whites. A student filed suit, claiming that the regulation prohibits legitimate research, and his view was upheld by a federal judge.[134] A federal court has also struck down a speech code at the University of Milwaukee.[135]

In 1987, the University of Connecticut established what was probably the most bewilderingly broad "sensitivity" code at any school in the country. In addition to the usual slurs, it forbade "inappropriately directed laughter" and "conspicuous exclusion [of another student] from conversation." Only after a student sued the university did it limit its speech ban in 1991 to words "inherently likely to provoke an immediate violent reaction."[136] Speech codes may well increase tension and edginess rather than relieve them. A student at the State University of New York at Binghamton complains that "If you look at someone funny, it's a bias incident."[137]

One university, Brown, has already imposed the heaviest possible penalty—expulsion—on a student who violated its speech code. In a drunken outburst to no one in particular, a white football player, Douglas Hann, let fly with a series of obscene insults about blacks, Jews, and homosexuals. When a black student approached him to complain, he reportedly told her that his people owned her people.[138] Loutish though Mr. Hann's behavior was, Brown has hardly distinguished itself by expelling a student for expressing opinions.

There is some question as to whether speech restrictions are even legal. Some experts have argued that publicly funded universities cannot restrict speech and must abide by the terms of the First Amendment, whereas private colleges have more latitude. Congressman Henry Hyde of Illinois would like to settle the question once and for all. In March 1991, he introduced legislation in Congress that would outlaw speech codes.[139]

In any case, it is a sad day when our universities, which supposedly promote academic freedom and unrestricted inquiry, are binding their members with tighter restrictions than does society at large. In such an environment it is no surprise to learn that students keep unfashionable opinions to themselves. In 1991, one professor found that students at New York Law School would criticize affirmative action only if they were assured their opinions would be anonymous. On the record, they were all in favor of it.[140]

Entire courses have been dropped in the name of "racial sensitivity." Reynolds Farley, an acclaimed demographer at the University of Michigan, stopped teaching a popular undergraduate course, Race and Cultural Contact, after he was criticized for racism. His offense was to have read in class a self-deprecating passage written by Malcolm X, and to have discussed the southern arguments in defense of slavery. "Given the climate at Michigan," he says, "I could be hassled for anything I do or don't say in that class."[141] Other faculty members at Michigan have cut discussion of race-related subjects from their courses for fear of attack.[142]

Administrators come under just as much scrutiny as professors. In early 1992, 250 faculty and students at the City University of New York (CUNY) filed a racism suit claiming discriminatory spending. They argued that the State University of New York (SUNY) was getting more public money per student because it had proportionately more white students. Indeed it was; about 10 percent more. Was this proof of racism? The state university maintains expensive medical, dental, and technical schools. When these were taken out of the calculations, the city university was actually receiving *more* public money per student than the state university.[143]

One increasingly common way to combat alleged campus racism is to make all students take courses designed to sensitize them to the plight of minorities. In 1991, the University of California at Berkeley started making students study the contributions of minorities to American society.[144] English Composition is the only other campuswide requirement.[145] The University of Wisconsin campuses at Madison and Milwaukee, New York State University at Cortland, the University of Connecticut, Penn State University, the University of Michigan, and Williams College have also instituted race-relations requirements in the past several years.[146]

Courses like these often put the burdens of guilt and responsibility squarely on whites. As one satisfied student at Southern Methodist University put it, the purpose of a race-relations course he was taking was to show that "whites must be sensitive to the African-American community rather than the other way around."[147]

At Barnard College, teachers who assign readings from the works of "minority women" get cash rewards paid for by grant money.[148] The Ford Foundation recently announced grants worth $1.6 million to nineteen different schools to "diversify" faculties and course content.[149]

Many colleges that have not set up required courses make do with specialized orientation. There are no blacks at all at Buena Vista College in Storm Lake, Iowa, but it feels it must also combat racism. Special seminars are held every year. In addition, freshmen were put through a month-long immersion course on racism in 1990. At least one student was so struck by what he was taught that he reportedly wanted to travel to other parts of the country to see racism firsthand.[150] One wonders exactly what he expected to see.

In April 1987, Wellesley College in Wellesley, Massachusetts, commissioned a Task Force on Racism in response to incidents reported on *other* campuses—there had been no complaints at Wellesley. The task force duly reported that Wellesley was "covertly racist," so it committed itself to hiring more minority teachers, and now requires freshmen to take a course in non-Western culture.[151]

Harvard University recently put on a week-long program of AWARE seminars (Actively Working Against Racism and Ethnocentrism). John Dovidio, the keynote speaker, explained that all white Americans are racist, 15 percent overtly so and 85 percent more subtly. A black speaker, Gregory Ricks, explained that Ivy League colleges deliberately sap the confidence of blacks, and wondered if they were not practicing a particularly devious form of genocide. One professor suggested that teachers should edit out any facts from their lectures that might offend minorities, because "the pain that racial insensitivity can create is more important than a professor's academic freedom." Another professor agreed that teachers should have less freedom of expression than other people, because it is their duty to build a better world. Finally, Lawrence Watson, cochairman of the Association of Black Faculty and Administrators, had this advice for minority students: "Overreacting and being paranoid is the only way we can deal with this system. . . . Never think that you imagined it [racial insensitivity] because chances are that you didn't."[152]

Racial sensitivity can take many forms. The University of Michigan marked the 1990 celebration of Martin Luther King's birthday with a series of vigils, seminars, and lectures that involved virtually every department. Some of the offerings were nothing short of heroic. The classical studies department gave a talk called "Ancient Greece and the Black Experience," and the nuclear engineering department sponsored a session called "Your Success Can Be Enhanced by Positive Race Relations." The School of Natural Resources gave a lecture on "Environmental Issues and Concerns: The Impact on People of Color." University president James Duderstadt says, "We're reinventing the university for twenty-first-century America."[153]

Racism at Stanford

Stanford University has also been reinventing itself. It conducts intensive "sensitizing" seminars and requires them for all freshmen. Nevertheless, in the fall of 1988 Stanford was one of many campuses said to be afflicted with white bigotry. Newspapers and magazines repeatedly referred to a notorious "poster" incident, but they never explained what had happened. The episode is worth a close look.

Ujamaa House is Stanford's African-theme residence hall. In 1988 more than half of its 127 students were black. One evening in October there was a hallway discussion among undergraduates. One was a black, whom we will call QC. At one point QC claimed that all music in America has African origins. One of the whites asked about Beethoven. QC shot back that Beethoven was black. Several white freshmen, one of whom we will call Fred, openly doubted that.

Later that evening, Fred found a Stanford Orchestra poster with a big picture of Beethoven on it. With a crayon, he gave Beethoven an Afro and black features, and hung the poster outside QC's room. QC found it the next day and was "flabbergasted." Another black Ujamaa resident called it "hateful, shocking" and said she was "outraged and sickened."

Though he had heard no reaction to the poster, Fred, who lived in the dorm next door to Ujamaa House, began to worry that it might have given offense. He went to his teaching assistant for advice, but the T/A suggested he do nothing. "Let it blow over," he said.

Meanwhile, someone scrawled the word "niggers" across a poster advertising a dance at a black fraternity. Coming on top of the Beethoven poster, this caused much fury at Ujamaa House. A black resident T/A who suspected that Fred had defaced at least the Beethoven poster, went to Fred's room to ask him about it. To scare the truth out of him, the T/A said that Ujamaa students were talking about beating him up. Fred promptly admitted marking up the Beethoven poster. It was clear he had had nothing to do with the "niggers" poster. After an abusive grilling by the staff members of Ujamaa House, Fred decided that he would publicly explain his motives the day after next.

About a hundred people were at the meeting, including a thirty-eight-year-old black residential dean who was involved with minority affairs. Fred explained that when he first came to Stanford, he was shocked and offended by the emphasis on race. He said he had come from a multiracial environment but that race was not the central fact of life. He said he disliked what he called "ethnic aggressivity" and that the campus obsession with race was "stupid." A friend had been upset to meet a black student who insisted she would not consider marrying anyone but another black. He said he had defaced the Beethoven poster because it was a "good opportunity to show the black students how ridiculous it was to focus on race." He said the poster was "satirical humor."

A black student interrupted: "You arrogant bastard. How dare you come here and not even apologize. I want an apology." Fred made a perfunctory apology, which the blacks did not accept. There was then a clamor that Fred be expelled from the neighboring dormitory. The black dean came to Fred's defense and argued that the Beethoven poster was not a big deal, that Fred should stay. The dean said he had dealt with much worse than that in the sixties. The black students then turned on the dean, and attacked him repeatedly in a "loud and insulting manner." They later claimed that the dean had "stabbed them in the back."

QC stood up to attack the dean. He said it was arrogant of the dean to downplay the Beethoven poster and said he could not tolerate having Fred live next door. He accused Fred of "dogmatic racism" and of having used the poster to insult him personally. After a few minutes of this, QC started crying and moved toward Fred. He shouted something to the effect that in Chicago, where he was from, he could kill Fred for a thing like that. He then lunged at Fred and collapsed. Six or seven students carried him out of the room, "crying and screaming and having a fit."

The meeting then went to pieces, with about sixty students crying, some screaming, and others in a daze. In the midst of all this, some of the students continued to argue heatedly with the black dean, who finally agreed to expel Fred from the residence next door. The meeting finally ended.

Two days later, two of the white residents at Ujamaa found notices pushed under their doors that said: "Nonblacks leave our home/you are not welcome in Ujamaa." The same notice appeared on the bulletin board. Also that day, someone defaced the photo display of the freshmen in Ujamaa by punching holes in white faces. Several days later, a few signs turned up around campus that read: "Avenge Ujamaa. Smash the honkie oppressors!"[154]

This, in summary, is the "racial incident" that added Stanford to the list of campuses where white racism is on a dangerous upswing. In fact, the most poignant character in this sorry tale is the black dean. It is certainly ironic to have struggled to get where he is, only to be attacked by students half his age because he would not admire the depth of their suffering at the hands of "dogmatic racism."

Six months later, Stanford released a 244-page report on campus race relations. Because of incidents like the one at Ujamaa House, the report called for thirty new minority faculty, double the number of minority graduate students, twice as many courses on American race relations, and an obligatory undergraduate course in ethnic studies. The president quickly agreed to hire the thirty new minorities and double the number of minority graduate students, and promised to study the other proposals. Not satisfied with this, the Stanford Students of Color Coalition took over the president's office and would not leave until the police arrested them. The poster incident was on their lips.[155] In one of the postmortems that followed the takeover, a spokesman for the United Stanford Workers union accused the university of "wall-to-wall discrimination."[156]

The Beethoven poster incident took on a life of its own. Local newspapers referred to it repeatedly, as did *The New York Times*. Seven months after the fact, *The Times* was still dragging it out as the decisive example of white bigotry at Stanford.[157] *Harper*'s magazine denounced it.[158] It popped up again, a full year later, in *Newsweek,*[159] and yet again, eight months after that, in *The New York Times.*[160] Its most recent known appearance was in the *ABA Journal* of July 1990.[161] It refuses to die. Why is it that the Beethoven poster continues to be national news while the Arizona football players who *went to jail* for assaulting whites were scarcely heard of and quickly forgotten?

Stanford, along with many of our finest universities, has lost its bearings. Nevertheless, these schools are only reflecting the received wisdom of the day—that white racism is responsible for all the troubles that afflict black people. Universities are therefore determined to root out not only white racism but also the merest hint of what someone might construe to be white racism. The final step is to curtail debate and even suppress the truth if the truth might hurt feelings. Universities are thus helping build a society in which only certain views are legitimate and dissent is discouraged.

Amid all the talk of surging campus racism, the Carnegie Foundation actually spent a year studying it and published a report in the spring of 1990. It surveyed five hundred officials who are involved in the quality of student life, and asked them about trends in racial harassment on their campuses over the past five years. Eleven percent of the officials thought the problem was worse, while slightly more—13 percent—thought it was less of a problem. Thirty-five percent said there had been no change, and the largest number of all—40 percent—said it was not a problem at all. When the officials were asked how many racial or ethnic incidents there had been on their campuses in the past year, fully 78 percent said there had been none, and 12 percent said there had been one. That left 10 percent who reported there had been more than one.[162]

It does not sound as though there is a raging problem that can be cured only with required courses in race relations. But the findings do suggest why an ambiguous incident like that of the Beethoven poster was so widely reported: There is not much else to write about. If the charge of pervasive white racism is to stick, there must be examples of it. The same incidents can be written about over and over if necessary.

Racism at Every Turn

It is not only at universities, on the job, or at the hands of the police that blacks are said to face systematic discrimination. It is often claimed that they face it at every turn. Housing segregation, for example, is frequently cited as evidence of racism, and there is no question that many blacks live in all-black neighborhoods. Douglas Massey, who is the director of the University of Chicago's Population Research Center and has studied housing patterns, explains it this way: "discrimination in the housing market, discrimination in the lending market and the prejudice of whites."[163]

Mr. Massey may be a little hasty. The only accurate way to study housing prejudice is to send black and white applicants, under identical circumstances, to investigate the same housing opportunities. If the black is treated differently, it is presumably because of prejudice. The Commission on Human Rights of the state of Kentucky actually conducts studies of this kind. In a 1989 survey of fifty apartment complexes in seven cities, it found that blacks got different treatment in 9.8 percent of the time. That is 9.8 percent too often, but it means that whites and blacks were treated identically 90 percent of the time.[164]

The Urban Institute did a similar study, involving thirty-eight hundred visits to apartments and houses all over the country. They found that 15 percent of black renters were told that an apartment was not available even though the same apartment was offered to a white. Eight percent of black buyers were falsely told that a house was no longer for sale. This is hardly perfection, but it means that most of the time blacks do not face discrimination.[165]

Studies like these are always designed to find discrimination by whites; no one ever seems to test how white applicants are treated by homeowners or apartment managers of other races. California, which is increasingly multiracial, suggests an answer. In 1990, the Fair Housing Council of Orange County received 1,178 complaints of housing discrimination. The largest number of complaints were filed by whites, followed by blacks and Hispanics.[166]

There are many reasons other than discrimination that explain why blacks tend to live among other blacks. White neighborhoods are usually more expensive, and blacks may not be able to afford them. They may also think that white realtors, superintendents, and neighbors would be hostile, and sometimes they are. But it never seems to occur to the people who study housing patterns that many blacks prefer to live with blacks. Just as many prefer black-theme dormitories at universities, and just as they frequently socialize with each other at work, blacks are often more comfortable in black neighborhoods. Middle-class blacks who do choose to live in largely white neighborhoods may even be taunted for it by other blacks. Many affluent blacks deliberately refrain from moving into white neighborhoods they could afford because they want their children to have black playmates.[167] Moreover, it is a peculiar kind of patronizing to assume that all blacks want nothing more than to live next door to white people.

Some blacks not only prefer their neighborhoods black, they also want them to stay that way. A black journalist writes about a backyard gathering in an affluent, all-black Atlanta suburb. The party suddenly went silent when a realtor's car, bearing a white couple, cruised slowly down the street. "I hope they don't find anything they like," said one of the black guests in all seriousness; "otherwise, there goes the neighborhood."[168] The football player Jim Brown also once said that he did not want to live among whites.[169] Attitudes like this do not figure into public discourse. If the races are found to live apart from each other, the reason is always assumed to be white prejudice.

The charge of racism is frequently leveled against mortgage lenders. In a 1989 study of ten million loan applications, the *Atlanta Journal and Constitution* found that whites were approved 74 percent of the time while blacks were approved 50 percent of the time. The newspaper did not consider such things as the applicant's debt burden, credit history, value of the collateral, or size of the down payment, so the "study" means virtually nothing. This did not stop other newspapers from picking up the story, putting it on the front page, and running headlines saying that black applicants are twice as likely to be rejected as whites.[170]

When the federal Office of Thrift Supervision released similar statistics several months later, it expressly pointed out that without data on the financial positions of applicants, it was impossible to pin the difference on race. This did not stop members of the U.S. Senate Banking Subcommittee from immediately asking regulators for new ways to force banks to stop racial discrimination.[171]

The same empty drama was played out two years later, when the Federal Reserve Board released the same rough data showing the same disparities. Jesse Jackson immediately concluded that the figures confirmed "what we have known for decades: Banks routinely and systematically discriminate against African-Americans . . . in making mortgage loans."[172] In fact, in that year, the Fed's figures showed that Asians were *more* likely than whites to be granted mortgages.[173] No one appeared to notice; certainly no one argued that bankers are prejudiced in favor of Asians.

In a few cities, journalists thought to test the racism theory by finding out whether blacks were more likely to have loans approved if they applied to black-owned banks. In Houston, Texas, the city as a whole approved black applications 50 to 60 percent of the time. The one black-owned bank, Unity National Bank, approved them only 17 percent of the time.[174]

The curious thing about this whole controversy is that there is not even a theoretical reason why bankers should refuse to make profitable loans to black people. No one ever complains that white auto dealers or shoe salesmen refuse to do business with blacks. Are bankers somehow different from everyone else? Our elected representatives are prepared to believe that bankers systematically forgo profits in order to indulge prejudice. Like most Americans, they have never bothered to find out that black bankers are no more inclined to make risky loans than whites are.[175] Like Unity National Bank in Houston, they may be *less* likely to make loans to blacks, since they know they will not be accused of racism for turning down a risky credit.

The same blinkered thinking is behind the charge, repeated endlessly, that white cab drivers refuse to pick up black riders. Does anyone really think that a large number of white drivers will pass up what they think will be a peaceable, paying customer just because he happens to be black? One white New York City driver, who has heard the story about racist taxi drivers too many times, points out that in his city as many as seventeen drivers have been murdered by riders in a single year, that hundreds are beaten and wounded, and thousands are robbed or defrauded. Eighty-five percent of the six felonies committed against cabbies every day are by black men between ages sixteen and forty. As he explains, "Cab drivers have only one effective way of protecting themselves against the murderous thieves who prey on us. And that is to exercise experienced discretion in whom we pick up. . . . Half of New York's cab drivers are themselves black and act no differently from white drivers."[176]

Indeed, in a study conducted by Howard University in Washington, D.C., when similarly dressed blacks and whites tried to hail taxis, the blacks were seven times more likely to be refused a ride. But in the lawsuits against taxi companies that arose from these studies, *not one* of the "prejudiced" drivers was white; all were either African immigrants, native-born blacks, or Middle Easterners.[177] No driver, of any race, is likely to want to carry young black male passengers into parts of town that are known to be dangerous.

In only the first two months of 1991, Washington, D.C., cab drivers were robbed more often than in all of 1988 (the police did not have statistics for 1989 or 1990). A reporter interviewed more than a dozen city cabbies—all black—and found a near-uniform policy of not picking up young black men at night. The drivers knew they risked a $500 fine for discrimination, but as one explained, "I'd rather be fined than have my wife a widow."

The head of the D.C. Taxicab Commission said that robberies

and violence against drivers were a pity but that she would enforce the law. "Discrimination in this city, and that is what that is, blatant discrimination, will not be tolerated," explained Carrolena Key.[178] The very notion of racial discrimination takes on a strange new flavor when blacks who refuse to pick up other blacks because they fear for their lives are accused of it.

The medical profession is also said to be prejudiced against blacks. Recently, for example, it was reported that white dialysis patients are more likely to get kidney transplants than blacks. This was attributed to racism, and some newspapers even wrote despairing editorials about it.[179] But what are the facts?

First of all, organ transplants work best between people of the same race; one fifth of blacks have antigens that make them reject kidneys donated by whites. At the same time, blacks are only half as likely as whites to donate organs after they die, so the supply of black kidneys is small. This mismatch is even worse because blacks have kidney failure more often than whites and are several times more likely to be on dialysis. Even more important, whites who are still alive are *six* times more likely than blacks to donate a kidney voluntarily to a close relative—and a close relative's kidney is usually the best match. Finally, although the operation is usually free, postoperative treatment has generally cost $5,000 to $10,000 a year, a cost that wealthier whites may be better able than blacks to bear.[180]

Dr. Clive O. Callender is head of the Transplant Center of Howard University and is the nation's senior black transplant surgeon. He explains that one of the most common reasons why blacks refuse to donate organs is that *they are afraid the recipient might be white.* Whites do not seem to worry whether a black might get their organs; Dr. Callender points out that even at Howard, *80 percent* of the organ donors are white.[181]

Where is the "racism" here? In fact, the disproportion between the number of black and white kidney recipients—the problem that prompted charges of racism in the first place—is not very great to begin with. Though blacks suffer 28 percent of serious kidney diseases, they get 21 percent of the transplants.[182] If anything, one might conclude from the facts that the medical establishment is doing a remarkable job of finding kidneys for black patients despite built-in obstacles erected by blacks. Nevertheless, it is whites who are accused of racism.

A more fruitful approach has been pursued by the federal government. It recognizes that the problem is not white racism but an inadequate supply of black kidneys. In the San Francisco area, it has made a grant to the African-American Donor Task Force, which works through black churches to persuade blacks to donate organs.[183]

Sometimes the "racism" explanation for black/white differences is almost comical. *Money* magazine recently pointed out that even when blacks and whites have similar incomes, whites are two and a half times more likely than blacks to own financial assets such as stocks, mutual funds, or an Individual Retirement Account. The magazine quoted an insurance salesman who explained this by saying that stockbrokers do not like to go into black neighborhoods to make house calls.[184] Stockbrokers do not make house calls in any neighborhoods. Jesse Jackson was being just as ridiculous when he wrote in 1990 that the process of voter registration—perhaps a five-minute procedure that helps stop voter fraud—is a deliberate obstacle thrown up by whites to keep blacks from voting.[185] One writer explains that the reason people complain about welfare but do not object to widows receiving their dead husbands' Social Security benefits is that welfare mothers are likely to be black while most Social Security widows are white.[186] This fanciful view ignores the fact that most people see Social Security income as the just return on payments made during a lifetime of work, whereas they see welfare income as unearned and therefore less deserved.

"Environmental racism" is the name of a recently discovered form of discrimination. This is said to be the deliberate siting of potentially polluting factories or waste dumps in nonwhite neighborhoods. A National People of Color Leadership Summit on the Environment was held in Washington, D.C., in late 1991 to debate what to do about the problem.[187] By 1992 there were at least ten minority-based environmental groups charging officials with such things as "radioactive colonialism" and "garbage imperialism."

It would be no surprise if activists could show that nonwhites are more likely to be exposed to environmental hazards than are whites. If a city needs a site for a new incinerator, it will look for inexpensive land. Nonwhites have less money than whites and tend to live in less expensive places. Thus, if nonwhites really are likely to live closer to hazardous sites, there are probably economic reasons for it that have little to do with race.

In fact, there is not even the *appearance* of a serious case behind charges of "radioactive colonialism." The United Church of Christ has actually researched how hazardous waste landfills are sited. In 1987 it found that 78 percent were in areas that had more white than nonwhite inhabitants. Fifty-seven percent of blacks (and Hispanics) live near toxic waste sites, but 54 percent of whites do. Only 46 percent of Asians live near one,[188] but no one seems to argue that waste disposal is somehow arranged for their benefit.

"Environmental racism" is therefore an utterly spurious charge. Usually, cries of racism are based on some real difference between blacks and whites that could conceivably be due to racism. In this case, there is not even a difference; but that does not stop people from assuming that there is one and that racism must have caused it.

In fact, America is prepared to swallow accusations of racism that are even more preposterous. Blacks learned long ago that whites can be silenced and intimidated by accusing them of racism. White acquiescence has made the charge of racism into such a powerful weapon that it should be no surprise to find that a great many blacks cannot resist the temptation to wield it.

2

Charges of Racism

O RANGE COUNTY, A SUBURB OF LOS ANGELES, HAS A POPULA-
tion that used to be overwhelmingly white but has recently seen its nonwhite population rise to 35 percent.
There has been some friction as white neighborhoods
have lost their homogeneity. The *Orange County Register* has kept
a watchful eye on racial incidents, and in July of 1991 it published
a complete list of "hate crimes" committed in the county so far
that year. Here, verbatim and *in toto*, is the *Register*'s report of bias
crimes committed in the county during the months of April and
May 1991:

- A black woman, who with her white husband was featured in
  a newspaper article, receives phone calls asking, "What are
  you doing married to a white man?" [Race of caller(s) not
  specified.]
- A black woman hears racial epithets as she jogs in her neighborhood.
- A woman reports that her elementary school-age son is being
  harassed at school by a white child.
- A Cypress City Council member tells a League of Cities
  meeting, "I thought when they killed (openly gay San Fran-

cisco Supervisor) Harvey Milk, they would finally put some men back on the board."
- White students at a Fullerton high school throw golf balls into the campus quad, hitting Asian students.
- An Iranian family's home in Saddleback Valley is burglarized, and a swastika is scratched on their new BMW car.[189]

Each of these incidents was no doubt very disagreeable to the person who was its target, and Orange County decided to take them extremely seriously. Andy Romero, the county sheriff, announced in August of that year that police efforts to combat these crimes had been put "on a par with homicides . . . and disaster responses."[190]

That episodes like these should be put on par with murder and earthquakes shows how great the power of "racism" can be. Like all power, it can be misused.

Deflecting Criticism

Blacks find it convenient to accuse whites of racism under a variety of circumstances, but one of the most common purposes is to deflect criticism. It has become virtually impossible to criticize a black, especially any prominent or successful one, without provoking cries of racism.

Gus Savage, a black, six-term congressman from Chicago, has made a particularly colorful career out of charges of racism. Although he had one of the worst attendance records on Capitol Hill, and counted half a dozen bills honoring the boxer Joe Louis as his greatest legislative achievements, he routinely brushed off any criticism of his record, whether by whites or blacks, as "racism."[191] When his son was arrested in Washington, D.C., for driving an unregistered car without a license, he called it racism—even though the arresting officers, the police chief, and the city's mayor were all black.[192] He has referred to Ron Brown, the first black to be chairman of the Democratic National Committee, as Ron "Beige" because he has supported white candidates.[193]

Congressman Savage first became known to a national audience not because of race but because of sex. In March of 1989, during a visit to Zaire, he tried to force himself on a black Peace Corps volunteer. The volunteer finally escaped his maulings but was given a medical evacuation back to the United States, where she underwent therapy for sexual assault.

When asked by a reporter about this incident, Congressman Savage replied, "stay the f—— out of my face." He claimed that the attention paid to the incident was part of a white conspiracy. "Black leadership is under attack in this country," he explained, likening himself to Martin Luther King, "and I'm the No. 1 target."[194] Several months later, when the House Ethics Committee censured his behavior, the congressman explained it this way: "Because of the extreme racist resentment of any influential African-American man defying white authority . . . I expect further persecution of me by white media and coconspiring government agents."[195] One of his favorite replies to questions from white reporters was to call them "white racist mo——fu——s."

Once, when a reporter from the *Washington Times* approached Mr. Savage just a few steps off the House floor, the congressman let fly with this unprovoked tirade:

> I don't talk to you white motherf——s. . . . You bitch motherf——s in the white press. . . . F—— you, you motherf——ing a——hole . . . white devils.

This exchange was witnessed by a Capitol policeman and a reporter for *USA Today*.[196] When it was suggested to Mr. Savage that his own actions smacked of racism, he explained that that was impossible because only whites could be racist.[197]

In 1990, Mr. Savage faced what should have been a very tough race against Mel Reynolds, Illinois' first black Rhodes scholar and by all accounts an able man. Nevertheless, most of Chicago's black leadership was behind Mr. Savage, as were black activists around the country. One of Mr. Savage's aides explained that Mr. Reynolds was a tool of the antiblack movement and was working "to undermine strong black leadership." The incumbent told voters that their choice was between "white and right."[198]

This sort of talk didn't prevent prominent black congressmen—House whip William Gray and Representative Charles Rangel—from going to Chicago to campaign for Mr. Savage,[199] who beat his opponent handily, 52 to 43 percent. One of his constituents explained the victory: "Anything you read in the white media, if they're attacking a black man, he must be doing some good."[200]

Mr. Savage's congressional career came to an end only in 1992, when his district was redrawn. On his third attempt, and with the help of white voters, Mr. Reynolds finally unhorsed the incumbent —after death threats and even a murder attempt.[201] In his usual style, Mr. Savage blamed his loss on "the white racist press and racist, reactionary Jewish misleaders."[202]

Mr. Savage is not alone. The black mayor of Atlantic City, New Jersey, also has consistently made race part of his politics. When, in July of 1989, Mayor James Usry and thirteen associates—most of whom were black—were arrested on bribery and corruption charges, he quickly organized a chorus of accusations. "We feel it's an attempt to dismantle our black leadership," said a black community leader. A former city councilman said, "They [whites] can't vote Usry out, so they're looking for any way to get him out." If anything, blacks should have been pleased to see the leadership cleaned out. In the eleven previous years, the population of Atlantic City had plummeted, while welfare cases doubled and violent crime tripled. Parts of the city look like bombs hit them, and a national magazine called it the most unlivable city in America.[203]

In the summer of 1990, Mayor Usry was forced into a runoff election against a white candidate. Although there was no evidence to suggest this, former comedian Dick Gregory stood at the mayor's side and claimed that whites had "rigged" voting machines so as to steal the election. Mayor Usry did not even try to win white votes. His campaign literature, which was distributed only in black wards, urged people to vote for him because of "the color of my skin."[204] The appeal worked; Mayor Usry was returned to office.

In 1990, federal investigators looked into the misuse of a secret Detroit police fund that was used for undercover drug purchases. The police chief of fourteen years, William Hart, was alleged to have taken as much as $2.6 million from the fund. It was reported that stolen cash had fluttered down from the ceiling of the police chief's home when a workman was doing repairs. Mayor Coleman Young of Detroit claimed that the investigation was part of a racist vendetta against him and the black police chief.[205]

Mayor Richard Arrington of Birmingham, Alabama, was cited for contempt of court when he refused to turn over certain papers in a federal corruption investigation. Rather than comply with the order, Mayor Arrington sent letters to a host of national and local organizations, inviting them to participate in a seminar on "the selective prosecution and harassment of black leadership." His supporters claimed that any investigation of Mr. Arrington was driven by a "Ku Klux Klan mentality." When a federal judge ordered him to spend Thursday through Monday of every week in jail for the next eighteen months or until he turned over the papers, Mayor Arrington deliberately gave his punishment the trappings of civil rights martyrdom. He led hundreds of demonstrators, some of them draped in chains, down the same streets through which Martin Luther King led civil rights marches in 1963. Even blacks were dismayed by a transparent attempt to turn a personal predicament into a civil rights struggle.[206]

Likewise, in New York, when David Dinkins, the black mayor-elect, was investigated by tax officials for revaluing at $58,000 a portfolio of stock he had previously valued at $1 million, prominent black groups complained that the inquiry was racist.[207] When, in the following year, Mayor Dinkins was criticized for the way he was handling New York City's increasingly pinched finances, his supporters accused critics of racism. "They cannot live with the fact that an African-American is mayor," said one.[208]

Blacks took up the same cry in 1992, when Mayor Dinkins's campaign finance chairman, Arnold Biegen, was indicted on charges of grand larceny and falsifying business records. Once again, this was seen as evidence of selective harassment of black officials—despite the fact that Mr. Biegen is white.[209] In the same year, the press discovered that Laura Blackburne, a black Dinkins appointee to run the New York Housing Authority, had spent public money with remarkable determination. Although she was in charge of finding housing for New York City's poor, she apparently saw no irony in spending $345,000 to renovate her offices, nor in staying in $300-a-night hotel rooms in Washington, Chicago, San Antonio, and Boston. Miss Blackburne openly defied Mayor Dinkins's orders and spent public money to travel to South Africa, and her spending on other official business trips was notably lavish.[210]

Blacks insisted that the inevitable outcry against Miss Blackburne was racist. Mary Pinkett, a black member of the City Council, claimed that blacks were once again being "in a sense lynched . . . in the press." At least three other black City Council members joined in the chorus of accusations, as did a black state senator from Manhattan.[211] Some blacks are, themselves, so blinded by race that they cannot conceive of whites criticizing blacks for any reason other than color.

Even when a black is duly tried and found guilty, he may simply dismiss due process as an exercise in racism. When former New York State senator Andrew Jenkins was sentenced to a year in prison for money laundering, he claimed that he was the victim of "a vendetta" against black elected officials.[212] The U.S. Congress spent two years investigating a black federal judge, Alcee Hastings, before the full Senate voted to remove him from the bench on a bribery charge. Naturally, Judge Hastings's supporters detected racism in the proceedings and complained loudly about it. Undaunted, Judge Hastings announced plans to run for governor of Florida.[213] When a black New Orleans judge was convicted of scheming to split a $100,000 bribe from a drug smuggler—the first federal judge ever to be convicted of bribe-taking—his lawyers claimed that he and his bagman were both singled out for prosecution because they are black.[214]

Marion Barry, the black mayor of Washington, D.C., was long beset by scandal: patronage, women, mismanagement. His administration was a shambles, but he always fended off criticism with accusations of racism.

Almost one in five voters in Mayor Barry's city were on the municipal payroll—about three times the national average. During his twelve years in office, Mayor Barry boosted the number of city bureaucrats by 27 percent, while the population of the District of Columbia fell by thirty thousand.[215] Many of these workers were flagrantly incompetent. Although Washington had nearly twice as many housing bureaucrats per public-housing resident as Baltimore or Detroit, one fifth of the public housing was vacant because it was waiting for repairs. The waiting time for a unit was seven years. Emergency services were so arrogant and lazy that calls to 911 sometimes weren't even answered and an ambulance might not show up until the next day.[216]

Ten key officials in the city administration—including Mayor Barry's top deputy—were convicted of financial crimes. In the last three years of his tenure, judges had cited the city no less than seven times for systematic mistreatment of people in its care: juvenile delinquents, prisoners, the mentally retarded. In 1989, *Washington Monthly* bluntly called the Barry administration "the worst city government in America."[217] Equally disheartening were the increasingly well-substantiated stories about the mayor's crack cocaine habit. In a city in which the drug was blighting thousands of lives, rumors of drug use at City Hall were a blow to morale.

Mayor Barry stayed in office thanks to near-monolithic support from blacks that was held together with well-timed charges of racism. Even in the face of dismaying incompetence, whites scarcely dared criticize such a prominent black. When the *Washington Post* finally overcame its reluctance and attacked him, Mayor Barry blamed the "white press" for "a new style of lynching."[218] By early 1989, many people heartily agreed when one columnist wrote, "color Barry white, and he would, as he should, be swiftly gone."[219]

A year later, Mayor Barry was defending himself against attack by comparing himself to Jesus and Gandhi, who were persecuted for the good that they did.[220] The balloon finally burst when the FBI used a former girlfriend to lure the mayor to a hotel room and then videotaped him smoking crack. Benjamin Hooks, who was then executive director of the NAACP, duly warned that the arrest might be part of a racist campaign by federal agents to harass black leaders.[221] The mayor even accused the government of trying to kill him by supplying him with crack that was "90 percent pure." At his indictment, Mayor Barry claimed that he was the victim of a "political lynching."[222]

Black Washingtonians seem to have believed him. Preachers did not take to their pulpits to denounce him as a bad example for young blacks. Not even Jesse Jackson, who styles himself a champion against drugs, had a single word of criticism. No crowds marched on City Hall to insist that the mayor step down. No prominent city officials resigned in protest. Instead, T-shirts began to appear around town that said, "I've seen the tapes and the bitch set him up."[223] Washington's three black weeklies continuously promoted the view that the arrest was a dirty, racist trick.[224] When the black-owned *Capitol Spotlight* started running wildly accusatory stories claiming that the Barry indictment was just the beginning of a massive white plot to unhorse black leaders and imprison black men, its circulation jumped by a third.[225] New York's *Amsterdam News* thundered against a government "vendetta" against "Black public officials throughout the country who have dared to speak out against injustice to minorities. . . ."[226] Benjamin Hooks went on to call the Barry prosecution "Nazilike."[227] George Stallings, founder of his own breakaway black Catholic church, claimed that the greatest mayor Washington had ever had was felled by a racist government because he was "too intelligent and too black."[228]

Perhaps most surprising to whites was Mayor Barry's rapturous welcome at a conference of black mayors in April 1990. He had just returned from a stay at a drug treatment center, to which he had disappeared shortly after his arrest. Jesse Jackson, who was at the conference to deliver the keynote address, called him up from the audience to the podium. Four hundred black mayors rose from their seats to give the arrested and indicted Marion Barry a standing ovation. Mr. Jackson, with no apparent sense of irony, then proceeded with his keynote address on drug policy.[229] Later, Mayor Barry held a press conference during which he criticized federal officials for not working closely with him to fight the crack epidemic in Washington.

Columnist Mike Royko was one of several commentators who were disgusted by the news conference and baffled by the ovation.[230] He need not have been baffled. What explains the ovation is probably the same thing that kept Congressman Savage in office for so long: The more a black is criticized by whites—no matter how legitimately—the more he will be applauded by many other blacks.

Mayor Barry understood this perfectly. As he went to trial on fourteen counts of cocaine possession and lying to a grand jury, he boasted that it would be impossible to find a Washington jury that would convict him, no matter what the evidence. "All it takes," he said, "is one juror saying, 'I'm not going to convict Marion Barry —I don't care what you say.' "[231] Jesse Jackson continued to lecture the citizens of Washington on the need to raise a legal defense fund for the mayor and to find him a new job. He also spoke of lucrative "book possibilities."[232]

After a long and highly publicized trial, Mayor Barry's assessment of black jurors' unwillingness to convict a fellow black was found to be almost exactly correct. In spite of overwhelming evidence against him and even an open court admission from his defense lawyer that the mayor had used crack, the panel of ten blacks and two whites convicted him of only one charge, of cocaine possession. On an astonishing ten of the fourteen charges, the jurors could not reach agreement.

The verdict was so surprising that Thomas Jackson, the judge who tried the case, made a highly unusual public statement about the behavior of the jurors. He told a Harvard audience that he had never seen a stronger case for the prosecution and that he was convinced a group of black jurors had been determined from the start not to find the mayor guilty. He thought that they must have lied during jury selection in order to convince the court that they would consider the evidence with an open mind.[233]

Newspaper reporters learned independently that a bloc of five black jurors consistently held out for acquittal. They claimed that the government had manufactured evidence and coached witnesses to lie. There were occasions during deliberations when a pro-acquittal black accused another black, who was leaning toward conviction, of not sufficiently identifying with her race. One black juror urged others to read a book about white oppression of blacks before they voted on the charges.[234]

It is, of course, wholly illegitimate to permit notions of racial solidarity to influence a legal finding of fact, and many decent blacks were disgusted by the jury's behavior. As black columnist Carl Rowan put it, "These jurors were saying: The mayor may be a cocaine junkie, a crack addict, a sexual scoundrel, but he is our junkie, our addict, our scoundrel, and we aren't going to let you white folks put him in jail."[235]

The jury's behavior was pure race loyalty of the kind that explains why blacks never got together to throw the mayor out long ago. They could not bear the thought of organizing to unseat a fellow black, especially one who had been criticized by whites.[236] His flagrant corruption meant less to them than his race.

Many Washington blacks also apparently feared an alleged white plot known as "The Plan." They believed that whites were secretly scheming to regain political control of the District and that Mr. Barry's removal was to be the first step. Part of "The Plan" was said to include planting drugs and guns in black neighborhoods so that young men would destroy themselves and each other.[237]

Across the country, more and more black jurors are behaving just as Mayor Barry predicted: They are refusing to convict blacks, no matter what the evidence. When black congressman Harold Ford of Tennessee was tried on bank fraud charges, his jury also split along race lines, with eight blacks voting to acquit and four whites voting to convict. A white columnist compared this outcome to that of the Barry trial and was brave enough to ask this hard question: "Will black juries convict black defendants, especially for crimes against whites?"[238] Jesse Jackson appears to think that they will not and should not. When the government decided to retry Congressman Ford, he told a Memphis crowd of fifteen hundred, "It is the Justice Department that is on trial."[239] Mr. Jackson has likened the alleged antiblack "pattern" of prosecutions to the days of slavery, when any strong or free-thinking black man was, according to Mr. Jackson, put to death as an example to keep other blacks subservient.[240] Thwarting "white justice" thus becomes a duty.

The same thinking can be found during the trials of common criminals. Ricardo Pouza, a Miami black, confessed to having killed a Cuban immigrant during a $25 stickup. Witnesses corroborated his confession, and physical evidence matched everyone's account. Two successive trials resulted in hung juries: Whites voted to convict and blacks voted to acquit.[241] In Hartford, Connecticut, a black named Joe Lomax finally went free after three hung juries failed to convict him of murder. Once again, the voting was split along racial lines.[242]

Of course, one could argue that it was the white jurors who were driven to convict innocent blacks through sheer racial animus. Nevertheless, in all these cases, as in the trial of Mayor Barry, the evidence of guilt seemed overwhelming to most observers. Moreover, if it were whites who were voting by race rather than on the facts, one would expect to find frequent reports of whites acquitting fellow whites despite clear evidence of guilt. Such reports are exceedingly rare. Instead, it is blacks who accuse the justice system of systematic bias and who appear to think in terms of race first and the facts second.

But to return to the subject of black officials charged with wrongdoing, there is a dreary inevitability about their cries of racism, no matter how astonishingly corrupt or incompetent they may have been shown to be. Carl Green was a $94,614-a-year vice president of the New York City Transit Authority. In 1992 he was charged with what newspapers called a "textbook case" of nepotism. His two sons, his girlfriend's two nieces, his top aide's daughter, and a swarm or other relatives and friends all suddenly found jobs at the Transit Authority. John Pritchard, the inspector general for the Metropolitan Transportation Authority, conducted a careful investigation of Mr. Green and recommended that he and three of his subordinates be fired. It seems to have made no difference to Mr. Green that the inspector general is black; Mr. Green claimed to be a victim of racism.[243]

In 1988, New York City was shocked by revelations about its local school boards. One black principal, Matthew Barnwell, was late or absent nearly four out of five school days. When he did show up, he was often drunk and spent the day watching television game shows. Staff who didn't have connections bought their way into jobs. One quarter of Mr. Barnwell's teachers were regularly late or absent, and his mostly minority students fared miserably. This man kept his $60,000-a-year job for sixteen years and got into the news only when he was arrested for using crack cocaine.

In New York City, school boards are decentralized to an unusual degree. Charges against Mr. Barnwell could be brought only by his local board. At the time he was arrested, Mr. Barnwell's *entire board* was under investigation by the district attorney for taking drugs, stealing school property, and cooking the books.[244]

At another local board, one member was a heroin addict who had been evicted from her apartment and lived in a cardboard box. Classroom aides often got their jobs through patronage, and some were illiterate; they could not even fill out job application forms. One acting principal drove a van up to the school and loaded it with stolen pads, notebooks, pencils, and other school supplies. A five-year-old child was found in a Bronx elementary school cafeteria carrying a loaded pistol. As scandal followed scandal, board members predictably charged that it was all a racist campaign to make blacks and Hispanics look bad.

Almost too excruciating for anyone to point out was that New York's school boards were decentralized only in 1970, after blacks and Hispanics charged that the largely white central bureaucracy was ignoring their special needs.[245] But perhaps most unfortunate of all were the results of school board elections held in these jurisdictions just a few months after the scandals. Only 7 percent of eligible voters turned out—an all-time low—and virtually all the incumbents were reelected.[246]

In Detroit, where 40 percent of the students do not finish high school, one school tried holding a lottery to encourage attendance: Students could win up to $100 just for handing in class registrations. In 1987 the district recorded 14,009 "illegal acts" on school grounds, including 137 cases of students carrying guns. While schools scraped for money, board members flew first class and rolled up to board meetings in chauffeur-driven cars. A seventeen-year veteran board member brushed off the growing criticism: "I know racism when I see it," he said.[247]

In early 1990, school boards tried to dismiss black superintendents in Boston and in Selma, Alabama. In Selma, black students charged racism, demonstrated, occupied school buildings, and threatened violence.[248] In Boston, the president of the local chapter of the NAACP accused the school board of "a blatant act of racism." A white board member wearily explained that, yes, the superintendent had been treated differently because he was black. "He wouldn't have been here as long as he was if he wasn't black," she said; ". . . [We] had to think twice before firing a black."[249]

The trusty technique of the well-timed accusation surfaced once again during the long-running congressional inquiry into corruption at HUD during the Reagan administration. DuBois Gilliam, a onetime aide to former secretary Samuel Pierce, told how he used race to cow and discourage investigators. After admitting that he had distributed millions of dollars in housing grants on the basis of pure favoritism, he explained that since he was black, Secretary Pierce was black, and other high HUD officials were black, he had only to charge racism to intimidate investigators.[250]

One of the saddest cases of a black person trying to shout down his accusers with charges of racism was that of U.S. Supreme Court justice Clarence Thomas. Throughout his career, Judge Thomas had held firm to the view that blacks should not expect preferential treatment and that civil rights groups should concentrate on black self-help rather than on blaming whites. In a 1984 newspaper interview, for example, he said that all civil rights leaders do is "bitch, bitch, bitch, moan, and whine."[251]

And yet, when his elevation to the U.S. Supreme Court came under serious threat from a woman who accused him of sexual harassment, not even Judge Thomas could resist using the mighty psychological weapon that America has put into the hands of all blacks. When his back was to the wall, he insisted that the attack on his character was "a high-tech lynching for uppity blacks."[252]

This was a particularly improbable charge because his accuser, Anita Hill, was black. Furthermore, the people who most opposed his nomination were liberals who would have been delighted to see a black justice replace Thurgood Marshall. They were opposed to his politics, not to his race. Even men who claim to despise "bitching and moaning" may resort to it if the prize is great enough.

It would be refreshing to hear of prominent blacks who have been fired or seriously criticized without provoking charges of racism, but it rarely seems to happen. And since the charge of racism is such a potent and effective one, there must surely be blacks who

[250] Philip Shenon, "Ex-Aide Asserts Pierce Misused Grants," *The New York Times,* (May 5, 1990), p. 8. *The New York Times* mentions only the corrupt use of funds. Mr. Gilliam's explanation of how he threw investigators off the trail was quoted in *The McNeil-Lehrer Report* of May 4, 1990.

remain in positions where they do not belong because whites are afraid of the outcry that would meet any attempt to remove them.

The executive editor of *The New York Times* once explained his reluctance to fire blacks:

> I know that when a woman screws up, it is not a political act for me to go fire them. I cannot [easily] say that with some of our blacks. They're still precious, they're still hothouse in management [*sic*], and if they are less than good, I would probably stay my hand at removing them too quickly. It's still a political act and it would hurt the organization in a larger sense. . . ."[253]

The Impulse to Accuse

Cries of racism need little provocation. Shortly after the presidential election of 1988, two blacks wrote on the editorial page of *The New York Times* about Jesse Jackson: "If he were not black, he would now be the President-elect."[254] In other words, Mr. Jackson's policies were the ones Americans really wanted, but white voters were so blinded by bigotry that they voted against their own interests. It is unlikely, of course, that anyone of any race could have been elected on Mr. Jackson's platform. Many people suspect that he got as far as he did only because he was black. This off-the-shelf accusation of white racism is therefore both groundless and insulting.

In 1989, a black Massachusetts state senator introduced a bill in the state House that would require the taxpayers to make reparations to blacks on account of slavery. Even in liberal Massachusetts, this idea met opposition. David Hall, head of the state chapter of the National Conference of Black Lawyers, says that the opposition is "strong evidence of how deeply racism still flows within the veins of this society."[255]

When blacks want something, it is "racist" to oppose them. The black columnist Carl Rowan, for example, says that anyone who opposes statehood for Washington, D.C., is a racist.[256] When the city of New Orleans voted to establish term limits on City Council members, long-serving black councilmen insisted that it was a racist plot to deprive blacks of "experienced" politicians.[257]

Governor Mario Cuomo of New York was the victim of similar thinking in 1991, when he tried to make up a $6 billion gap in the state budget. After a great deal of study and agonizing, he proposed to make up the difference with $1.5 billion in increased taxes and $4.5 billion in spending cuts, some of it in social programs. This earned him the accusation from Arthur Eve, the highest-ranking black legislator in the state, that Governor Cuomo presided over "the most racist state in the union." Assemblyman Eve went on to tell a black audience that the governor's policies were "killing you and your children."[258] Essentially, racism is anything that blacks say it is, and anyone whom they accuse of it is *ipso facto* guilty.

The black poet Amiri Baraka (formerly LeRoi Jones) sought tenure at Rutgers University. When it was denied in March 1990, he claimed that his appointment was blocked by "white supremacists" on the faculty. "We must unmask these powerful Klansmen," he told a rally of 250 supporters. "Their intellectual presence makes a stink across the campus like the corpses of rotting Nazis." Mr. Baraka did not identify any of the "white supremacists" by name.[259] Likewise, when *Do the Right Thing*, by the black director Spike Lee, failed to win the top prize at the Cannes Film Festival, Mr. Lee explained that this was because of racism.[260]

Sometimes charges of racism are genuinely difficult to understand. In April 1991, the ABC network broadcast a flattering four-hour series on the life of the black U.S. Supreme Court justice Thurgood Marshall. A black journalist, Richard Carter, wrote in *The New York Times* that the series was "an insult to African-Americans." Why? Thurgood Marshall is a light-skinned black, but Sidney Poitier, who played him in the series, is dark-skinned. Not to have matched Justice Marshall's skin color more closely was apparently an act of disrespect.[261]

At the National Medical Association's 1989 convention, a panel of black doctors concluded that white people are largely responsible for the fact that black Americans have poorer health than whites. As Dr. John Chissell of Boston explained, "We live in an intensely racist society that teaches us to hate ourselves. . . ." This reportedly leads to "low self-esteem" and to poor health.[262]

One black theorist, who is the dean of the School of Humanities and Social Sciences at Savannah State College, has concluded that drug addiction and alcoholism are not natural to blacks but foisted upon them by white people. He even argues that whites themselves suffer from these problems mainly because their minds have been unhinged by the exertions of racism.[263]

Blacks have grown so accustomed to making charges of racism that it sometimes seems like an unconscious reflex. Black state senator Valmanette Montgomery of Brooklyn recently refused to accept a Hispanic student intern for her legislative office and insisted instead on a black. When the head of the intern program at the State University of New York made her refusal public, she denied nothing but promptly accused the university official of, yes, racism.[264]

In January 1992, the Hertz car-rental company announced that it was adding stiff surcharges to rentals in Brooklyn and the Bronx. This was an attempt to try to make up for the $45 million it had lost in the previous three years due to lawsuits, wrecks, and stolen cars. Mayor Dinkins promptly accused the company of "racism," since these parts of the city have large black populations.[265]

In a recent study in the Chicago area, 14 percent of blacks and 9 percent of whites agreed with the view that blacks have less "inborn ability to learn than whites." The fact that more blacks than whites expressed this "racist" view was, somewhat paradoxically, attributed to white racism. Larry Bobo of the University of California explains that whites have established a "pervasive ideology" of black inferiority. "An entire society is built around it," he says.[266] It seems odd to argue that whites have somehow made blacks believe something that most whites, themselves, claim not to believe.

Robert McIntosh is an Arkansas man who has tried several times to burn the American flag in the hope of calling attention to social problems. Shortly after June 1989, when the U.S. Supreme Court upheld flag burning as a form of free speech, he announced that he would celebrate the Fourth of July by burning the flag on the steps of the Arkansas State Capitol. He was prevented from doing so by outraged citizens. Because of several attempts like this, Mr. McIntosh attracted nationwide media attention and many death threats. Mr. McIntosh, who is black, does not believe that the furor was over the flag at all. "It was caused by racism," he says.[267]

Andrew Jenkins, the black superintendent of Washington, D.C.'s, school district, was fired in his third year on the job. He accused the school board of racism—even though eight of the eleven board members were black.[268]

In Dallas, Texas, Judge Jack Hampton of the State District Court got into trouble for remarks from the bench about homosexuals, whom he called "queers." He was then attacked by minority groups for . . . racism. "What other prejudices does he harbor . . . ?" asked the head of the Mexican-American Bar Association. "The only difference between the Ku Klux Klan and Judge Hampton is that one wears a white robe and the other a black robe," said a black county commissioner.[269] Mayor Dinkins of New York has also argued that anyone who disapproves of homosexuals is likely to be a racist as well.[270]

Sometimes the stock appeal to white wickedness can take a very ugly turn. In 1988, a black murderer tried to pin his crime on whites by carving the letters KKK on the victim's leg.[271] Likewise, in May 1991, when Andrew Denton robbed and ransacked his aunt's home in Milton, Massachusetts, he and his confederates wrote racist graffiti on the wall to make it look as though whites had done it.[272]

A much better-known case of this type was that of Tawana Brawley. The entire nation was mesmerized by the story of this sixteen-year-old. In November 1987 she was found in a garbage bag, smeared with dog feces and with the words "nigger" and "KKK" written on her body. She claimed she had been abducted and repeatedly raped by a gang of white men. Believers in white racism rallied to these charges in full cry. A special prosecutor was

---

[272] Andrea Estes and Sarah Koch, "Cops Nab Five Blacks in Milton Burglary," *Boston Herald* (May 25, 1991), p. 1. Although blacks frequently stage "racist" incidents for their own benefit, it is impossible to get an accurate idea of how common they are. A well-documented, self-published study of the phenomenon is available: Laird Wilcox, *The Hoaxer Project Report*, Editorial Research Service, P.O. Box 2047, Olathe, KS 66061.

appointed, on the assumption that a racist system would never deliver justice.

But Miss Brawley, on advice from her black lawyers, refused to cooperate with police. Her lawyers likened the prosecutor, a long-time civil rights activist, to Hitler, and called him a "moral beast." They accused him of masturbating to seminude photos of Miss Brawley, and called Governor Mario Cuomo of New York a racist and a dog. They managed to spin out this distasteful farce for nine months before a grand jury finally concluded that Miss Brawley had done herself up in the garbage bag and then invented the rapes. She apparently thought this would be a convincing way to explain to her violent parents why she had not come home that night.[273] This sorry circus would not have gone on for nearly as long but for America's readiness to believe charges of racism.

Many blacks still believe Miss Brawley's story. She has made repeated public appearances as a martyr to the cause of black liberation. Two years after the incident, Louis Elise, president of the Boston chapter of the NAACP, told a television audience he was still convinced she had been raped by white policemen.[274]

Some sympathetic whites seemed to think it did not matter either way. As anthropologist Stanley Diamond explained in *The Nation,* "It doesn't matter whether the crime occurred or not . . . [since it was] the epitome of degradation, a repellent model of what actually happens to too many black women. . . ."[275] In fact, as we will see below, rape of a black woman by a white man is one of the rarest of crimes, whereas rape of a white woman by a black man has increased greatly over the past few decades. In 1988, for example, there were 9,406 reported cases of whites being raped by blacks, whereas there were *fewer than 10* reported cases of blacks being raped by whites.[276]

Some of the saddest—and most hurtful—charges of racism are directed at whites who are doing their best to help blacks. When former Surgeon General Everett Koop warned blacks that high consumption of cigarettes made them more likely than whites to get lung cancer, he was immediately branded a racist.[277]

The San Francisco AIDS Foundation got in the same kind of trouble when it produced posters warning blacks about the connection between drug-related promiscuity and AIDS. In one part of the two-panel poster, two black men are smoking crack, while a black woman looks on in the distance. In the second panel, a young black man holding a crack pipe is standing in front of a black woman. The woman's legs are apart and she is raising her dress. The poster brought down such wrath that it had to be junked. Cecil Williams, the most famous black preacher in the city, said, "The poster is an affront to black women. It's exploitative and dehumanizing." The AIDS Foundation meekly observed that it had consulted with black, recovering drug addicts before it made the poster, but promised to try again with something less offensive.[278]

The connection between cigarette smoking and cancer is well known, as is that between crack cocaine and AIDS. What is racist or exploitative about calling this to the attention of blacks—especially when they suffer more from the consequences than whites do? Apparently the preferred way to persuade blacks to stop smoking is to tell them that cigarettes are a racist plot. In 1992 a nonprofit group in New York announced an antismoking ad directed toward blacks that depicted a skeleton lighting a cigarette for a black child. The caption read: "They used to make us pick it. Now they want us to smoke it."[279] Once again, the evils of the world can be laid at the feet of whites.

Black Responsibility

So far we have examined aspects of white behavior that could make a real difference to black people. If blacks could not get jobs, were cavalierly arrested and shot by the police, were sought out by white criminals, persecuted in universities, hounded out of public office, and beset by racism at every turn, it would certainly hold them back. However, blacks suffer from terrible, self-inflicted wounds, for which whites can hardly be blamed.

Practically everyone has heard the awful statistics about black illegitimacy and teenage pregnancy. One study in Chicago, for example, found that of the many black fathers who had their first child out of wedlock, only 29 percent eventually married the mother. The figure for whites was 74 percent.[280] Nationwide, black children are much more likely than whites to be illegitimate. It is hard to see how malevolent whites manage to persuade black teenagers to get pregnant or talk black men into running out on their children. Since hardly anyone dares suggest that blacks themselves are responsible for this, and since today's whites cannot be blamed by even the most contorted logic, society blames yesterday's whites. Slavery must have destroyed the black family.[281]

Slavery, however, defines relations between blacks and whites about as accurately as colonialism defines relations between Britain and the United States. Female-headed families and black illegitimacy on a large scale are recent problems. Even before emancipation, most black children grew up in families with two parents.[282] In 1950, only 9 percent of black families were headed by one parent. By 1965, the number was 28 percent, and by 1970 it was 33 percent. Now fully half of all black families with children are headed by a single parent.[283] In 1959, only 15 percent of black births were illegitimate. In 1988, 61 percent were, and by 1992, the figure was approaching 70 percent.[284] The black family survived slavery, the Depression, urbanization, and the postwar migrations to the North,[285] only to collapse precisely when America was doing its best to do away with racial inequality.

We have heard over and over that blacks are the only people who were brought to America against their will, and that this terrible blow explains their failures centuries later. In fact, hundreds of thousands of European criminals and paupers were forcibly exiled to America, and Britain was still dumping its human refuse in America as late as 1885—more than a century after independence.[286] Other whites came to America in bondage as indentured servants. They ran away, were recaptured, and flogged just like slaves. One scholar estimates that more than half of the white immigrants to the thirteen original colonies came as bondsmen.[287]

But more to the point, it is exquisitely irrelevant whether anyone's great-great-great-great grandparents came to America by free will or not. No one chooses his birthplace, so except for first-generation immigrants, no one in America has any more choice over his homeland than do the descendants of slaves. This does not stop people from blaming slavery for everything from drug addiction to murder rates to illegitimacy.

It is not clear what destroyed black families. The stigmas against divorce and sex outside of marriage have faded for all Americans, and white families are falling apart, too, though not as rapidly. Perhaps it was that blacks, at the bottom of the social scale, had the fewest reserves against collapse. In any case, few whites have any idea what these stark statistics about illegitimacy mean for the texture of life for some blacks. Though it is a subject that most people approach, if at all, with the greatest delicacy, a 70 percent illegitimacy rate lies at the heart of many of the sorrows that black people face. The final two chapters of this book examine the catastrophic consequences of a society without families.

Help Must Come from Whites

When it comes to trying to solve social problems, blacks seem to turn instinctively to whites. In September 1990, a San Francisco group calling itself the Coalition for the African American Community Agenda staged a candlelight vigil in front of City Hall. It denounced the large number of shooting deaths of young blacks—virtually all at the hands of other young blacks—and, declaring a "state of emergency," demanded that city government stop the killings. The clear implication was that white city bureaucrats are to blame if blacks are shooting each other.[288]

The same thinking is at work on the other side of the country. In 1985, Mayor Ed Koch of New York appointed a fifteen-member, all-black commission to study the status of the city's blacks. Three years later, it produced a 336-page report that surprised no one. It found that blacks are "a community in crisis" and that they are "less educated, earn less, and have a higher rate of unemployment than whites." The commission asked for loan guarantees for black business, city deposits in black-owned banks, recruitment of more high-level blacks, job set-asides, community hiring halls for blacks, etc. As one black newspaper approvingly put it, the report bolstered the view that "many of the economic and social prob-

lems being experienced by blacks can be traced right to City Hall."
Mayor Koch praised the report.[289]

As is common in reports of this kind, there was no suggestion
that blacks should, or even could, get a grip on themselves. All
help is to come from whites or from the government. This reflects
a very common view among blacks. As one prominent polltaker
reports, "the greatest difference between blacks and whites in
polling [is that] the vast majority of blacks believe government can
solve *anything.*"[290] For many blacks, government is a symbol of
white America. White people could solve black people's problems
if they really wanted to. Since the government has not solved all
their problems, it must not want to.

Just how far this kind of thinking can go was clear after the
election of David Dinkins as the first black mayor of New York
City. One of Mayor Dinkins's first important appointments was
that of a black police chief. Nevertheless, in the first few months of
his term, there was a brief rise in civilian deaths at the hands of
police officers. This came as a shock to some of the new mayor's
black supporters. Rev. Herbert Daughtry of Brooklyn, who had
been prominent in the Dinkins campaign, expressed incredulity
that police should still be shooting at people now that the city had
a black mayor. He suggested that the deaths must be the "legacy"
of former white mayor Ed Koch.[291] If a prominent preacher can
be so naive as to think that the election of a black mayor will
somehow mean that police need no longer use their guns, it is easy
to imagine the faith that less sophisticated blacks must have in the
powers of government.

But even if America had a government of geniuses and every
white person were a saint, fatherless children with thirty-two-year-
old grandmothers would still have a good chance of staying poor
and going to jail. These children are not the victims of racism; they
are victims of irresponsible parents—irresponsibility that is ignored and excused by constant harping on white wickedness.
Blacks are done a great disservice when they hear from their own
leaders and from "honest" whites that City Hall is to blame for all
this. Of course, City Hall is now often run by blacks—in Los Angeles, Detroit, Washington, D.C., New York, Seattle, New Haven,
Cleveland, Philadelphia, Baltimore, and Newark, New Jersey, for

example—but there are always ways to shirk responsibility. As William Raspberry explains, "[Even] when both the victims and the victimizers are black . . . the tendency is to start looking for white people to blame."[292]

Crime and Race

The theory of white racism carries an enormous, impossible burden—the burden of explaining black tragedy. It is a theory based not so much on evidence but on emotion, evasion, and guilt. Because the evidence for systematic racism is thin, believers must always be on the alert for any indication of it. Because there is so much black tragedy that racism must explain, when the believers do find a certifiably evil act they wave the bloody shirt with a terrible fury—fury laced with a touch of relief at finding "proof" that their dark suspicions were right all along. This helps explain why racially motivated crimes committed by whites against blacks so frequently become front-page, national news. Two examples will do.

One evening in 1986, some white teenagers were driving a girl home when three blacks walked in front of their car and were nearly hit. A shouting match then ensued, a black shouted "F—— you, honky," another flashed a knife, and one reportedly stuck his head through a window and spat in the face of one of the whites. The whites drove away furious, and after dropping off the girl, returned with baseball bats. They brutally attacked one of the blacks and gave him an injury requiring five stitches. Another black was hit and killed by a car as he tried to escape.[293]

Since the attackers were white, the victims were black, and the word "nigger" was used, this incident became a national sensation known as Howard Beach. New York City could hardly talk of anything else. There was a flood of analysis and self-criticism. Blacks held rallies, marches, and demonstrations. Whites beat their breasts. Mayor Ed Koch, who presided over a city whose citizens were committing more than fifteen hundred murders every year, chose to call this one the most horrendous crime in all his

years in office. Blacks demanded, and quickly got, a special prosecutor to try the case, since the usual procedures were allegedly
shot through with racism and could not handle such a case
fairly.[294] The whites were, of course, duly convicted.

The second incident occurred three years later. A gang of bat-
swinging whites viciously attacked four blacks whom they thought
had come to visit a white girl in the mainly white Brooklyn neighborhood of Bensonhurst. One of the whites reportedly yelled, "To
hell with beating them up, forget the bats, I'm going to shoot the
nigger." He then pulled out a gun and shot a sixteen-year-old to
death.[295]

Although this incident was repeatedly described as one in which
whites were lying in wait to attack any blacks who came along, this
was not at all the case. They were looking for a specific group of
blacks whom they thought would be invading their "turf," and
repeatedly asked each other, "Are these the guys?" before attacking. The purely racial explanation for the killing is further weakened by the fact that one of the young men who helped round up
bats for the group was a Bensonhurst resident named Russell Gib-
bons, *who is black.* He was a close friend of one of the whites,
Keith Mondello, who was later convicted in connection with the
killing.[296] In fact, at the last moment, most of the whites realized
that they had surrounded two innocent men. When the actual
killer, Joseph Fama, pulled out a gun, whites in the group shouted
at him not to use it.[297] Race does not appear to have been the
exclusive motive.

All the same, this murder also provoked an outpouring of soul-
searching and analysis. Blacks used the incident as a pretext for
transparently antiwhite provocations. Black filmmaker Spike Lee
blamed all whites for the shooting and declared that Mayor Ed
Koch's finger was on the trigger of the murder weapon.[298] Black
demonstrators, chanting and waving signs, marched through Bensonhurst not just once but more than a dozen different times,
condemning the whole neighborhood.[299]

During another demonstration, marchers chanting, "What's
coming? War!" tried to block traffic on the Brooklyn Bridge.
When police tried to keep the bridge open, marchers attacked and
injured twenty-three officers.[300] Black activist Viola Plummer gave

a speech in which she vowed, "From this day forward, for every black child that we bury, we are going to bury five of theirs."[301] Even some middle-class blacks lost their heads. One wondered, in a *New York Times* guest editorial titled "Will I Be Next?," whether "white people secretly aspire to intern us all in jails or concentration camps—to permanently do away with us?"[302]

What is the meaning of incidents like these? They demonstrate that, without a doubt, there are some whites in America who do ugly things to blacks. However, in a nation of a quarter of a billion people, there will always be a few whites who do ugly things to blacks. The significance of the Howard Beach and Bensonhurst killings lies as much in the reactions to them as in the incidents themselves. If America were seething with white racism, this sort of thing would presumably be happening all the time. It is because it *so rarely happens* that Howard Beach and Bensonhurst became huge sensations. They were proof, they were The Real Thing, racism at its murderous worst. They were what the believers in white wickedness are hunting for.

Although many white Americans sense that crimes committed by blacks against whites are more common than the reverse, this is something that is rarely acknowledged publicly. The press treats interracial crime in the same way it treats race relations in general —so as to suggest that blacks are vastly more sinned against than sinning. In the case of interracial crime, this impression is created by giving huge publicity to crimes committed by whites against blacks while downplaying the same crimes when the races are reversed.

The misleading portrait of America that results from this kind of reporting has different effects on blacks and whites. It fuels an already exaggerated sense of grievance in blacks. It instills an exaggerated sense of guilt in some whites, while it sows mistrust among those who have some knowledge of the true proportions of interracial crime. All of these effects are dangerous.

Even a cursory search will bring to light little-known crimes committed by blacks against whites that would have been national news if committed by whites against blacks. For example, a month after the widely reported Bensonhurst shooting, an almost identical crime was committed in the Bronx by blacks. A white got out of his car to make a telephone call on East Tremont Avenue, in a racially mixed neighborhood. Two blacks approached and asked, "What are you white guys doing on Tremont? You don't belong here." In the argument that followed, one of the blacks pulled a gun and shot the white, wounding him in the stomach.[303] This incident provoked no marches, no outbursts, no hand-wringing, and hardly any press coverage. When a black minister who had been prominent in berating whites on account of the Bensonhurst killing was asked about the shooting in the Bronx, he replied, "I don't know that that's racism as I define it. . . . There's a difference between racism and revenge."[304]

There was not even the element of revenge in the death of white, twenty-three-year-old Danny Gilmore. One evening in July 1988 he was driving his pickup truck through a black neighborhood of Cleveland, looking for the freeway. A black man on a moped pulled out without looking and bumped the truck. He was uninjured, but a crowd of about forty black men soon showed up. People started pouring beer into Mr. Gilmore's truck. Someone tried to get into the cab and grab the keys. A scuffle broke out, and the blacks thrashed Mr. Gilmore. He broke away, stumbled in front of his truck, and collapsed on the street. One of the blacks started the engine, and as the crowd cheered him on, crushed Mr. Gilmore under the wheels of his own truck.

The black reporter for the *Cleveland Plain Dealer* who covered the killing immediately recognized it to be racial dynamite, but his white editors buried the story and, over his protests, suppressed the race angle. The killing got little local attention and no national coverage. The Cleveland homicide detective who covered the case explained it this way: "The mayor's office doesn't want us to have racial killings in this town, so Danny Gilmore's death wasn't a racial crime. And I'm the tooth fairy."[305]

A similar crime was committed in Philadelphia just a few months before the Bensonhurst killing. A gang of Hispanics, who had been prevented from crashing a white party, vowed to take revenge. A week later, they did. They were not able to find any of the people who had kept them out of the party, so they shot and killed the first white youngster they could find.[306] This incident was ignored by the national media.

Crimes of this type are part of American life, but they attract virtually no attention. In January 1991, a black man named Robert Herbert killed a white man named Mark Belmore. Earlier, Mr. Herbert and three other blacks had agreed among themselves that they would kill the first white person they saw. Mr. Belmore, a student at Northeastern University in Boston, was unlucky enough to be the first, and was stabbed to death.[307] It was strictly local news.

In February 1991, Christopher D. Peterson was arrested for murdering seven white people with a shotgun. Mr. Peterson, who is black, explained that he had killed for purely racial reasons, saying that he had "a deep-rooted hatred for white people."[308] This would certainly appear to be a far clearer and more spectacular example of a "hate" crime than the Howard Beach and Bensonhurst cases, but the incident was largely ignored.

In May 1992, three blacks were sentenced in a case that closely paralleled the famous Howard Beach incident. One night in 1990, the three had a heated exchange of racial slurs with a white man. Later that night they vented their anger on another white man, 21-year-old Robert Massaro, whom they attacked and beat. Mr. Massaro broke away and was chased into a lake, where he drowned.

The incident drew scant attention and the attackers were lightly punished. Each was fined $500, put on probation for three years, made to do community service, and given jail terms of up to one year. The contrast with the uproar over the Howard Beach case could not be more striking.[309]

In Tampa, Florida, on a Saturday night in May 1990, a dozen blacks showed up at a hangout popular with white teenagers. They were looking for a fight, were accommodated with some minor fisticuffs, and left vowing to return with reinforcements. An hour later, the blacks found some of the whites in a parking lot five blocks away and attacked them. The whites met the attack with their fists. The blacks then started swinging clubs, and when one opened fire with a pistol, the whites scattered. One of the whites did not get away in time, and was cornered by seven blacks. According to a woman who saw the attack from her window, the blacks beat the nineteen-year-old white to death with two-by-fours. "I could see a piece of wood come down and crack against his head," she said. She told police that with every blow, the assailants said, "Don't ever f——with us. Don't ever f——with us again." Police later found the attackers and charged four black adults and two juveniles with first-degree murder.[310]

In the Howard Beach incident, the whites who cornered a black could have killed him with their baseball bats but did not. They gave him an injury that took five stitches to close and then stopped beating him. The man who did die was hit by a car. The deliberate beating to death of a white in Tampa is local news, while the death of a black in New York is national news. When whites kill people for racial reasons it goes on the front page and is cause for agonized self-examination. When blacks (or Hispanics) kill whites for racial reasons, there is silence.

The 1991–92 trial of Hulon Mitchell, leader of the black, Miami-based Yahweh sect, brought to light what may be some of the most shocking antiwhite murders ever committed in the United States—but they remained mainly local news. Mr. Mitchell's cult was based on a theory of the white man as devil, which he spread in various ways. One was to show cult members—men, women, and children alike—the vilest possible pornographic videos of white women having sex with animals or black men. He would call the woman "Miss Ann" and claim that her degradation proved she was a she-devil.

He also gave a regular course in hatred of whites, which came to be known as the Killing Class. "How many of you would bring back a white head?" he would ask, and everyone would raise his hand. He would then shout, "One day, Yahweh is going to kill the white devil off the planet. We're going to catch him and we're going to kill him wherever we find him. All over America, white heads are going to roll!"[311]

A number of Yahweh sect members were ordered by Mr. Mitchell to seek out and kill white devils—and they did as they were told. Robert Rozier, a former Yahweh sect member and onetime professional football player, testified in January 1992 that he killed three "white devils" on instructions from Mr. Mitchell. It made no difference whom he killed as long as his victims were white.

The first two "white devils" were Mr. Rozier's roommates. However, Mr. Mitchell would not acknowledge these killings because Mr. Rozier failed to bring back the heads as proof. When it was pointed out that it was awkward to be seen walking about Miami with a human head, Mr. Mitchell relaxed the requirements and said he would be satisfied with an ear. Mr. Rozier took to riding the subways with a twelve-inch sword, looking for "white devils" to kill. When he finally got his man, he brought back an ear as a trophy. All told, members of the sect appear to have killed at least seven different "white devils," beginning in 1986, and ears or fingers were usually brought in as proof of a mission accomplished. Sect members also killed several blacks, but they were apostates and other sworn enemies. The sect killed white people out of pure racial hatred.[312]

Miami police were reportedly hesitant to pursue these crimes for fear that they would be accused of *racial and religious persecution*.[313] And, in fact, that is precisely the argument that defense attorney and former judge Alcee Hastings tried to make. He claimed that the prosecutions were racially motivated. In May 1992, a jury found Mr. Mitchell guilty of conspiracy to commit murder.[314]

Needless to say, there would be a coast-to-coast media din of unprecedented proportions if a white group were discovered to have engaged in ritual murder and mutilation of blacks. In fact, the Yahweh trial ran concurrently with the trial of the Los Angeles policemen who were videotaped beating Rodney King. Mr. King's name was constantly in the news and practically a household name; few outside of Miami had heard of the Yahweh cult.

Why do the media report antiblack crime so assiduously and ignore antiwhite crime? Because they are hypnotized by the myths they have helped to create. Since everyone has been led to believe that America is a fever swamp of white racism, the press must be very circumspect about reporting such things as the Yahweh killings, for fear of feeding that racism. Whites cannot be trusted with the truth about blacks because the truth might promote "negative stereotypes." There is no telling where that might lead. Whites might resort to lynching and mayhem if ritual murder of whites were reported as vigorously as a baseball-bat attack on a black. At the same time, the fever swamp might possibly be drained and civilized if whites are constantly reminded of their prejudices.

Thus, while the media strain every muscle to avoid every other "negative stereotype," there is one stereotype that can always be assumed, promoted, and circulated: that of the racist white person. Editors soft-pedal the news about antiwhite crime, give first-page treatment to antiblack crime, and then believe what they read in the papers.

In effect, people in the media cover race relations as if America had not changed in decades. Until the middle of this century, there always was the danger, especially in the states of the former Confederacy, that rumors of a black offense against whites would touch off retaliatory violence. However, no black man has been lynched in America for more than thirty years.[315] Moreover, it was as far back as the 1930s that the meaning of the term "race riot" changed. Until then, as in the Atlanta riots of 1906 and the Tulsa riots of 1921, it had meant mobs of whites attacking blacks. The turning point was the Harlem riot of 1935. Since that time, American race riots have consisted of mobs of violent blacks.[316] America has not seen a mob of whites on the rampage against blacks in more than half a century. The media seem not to have noticed.

The Statistics

In the soul-searching that follows crimes like those at Howard Beach and Bensonhurst, virtually no one cites the statistics on interracial crime. When whites do violence—rape, murder, assault—how often do they choose black victims? Shouldn't a nation of bigots target blacks most of the time? At least half of the time? Of course, it does not. When whites commit violence, they do it to blacks *2.4 percent* of the time. Blacks, on the other hand, choose white victims *more than half* the time.[317]

What about interracial murder? In those cases in which the race of the killer is known, blacks kill twice as many whites as whites

---

[315] It has been all but forgotten that whites were lynched as well as blacks. Between the years 1882 and 1962, a total of 3,442 blacks and 1,294 whites were lynched. The last white was lynched in 1957, and the last black in 1961. From 1947 to 1961, blacks were lynched at a rate of fewer than one a year. Harry Ploski and James Williams, eds., *The Negro Almanac*, 4th ed. (Bronxville, N.Y.: Bellwether Publishing, 1983), p. 348.

kill blacks. Black-on-white robberies and gang assaults are twenty-one times more common than white on black. In the case of gang robbery, blacks victimize whites fifty-two times more often than whites do blacks.[318]

The contrasts are even more stark in the case of interracial rape. Studies from the late 1950s showed that the vast majority of rapes were same-race offenses. Research in Philadelphia carried out in 1958 and 1960 indicated that of *all* rapes, only 3.2 percent were black-on-white assaults and 3.6 percent were white-on-black. Since that time, the proportion of black-on-white rapes has soared. In a 1974 study in Denver, 40 percent of all rapes were of whites by blacks, and *not one case* of white-on-black rape was found. In general, through the 1970s, black-on-white rape was at least ten times more common than white-on-black rape.[319]

Because interracial rape is now overwhelmingly black on white, it has become difficult to do research on it or to find relevant statistics. The FBI keeps very detailed national records on crime, but the way it presents rape data obscures the racial element rather than clarifies it. Dr. William Wilbanks, a criminologist at Florida International University, had to sift carefully through the data to find that in 1988 there were 9,406 cases of black-on-white rape and fewer than ten cases of white-on-black rape.[320] Another researcher concludes that in 1989, blacks were three or four times more likely to commit rape than whites, and that black men raped white women thirty times as often as white men raped black women.[321]

Interracial crime figures are even worse than they sound. Since there are more than six times as many whites as blacks in America, it means that any given black person is vastly more likely to commit a crime against a white than vice versa. For example, though the actual likelihood is exceedingly small, the average black person is 12.38 times more likely to kill a white than the average white is to kill a black.[322] When it comes to gang robbery, the average black is an astonishing 325 times more likely to take part

[322] To simplify the calculation, assume that America has a population of 100, of whom 75 are white and 12 are black (very close to the correct proportions). If blacks kill 10 whites and whites kill 5 blacks, the likelihood of a black killing a white is 10 divided by 12, or 0.83. The likelihood of a white killing a black is 5 divided by 75, or 0.067. The likelihood for blacks, 0.83, is 12.38 times greater than the likelihood for whites, 0.067.

in a gang attack on a white than a white is to take part in a gang attack on a black. If we accept an extremely conservative estimate —that black-on-white rape is ten times as common as the reverse —the average black man is 64 times more likely to rape a white woman than is the average white man to rape a black woman.

How much of these differences are due to antiwhite racism? No one knows. When a black man kills or robs a white man, no one asks whether his motives were racial. Government commissions, watchdog groups, "civil rights" activists, and editorial boards are not constantly on the alert for black racism.

This is because black racism does not carry the heavy burden of having to explain America's greatest social problems. When a white acts viciously toward a black, the incident takes on huge significance, as part of the miasma of white hatred that is said to be making blacks fail. It falls into a class of acts for which ready-made explanations and consequences are endlessly repeated.

When blacks act viciously toward whites, it is usually considered a matter between two individuals. The evil begins and ends with the actor and his victim, whereas the same act, only with the races reversed, reverberates through society. America is outraged by white racism; it merely averts its eyes from black racism.

Moreover, since black racism sits uncomfortably alongside the whites-are-responsible theory of black failure, it is best not to acknowledge it at all. When a white kills a black, it is racism; when a black kills a white, it is homicide. If black racism must be discussed at all, it can be excused as a consequence of centuries of white racism. Of course, many blacks blandly maintain that there can be no such thing as black racism.

It is only very recently, with the passage of laws requiring police departments to keep records of "hate" crimes, that some indication of the racial motivation of black-on-white crime has officially come to light. Of course, it is not always easy to know what motivates interracial crime, and police departments have generally had to rely on statements from victims about what the attacker said. As one might expect, there is considerable pressure to scrutinize white-on-black crimes for signs of "bias," if only because they are rare. The mass of black-on-white crime often goes unexamined. One newspaper even wondered in an editorial why the term "bias crime" seemed to be applied only to crimes in which whites attacked blacks.[323]

What, after all, is one to make of a news story like this, here reproduced in full:

> **"Wilding" attacks:** San Diego police are investigating 50 unusually savage assaults that they liken to New York City's notorious "wilding" attacks, perpetrated by youthful robbers for the sake of committing violence.
>
> Police said the young attackers are black and their victims, 46 men and four women, are white. The victims were attacked in the Hillcrest and North Park neighborhoods.
>
> There is no evidence they are hate crimes, Detective Steve Baker said.[324]

Particularly among blacks, there is great resistance to calling a crime committed by blacks against whites a "hate" crime. For example, Rev. Timothy Mitchell of the Ebenezer Missionary Baptist Church in New York had this to say about the rape of a fifteen-year-old white girl by two black men:

> Rape is rape; white or black. I read that the child says one of the black men told her she was being raped because she was "the perfect white girl" and that he asked, "Have you ever been kissed by a black man?" If he had called her a white epithet or said, "I'm gonna fix you for what is happening to my people," then it's bias. But I don't think based on the statements she claims were made to her, that this is a bias case.[325]

Despite this reluctance to categorize attacks by blacks as "hate crimes," the statistics that have begun to trickle in paint a grim picture. In the state of New York in 1990, whites were nearly twice as likely as blacks to be victims of hate crimes.[326] Once again, given that there are only one fifth as many blacks in the state as there are whites, it is clear that a vastly larger proportion of blacks than whites commit "hate crimes."

There is a certain irony in the fact that statistics like this are available at all. New laws on "hate crimes" have usually been passed in the wake of heavily reported—but uncharacteristic—crimes committed by whites against minorities. The New York State data were probably a surprise to many people who learned of them. Few learned of them, however, because the news was scarcely reported. The fact that blacks are far more likely to commit "hate crimes" than whites is a fact for which there is simply no room in the conventional view of how American society works.

Sadly, anyone who had regularly skimmed the New York City police blotter would not have been surprised by the "hate crimes" report for 1989. There has been plenty of crime that was clearly antiwhite. A gang of black passengers drags a white boy to the back of a city bus, where they kick, punch, and rob him, repeatedly calling him "white boy."[327] Ten teenage black girls in New York are arrested for a week of attacks on forty different white women, in which they ran down Broadway jabbing them with push pins "to see their reaction."[328] Ten blacks approach two white women in an automobile. One says, "If you're looking for white women to kill, here's two now," and the blacks throw rocks and bottles at the car.[329] Two white girls are waiting for the subway. They are approached by one Hispanic and four black girls. A black says, "What are you white b——s looking at?," grabs an umbrella from one of the white girls, and beats her with it.[330] Twenty black thugs go on a violent rampage through a subway train. "Get the white guys; leave the brothers alone," says one, and they proceed to do just that.[331]

There are many incidents like this in any large city, but they are lightly reported and never result in protest marches into black neighborhoods or in antiblack rampages. Nevertheless, one white high-school student who lives in New York City did reflect in *The New York Times* about a group of blacks who attacked him and broke his nose. He did not, however, complain about black racism. "Getting attacked because of my race made me look at myself and

---

[331] Jim Dwyer, "Giving Violence a Brand Name," (New York) *Newsday* (November 2, 1989), p. 4. The general impression of New Yorkers that most street crime is committed by blacks and Hispanics—whether against whites or against each other—is correct. Although blacks and Hispanics together make up about half of the city's population, they account for 95 percent of the city's jail inmates. William Glaberson, "One in Four Young Black Men Are in Custody, Study Says," *The New York Times* (October 4, 1990).

understand what I symbolize to others. It doesn't matter that I have not a single racist bone in my body; too many white people before me did." This boy did not condemn the attack because it was racist; he *excused* it because it was racist. His solution? Vote for Jesse Jackson.[332]

Only a few recent antiwhite outbursts have gotten much notice. One was a black riot in the Crown Heights section of Brooklyn in the summer of 1991. It was set off by a traffic accident. A Hasidic Jew, driving in convoy through a black neighborhood, fell behind his party and ran a red light in an attempt to catch up. His car was hit by cross traffic, jumped the sidewalk, and smashed into two black children. When Yosef Lifsh got out of the car to see what had happened, he was immediately surrounded by angry blacks. They beat Mr. Lifsh and tore his watch off his wrist and his wallet out of his pocket. When a bystander tried to use Mr. Lifsh's cellular telephone to call the police, another grabbed it and ran. Others stole things out of the car.[333]

The police and two ambulances—one from a private, Hasidic service and the other from the city—arrived almost simultaneously. Police directed the Hasidic crew to take care of Mr. Lifsh, who was bleeding profusely and needed eighteen stitches on his face and head. The city ambulance took the black children to the hospital, where one of them died.

Blacks began to converge on the scene and spread false reports that the Hasidic paramedics had given the Jewish driver first aid but had deliberately ignored the badly injured black children. A mob started throwing rocks and bottles at police, who were trying to restore order. Three hours after the accident, rampaging blacks fell upon a Jew dressed in classic Hasidic garb. Twenty or so surrounded the hapless Yankel Rosenbaum and chanted "Kill the Jew" while a sixteen-year-old stabbed him to death.[334]

Two more days of rioting followed, during which gangs of blacks looted stores, burned two buildings, destroyed parked cars, and chanted "Hitler was right." Blacks attacked at least six white journalists who were covering the riots. Dozens of police were injured, and both Mayor Dinkins and New York City's black police chief narrowly escaped violence when they came to Crown Heights to preach calm.[335]

Prowling mobs pulled passing white motorists from their cars and thrashed them. One of their targets was columnist Jimmy Breslin, who had taken a taxi to Brooklyn to see what was happening. A shout went up that there was a white in the car, and a crowd of black children smashed the windshield and swarmed into the taxi. The black cab driver took to his heels while Mr. Breslin was robbed, beaten, and stripped to his underwear. He was knocked down, and thinks he might have had his brains dashed out with a baseball bat if a large black man with a knife had not appeared and forced the young robbers to leave.[336]

The rioting did not finally stop until the mayor decided to get tough and send two thousand riot police to Crown Heights.[337] Afterward, *The New York Times* editorialized about the need for "continuing efforts to ease race relations." It urged the city to "foster communication between blacks and Hasidim."[338]

Did a lack of "communication" provoke riots in Crown Heights? It is true that a black child was run over by a Jewish driver, and though there may have been negligence, this was certainly not a deliberate killing. As it happens, in October 1989 a black driver hit and killed a Jewish child. In January 1990, a black man ran over and killed an eighty-nine-year-old Jewish man. In neither case was the driver molested. In neither case were there disturbances.

Blacks and Hasidic Jews do not always get along in Crown Heights, but there is no possible lack of "communication" that can justify murder, riot, arson, or pulling whites from passing cars and beating them. The riots were not so much expressions of legitimate grievance as outbursts of lawlessness and hatred.

Another black-on-white crime that got even greater attention was the case of the Central Park jogger. In April 1989, a white woman jogging in Central Park was gang-raped, beaten to within an inch of her life, and left for dead by a roving group of young blacks and Hispanics. She was so badly mangled that when the police called in her boyfriend to identify the unconscious woman, he could recognize her only because of her ring. This crime was met with a torrent of press commentary, but no marches, demonstrations, or "revenge." Despite the fact that some of the hoodlums had said "Let's get a white girl" before attacking, many commentators urged readers not to think of the crime as racially motivated at all.[339] The widespread black response to this crime, and to the trial that followed, was so spiteful that even the most resolutely accommodating whites were astonished.

As is customary in cases like this, the press voluntarily refrained from publicizing the name of the victim. As Jerry Nachman of the *New York Post* explained, "What we want to avoid is, a year from now, she buys a blouse from Bloomingdale's and hands her credit card to the clerk who says, 'Oh, yeah, you're the one who got gang-raped in Central Park.' " Black newspapers, which generally follow the same rule, deliberately published the name of the white jogger.[340] Black-owned radio station WLIB also broadcast her name.[341]

Despite videotaped confessions that left little doubt about the guilt of the accused rapists, black newspapers described the trial as a racist farce. The *Amsterdam News* repeatedly used the word "lynching" in its headlines, and described the prosecutor and grand jury as "little better than lynch mobs," with police lined up "to do the lying and dirty work."[342] The paper's publisher, William Tatum, explained what was going on:

> The truth of the matter is that there is a conspiracy of interest attendant in this case that dictates that someone black must go to jail for this crime against the "jogger" and any black will do. The rationale being the belief that blacks are interchangeable anyway."[343]

The *City Sun,* apparently miffed at *New York Post* columns that criticized black papers for their coverage of the trial, began calling the *Post* "New York's apartheid paper."[344]

The trial was attended by a faithful group of black demonstrators who treated the defendants like heroes and accused the justice system of racism. When the rape-victim jogger arrived to testify, still disfigured and unsteady, they screamed that she was a whore and that she had been raped by her boyfriend.[345]

The prosecutor, Elizabeth Lederer, was repeatedly threatened by defendants and their supporters.[346] After the inevitable guilty verdicts were announced, black spectators at the trial shouted curses and insults at the jogger, who was not there, and at the prosecutor. Blacks in the hallway of the courthouse shouted "filthy white whore," "white slut," and "People are going to die."[347] The prosecutor had to be protected by an escort of twelve policemen as she left the courthouse, but about two dozen blacks followed her, shouting, "liar," "prostitute," and "You're gonna pay."[348]

Thomas Galligan, the judge who presided over the jogger trials, received repeated anonymous death threats. He sentenced one man, who publicly threatened him, to thirty days in jail for contempt of court.[349]

But perhaps the low point in the entire trial was a one-day appearance by Tawana Brawley. The perpetrator of a spectacular rape hoax came to congratulate and show solidarity with the hero/ martyrs on trial for a very real rape and near-murder. A spokesman for Miss Brawley explained that she had come to court to "observe the differences in the court system between a white and a black victim."[350]

After the trial ended, even prominent blacks doubted whether the defendants were guilty. Hazel Dukes, chair of the NAACP board of directors and chief of New York City's Off-Track Betting Corporation, said there had not been enough evidence to convict. Rev. Calvin Butts, pastor of one of the most important churches in Harlem, told his congregation that there was much to be learned by comparing the jogger case with that of Tawana Brawley, that what was thought to be insufficient evidence when a black is raped by whites is perfectly good evidence when a white is thought to have been raped by blacks.[351]

One of the strongest expressions of the popular black view of the trial was a guest editorial in the *Amsterdam News* that appeared long before the jury had reached its verdict:

> [I]t strikes me as utterly ironic and hypocritical that, as in most court cases these days, a group of white people can sit in judgment of [sic] diminutive young Black males and pretend that they are about the business of "justice."
>
> Considering the fact that not one of the whites . . . judge, jury, security guards, lawyers, have ever had their "racism quotient" measured; and each one has been conditioned by

an admittedly institutionally racist society; I sit on this hard wooden courtroom bench in agony—hardly able to contain my outrage and anger at what I know in my gut is a continuing obscene exercise in public masturbation, with Black lives and psyches as the seemingly endless fodder in a system set up by white males for the benefit of white males.[352]

Needless to say, no white-owned newspaper expressed similar agony when the Bensonhurst case was tried before a black judge. Nevertheless, this editorial only expresses, if somewhat intemperately, our society's prevailing views of race. We have created a climate in which much that goes wrong for blacks is assumed to be the fault of white people. Society is said to offer blacks neither opportunity nor justice.

Genocide: Escalating the Charges

Blacks have a great deal to gain through charges of racism. From convicts to college students to congressmen, they can make race the basis for excuses and special treatment, while whites listen humbly to accusations they know to be false. Blacks also recognize that they themselves are virtually immune to charges of racism, no matter how spiteful their behavior. Cries of racism have become so common, though, that they may be losing their effect. To draw attention, it may be necessary to escalate the charge.

In 1988, over half of the two hundred thousand heroin addicts in New York were found to be infected with the AIDS virus. The virus spreads when addicts share dirty needles. Late that year, after much soul-searching, New York City began an experimental program of handing out clean needles. As it happens, most of the heroin addicts are black or Hispanic, so Harlem city councilman Hilton Clark proceeded to describe the free-needle program as "a *genocidal* campaign against the black and Hispanic people."[353]

Mr. Clark may be opposed to helping addicts continue with their illegal habits, even if the goal is to fight AIDS. However, if he believes that the experimental needle program is a systematic attempt to exterminate blacks and Hispanics, he is, to put it politely, mistaken.

In early 1992, thousands of Haitian boat people tried to enter the United States, claiming to be political refugees. When the U.S. Supreme Court ruled that they were economic migrants and therefore could be returned to Haiti, Jesse Jackson was only one of several black commentators who called the government's policy "genocidal."[354]

One recent issue of *The Black Scholar* carried a major story that blamed white society for the rate at which black men kill each other and die of drugs. The title of the story? "Black Male Genocide: A Final Solution to the Race Problem in America."[355] The author has a Ph.D. and teaches sociology at the University of California. Black civil rights activist Ossie Davis, in a recent article in *The Nation,* writes that young black men are "under genocidal siege" by white society.[356]

The chairman of the black studies department at the University of California Santa Barbara writes that "in 1990 it is possible to be more optimistic about the situation of blacks in South Africa than their American counterparts."[357]

Vivian Gordon, a professor of African-American studies at the State University of New York at Albany, is a specialist on the black family. "I believe black men are a hunted and endangered species," she says. "You kill off the male and leave the woman vulnerable and without a partner. They have done everything to devastate us by devastating our men."[358] Is there any doubt about whom Professor Gordon means by "they"?

Roger Wilkins, professor of history at George Mason University, says, "Black people know there is an enormous amount of racism that results in the decimation of their communities."[359] William Cavil of the Institute for the Advanced Study of Black Family Life and Culture, in Oakland, California, sees racist conspiracy as the only explanation for black failure. Barbara Sizemore, a black studies professor at the University of Pittsburgh, goes farther: "I no longer think it's a conspiracy. . . . I call it outright war."[360]

It has slowly begun to dawn on white people that a great many blacks—and not just cranks—actually believe this talk of genocide.[361] The National Urban League has concluded that drugs are sold to blacks as part of an extermination campaign by whites. "It's almost an accepted fact," says the publisher of a Brooklyn-based black weekly, the *City Sun*. A youth coordinator in Selma, Alabama, says, "Most blacks believe in their hearts that crack was put here by whites to wipe us out." Black filmmaker Spike Lee also believes that whites are deliberately trying to make nonwhites use drugs.[362] Rev. Joseph Lowery, president of Martin Luther King's old organization, the Southern Christian Leadership Conference, sees the drug problem this way:

> African-Americans are pretty much convinced that there is a national assault on black life. . . . The market place for drugs is very intentionally placed in the black community. Because wherever the marketplace is, that's where the war zone is, so they can kill each other.[363]

Of course, underground markets cannot be "placed" anywhere. They simply follow demand.

Other blacks think that AIDS was developed by the U.S. government and tested on homosexuals before it was unleashed on blacks. Late in 1991, actor Bill Cosby announced that he had joined the growing number of blacks who believe that AIDS was developed "to get after certain people." He was entirely candid about having no proof. "I just have a feeling," he said.[364]

There was only conjecture as to how many blacks believed this sort of thing until CBS News and *The New York Times* did a poll to find out. A quarter of all blacks were convinced that the government was deliberately supplying drugs to blacks in order to destroy them, and another 35 percent were not sure, but thought such a plan was possible. Thirty percent of blacks thought either that AIDS had been deliberately invented by the government to kill blacks, or that there was at least a chance that this was true. Nearly 80 percent were either convinced that there was a racist,

[361] If there is any effort to practice genocide on American blacks, it is a complete failure. Every black generation is 17 percent larger than the preceding one. Every white generation is 10 percent smaller. At these rates, the number of blacks will equal the number of whites in 180 years. Boyce Rensberger, "Demography: The Shifting U.S. Racial Mix," *The Washington Post* (January 1, 1990), p. A2.

government campaign to discredit black elected leaders, or thought it possible that there was such a campaign.[365] According to a 1990 poll of black churchgoers conducted by the Southern Christian Leadership Conference, 35 percent believed that AIDS was a form of black genocide and 30 percent said they didn't know what to think.[366]

Even whites who are willing to listen to virtually any other charge of white racism choke on the idea that the U.S. government is trying to exterminate black people. This is clearly not an insignificant aberration in black opinion.

If nearly twenty million blacks are so suspicious and deluded as to think their government may be trying to exterminate them with drugs and AIDS, what else are they prepared to think? Will they not see "racism" in any white gesture, no matter how well-intentioned?

Fears of this kind have real consequences. Brooklyn Bottling is a soft drink manufacturer with a brand called Tropical Fantasy. Late in 1990, someone started the rumor that Tropical Fantasy was being secretly made by the Ku Klux Klan and was laced with an ingredient that would sterilize black men. Who would believe this nonsense? Plenty of people. Before long, Tropical Fantasy's sales fell 70 percent.[367]

Here are some excerpts from an opinion piece written by a black student in the college newspaper of Penn State University. After citing "proof" that AIDS is a "diabolical plot to exterminate black people," he goes on to say:

> After looking at all of the evidence there is only one conclusion: white people are devils. . . . I believe that we must secure our freedom and independence from these devils by any means necessary, including violence. . . . To protect ourselves we should bear arms (three handguns and two rifles, maybe an M-16) immediately and form a militia. . . . So black people, let us unite, organize and execute.[368]

Execute? What accounts for words like this from a young black man attending a well-known university? Why would someone who grew up in an era not only of civil rights and integration but also of affirmative action write these things?

This man's hatred, and his delusions of genocide, are not so freakish as they seem. They are natural consequences of endlessly repeated charges of white racism. They are natural consequences of the resentment that a largely white society systematically instills in blacks. If employers, schools, the police, realtors, bankers, and practically everyone else are said to be discriminating against blacks at every turn, why not the government? By publicizing and magnifying every act of "racism," by constantly harping on the sins of slavery and segregation, we have built a mood in which virtually any kind of white wickedness becomes plausible, especially to blacks. Much of what is said about race becomes reflex rather than reflection, and facts are a troublesome irrelevance.

But what are the facts? Differences in income between black and white men are said to prove racism, but the fact that black women earn just as much as white women is deliberately ignored. The preference of American blacks for white dolls is said to prove racism, but the same preference by blacks in Trinidad goes unexplained. The fact that killers of whites are more likely to get the death penalty proves racism, but the fact that white killers are more likely than black killers to get the death penalty is ignored. The South has the reputation of being more racist than the North, but no one seems to notice that Minnesota jails blacks at seven times the rate that Mississippi does. A researcher can find no evidence that white judges hand out longer sentences to black convicts, but concludes that sentencing is racist anyway. When blacks are denied mortgages more often than whites are, it is proof of racism; when whites are denied mortgages more often than Asians, there must be some reason other than race. The Bensonhurst killing proves that white people are racist, but the fact that blacks are far more likely to kill whites than vice versa means nothing. If black men committed suicide twice as often as white men, it would surely be attributed to despair over racism. In fact, white men commit suicide twice as often as black men,[369] but scarcely anyone stops to wonder why. Sifting through the charges of racism may be a wearying task, but it is a necessary first step in understanding the assumptions that govern conventional thinking about race.

It is easy to understand why blacks make such charges, but why do whites submit to them? Why do they accept racism as an explanation for things it cannot possibly explain?

Part of the reason is force of habit. When blacks were chattel, whites were clearly responsible for their circumstances. When they were unable to vote, whites were responsible for their powerlessness. When they were barred by law from education and employment, whites were responsible for their poverty. Today, none of these things is true; yet blacks and whites alike often continue to act as if they were. Habits of the mind are the most difficult to shed, and an old error is always more popular than a new truth. White racism is a simple, lazy answer to a difficult question.

Another reason why racism is so readily accepted as the explanation for black failure is that there appears to be no acceptable alternative. If whites are not forcing blacks into misery, they must be bringing it upon themselves. If whites are not holding blacks down, it might mean that they have risen as far as their inherent limitations permit. The possibility of black inferiority is the unacknowledged goblin that lurks in the background of every attempt to explain black failure. Part of the shrillness with which white racism is denounced stems from the belief that any letup in the struggle against it might leave room for a theory that is too dangerous to be contemplated.

Another reason has been the good intentions of whites. Despite what black activists so confidently maintain, for the past several decades the majority of whites has genuinely wanted black progress. They certainly did not want blacks to languish in ghettos, go on welfare, or commit crimes. What could white people do to help blacks? Given America's tortured history, the most obvious way was simply to stop hurting them, and the obvious way to do that was to eliminate racism.

Once the nation had made the elimination of racism a national goal, there could be no harm in denouncing racism—the more often the better. Even charges of racism that made no logical sense could be accepted and encouraged, because racism was a bad thing and it was proper to criticize it. One could not be too thorough about denouncing a national evil, and the momentum of the struggle built up relentlessly. Its culmination is the meticulous policing of speech and thought that is common on college campuses. Fighting "racism," however it is defined, has become a way for whites to side with the angels and feel virtuous.

At the same time, it is widely assumed that if the struggle against racism is not maintained at fever pitch, white people will promptly relapse into bigotry. Thus a great deal of the criticism of whites is justified on the grounds that it will forestall *potential* racism. The process becomes circular. Since whites are thought likely to turn racist if not constantly policed, it is legitimate to denounce acts of racism they *might* commit as if they had already done so. In this climate, all charges of racism must be taken seriously because they are *potentially* true. Even if a specific accusation of racism may not be factually true, it is *morally* true, because of the constant potential for white bigotry.

Finally, the race-relations industry has developed a huge infrastructure of people whose careers depend on the discovery and extirpation of white racism. Governments at every level—local, state, and federal—are staffed with civil rights specialists and equal employment officers. So are universities and private corporations. Presiding over the entire enterprise are the federal Equal Employment Opportunity Commission, the Civil Rights Commission, the Civil Rights Division of the Department of Justice, and the Office of Federal Contract Compliance Programs.

Most of the time it is the same people who both report to the public on the extent of racism and who are charged with combating it. The greater and more determined their foe appears to be, the more likely they are to win admiration, grant money, and additional staff. Thus the organizations that monitor "racism" have a strong motive for finding and publicizing as much of it as possible.

Teaching Hatred

One thing that whites lost sight of was that although constant denunciations of racism were primarily meant for white ears and were supposed to change white behavior, they had an enormous influence on blacks. For example, it is often claimed that because of white racism, society teaches blacks to hate themselves. No one ever spells out, in practical terms, just how society does this, but the prevailing view is that whites somehow manage to teach blacks to hate themselves. In fact, if anything, our society teaches blacks to hate whites. At every turn, blacks are told that whites are responsible for their problems. At every opportunity blacks are reminded of slavery. Virtually every failure by blacks—be it crime, poverty, drug-taking, or even cigarette smoking—is said to be the work of white people.

This constant reminder of the sins of the white man is supposed to root out white racism and bring about social harmony. Instead, it only gives blacks reasons to hate whites. If whites were guilty of one tenth of the evil that the doctrine lays at their feet, blacks would be justified in hating whites. Clearly, not all of them do. However, the blacks who called the Central Park jogger a whore hate white people. The Crown Heights rioters who killed Mr. Rosenbaum, and the blacks who set out to kill the first white person they could find, hate white people. The people in the Yahweh cult hate white people. The blacks who talk about genocide have, at the very least, a profound distrust of white people, and former congressman Gus Savage certainly appears to hate white people. Outside of small, extremist groups that are condemned by all segments of society, it would be difficult to find whites who openly hate blacks with the visceral, consuming intensity with which these black people hate whites.

Doctrine holds that white society is seething with hatred for blacks. The very reverse is true. With the best of intentions and for the best of reasons, America has done everything within its power to encourage blacks to hate whites.

3

Asians

*I*F WHITE RACISM WERE BLIGHTING THE LIVES OF BLACKS, HOW would it be affecting other nonwhites? Should it not be a terrible obstacle for Asians as well?

Asians have faced fierce discrimination in America, but this has not stopped them from working hard and getting ahead. In fact, they have been so successful in "racist" America that whites have even begun to complain about Asian achievement. Whether one looks at Japanese and Chinese, who have been in America for generations, or Koreans and Vietnamese, who have arrived more recently, Asians have been remarkably successful.

The Legacy of Prejudice

In many respects, Asians have suffered as much prejudice as any group. In 1790, Congress excluded both blacks and Asians from citizenship by forbidding the naturalization of anyone who was not a "free white person." Blacks, but not Asians, became citizens in 1870, when Congress authorized the naturalization of "aliens of African nativity and persons of African descent." The 1879 Constitution of California continued to deny the vote to "natives of China, idiots and insane persons,"[370] and as late as 1914, the U.S. Supreme Court upheld the principle that citizenship could be denied to foreign-born Asians.[371] Chinese were not allowed to become naturalized citizens until 1943, and denial of citizenship was symbolic of the concrete obstacles Asians faced every day.

Chinese started coming to the United States in the 1850s and settled mainly in California. They aroused immediate resentment because of their willingness to work for low wages, and the California legislature promptly rolled out a series of anti-Chinese laws that seem incredible today. In 1855, the state levied a $55 per person entry tax on Chinese immigrants. Since this did not stop the flow, California passed a more drastic law just three years later. All people of Chinese or "Mongolian" descent were barred from entering the state except in cases of shipwreck or accident. Survivors were to be expelled as soon as they recovered.

In 1861 the state turned on the Chinese who were already in California by passing a tax on foreign miners. In theory, the tax applied to all foreigners but was collected only from Chinese. The next year, the state passed a monthly tax of $2.50 on all resident Chinese over age eighteen who were not producing sugar, rice, coffee, or tea. Cities passed their own anti-Chinese laws. San Francisco levied a quarterly license fee of $15 on all laundries that did not use a vehicle—that is to say, on Chinese laundries. Anyone who sold vegetables door-to-door from a wagon had to buy a $2.00 license; anyone who went on foot had to buy a $10 license. Perhaps most insulting was the "queue ordinance," according to which anyone convicted of a crime was given a mandatory haircut —loss of his pigtail was a great disgrace to a Chinese.[372] From 1854 to 1874 Chinese were barred by law from testifying as witnesses against whites.[373]

As if pressure from the surrounding white population were not enough, Chinese and other Asian immigrants had a severe internal social problem. Virtually all early immigrants were men. Since they were rejected by respectable white women, they were celibate for decades or consorted with prostitutes. Asians often returned to their home countries to seek wives only after they were firmly established in America. These pressures could easily have led to unstable families, but they did not.

Although plain racism and resentment against low-wage labor were the main sources of anti-Chinese feeling in California, Americans whose jobs were not threatened sometimes opposed Chinese immigration for humanitarian reasons. Chinese coolies were brought to the New World in gangs and were worked mercilessly by their Chinese overseers. In the 1870s they were still being shipped to the Caribbean, practically as slaves, where they were bought and sold in "man markets" as if they were animals. Like many other Americans, President Ulysses S. Grant objected to Chinese immigrants because they came to America in conditions so close to those of the black slaves he had helped free.[374]

Thus when the U.S. Supreme Court ruled that immigration control was not a state but a federal responsibility, both racialists and humanitarians backed the anti-Chinese law of 1882. This measure barred immigration for ten years and denied naturalization to Chinese already in the United States. The ten-year restriction was renewed in 1892, and the ban on immigration and citizenship continued right up through the Second World War. Only in 1943, when the United States found itself allied with China in the fight against Japan, were these laws excluding Chinese finally repealed. Congress set an annual immigration quota of 105 people, and resident Chinese were finally granted the right to apply for citizenship.[375]

Throughout this period of constant prejudice and persecution, Chinese worked hard, saved their money, and built better lives for themselves. By the time they had full, legal standing in this country, many Chinese had incomes comparable to those of native-born whites. By 1969, Chinese as a group outearned Italian, German, and even Anglo-Saxon Americans.[376]

During the 1960s, Chinatown was the part of San Francisco with the most unemployment and poverty, the highest rate of tuberculosis, the least education, and the most substandard housing. Nevertheless, in 1965, *only five* people of Chinese ancestry went to jail in the whole state of California.[377]

Japanese came to America later than Chinese, since their government prohibited emigration until 1885. As soon as they arrived, they found that strong anti-Chinese feelings quickly transferred to them. Most were shunted into jobs as unskilled, low-paid field hands and lived in squalor. They, too, were willing to work for less than the prevailing wage and quickly raised the ire of whites. Just as southern whites passed Jim Crow laws to keep blacks out of certain professions, so Californians passed their own laws to keep out Japanese.

Although there were far fewer Japanese than Chinese immigrants—only about twenty-four thousand in the entire United States by 1900—anti-Japanese sentiment was whipped up by the Japanese and Korean Exclusion League, founded in San Francisco in 1905. President Theodore Roosevelt responded in 1907 by persuading the Japanese government to withhold passports from anyone who wanted to emigrate to America.[378]

None of this stopped the Japanese from living frugally and saving money. Many Japanese bought farms, and their hard work began to threaten white farmers. In 1913 the California legislature voted, by an overwhelming majority, to prohibit ownership of farmland by noncitizens.[379] This law was upheld by the U.S. Supreme Court, and soon ten more western states passed similar laws.[380] This did not stop the Japanese either. They went into partnerships with whites, set up dummy holding companies for Japanese farms, and kept on working.

Californians saw Japanese farmers as much more than economic threats. In 1921, California state Senator James Phelan wrote, "The state, therefore, is obliged as a simple matter of self-preservation to prevent the Japanese from absorbing the soil, because the future of the white race, American institutions, and western civilization are put in peril. . . ."[381]

During the Second World War, just when Chinese were finally being granted the right to apply for naturalization, Japanese were subjected to one of the most spectacular violations of civil rights in living memory. Soon after Japan attacked Pearl Harbor in 1941, Japanese Americans living in the continental United States were rounded up and sent to concentration camps. Here they were kept behind barbed wire and guarded by soldiers. The property they left behind was either stolen or sold at a sharp loss. At the time of the evacuation, the Federal Reserve Bank estimated Japanese property losses at $400 million[382]—a figure that, today, would be many billions.

This wholesale internment was far worse than anything done to blacks then or since. Many of the men, women, and children who were rounded up are still living today. If any group in America had wanted to give up, blame white society, and try to live off its victim status, the Japanese could have. Instead, when the war was over, they went back to what was left of their lives and started over. Twenty-five years after the war, they had long since caught up with white society and, as a group, had incomes 32 percent above the national average.[383]

Asian Americans have not tried to blame others for their troubles or shirk responsibility for their own success or failure. They have looked to their own resources to succeed. White America has clearly oppressed them in the past, just as it has blacks. Some people have argued that Asian immigrants have the advantage of starting out fresh when they get to America, whereas blacks must constantly drag the baggage of slavery and oppression behind them. This obviously does not apply to the descendants of Asians who came to America a century ago practically in bondage and who, in many cases, were treated as badly as blacks. If racism is such an obstacle to success in America, why have Asians overcome it while blacks have not?

Asians Today

The achievements of more recent Asian immigrants have been well publicized. Everyone has heard of Vietnamese children who came to America unable to speak English and then, a few years later, graduated at the tops of their high-school classes.

If anything, when blacks and Asians mix in America today, it is the Asians who suffer because of their race. Many black criminals, for example, single them out as preferred robbery targets. Asians are often physically small and not likely to resist a mugger. New immigrants may not speak much English and not know how to report a crime. Asians also tend not to use credit cards but to carry cash. As a result, in New York City, subway robberies of Asians leapt 204 percent from 1987 to 1989, while robberies of non-Asians went up 63 percent. Deliberate targeting of Asians by blacks has become such a problem that New York police have instituted a special detail of undercover Asian policemen to act as decoys and to arrest muggers.[384]

A more widespread form of Asian mistreatment by blacks occurs when Asian success and black failure are found side by side in the same neighborhood. In many big American cities, recent Korean immigrants have opened thriving grocery stores. They have been welcomed in white neighborhoods. In black neighborhoods, Koreans likewise create retail trade, liven up desolated streets, and help save neglected city blocks from decay. Even on Harlem's main, commercial avenue, West 125th Street, Koreans now own three times as many businesses as blacks.[385]

Rather than appreciate what Koreans have done for dying neighborhoods, many blacks dislike them for their success. In city after city, blacks have called Korean merchants parasites and profiteers and have boycotted their stores. In 1988, in the Bedford-Stuyvesant section of Brooklyn, demonstrators chanted, "Boycott, boycott, close 'em down. Pass 'em by, let 'em die. Koreans out of Bed-Stuy."[386]

In a remarkable twist of logic, black boycotters accused the Koreans of racism. "It's racist that we don't own any businesses," said one black organizer; "This is a conspiracy against the black community." When a group of black businessmen in Bedford-Stuyvesant tried to work out a coexistence agreement with Koreans, other blacks accused them of selling out.[387] Blacks have been putting racial pressure of this kind on Korean shopkeepers for at least eight years.[388]

The Brooklyn Boycott

Recently the same drama was played out all over again, this time in the light of increasing publicity about the crudely racial character of the boycotts. It was one of the most malodorous stories to come out of New York in a long time and is worth looking at in some detail.

On January 18, 1990, a Haitian immigrant was involved in an altercation in a Korean-owned grocery store in a mostly black neighborhood in the Flatbush area of Brooklyn. She claimed that the Korean owners attacked her without provocation, knocked her to the ground, and kicked her. The Koreans say that the woman produced only two dollars for a three-dollar purchase and started shouting when the owners asked for the full amount. They say she spat at the cashier, cursed her, and started knocking over counter displays. When a salesman put his hands on her shoulders and asked her to leave, she dropped to the floor and started screaming. Whatever actually happened, the word quickly circulated among blacks that Koreans had thrashed a black woman.[389]

Activists started a boycott, not only of the grocery, but of a Korean-owned fruit store across the street. A knot of demonstrators took up a position on the sidewalk in front of the stores, and acted as a perpetual picket line. They passed out leaflets urging blacks not to buy from "people who don't look like us." They cursed the Koreans whenever they left the store, and vowed not to stop the boycott until the owners closed their shops and left the neighborhood. Under this kind of intimidation, patronage dropped to near zero. Some moderate Haitians who urged a peaceful resolution got death threats.[390]

By April, as the weather got warmer, the number of activists/ demonstrators grew. Young black toughs reportedly started showing up at other Korean stores and threatened more boycotts if they were not paid off.[391]

The press in New York City is so sensitive about race and so unwilling to write unfavorably about blacks that it ignored the boycott for *more than three months.* It was not until April that the *New York Post* first broke the silence and began to write about it. By May, the racial character of the boycott was so clear that pressure began to mount on the black mayor, David Dinkins, to do something about it. After much dithering and pious talk about not "taking sides," he finally brought himself to call the boycott "inappropriate" and "intimidating."[392]

For those who wondered why the mayor had waited so long to

criticize the boycotters, the furious reaction among blacks gave the most likely answer. Black newspapers called the mayor an "Uncle Tom." The city's largest black-owned radio station was flooded with on-the-air calls from blacks blasting the mayor. They accused him of being a tool of the white, Jewish establishment and called his criticism of the boycott an affront to all blacks. The calls were so vicious that the station's owner, who is a friend of the mayor, called them "racist"—a curious characterization of a feud between blacks. He threatened to close the station down rather than "see it used by blacks to attack blacks."[393]

Meanwhile, a Brooklyn judge concluded that it was threatening and disruptive for as many as a hundred pickets to plant themselves right in front of the Korean grocery. He ordered the demonstrators to stay fifty feet away from the store and ordered the police to enforce the ruling. New York's black police commissioner, Lee Brown, refused. When another judge confirmed the original fifty-foot order, Mr. Brown *appealed* the decision. Not until September 17, when an appellate court ruled unanimously in favor of the fifty-foot decision, did he enforce the rule.[394]

Even the city's Human Rights Commission, whose job is to ensure civil rights, said that it planned to look into the "underlying causes" of the dispute—lack of economic opportunity—rather than take sides.[395] Former mayor Ed Koch wrote that if he were still mayor, he would order the Human Rights Commission to sue the demonstrators.[396]

As the boycott wore on, it drew public attention to other anti-Asian incidents. Just a few blocks from the boycott site, some black thugs attacked several Vietnamese, whom they had mistaken for Koreans. They fractured the skull of one of the Vietnamese with a hammer, and it took thirty-seven stitches to close the wound.[397] As if the racial theme were not clear enough, black activist "Sonny" Carson called for a boycott of all Korean stores in the city and promised that "in the future, there'll be funerals, not boycotts."[398]

By now, New York papers were wondering whether incidents like these were not deliberately staged as pretexts to drive Koreans out of black neighborhoods. The *New York Post* drew parallels with the Tawana Brawley case, in which phony charges of a racist attack led to months of posturing and provocation.[399]

Many blacks were likewise outraged by the boycotts, and some began to defy the picketers. One of the bravest was Fred McCray, a teacher at Erasmus Hall High School, four blocks from the boycott site. He took thirty students to the store to buy apples. The children had planned to make a little speech to the demonstrators about peacemaking, but they never got the chance. Men in the crowd screamed and cursed at them and threatened to kill Mr. McCray. The shaken students nevertheless managed to get away with their apples. Mr. McCray and his family got further death threats, and he felt himself in such danger that he transferred to another school.[400]

Roy Innis of the Congress of Racial Equality (CORE) also stood up for the Koreans. He accused Mayor Dinkins of "racial cowardice" and of "acquiescing to lawbreaking." He offered to let the Korean grocers use his legal team free of charge.[401]

One of the most unsavory elements in the entire story was the report of a panel appointed by Mayor Dinkins to look into the boycott. It lauded the Dinkins administration's handling of the incident and concluded that whether or not the boycotters had a legitimate grievance, the boycott itself was not racially motivated. It ended with the astonishing observation that the only real problem was that the white district attorney had not prosecuted the Korean storekeepers for their attack on the black customer. With the crude racism of the boycotts by now flagrantly evident, the report was met with hoots of derision.[402]

About one month after the report appeared, the black woman, Laura Blackburne, who headed the panel that wrote it was appointed to a $110,000-a-year job as head of New York City's Housing Authority (see previous chapter). News surfaced that she had been under consideration for the job at the time she was appointed to the panel, and editorialists grumbled that the prospect of this plum post had obviously tainted her findings. The New York City Council then issued its own report on the boycott, concluding not only that the demonstrators were obviously racist but that the mayor's "fact-finders" had been hopelessly biased. Besides the compromised Miss Blackburne, two of the five other black panel members were suspect from the outset. One was the wife of a prominent black minister who had publicly supported the boycott, and another had said even before his appointment that he would try to have one of the boycotted stores shut down.[403]

In September, after eight months of boycott, things finally began to look up for the Koreans. The police commissioner grudgingly started enforcing the fifty-foot rule, and customers began to trickle back.[404] A detail of no less than four hundred policemen had to be assigned to the stores to enforce the court order.[405]

With the demonstrators a safe fifty feet away, Mayor Dinkins finally crossed the line and bought a few dollars' worth of groceries at the two Korean stores.[406] The mayor's gesture brought out yet more shoppers. The next day, enraged demonstrators, trying to stop the flow of customers, violated the fifty-foot limit and chanted, among other slogans, "Death to all white men." Eight were arrested.[407]

The boycott dragged on into 1991, though more people began to cross the line. In February the Korean storeowner was acquitted of assault charges on the black shopper. Just a few hours after the verdict was read, the picketers were back at their posts, demanding that the store be closed.[408] Ten picketers marched into the store, surrounded the owner, made imaginary pistols with their hands, and said, "Die, die."[409]

This appears to have been the picketers' last hurrah. There were further incidents, but the momentum of public feeling had turned against them. What, however, were white and Asian New Yorkers to make of this incident and of the way the black administration handled it? Both the boycott and the city's gingerly handling of it reeked of unfair treatment.

Once he was officially vindicated and the boycott was broken, the Korean owner felt he had done his duty. A year of boycott and threats had turned his jet-black hair completely gray. He sold his store to another Korean and moved away.[410]

New York is hardly the only city in which blacks have put racial pressure on Korean storekeepers. In Washington, D.C., eleven Korean-owned shops have been firebombed in a single black neighborhood in just two years.[411] In Philadelphia, when a Korean storekeeper shot a black in what the district attorney called a self-defense killing, his store was firebombed, and he was threatened with such continuous violence that police officers were sent to protect the store twenty-four hours a day. Black protesters insisted that the store be shut down and that all Korean businesses in the area be driven out.[412]

In Chicago, a black women's organization boycotted Korean grocers to force them to stock black-made products. Although the stores are mom-and-pop operations, the women also demanded that the Koreans hire black clerks. In Chester, Pennsylvania, black shopkeepers organized a boycott against Asian merchants and petitioned the mayor to keep them out.[413]

In Los Angeles, immigrants from Korea have often been unable to open shops anywhere but in the South-Central area, where rents and property prices are relatively low. Many have had to work sixteen-hour days to make ends meet,[414] but there has been constant friction with black patrons. An activist group called the Brotherhood Crusade has succeeded in closing down two Korean stores through threats and boycotts,[415] and other Los Angeles stores have been firebombed and vandalized.[416]

In 1991, the rap musician Ice Cube (O'Shea Jackson) put an anti-Korean message on one of his albums, *Death Certificate:*

So don't follow me up and down your market
or your little chop suey ass will be a target.
So pay your respects to the black fist
or we'll burn your store right down to a crisp.[417]

Later that year, Mr. Jackson's album was number two on *Billboard*'s album chart and went on to sell more than a million copies.[418]

In the spring of 1992, during the Los Angeles riots that followed the acquittals of the four police officers who beat Rodney King, blacks appear to have followed Mr. Jackson's hateful advice. During the riots, looters and arsonists deliberately sought out Korean-owned stores for destruction. In Korea Town, 80 percent of the businesses were damaged.[419] In all, 1,839 Korean-owned businesses were burned or looted.[420] Even the Korean consulate came under attack.[421] It is tragic that blacks, who persist in blaming white racism for their own problems, use overtly racist tactics against another group.

In New York, some Koreans, who have been among the most energetic and hardworking immigrants to the area in recent years, have decided that the trip was a mistake. In 1991 they were returning to Korea at the rate of fifty families a month.[422] One who stayed behind wondered if Koreans have been mistaken in thinking that "being quiet and working hard is supposed to be the way to go." She suggested that Koreans would be better off if they banded together along openly racial lines, just as blacks do. "What we Korean Americans need is a Korean Al Sharpton," she concluded.[423]

What very few people dared point out is that it was the bad luck of the Koreans to have suffered racial discrimination at the hands of *blacks*. If whites had boycotted Korean (or black-owned) stores with chants of "Let 'em die" or circulated fliers urging whites not to buy from "people who don't look like us," the nation would have gone into convulsions. State legislatures would have passed laws to make the boycotts illegal. The police would not have had to enforce court orders against the boycotters. They would have had to protect them from crowds of angry counterdemonstrators.

Many blacks must know that newly arrived Asians are a powerful threat to the theory of white racism. When these nonwhites with little education, who hardly speak English, get ahead through determination and hard work, it undercuts blacks' excuses. Asian successes are galling for another reason. Asians never had black slaves, never supported the KKK or joined lynch mobs. It is hard to persuade Korean grocers to go along with special treatment for blacks in the name of historical redress.

A few blacks are keenly aware of how different the expectations of blacks and Asians are, and how damaging this is for blacks. *Washington Post* columnist William Raspberry says this:

[Blacks] expend precious resources, time, energy, imagination and political capital searching, always successfully, for evidence of racism, while our problems grow worse. . . . It is clear that recently arrived Asian Americans spend none of their time proving that white people don't love them. The difference between us and them is in our operating myths. Our myth is that racism accounts for our shortcomings. Theirs is that their own efforts can make the difference, no matter what white people think.[424]

Many blacks, of course, reject the suggestion that they should work to get ahead as Asians do. *The Black Scholar* has a typical response: "The perspective that blacks should be like other ethnic groups that succeeded without the benefits of affirmative action but through hard work is a restatement of the bootstrap thesis—a fallacious, biased, and ahistorical view."[425]

If not in so many words, white America has agreed that it is fallacious, biased, and ahistorical to expect blacks to take full responsibility for themselves. And that is why, almost exactly one hundred years after America abolished one "peculiar institution," it established another: affirmative action.

4

Affirmative Action in Education and Employment

*A*FFIRMATIVE ACTION HAS A TANGLED HISTORY THAT illustrates the legal and moral dilemmas of race. It has proud roots—the struggle during the 1950s and 1960s that abolished legal discrimination—but it has born a bitter fruit. It is the practice of discrimination in the name of equality, of injustice in the name of justice. Perhaps nowhere else in our society have good intentions gone so sadly wrong, and good sense been driven so completely from the field.

The original impetus for affirmative action was understandable. If racist barriers had kept large numbers of talented blacks from getting good jobs or going to good schools, such people could surely be found with little effort. Once found and given equal opportunity, they would succeed at the same rate as whites. If there was to be preferential treatment, it would be nothing more than the small effort it might take to find qualified blacks.

Things were not so simple. Even before the civil rights laws, gifted blacks had found routes to success. The reservoir of competent but excluded blacks that universities and employers hoped to find was very much smaller than expected. If blacks were to be represented at universities and on work forces at anything even approaching their numbers in the population, standards would have to be lowered for them.

This step could be justified by past racism. If a job applicant did not meet professional standards, it need not mean he was unable to do the job. He might have been kept out of a good university because he was black, and with a little on-the-job training, he would soon be a capable worker. The same was true for college admissions. Black applicants had presumably been forced to go to inferior high schools, so with a little catch-up work, they would become solid students. This thinking could be applied to junior high school, grade school, even to preschool home life. Past racism made it impossible for blacks to benefit from strictly equal opportunity, so it was only fair to weight the scales a little in their favor.[426]

In some cases, blacks may have quickly caught up with the mainstream, but all too often they did not. What might have been intended as a temporary relaxation of standards hardened into permanent racial preferences. The gap in black/white achievement refused to go away, and what came to look more and more like reverse racial discrimination had to be justified by claiming that the persistent racial gap in achievement could be due only to persistent white racism.

Affirmative action preferences for blacks are now nearly a quarter century old but show no signs of fading away. Indeed, they are more entrenched than ever, and the hypocrisy and bitterness to which they give rise are fatal to any hope for amicable race relations.

---

[426] The idea behind Head Start was that poor blacks were at a disadvantage from the beginning. A boost during the early years would enable them to take advantage of equal opportunities and compete successfully with whites. Head Start is discussed in Chapter Eight.

The Legal Basis

The legal basis for affirmative action is the Civil Rights Act of 1964. The act followed a well-established trend in our thinking about race. By then, a clear majority of Americans had come to realize that racial discrimination was wrong and demeaning to everyone. There was still local support for certain kinds of discrimination, especially in housing, but the climate was right for Freedom Riders, peaceful sit-ins, and "I Have a Dream." Though popular mythology dates all progress for blacks from the passage of the Civil Rights Act of 1964, upward trends in black employment, income, and educational opportunities were already well established by then.[427]

The first antidiscrimination laws actually date from thirty years before the Civil Rights Act of 1964, and were passed during the New Deal. The Public Works Administration required contractors to set black hiring quotas.[428] The first black federal judge had been appointed by Franklin Roosevelt in 1937, and a black congressman became the head of the Government Operations Committee in 1949. During the Second World War, four Merchant Marine ships had black captains who commanded white crewmen, and several ships were named after a black seaman who died heroically in the service. In 1945, a black officer was first put in command of a U.S. military base. In 1948 President Truman issued Executive Order 9981, requiring equal treatment of the races in the military, and set up the Fair Employment Practices Committee to oversee civilian employment. In 1940 black author Richard Wright's *Native Son* was a Book-of-the-Month Club selection, and in 1950 Gwendolyn Brooks won the Pulitzer Prize for poetry.[429] When Congress voted the Civil Rights Act of 1964, it hardly changed the mood of America; it bowed to it.

[427] Thomas Sowell, *Civil Rights: Rhetoric or Reality?* (New York: William Morrow & Company, 1984), pp. 49–51. By 1916, America had already gotten its first black millionaire: Madam C. J. Walker, born just four years after emancipation, made a fortune selling beauty products for blacks. Audrey Edwards and Craig Polite, *Children of the Dream* (New York: Doubleday, 1992), p. 17.

The clear intent of Congress was to remove race as a consideration in the professional lives of Americans, and its famous Title VII was written to end discrimination in employment. Section 703(a) forbade any employer to "limit, segregate, or classify his employees in any way which would deprive or tend to deprive any individual of employment opportunities or otherwise adversely affect his status as an employee because of such individual's race, color, religion, sex, or national origin."

The law was wordy but clear. Nevertheless, some lawmakers worried that the act could be used to justify reverse discrimination, or racial quotas in hiring. Senator Hubert Humphrey, who was one of the bill's most powerful backers, stoutly denied that the act could be interpreted that way: "[T]itle VII does not require an employer to achieve any sort of racial balance in his work force by giving preferential treatment to any individual or group," he said.[430] He even promised on the floor of the Senate that he would physically eat the paper the bill was written on if it were ever used to require corrective hiring preferences.[431] Congress put in Section 703(j) of Title VII just to make things perfectly clear:

> Nothing contained in this title shall be interpreted to require any employer . . . to grant preferential treatment to any individual or to any group because of race, color, religion, sex or national origin of such individual or group on account of an imbalance. . . .

America had legally dismantled the color barrier.

The government's first use of the phrase "affirmative action" was not a departure from the intent of the law. Shortly after the Civil Rights Act was passed, President Johnson issued Executive Order 11246, which established color-blind hiring rules for federal contractors. It says, "The contractor will take affirmative action to ensure that applicants are employed, and that employees are treated during employment, without regard to their race, color, religion, sex, or national origin." Here, too, the emphasis was on *equal* treatment, not on special preferences.

The first government mandate for racial preferences was what came to be known as the "Philadelphia Plan," instituted by the

Department of Labor in 1969. Government contractors in that city were told that if they did not come up with minority hiring goals, their bids would not even be considered. For the first time, private employers were on notice that an absence of discrimination was not enough; they had to employ a certain number of nonwhites through race-conscious hiring schemes. Since race-consciousness in hiring was the very thing that the Civil Rights Act of 1964 had prohibited, the Nixon administration had unilaterally repealed an act of Congress.[432]

It is interesting to note how quickly the very people who had argued that race was irrelevant changed their minds. In the famous 1954 legal brief it filed in the school desegregation case of *Brown* v. *Board of Education*, the NAACP had professed its "dedicated belief . . . that the Constitution is color-blind" and that "the 14th Amendment compels the states to be color-blind in exercising their power and authority."[433] As soon as there was a chance that blacks might benefit from reverse discrimination, the NAACP forgot all about the color-blind Constitution. "Civil rights" leaders became revisionists and reversed the movement's goals. As one scholar puts it:

> The revisionists purveyed a civil rights agenda in name only. The shift in focus was deceptively subtle, relying upon familiar terms with broad support such as "freedom" and "equality." In reality, however, the revisionists embarked upon an ambitious new program of social engineering and wealth redistribution that is profoundly antithetical to the traditional civil rights vision.[434]

This change in direction went largely unchallenged: "The head-spinning swiftness with which the former champions of color-blindness embraced color-consciousness once someone else's ox was being gored would have been comic were it not so tragic."[435]

---

[432] Robert Detlefsen, *Civil Rights Under Reagan* (San Francisco: ICS Press, 1991), pp. 25–28. This book is a brilliant, closely reasoned explanation of how antidiscrimination laws were turned into tools of discrimination. It also points out that although Lyndon Johnson is usually thought to have overseen the establishment of affirmative action, it was actually Richard Nixon who did so.

The goal of the "civil rights" movement changed from equality for all to preferences for some.

Even more astonishing is that white society went along with this. America had just done something that few nations ever do: put an official, legal end to discrimination against minorities. Now blacks were asking America to do something no nation on earth had ever done: officially discriminate in favor of minorities. How could whites be made to accept this? The following theory is as good as any:

> It is one thing—and difficult enough—to convince a majority to support equal rights; it is yet another to convince it to volitionally subordinate its own rights in favor of the minority.
>
> The rationale advanced for such a subordination was guilt —white Americans were adjudged guilty of imposing the condition of slavery, and were held responsible for its manifestations, which were viewed to encompass every conceivable malady afflicting blacks. In order to redeem itself, the majority was called upon not only to ensure freedom and opportunity for blacks but to furnish "reparations" as well.[436]

When it became clear that merely ending legal discrimination would not lead to quick parity, a new set of arguments arose to justify a new form of racial preferences: Slavery was a terrible thing that whites did to blacks. Slavery and racism have ever since been the reasons why blacks do not get ahead. All whites must take responsibility for these crimes, whether or not their ancestors owned slaves or discriminated against blacks. Therefore, society will now compensate blacks for these crimes even if it means penalizing whites.

As a theory of justice, this is a shambles. Whites are guilty simply because they are white. A black gets preference over a better-qualified white because some whites, at some point in the past, discriminated against some blacks. It makes no difference if neither the black nor the white was ever within a hundred miles of an act of discrimination.

Normally, a man is innocent until proven guilty. Under affirmative action he is guilty without trial or appeal. Even if a white job-seeker were to prove himself completely innocent of discrimination, he is guilty simply because he is white. A white man can therefore be guilty—and punished—even if proven innocent. A white immigrant to this country can be penalized because white people he is not even related to once owned slaves. This is dangerous nonsense of precisely the kind that Hubert Humphrey assured us was unthinkable. And yet it is now institutionalized.

Supporters of affirmative action argue that this is not what is really happening. They insist that preferences for women and minorities do not mean discrimination against white men. It is hard to understand, even in theory, how preference for one group is possible without prejudice against another. Preferences for whites have *always* been called discrimination against blacks. If a certain number of slots are held aside for blacks, they are not available to whites.

Nevertheless, many people use the terms "affirmative action" and "equal opportunity" which are exact opposites, as if they had identical meanings. Benjamin Hooks has written that the American revolutionaries who dumped tea into Boston Harbor were seeking equal opportunity and that the tea party was therefore an early blow for affirmative action. He goes on to argue: "[A]ffirmative action is simply any action taken to ensure, or affirm, equal opportunity for oppressed or previously disadvantaged groups. What's wrong with that?"[437]

Affirmative Action at Work

Larry Gatt grew up in San Francisco and always wanted to be a fireman. The Fire Department had always hired firemen in what it thought to be the fairest possible way. Every four to six years, it gave a test, and hired the people with the best scores.

Firemen must have brains as well as brawn. They must understand chemical fires, gas fires, and toxic discharges, and use the best technique to stop the blaze. They must give first aid to people who are burned, electrocuted, drowned, shot, or mangled on the highway. They must also be strong enough to hack their way through doors, sprint up stairways, and carry unconscious people down ladders. San Francisco therefore had two tests, one written and the other physical, with a weighting of 60:40 in favor of brains over brawn. The department gave the written test first.

Mr. Gatt was eligible to take the test in 1982, a year when the department was under court order to hire minorities. No discrimination had been proven, but the department did not have enough minorities. Seven thousand people signed up for the written test, and thirty-five hundred actually took it. The department had made a strong effort to advertise the test to minorities. It managed to sign up a good number of blacks, but only a reported 20 percent of them showed up for the test. The department knew it had a problem as soon as the tests were graded: Not enough blacks had passed. The department dropped the passing score from 70 to 60, crossed its fingers, and gave the physical test. Theoretically, if most of the whites who had passed the written test failed the physical test, while most of the blacks passed, the department might have had enough minorities to satisfy the court.

It did not work out that way. Once the scores were combined, if the department had worked its way down the list to get the two hundred people it needed, it would have ended up with far too many whites. Of the fifteen hundred people who passed both tests, Mr. Gatt was number forty-three. He would have gotten a job. The department showed the results to the court. It pointed out that it was not the department's fault if blacks did not show up for the test, or failed it if they took it. The court did not care. It wanted more blacks on the force.

The department swallowed hard and threw out the results of the written test. It ended the practice of hiring firemen for both brains and brawn, and decided to hire on brawn alone. It made a ranking of 190 men based only on the physical test. Mr. Gatt was still on that list, but he had dropped from forty-third to ninety-fifth. He still had a chance.

The department finally hired only thirty-nine men, and two thirds of these were minorities. Even on the list of brawn alone, it was only the whites who were hired strictly according to rank order. The department picked blacks who ranked lower than whites in order to get enough minorities. The department stopped far short of hiring the number of men it needed because the process had become so politicized and unsuitable.

Mr. Gatt did not get a job. He has since taken the test again. He has continued to be passed over so the department could hire minorities. He has never achieved his childhood ambition, to work for the San Francisco Fire Department. Mr. Gatt, like many whites who have been pushed aside in the name of affirmative action, is bitter. "I don't care who gets the job," he says, "so long as he's chosen fairly. They made a mockery of the test—they just hired the people they wanted."

Mr. Gatt points out that this is not the only time that white firemen face discrimination. "It doesn't end at the front door," he says. "It follows you for your whole career, with promotions and everything." In fact, the fire department found that once they were hired, minorities did not do as well as whites on the examinations for promotion to lieutenant. Once again, under court order, it devised a special grading system so that minorities could pass, and promoted them over the heads of whites who had scored higher. The department went even farther. It decided that the original test, which white firemen passed in greater number than blacks, must have been discriminatory. Blacks who had taken the old test therefore got promotions and tens of thousands of dollars in back pay.

It is not hard to imagine what this does to the morale of a fire department. Can veterans be happy with new recruits who are hired, not because they are qualified, but because they are black? Can whites help feeling cheated when they see less-qualified blacks promoted over them? Whites who might make excellent fire fighters will think twice about a job with a biased employer. San Francisco's fire department will not be as good as it could be. And finally, biased hiring patterns devalue the accomplishments of blacks who could have made it on ability alone.

What goes on in San Francisco is typical of fire and police departments across the country. Freddie Hernandez, a Hispanic lieutenant in the Miami fire department, explains how things work: "We hire 60 percent Hispanics here, regardless of qualifications.

. . . They just have people take a test, and they pick minorities [even] from the bottom of the list."[438]

In Detroit, a federal court upheld a promotion scheme that established two lists for police officers, one black and one white. Half of all promotions must be black, with the best candidates chosen in equal numbers from the two lists. Blacks compete for promotions only against other blacks.[439]

Detroit made no pretense of making blacks compete against whites for promotions. Other fire and police departments have tried to stick to the old way of promoting officers strictly according to test results, but are under court order to promote a certain number of blacks. Usually it is impossible to do both. When promotion examinations are used, blacks do not pass in sufficient numbers to satisfy affirmative action requirements.

The universal explanation for this is that the promotion tests are racially or culturally biased. Presumably, if a test suffers from cultural bias, someone familiar with the cultures involved could go through it in advance and eliminate bias. This has been attempted many times, but blacks still do not pass these tests at anything like the same rate as whites. Perhaps people are trying to remove something that is not there. In 1982, the National Academy of Sciences did a thorough investigation of cultural bias on standardized tests and strongly discounted the notion that there even is such a thing. Nevertheless, this study has been widely ignored,[440] and cultural bias stands alone as the explanation for why blacks and Hispanics do less well on tests than whites and Asians.

When it comes to a policing exam given to professional policemen, it is difficult to imagine what form cultural bias could take. This has not stopped cities from taking great pains to correct it. San Francisco spent nearly $1 million over a period of nearly five years trying to devise a test that minorities could pass in equal numbers to whites. The city never got one. In 1991 a judge ordered that twenty-two nonwhites be promoted over the heads of whites who had gotten better scores on the new, presumably bias-free test.[441]

For ten years, New York City police battled lawsuits claiming that biased tests prevented minorities from getting deserved promotions to sergeant. Finally, in 1989, the department hit upon the idea of inviting black and Hispanic officers to help design the test, thus eliminating bias. Even so, less than 2 percent of the blacks who took it passed; 95 percent of all promotions to sergeant were non-Hispanic whites. The department braced itself for another round of lawsuits.[442]

Something else the New York City police have tried is to replace the pencil-and-paper test for sergeant with a video-based test. The theory was that *any* written exam was biased against blacks. This proved no better than the traditional exam at giving equal pass rates. When the results were announced, both black and Puerto Rican spokesmen denounced the test as biased.[443]

In 1992, the city's fire department took a different approach. It decided that minorities do less well than whites on multiple-choice tests because of "test anxiety." The city paid a consultant to devise a test in which candidates got three choices rather than just one to pick the right answer. Getting the right answer as the first choice was to be worth a full point, with a half point and a quarter point awarded to anyone who got the right answer as second or third choice, respectively. Besides reducing "test anxiety," another effect of this would be to narrow the gap in test scores between people who know the right answer and people who do not. More minorities might thereby get a passing grade.[444]

One way to squeeze bias out of a test is to make it so easy that anyone can pass it. New York's Sanitation Department indulged in an enormous waste of time when it gave a test on which 23,078 applicants out of 24,000 got *perfect scores.*[445] Presumably, the department could then claim to have hired only those minorities who got the highest possible score.

Since it has proven impossible to design meaningful tests that do not give "biased" results, the Houston Fire Department worked out a court-approved method to eliminate bias *after a test was taken.* In 1991 it gave a one-hundred-question test for promotions, with a passing grade of 70. Whites got better scores than blacks. The court agreed that the department could then study the results and throw out questions that minorities were more likely than whites to get wrong. The reasoning was that if they got them wrong, they must have been biased, even if no one could have known that in advance.

The department farmed the test scores out to a private consulting firm, which duly eliminated twenty-eight questions. This meant that thirty-two people who had originally passed now had failing grades. They were twenty-four whites, four blacks, three Hispanics, and one Asian. After the test was rescored, thirteen people who had originally failed were found to have passed: five blacks, four Hispanics, and four whites. Since eight minorities had been knocked off the pass list but nine had been added to it, the exercise resulted in a net gain of one. Naturally, the people who had been knocked off the pass list, including the minorities, were hopping mad, but the Houston fire chief got one more minority promotion out of the exercise.[446]

This was plain hard luck for the blacks who got the right answers on questions that were supposed to be "biased" against them, and it was a piece of good luck for the whites who got the *wrong* answers on questions that were supposed to be "biased" *in their favor.* This sort of foolishness makes a joke out of what is supposed to be an objective procedure, but some people would do double backflips if that were what it took to get the right number of black promotions.

The entire debate about cultural bias must seem faintly surreal to Darryl Hayden of Indianapolis. In 1985, out of 1,250 applicants for jobs as fire fighters, he got the highest test score. Cultural bias appears to have been no obstacle to him, despite the fact that he is black.[447]

Nevertheless, cultural bias has been an effective tool for justifying affirmative action. Between 1970 and 1990, fully 41 percent of all new police officer jobs have gone to blacks, a number that is nearly three and a half times as great as the percentage of blacks in the general population.[448] In 1960, 2.5 percent of all firefighters were black; by 1990, 11.5 percent were black.[449]

The federal government has had no better luck at designing an examination that blacks and whites can pass at equal rates. In the 1970s it used something called the Federal Service Entrance Examination. Although blacks got extra points because of their race, their pass rates were disproportionately low. At great expense, the government designed a new test, called the Professional and Administrative Career Examination (PACE), which was to be free of bias. Apparently it was not; 42 percent of white applicants passed it but only 13 percent of Hispanics and 5 percent of blacks did. So in 1982 the government scrapped PACE and gave up testing. It instituted a more subjective system of interviews and evaluations to make it easier for the government to hire nonwhites. In 1987 a federal judge ruled this new process "arbitrary and capricious," but since it resulted in a satisfactory number of minority hires, it continued to be used.[450]

Six hundred thousand dollars later, the government produced yet another set of tests, which were given for the first time in June 1990. These have less academic content than PACE and call for a considerable amount of subjective "biodata." As the government puts it, half of the two-part test "evaluates how well you have used the opportunities you have had in school, work, or outside activities."[451] The results were to be scrutinized for a period of five years, with an option to scrap the tests if they proved to be "biased."[452]

In 1990, the New York City school system gave up on the merit system and decided that the racial mix of its teachers must reflect the racial mix of all potential teachers. The new system would allow the chancellor to suspend any school board that did not meet affirmative action targets.[453] Robert F. Wagner, president of the Board of Education, explained that although the experiences of other school districts across the country suggest that it is very difficult to find good minority teachers and that the effort was not likely to help students very much, it was important not to give even the appearance of discrimination.[454] In other words, Mr. Wagner was defending an expensive, difficult undertaking that would probably show few results and that would discriminate against whites. It was necessary so as to avoid the *appearance* of discriminating against blacks.

White teachers face discrimination when staff are cut. In Boston, for example, when thirteen hundred teachers had to be laid off in the early 1980s, a federal judicial order overturned the school district's seniority rules. Thus, while whites with up to fifteen years' experience were being laid off, the school district continued to hire new black teachers. Whites tried twice to appeal this injustice to the U.S. Supreme Court; both times the Court refused to hear the case.[455]

The Santa Clara County Transportation Agency, in California, has set out to produce a work force that mirrors the surrounding population in every respect. For all jobs in which blacks are under-represented, they must be hired in strict preference to whites, as long as they meet the minimum qualifications. Nobody has ever shown that in the past the county discriminated in its hiring, but the agency got Supreme Court approval for its program in 1987. What is the significance of plans like this?

> [They] squarely endorse coerced equality of result over equal opportunity, and group rights over individual liberty. . . .
> [The message it sends blacks is that] above a certain minimal threshold of competence, gradations in qualifications are insignificant and may properly be supplanted by race . . . that for some, the highest standards of excellence are unnecessary.[456]

Is this the kind of society we want to build?

In this climate, it is no wonder that a few whites are scouring their family trees for the odd black or Hispanic ancestor. Between 1986 and 1988, eight people in the Boston police department had their "minority" status challenged. In 1988, the fire department launched an investigation of the bona fides of its minority employees after anonymous tipsters accused whites of making fraudulent racial claims.[457]

In San Francisco as well, affirmative action programs have spurred an intense interest in genealogy. Firemen and policemen have started claiming to be members of one or another protected group, since it can mean automatic promotion or pay raises. There have been challenges and counterchallenges and numerous accusations of "ethnic fraud."

Attempts to cash in on affirmative action have highlighted not only how arbitrary the practice is but even how arbitrarily the protected populations are defined. Essentially any nonwhite can get preference, including recent immigrants. However, since Hispanics are often defined as "Spanish-surnamed," white Spaniards are a federally protected group, even though Portuguese, for example, are not. This means that South Americans, even those descended from European immigrants, get preferences—except for those Brazilians who do not happen to be black. They have Portuguese surnames, so are treated like native-born whites.[458] Presumably this makes sense to someone.

Latin Americans have been particularly resentful of the fact that Spaniards qualify for affirmative action. They claim that only New World Hispanics have suffered enough to deserve racial preferences, and have called for the establishment of "ethnic purity panels" to determine how the racial spoils will be distributed.[459]

Increasingly, the spoils are so great that some white parents have pushed their children into the racial masquerade. In San Francisco, court-ordered desegregation plans set an upper limit on the number of white children who may attend the best schools. According to their enrollment forms, white children have suddenly started turning black, Hispanic, or Asian.[460]

Tortured Logic

Whites who defend affirmative action have to pretend that there is no injustice in it. J. Stanley Pottinger was once in charge of affirmative action at the Department of Health, Education, and Welfare (HEW, now the Department of Health and Human Services). When someone told him that affirmative action might mean discrimination against whites, he replied: "That is balderdash. That is the biggest crock I have ever heard. It is the kind of argument one expects to hear from a backwoods cracker farmer."[461] Mr. Pottinger seems to have had prejudices of his own against rural whites.

More recently, President George Bush's appointee as chairman of the U.S. Civil Rights Commission, Arthur Fletcher, painted himself into a similar verbal corner. In the same breath with which he denounced racial quotas he said that "specifying the number of person-hours to be worked by minorities and women" was a "typical contracting practice," of the sort required by the government.[462]

It is interesting to see the tortured reasoning that even our highest court has used to turn the Civil Rights Act inside out. Justice Blackmun, for example, has argued: "In order to get beyond racism, we must first take account of race. . . . And in order to treat some persons equally, we must treat them differently."[463]

As we saw above, Section 703(j) of the Civil Rights Act states clearly that it does not require employers to hire by race in order to even out a numerical imbalance. Congress thereby intended to forbid race-conscious hiring of any kind. However, in the famous case of *Weber* v. *Kaiser Aluminum,* the U.S. Supreme Court justified reverse discrimination on that very section. It ruled that since the act does not *require* race-based hiring, it therefore does not *forbid* it. That makes it legal.[464] Amazingly, racial quotas were blessed by the Supreme Court in the name of the very section of the law that was drafted to lock them out.

Justice William Douglas once explained his opposition to affirmative action to Justice Thurgood Marshall, the first black to be appointed to the Supreme Court. Douglas said he thought discrimination against whites was just as unconstitutional as discrimination against blacks. In a flourish of high legal reasoning, Justice Marshall replied, "You guys have been practicing discrimination for years. Now it is our turn."[465]

Justice Marshall was at least being honest. So were Mary Berry and Blandina Ramirez, both appointed to the Civil Rights Commission by President Jimmy Carter. In 1984 they issued a joint statement explaining that civil rights laws were not passed to protect the rights of white men and do not apply to them.[466] There was a similarly straightforward acknowledgment of the inherent injustice of affirmative action in a 1990 decision by Justice William Brennan, in which he wrote, "innocent persons may be called upon to bear some of the burden of the remedy [of past discrimination]."[467] So long as the innocent victims are white, Justice Brennan was saying, "equal opportunity" has been granted.

Not all judges are fooled by affirmative action. Chief Justice Warren Burger wrote in a dissent from a decision upholding reverse discrimination that "discriminatory preference for any group, minority or majority, is precisely and only what Congress has proscribed."[468] Justice William Rehnquist, likewise writing in a dissent, called the reasoning that transformed civil rights into affirmative action a "tour de force reminiscent not of jurists . . . but of escape artists, such as Houdini . . ."[469]

Escape-artist logic works for companies as well as for individuals. In 1989, thirty-six states and nearly two hundred local governments had minority "set-aside" programs, which awarded a fixed percentage of all contracts to companies owned by nonwhites or women.[470] It did not matter if another company could do the job better or cheaper.

Set-asides invited cheating. When there were not enough legitimate minority businesses, the "company" that got the contract might have been nothing more than a shell with a nonwhite face, which took orders for white "subcontractors." When the U.S. Department of Transportation studied the problem from 1982 to 1984, it found that half of the road-construction companies that got set-aside work were ineligible or questionable.[471]

The Supreme Court Steps In

Of all the various forms of affirmative action, minority set-asides were the first to be weakened by the Supreme Court's attempt to return to genuinely race-neutral principles. In January 1989, it ruled that the city of Richmond, Virginia, was discriminating against whites when it decided to reserve 30 percent of all city contracts for companies owned by nonwhites. The Court did not, however, do away with the principle of racial set-asides. It merely restricted them to cases in which past prejudice could be proven. Moreover, its ruling applied only to local governments. It therefore let stand the 10 percent federal set-aside program.[472]

The inefficiencies of set-asides became immediately obvious after the Court ruling. In Philadelphia, before the ruling black-owned companies were getting 25 percent of the city's contracts. When normal competitive bidding was restored, blacks got 3.5

percent. Many black-owned companies had been established deliberately to take advantage of set-asides. They were not accustomed to real competition, and when the artificial revenue of set-asides was taken from them, they failed.[473]

The city of Atlanta likewise saw a sharp drop in minority contractors when it returned to normal competition.[474] The city promptly allocated $500,000 for a project to find evidence of past discrimination so it could keep its set-asides going.[475] That is to say, it spent taxpayer money in an effort to demonstrate its past discrimination so it could now practice a new form of discrimination. Half a million dollars brought in an eleven-hundred-page report that covered the city's contracting history all the way back to the Civil War.[476] Why did the city search for racism so far back in the past? Perhaps it is because any discrimination that occurred within the past twenty years would be "discrimination" *under a black city government;* no white has been mayor of Atlanta since the election of Maynard Jackson in 1973.

The hunt for past discrimination was common all over the country. Durham County, in North Carolina, paid a minority organization $62,000 to find evidence of past discrimination so it could continue with set-asides.[477]

In late 1990, New York City announced it was paying for a "huge" study that would prove past discrimination and thereby permit a resumption of set-asides. The city's lawyers explained that they needn't prove that the city discriminated intentionally, only that contracting practices had a "discriminatory impact."[478] No racial discrimination in the city's contracting process appears to have been found. Nevertheless, the 25 percent of the companies that compete for city business and were owned by minorities or women were found to be getting only 7 percent of the dollar volume of contracts.[479] As a result, Mayor Dinkins made the sphinx-like announcement that although the set-aside program would not involve quotas, 20 percent of city contracts would henceforth go to

---

[479] This is not a comparison of like with like. If minority- and woman-owned businesses tend to be smaller than those owned by white men, it does not make sense simply to compare the number of companies with the total spent by the city. A fairer comparison would be to compare sales to the city as a proportion of total sales. Such a comparison could conceivably have shown that nonwhite firms were *over*represented in their dealings with the city.

companies owned by minorities and women.[480] The very notion of discrimination wastes away to nothing when numbers alone are used to prove that a city administration "discriminated" against black contractors and is therefore justified in establishing set-asides that discriminate against white contractors.

The city of San Francisco avoids the word "set-asides," but in late 1990 it announced a "goal" of awarding 12 percent of all city contracts to black-owned firms. Then-Mayor Art Agnos circulated an order to city department heads threatening to slash their budgets unless they found more minority suppliers.[481]

Presumably, the justification for set-asides was that minority contractors had faced discrimination in the past. Such programs went on for decades, and if it was discrimination that kept minority entrepreneurs from getting started, set-asides certainly gave them the chance. The National Association of Minority Contractors reports that thousands of minority-owned businesses went under in the year following the end of set-asides.[482] The fact that they have been unable to compete in the open market is the strongest possible evidence that the problem was one of inefficiency rather than discrimination.

Many large city governments are run by blacks, so there is little reason to think that racism is thwarting black companies that do business with them. When set-asides were in full swing, black construction firms got 93 percent of their business from public sector jobs.[483] If, after set-asides are ended, they are unable to get business from black-run, black-dominated city governments, racism is clearly not the problem.

In June 1989, the Court handed down two more important rulings on affirmative action. In the first, it made it more difficult for minorities to base charges of discrimination on a purely numerical analysis of a work force—that is to say, in cases where there was no evidence at all of deliberate discrimination. In the past, if an employer had a racially unbalanced work force, he had to prove, in court, that the imbalance was a result of job requirements that were "essential" to get the job done.

For example, requiring a high-school diploma for certain jobs could put a work force out of balance, even if the requirement were applied impartially to blacks and whites. This is because more whites than blacks graduate from high school. When an impartially applied standard affects the races differently it is said to have a "disparate impact." Once a disparate impact had been shown, an employer had to prove that the diploma was not just desirable but *essential* for getting the job done. In the usual, guilty-until-proven-innocent way, the burden of proof was on the employer to show that he was not using the job requirement as a cover for racism. Faced only with circumstantial evidence of prejudice—numbers—an employer was guilty until he convinced a court otherwise. In no other kind of judicial proceeding do American citizens bear the burden of proof in the face of strictly circumstantial evidence.

In some cases, rigid "disparate impact" thinking has lead to the complete elimination of some standards. In the past, most fire and police departments turned down applicants who had been dishonorably discharged from the military or who had conviction records. As a legal manual for fire departments explains, that was found to be racial discrimination:

> The EEOC has ruled that a requirement that applicants who have served in the armed forces must have an honorable discharge is not a valid prerequisite. The reason is that twice as many blacks receive dishonorable discharges as whites, indicating "racism" as the most significant factor in this disparity. The commission also has ruled that arrest records cannot be used to disqualify applicants, as experience shows blacks are arrested substantially more frequently than whites in proportion to their numbers.[484]

Of course, these rules do not apply only to fire departments; they apply to all employers.

Until the Supreme Court's 1989 ruling, any employer who simply wanted the best work force, without regard to race, automatically fell afoul of the law if more-than-minimum job standards

[484] Timothy Callahan and Charles Bahme, *Fire Service and the Law* (Quincy, Mass.: National Fire Protection Association, 1987), p. 56. See Chapter One for an analysis of "racism" in the criminal justice system. There is no reason to believe that the military discharge system is any more "racist."

meant that nonwhites were underrepresented. This was just the sort of foolishness that would have required Senator Humphrey, were he still alive, to eat the Civil Rights Act of 1964. Many companies just gave up and promised to make their work forces mirror the racial composition of the surrounding population. This was the only way to avoid lawsuits. Race became as important a hiring factor as ability, and employers who had never discriminated against anybody were forced to discriminate against whites.

President Carter's appointee as chairman of the Equal Employment Opportunity Commission, Eleanor Holmes Norton, as much as told employers what their options were. Unless they had a racially balanced work force, the EEOC might sue them. If they had enough nonwhite employees, the EEOC would leave them alone.[485]

U.S. Supreme Court Justice Antonin Scalia understood perfectly that the threat of expensive litigation was enough to make employers hire by racial quota, even if it meant a lower-quality work force and discrimination against whites:

> . . . the *failure* to engage in reverse discrimination is economic folly, and arguably a breach of duty to shareholders or taxpayers, wherever the cost of anticipated Title VII [discrimination] litigation exceeds the cost of hiring less capable (though still minimally capable) workers. . . . A statute designed to establish a color-blind and gender-blind workplace has thus been converted into a powerful engine of racism and sexism, not merely *permitting* intentional race- and sex-based discrimination, but often making it, through operation of the legal system, practically compelled.[486]

If an employer were so foolish as to ignore race and hire only the best-qualified workers, it could be seen as a betrayal of stockholders' interests. This was because the gains of having competent workers could be wiped out if the company had to fight a discrimination suit—brought by the EEOC at taxpayers' expense. Linda Gottfredson of the University of Delaware points out that Supreme Court cases of the late 1960s and early 1970s had essentially forced employers to institute racial hiring quotas but they did not dare admit to this for fear of reverse-discrimination law-suits.[487]

The new Supreme Court ruling of *Ward's Cove Packing* v. *Antonio* gave employers some relief. First of all, it shifted the burden of proof. If a work force were out of balance, it would be the responsibility of those claiming discrimination to show that a job standard was unfair. Also, the Court ruled that employers could set standards that go beyond what is starkly "essential" as long as the standards were legitimately related to a business need. If all this seems obvious and unremarkable, something else is just as obvious: The ruling did not take away a single remedy from victims of demonstrated prejudice.[488] It concerned only unintended, unproven prejudice.

The second June 1989 ruling in this area by the Court was directly related to the first. Many employers, including those who had discriminated against nonwhites as well as those who had been guilty strictly on the basis of numbers, had signed consent decrees agreeing to balance their work forces. Since nonwhites were seldom as qualified as whites, the only way to do this was by discriminating against whites. This was exactly what the San Francisco Fire Department was doing to Larry Gatt. Whites like Mr. Gatt were not allowed to sue on grounds of racial prejudice, because the affirmative action programs were undertaken under the protection of court-approved consent decrees.

The Supreme Court, ruling on a case involving the Birmingham, Alabama, Fire Department, decided that this was wrong. The Court found that any agreement an employer made with minority groups could not bind the employer's relations with people who were not involved in the agreement. In other words, a company could not promise favors to minorities if it meant damaging the interests of whites. The Court did not go so far as to say that affirmative action programs should be immediately dismantled. It said only that if a white person were the victim of one, he had the right to sue.[489]

Plenty have. Within the first twelve months after the Birmingham ruling, whites filed reverse-discrimination suits in Boston, Chicago, Cincinnati, Memphis, Oakland, Omaha, and San Francisco. In Atlanta, white firemen who proved that they had suffered from court-ordered racial prejudice won back pay and seniority rights.[490]

There was a certain irony in the Supreme Court's ruling against the Birmingham fire department. The department's antiwhite hiring practices had been defended by the crack New York law firm of Cravath, Swaine & Moore, which lavished twenty-two hundred partner-hours and seventeen thousand associate hours—all pro bono—on the case. Cravath appeared to believe strongly in affirmative action—at least for other people. The firm has never had a black partner, and there are only 5 blacks among its 224 associates.[491] The population of New York City is one quarter black, and one wonders how Cravath would feel if a judge ordered it to match that figure in all its own hirings and promotions.

For people who think that civil rights mean special favors for nonwhites, the Supreme Court's rulings were a blow to civil rights. Benjamin Hooks, who was then executive director of the NAACP, echoed the views of most black leaders when he called the rulings "a disaster for all those committed to equal employment opportunity."[492] "The court has run amok," lamented Ralph Neas, executive director of the Leadership Conference on Civil Rights.[493] T. J. Jemison, head of the largest black church in America, the 7.8-million-member National Baptist Convention, said of the Supreme Court justices, "They call themselves strict constructionists, but I call them strict segregationists."[494] A *New York Times* editorial charged that "the Court majority displays an icy indifference . . . to the hopes of discrimination victims. . . ."[495] *Business Week* likewise warned that "The Court is moving down a treacherous road," and blasted its lack of support for "plans aimed at ending racial discrimination."[496] Republican and Democratic congressmen alike, claiming that this was an end to remedies for discrimination, promised new legislation to put the muscle back into affirmative action.[497]

---

[497] See, for example, Congressman Don Edwards' remarks in Aaron Epstein, "High Court Deals Blow to Affirmative Action," *San Jose Mercury News*, (June 13, 1989), p. 1A. See also H.R. 2598, introduced by Republican congressman Tom Campbell, approximately one week after the Court's decision in *Ward's Cove Packing* v. *Antonio*. The stated intention of the bill was to nullify that decision. [Congressman Campbell press release dated June 14, 1989, and open letter dated June 12, 1989.] Democratic senator Howard Metzenbaum was also quick to introduce a new civil-rights bill to correct what he called "the court's retreat

These people were using language in a very strange way. The remedy for discrimination remained what it always was: to eliminate it. Whatever Mr. Hooks may have said, the Court's rulings were not a disaster for equal employment opportunity, but a return to it. *Business Week* notwithstanding, an end to racial discrimination was exactly what the Court intended. However, as one of the few syndicated columnists who approved the decisions put it, " 'Civil rights' groups . . . think that the way to fight racial discrimination is with racial discrimination and that anyone who disagrees is a racist."[498] "Equal opportunity" is Orwellian code for *un*equal opportunity.

Lost in the din of criticism was the fact that the Supreme Court decisions took nothing whatsoever away from someone who could show real discrimination. Nonwhites who suffer actual job discrimination have powerful means of redress and can win large cash settlements. Deliberate discrimination certainly happens in America, and the courts had been punishing it for years. They will continue to do so.

The controversy over the Supreme Court decisions was about "unintended" discrimination—if there can actually be such a thing —that is to say, the consequences of standardized, race-neutral hiring policies. To equate these with deliberate exclusion of nonwhites from the work force is either colossal ignorance or irresponsible provocation. That the two were repeatedly equated and that this went largely unchallenged is eloquent proof of the depth of America's confusion about race.

In October 1990, Congress passed a new Civil Rights Bill. As its staunchest supporter, Senator Edward Kennedy, explained, its avowed purpose was to circumvent the series of Supreme Court decisions that had weakened affirmative action. The bill reinstated the prohibition against job standards that were anything above the minimum, and made employers once again guilty-until-proven-innocent if their work forces did not match the racial hue of potential employees. It broke new ground by providing not only for restitution in the case of job discrimination but also by opening the door to massive punitive damages. These would have applied

---

from equal opportunity." Joe Davidson, "Civil Rights Groups Turn to Congress to Overcome Recent High Court Rulings," *The Wall Street Journal* (July 14, 1989), p. A5.

even to employers whose racially unbalanced work forces were the result not of deliberate discrimination but of job qualifications that were found to be excessively demanding.

Although the bill specifically absolved employers of any requirement that they hire by quota, its effect was to make quotas unavoidable. It was a little like a building code that requires an electric power company to lay its wires underground but thoughtfully exempts them from the *obligation* of digging holes. In both cases, what the law required was probably not possible without resorting to what the law piously claimed not to require.

As usual, despite the fact that it is a thirty-eight-thousand-employee business, Congress exempted itself from the requirements of the bill. As Senator Warren Rudman of New Hampshire pointed out, the law might encourage "frivolous lawsuits." "It is absolutely essential," he went on to say, "that, as to our legislative employees, we have an absolute right without outside review by anyone of what we do." He concluded that Congress was different from a mere farm or factory and that its work must not be trammeled by the "civil rights" straitjacket he was prepared to order the rest of the country to wear.[499]

Thus Congress tried to shackle the country with employment rules it knew it would itself find intolerable. The Civil Rights Act of 1990 was vetoed by President George Bush and fell short of a Senate override by a single vote.[500] Nothing daunted, the forces that backed the bill promptly introduced a virtually identical one at the beginning of the 1991 Congress, and President Bush signed it into law late that same year.

The new law, which applied to women and religious minorities as well as racial minorities, left certain key concepts deliberately vague. An employer had to prove that a job standard with "disparate impact" was "job-related" and had a significant relationship to "business necessity." It was to be up to the courts to decide what those phrases meant.[501] The litigation nightmare began without delay: The first suit brought under the new law was filed within a week of the President's signature.[502] Some economists have speculated that since the law specifically exempted businesses with fewer than fifteen employees, some small companies might limit their growth so as to stay out of its clutches.[503]

The new law also reinstated the inviolability of court-ordered affirmative action programs. Once again, whites had no recourse in the face of blatant discrimination as long as the discrimination was ordered by a court. Some commentators thought this provision, which deprived whites of due process, was clearly unconstitutional.[504]

Congress, which had finally came under criticism for constantly exempting itself from the employment laws it passes for the rest of the country—including the Equal Pay Act and a variety of occupational health and safety acts[505]—made a stab at applying the law to itself. The House simply gave up and exempted itself as usual.[506] The Senate preened itself on a provision that would send employment discrimination cases before a Senate ethics committee, but the measure was largely a sham. Unlike other employers, who must go to trial before a jury, senators would be investigated by an ethics committee of their peers that has a consistent record of cowardice and leniency. As Senate majority leader George Mitchell explained, it would be an unfair burden on legislators "to look at mechanically duplicating the procedures used in the private sector." Once again Congress refused to live by the laws it passed for the rest of us.[507]

The obvious reason Senator Mitchell wanted to avoid the law is that by its own standards Congress is a blatant discriminator. Of the eighty-two hundred powerful jobs in Congress that influence legislation, only 3.7 percent are held by blacks. Nearly half of all minorities who hold such jobs work for the forty-four minority legislators.[508] Clearly, congressmen do not want to be forced to cut job standards to the bone, or have their staffs reflect the racial composition of 66-percent-black Washington, D.C.

Why did President Bush sign into law a bill that was, if anything, more quota-oriented than the one he vetoed? He appears to have been influenced by the success of former Klansman David Duke's substantial showing in a failed attempt to become governor of Louisiana. Though he was repudiated by President Bush and by virtually all prominent Republicans, Mr. Duke claimed to be a Republican. President Bush may have been trying to distance himself from Mr. Duke, though his approval of a bill that many people considered antiwhite only added to the very grievances that make people support someone as disreputable as Mr. Duke.[509]

Another reason may have been the furor that was stirred up among blacks and women by the Justice Clarence Thomas nomination hearings (see Chapter Three). Republican senator John Danforth dismissed complaints about the bill as "technicalities" and argued that it was necessary to appease angry blacks and feminists.[510]

Thus racial preferences once more have a firm legal basis. Often employers who do not want to hire by race have no choice. The U.S. Labor Department does not approve government contracts with companies that do not practice affirmative action—that is 325,000 firms and an estimated 16 million to 25 million employees. Contractors must file detailed racial breakdowns of their employees, and the department sends some of its 685 inspectors around to look into things if there are not enough nonwhites. The FCC can revoke licenses of broadcasters if they do not practice affirmative action. All colleges, local governments, and police departments that need federal money feel the same pressure. Thirty million to 40 million workers thus come directly under the federal racial quota system.[511] The Federal Equal Employment Opportunity Commission keeps everyone else in line.

Since numbers alone are enough to convict an employer, its "crime" has little relation to anything most people think of as discrimination. When no one has been shown to have done anything in particular to harm nonwhites, the solution to this kind of "discrimination" cannot be the simple elimination of a harmful practice. Instead, preferential policies must be established—in the name of a law that was passed specifically to forbid racial preferences—to bring the number of nonwhite employees up to a satisfactory level.

One problem is figuring out just what level is satisfactory. Liberty National Bank & Trust Co. of Louisville, Kentucky, has long had a reputation as a model employer of minorities. In 1989 it made a concerted effort to hire black tellers and clerical staff. Sixteen percent of the two hundred such employees the bank hired that year were black. Since this was a higher percentage than the proportion of blacks in the Louisville work force, the bank thought it had done very well.

Not so. The Labor Department discovered that 32 percent of the applicants for those jobs were black, so the bank broke the law by hiring too few of them. In 1991 the bank was ordered to offer jobs to eighteen blacks it had turned down two years previously. Whether or not they accepted the jobs, they were to be paid the amount of money they would have earned had they taken jobs in 1989—a total of $277,833—minus whatever money they might have made if they had, in the meantime, taken other jobs.

Liberty National Bank did not discriminate against black applicants; in fact, it made a special effort to attract them. Nevertheless, by turning away blacks whom it thought unsuited for the jobs, it was guilty of discrimination.[512] This is the situation that has been codified by the Civil Rights Act of 1991.

Sometimes the Labor Department makes affirmative action demands that are so stupid they are difficult to believe. One small Kansas City construction company had fifteen hourly employees, of whom three were nonwhite. Among these hourly employees were two truck drivers, both of whom were white, so in that job category it had a lily-white work force. It duly got a letter from the Labor Department saying it had "failed to exert adequate good faith efforts to achieve the minimum minority utilization goal of 12.7 percent for truck drivers. . . ."[513]

Like many other companies, Sears Roebuck has been sued by the Equal Employment Opportunity Commission for "discrimination" because it had an unbalanced work force. It decided to defend its good name rather than negotiate a settlement, but it had to spend *more than $20 million* before it was completely exonerated. Its actual court trial alone, in 1984 and 1985, lasted more than ten months. When it was all over, what did Sears have to show for its time and money? Precious little.[514] Its ordeal was not about discrimination; it was about statistics. Other companies faced with such suits have decided that it is safest and cheapest simply to hire by skin color.

Thus, when employers are reported to have settled "discrimination" cases, chances are that no intentional discrimination has ever been demonstrated. They have been convicted on the basis of numbers. In 1991, for example, Northwest Airlines agreed to spend $3.5 million to accelerate the hiring and promotion of blacks. It also agreed to finance scholarships for black trainees and to pay hundreds of thousands of dollars to blacks who claimed discrimination. It also agreed to pay for hearings in which thousands of nonwhite employees could make their cases for jobs and promotions. The airline admitted no discrimination; the case against it was based on numbers.[515] The airline *may not* have discriminated.

Any hiring system that hands out jobs on the basis of race rather than qualifications weakens the economy. America's international competitiveness is being seriously challenged. That in such times our Congress can still vote to carry on with such a debilitating, unjust system shows the extent to which our representatives—and our nation—have been mesmerized by race. As Thomas Sowell points out, "some congressmen probably would vote for a declaration of war against Canada if it were contained in a bill with the words 'civil rights' in its title."[516] Many lobbyists and business groups who thought that the new law was disastrous soft-pedaled their criticism because "race" and "civil rights" are words with such totemic value.[517] As always, underlying the entire debate on employment was the assumption—so universally subscribed to that it scarcely needed articulation—that white employers are inveterately unfair to blacks and must be constantly watched.

Other Government Policies

During the debate over the new civil rights law, many people lost sight of the fact that there are myriad government affirmative action programs that were untouched by the 1989 U.S. Supreme Court decisions. Section 8(a) of the Small Business Act, for example, mandates noncompetitive, sole-source contracting for companies owned by "economically disadvantaged" minorities. This is another form of set-aside. To be considered "disadvantaged" a contractor has to have a personal net worth of under $750,000. The average American family, presumably not disadvantaged, has a net worth of $78,000. The average black family has a net worth of $20,000 and the black median is only $3,397. The average net worth of the minorities who benefited from 8(a) was $160,000, more than twice the national average. In 1988 the 8(a) program handed out $3.2 billion to such "disadvantaged" minorities.[518] In 1991 there were thirty-six hundred beneficiaries of 8(a) programs.[519]

A 1980 law directs the Small Business Administration to "graduate" minority businesses from preferential programs after a certain period. The Reagan administration tried to do this but was thwarted by Congress. Opponents to "graduation" noted that without government handouts, the black firms would fail.[520] One wonders about the wisdom of fostering black companies that can never be weaned from the preferential teat.

The SBA's loans, including those to minority companies, have essentially gone unaudited. Inevitably, money has gone astray. When the *Los Angeles Times* did an informal survey of minority firms that the SBA listed as "current" 8(a) beneficiaries, it found that 22 percent could not be reached or had gone out of business.[521]

The Federal Bureau of Investigation runs its own formalized affirmative action program. On combined written and oral exam scores of 100, blacks get 5 extra points because of race. Since there are about eight thousand applicants every year for six hundred positions, every point makes a big difference. According to Hugo Rodriguez, who worked for the FBI from 1978 to 1987 as a minority recruiter, the agency ignores the scores if nonwhites do not score high enough. "Somehow they would decide they want so many blacks, or so many Hispanics," he says. "Then they would go down the list until they got that number."[522]

The State Department has long practiced various forms of affirmative action. Aspiring diplomats who could speak a foreign language were favored for jobs until it was pointed out in the 1960s that few blacks speak foreign languages. Now the U.S. diplomatic service may be the only one in the world that does not even consider foreign-language ability when it makes hiring decisions. By 1979 the department was even more worried about a dearth of blacks, so it created a "near pass" category on its examination for minorities. Although 70 is the passing score for whites, blacks have reportedly been admitted with scores in the mid-50s.[523]

Wherever there is government there is likely to be affirmative action. A report by the General Accounting Office on the Peace Corps, for example, found that minorities tend to think of the corps as white and middle-class. Consequently it has started a special program to recruit minority volunteers and now has a recruiting staff that is one-fourth nonwhite.[524] Even the National Gallery in Washington, D.C., has a minority internship program that is not open to whites.[525]

Private Sector Affirmative Action

Many private companies, whether required to by law or not, give minorities a leg up. Walt Disney Studios has a special program to get minorities into the screenwriting business. In 1990 it announced fellowships for twenty-seven nonwhite writers who were to work with the studio's creative teams, and it sent letters to agents asking for more material by minorities. Warner Brothers started a similar minority fellowship program in the 1970s, and 20th Century-Fox has a special outreach program to find black writers for its television programs.[526]

The American Society of Newspaper Editors recently voted to reaffirm its goal for nonwhite employment by the year 2000: 23 percent of all employees, or the same percentage as in the nation's population at large. The society has endorsed hiring quotas. After a flap over an editorial that offended black readers, the *Philadelphia Inquirer* took the lead by announcing that henceforth fully *one half* of its newsroom hires would be nonwhite.[527] David Lawrence, who became the newspaper society's president in 1991, announced that he would make minority hiring the top priority of his term in office.[528]

To meet goals like this, a large number of newspapers have set up recruitment and intern programs exclusively for nonwhites. Dow Jones has a minority reporting intern scholarship program for college seniors, and high school journalism workshops for younger minorities. Special scholarships and internships for non-whites are offered by Knight Ridder Newspapers, Cox Enterprises, and such papers as the *Boston Globe, The New York Times,* the *Hartford Courant,* the *Modesto Bee,* the *Philadelphia Inquirer,* the *Nashville Banner,* and the *Seattle Times.* Even a small newspaper such as the *Asbury Park Press* in New Jersey has offered minorities-only scholarships for ten years.[529]

Recently a group of forty-three regional and national papers set up the Task Force on Minorities in the Newspaper Business.[530] One of the task force's publications is called *Journalism Career Guide for Minorities.* Along with conventional advice on how to prepare for a job as a reporter, the booklet contains long lists of university scholarships open only to nonwhites, addresses of minority recruiters all around the country, summaries of minority training programs, and organizations that make journalism grants specifically earmarked for minorities.[531]

In late 1990 the task force organized a job fair in a downtown Pittsburgh hotel to attract nonwhites into the newspaper business. Twenty-three different news organizations were represented at what was one of twelve such racially exclusive events expected to be held around the country.[532]

Some companies are more zealous in hiring minorities than others. Corning, Inc., has tied its executive bonuses largely to how many minorities and women a manager can hire and promote. It sets aside well-paid internships exclusively for minorities. It makes all its managers take a two-day course that is supposed to help them combat racism. The company has done everything possible to make the little town of Corning, New York, where it is headquartered, a comfortable place for blacks. It persuaded local broadcasters to carry black programs, and it leaned on the local high school to hire black teachers and administrators. It even brought a black hairdresser to town. The chairman of Corning professes to dislike quotas but says "I don't know any way around them." This is all done in the name of fighting "discrimination," but as not a few white employees have noted, the effect is to discriminate against whites.[533]

When Kentucky Fried Chicken does an executive search, it makes blacks compete only with other blacks rather than with whites. It asks headhunters to come up with three separate lists of candidates: one of black men, another of white men, and a third of women. It then hires the best person from each list.[534]

Now that the Soviet threat has disappeared, tens of thousands of military personnel will be leaving the armed forces. Southmark Corporation, which runs 7-Eleven stores, is specially targeting these people to make them store managers and franchisees—as long as they are nonwhite. During 1992 it also planned a large minority-directed ad campaign to recruit nonwhites. Jeanne Hitchcock, Southland's manager of urban affairs, explained that the company anticipates a constant increase in minority participation: "We consider this an ongoing process. What we raise [the percentages of nonwhite managers and franchisees] to, we'll consider it progress and move on."[535]

The Mead Corporation calculates executive bonuses, in part, according to how many blacks have been hired and promoted.[536] Xerox does the same.[537] Money talks. Fourteen percent of Xerox executives at the vice president level and above are black[538] —more than the black percentage in the nation's population. In 1990, DuPont wanted 45 to 50 percent of its college recruits to be women or minorities; ultimately 65 percent were.[539]

Although affirmative action is usually described as a "goal," its nature quickly changes. Lawrence Ashe is a lawyer who has frequently been involved in discrimination suits. As he explains it, "A goal is like anything else in corporate America. It becomes an order. . . . [I]f you get a $5,000 bonus for meeting affirmative action goals, you will meet them."[540]

Gilbert Tweed, an executive headhunting firm in New York, reports that 14 percent of its searches in 1991 were specifically for minorities or women.[541]

In a recent survey of *Fortune* 500 CEOs, only 14 percent said their companies ignored race and hired strictly on merit. Inevitably, to meet hiring goals, executives often end up poaching each other's blacks. Forty-eight percent complained that their best minorities are snatched away by competitors.[542] Black entrepreneurs, who would like to hire other talented blacks to help them run their businesses, face the same problem: The most promising blacks are lured away by established white companies that can afford to pay higher salaries.[543]

A common way to hire blacks is for companies to participate in minority job fairs. They pay a fee to set up a booth at an event that will be open only to nonwhites. A recent minority fair in Manhattan had a blue-ribbon list of sponsors that included IBM, Campbell Soup, Colgate-Palmolive, and Xerox.[544] Fairs like this are held all across the country.

Black engineers are in particular demand because they are so scarce. In the spring of 1991, despite the first economic recession in close to a decade, there were 225 different companies vying with each other to hire Howard University's 125 engineering graduates. The demand for black graduates is so high that Howard's placement director, Samuel Hall, tells companies that if they want a chance merely to conduct interviews, they should agree to support the school with money and other resources.[545]

These days it is not enough simply to hire blacks. They must be visible in positions of authority. Unfortunately, so many companies have pushed minorities forward because of race rather than ability that some whites doubt the qualifications of black managers. This problem has given rise to a new kind of consulting. Capital Cities/ABC, Scott Paper, and Westinghouse are all paying for help in getting at least five minorities or women into high positions without giving the appearance of using quotas. Terry Simmons of New Hope, Pennsylvania, charges them each $125,000 to accomplish the promotions within two years.[546]

During the debates on the Civil Rights Bill of 1991, a few congressmen voiced some of the broadly felt, popular opposition to affirmative action, but some corporate executives brushed it aside. "It doesn't slow us down at all," said Donald Keough, president and CEO of Coca-Cola: "We just don't pay attention to the politicians." Wilfred Oliver, director of minority business development at Kodak, says, "We would do it [affirmative action] whether it was the law or not."[547]

Hiring by race is now so thoroughly ingrained in most companies that they would not know how to stop doing it. Alfred Blumrose, a former official at the Equal Employment Opportunity Commission, puts it this way: "Affirmative action programs are so much a part of the way industry operates today that to try to deestablish them would create enormous difficulties." Furthermore, if a company dismantled an affirmative action program, this could be cited in a lawsuit as intent to discriminate.[548] When racial preferences for nonwhites become the norm, a return to equal treatment is usually called discrimination.

The situation is even more complicated than this. In 1985, under prodding from officials appointed by President Ronald Reagan, the U.S. Justice Department tried to abolish the requirement that government contractors set minority hiring goals. Discrimination against nonwhites would still be illegal, of course, but companies would no longer be required to discriminate against whites. To the astonishment of the department, the National Association of Manufacturers, the quintessential representative of "big business," lobbied strongly against abolishing the requirement.

Why would they oppose the elimination of a regulation? First of all, they recognized the strong undercurrent of resentment whites feel for racial preferences that work against them. Whites have already begun to challenge them. If the government dropped its affirmative action *requirements* and companies continued to practice them anyway, they might be easy targets for law suits from disgruntled whites.

The obvious solution would then be to get rid of affirmative action altogether. The problem with this was that by 1985, large companies had well-entrenched affirmative action bureaucracies. Many of these were staffed by nonwhite activists who could not easily be fired or transferred. At the same time, any company that dismantled its preference programs was likely to face the fury of the civil rights establishment and the possibility of demonstrations and boycotts.

The elimination of a regulation would thus have forced companies to choose between two painful alternatives: either continue with affirmative action and face lawsuits from whites, or abandon affirmative action and provoke the wrath of nonwhites. The big business lobby prevailed, and its clients were spared this unpleasant choice.[549]

Lowering Standards

Companies are under such strong pressure to hire blacks that they sometimes have to lower their standards to do so. A number of techniques have been devised to make it appear that this is not happening. One of the most underhanded is to "correct" the results of employment tests by "race-norming" them. The technique is simply to give blacks or Hispanics higher marks than whites for the same number of correct answers.

The General Aptitude Test Battery (GATB) is a test that is widely used to assess a job candidate's fitness for a job. If test results were not adjusted for race, blacks would consistently be outscored by whites, and employers would be forced to abandon the test because of its "bias" and "disparate impact." Since it is a test of *general* ability and not one that measures the precise, minimal qualifications for a specific job, it fell afoul of the prohibition against discriminatory testing that resulted from Supreme Court decisions of the early 1970s. Nevertheless, it had been in use since 1947 and was widely acknowledged to be an excellent means of determining aptitude for a large number of different jobs. It would have been a shame to junk it.

In 1981, the U.S. Department of Labor "solved" the problem by establishing a new way to score the test: Candidates were compared, not with all other test-takers, but only with people of their own race. For example, if a black, a Hispanic, a white, and an Asian each got the same raw score of 300, the black would be ranked in the eighty-seventh percentile, the Hispanic in the seventy-fourth, with the white and the Asian together in the basement in the forty-seventh percentile. According to the Department of Labor, the test could then be used to give the job to the black, since test bias had been corrected by race norming.

By 1986 about forty U.S. state governments and myriad private companies were race norming their test results. Of the estimated sixteen million candidates whose scores have been adjusted this way,[550] virtually none was ever told about it. Many employers who hired workers through state employment agencies—companies such as Philip Morris, Canon, Nabisco, and Anheuser-Busch—got race-normed candidate profiles whether they knew it or not. As a result, less-qualified blacks and Hispanics got the jobs that should have gone to whites and Asians.[551]

A few whites nevertheless got wind of this system and began to complain. In Chicago, white police officers sued to put an end to what they charged was "clandestine and covert manipulation of [GATB test] results."[552] The National Academy of Sciences was commissioned to do "a thorough, scientific evaluation" of race-norming and determined in 1989 that it was entirely correct and justified, *even though there was no detectable bias in the test.*[553]

Nevertheless, since that time, race-norming has gotten some publicity—all of it bad. In July 1990, the then secretary of labor, Elizabeth Dole, suspended use of the GATB for a two-year period of review,[554] and the Civil Rights Bill of 1991 banned race-norming.[555]

Race-norming was, of course, nothing more than a cover for racial hiring quotas. The principle was that any test that did not give identical results for every racial group must be either deliberately rejigged to do so or be thrown out. The new Civil Rights law left the GATB in legal limbo. Race-norming was illegal, but so was disparate impact. That meant the GATB had to go into forced retirement unless someone hit upon some Solomonic solution.

Private test-makers were in trouble, too. When the government first forbade employment tests with disparate impact, they quickly devised their own race-norming scales. The Wonderlic Personnel Test, for example, was advertised for years as "federally approved as eliminating possible disparate impact upon Minority Applicants." The scoring manual came with an "Ethnic Conversion Table" for boosting the scores of nonwhites.[556]

Employers *like* standardized tests. Given the choice between doing without them completely and using unfairly race-normed tests, they actually prefer race-norming.[557] According to Tom Muller, president of the Employers National Job Service Council, many of the companies he represents hope to get race-norming reinstated.[558] One of the great, unsung ironies in the demise of standardized tests is that they were originally devised so employers could judge by objective assessment standards rather than the subjective impressions of personal preference. Since it has been impossible to devise meaningful, standardized tests that do not have disparate impact, America has returned to the era of subjective impressions, but with the addition of racial quotas (see the following chapter). Since it appears that America is to have racial quotas one way or another, the country would be better off being frank about it. Open race-norming at least lets an employer compare whites with whites and blacks with blacks.

Although it is clear for all to see that standards must be lowered if minorities are to be hired in numbers sufficient to meet affirmative action requirements, it is dangerous to say so. In 1990 a California transit executive took part in a transportation study group. In arguing that some of the beneficiaries of preferential hiring were not adequately qualified, he reportedly used the expression "inept minorities and women." The man was suspended from his $90,000-a-year job and was given "sensitivity and awareness training."[559]

Some companies try to forestall candor and the embarrassment that ensues by routinely giving their white employees "sensitivity training." Charles King is a black man who has been running racism seminars for twenty years. He charges corporate clients $275 per person for his two-day sessions. His central message is that bad race relations are the fault of white people, whether they know it or not. "Whites cannot perceive their racism," he says, "because racism is by definition the normal practices, customs, and habits of a majority group that tend to disadvantage a minority group."[560]

Sometimes the very steps companies take to "sensitize" their white employees can come back to haunt them. When minority and women employees sued Lucky Stores for discrimination, they discovered that notes had been taken during "sensitivity workshops." Managers had been asked to think of negative stereotypes and discuss them. They thought up the obvious ones. Judge Marilyn Hall Patel of the federal court in San Francisco ruled that records of these sessions could be used in court as evidence of bias.[561]

Other companies take a more low-key approach with their

white employees. Lewis Griggs is a white consultant who gives seminars to executives on managing "diversity." More than a thousand companies have bought his seven-part video, which emphasizes the importance of getting along with people from different cultures. Some companies sponsor "celebration workshops" in which whites eat ethnic food, watch ethnic dances, and try to develop their understanding of different peoples.[562] DuPont has even paid for black managers to hold conferences on how African-American culture can improve profits.[563] It is not clear what good any of this does, but corporations are certainly trying very hard to do what they think is right.

Many companies make donations to explicitly black charities, such as the United Negro College Fund. Procter & Gamble Company has been sponsoring large-scale family reunions in various American cities. Only black families get support.[564] In 1990 Hughes Aircraft Company spent $1.5 million on financial aid and laboratory equipment for black colleges.[565] In 1991 Coca-Cola agreed to spend $1 million to $2 million to support Black Expo USA, a series of trade fairs designed to help black entrepreneurs get started. Pepsi had been the previous sponsor, but Coke offered more money.[566]

The Big Three automakers all make special efforts to help blacks become car dealers. They offer minorities intensive, one- or two-year programs that include classroom training and sessions with established dealers. Once minorities have finished the program, the automakers finance up to 85 percent of the cost of the dealership. Whites have to find their own financing for a dealership, which can cost from $400,000 to $2 million.

Ford and General Motors go even farther and put the initial investment of a new minority dealer into an escrow account for the first six to twelve months. This is the most dangerous period for a new business, and if it goes broke, the investment can be returned to the dealer. Whites who start a dealership lose their investment if the business fails. The automakers also pay for consultants to advise black dealers on how to advertise, cut costs, and get more profit out of service departments. Partly as a result of preferential efforts like this, the number of Big Three auto dealerships owned by minorities rose from 243 to 629 in the decade to 1991.[567]

Companies are also trying very hard to do business with minority-owned firms, though they may have a hard time finding them. Many regional organizations have been established to make introductions, and a few private companies have gotten into the game. A black-run outfit called Univex will introduce executives to minority suppliers—for a minimum retainer of $4,000 a month.[568] There are also publications that specialize in taking help-wanted ads directed toward blacks. There is so much demand for minority employees that they can charge several times more for an ad than their circulation base would normally warrant.[569]

The National Minority Supplier Development Council makes similar introductions, for which it charges its three thousand public and corporate clients $30,000 a year.[570] It also manages a fund to provide working capital for minority businesses, to which Ford Motor Company recently gave $750,000 and Boeing gave $1 million.[571] In the era of affirmative action, this is just another cost of doing business.

There are many regional equivalents to this organization, usually formed as voluntary groups by local businesses. The Kansas City Minority Suppliers Development Council, for example, is chaired by the president and CEO of Kansas City Power & Light Company. He has set up the Adopt-a-Business program, under which white-owned companies take minority vendors under their wings and give them marketing, sales, financial, and management advice. The council is also setting up a revolving loan fund that will be open only to minority businesses.[572]

Sometimes companies go to comical lengths to secure "minority" suppliers. The Frito-Lay company spends millions of dollars a year on bags for its potato chips but was worried that it did not have a single nonwhite bag supplier. It therefore persuaded one of its white suppliers to spin off one of its bag plants as a joint venture, to be 51 percent owned by a black man. The entire deal was orchestrated and supported by Frito-Lay, which now can claim that it has a minority supplier.[573]

New York Telephone Company, NYNEX, takes a curious approach toward its suppliers. In the last weeks of 1990, the head of its Affirmative Action Division, Juan Rodriguez, sent a letter to the several thousand companies with which NYNEX does business. In it he wrote, "It is our intention to insure equal opportunity in all aspects of business operations, including purchasing of goods and services." To that end, Mr. Rodriguez then asked all vendors to fill in a form indicating what percentage of the company was owned or operated by nonwhites.

Would not equal opportunity be more likely if NYNEX knew nothing about minority ownership or operation? Would that not be the best way to ensure that race was *not* a factor in purchasing decisions? Though Mr. Rodriguez claimed that the purpose of the letter was "to update our vendor database," it is difficult not to conclude that, as head of his company's Affirmative Action Division, he was gathering data in the interests of *un*equal opportunity.[574]

Unlike private companies, federal and local governments do not have to worry very much about profits and efficiency. They have therefore been even more willing to hire poorly qualified workers through reverse discrimination. Nearly one in four black workers is employed by government, while the figure for whites is fewer than one in seven.[575] Fully half of all black professionals and managers work for government at some level.[576] Of the top executive appointments at President Bush's Department of Health and Human Services, at one time fully 70 percent were black, Hispanic, or female.[577] Are we really to believe that they were all chosen strictly on merit?

When the city of Mobile, Alabama, hired a black police chief and a black director of public safety, it did not even pretend that the men were hired for their competence. "We hired these men to make a progressive statement about Mobile," said Mayor Michael Dow.[578]

Many studies have shown that private companies are more efficient at many of the things governments do. However, there has been great resistance to cutting back the role of government because that would put pressure on black jobs.[579] Government services are therefore more expensive and inefficient than they need be.

Grant-making bodies have long channeled funds along racial

lines. Many black and Hispanic organizations receive crucial funding from the Ford and Rockefeller foundations. A large number of arts councils give both public and private money to ethnic dance, theater, and other arts groups. The National Endowment for the Arts has begun to penalize grantees that do not show enough minority representation.[580] The Rockefeller and Ford foundations reportedly plan to phase out their support for traditional European art forms altogether so as to concentrate on non-Western arts.[581]

Entirely typical of race-based grant-making was the 1990 announcement of a series of gifts by the Boston Foundation. It released $200,000, to be divided among fifteen Boston-area social service organizations for the sole purpose of hiring nonwhite employees.[582] The foundation also makes grants for the arts, but only for projects that show "cultural diversity."[583]

On Campus

Schools and universities play the same racial preferences game. After a slow start in the late 1960s, campus affirmative action was soon widespread. By the start of the 1990s, when a few voices in the rest of society were at least being raised about the morality and efficacy of reverse racism, preferences were so thoroughly embedded in the fabric of the academy that some universities could barely move a muscle unless it could be demonstrated to be in the interests of "diversity."

The Department of Health, Education, and Welfare was one of the first federal agencies to jump on the reverse discrimination bandwagon. In 1971, for example, HEW threatened to withhold federal grants permanently from Columbia University—not because Columbia had been shown to discriminate or had even been accused of discriminating. It simply had not come up with an acceptable affirmative action plan to atone for sins it might not even have committed.[584]

Even when faculty hiring committees could show that they had interviewed plenty of blacks, they still had to justify themselves if they did not hire them. This meant letting government bureau-crats root through confidential notes and minutes to see if anyone had expressed a tainted opinion. This was during the Vietnam War, when campuses were suspicious of a Republican administra-tion as never before. Even Berkeley, home of the high priests of protest, submitted without a whimper. "One might imagine the faculty would be in an uproar, what with Nixon's men ransacking the inner temple. But no. . . . [T]he faculty is silent," wrote one bemused academic.[585]

On some campuses today, the campaign to train, hire, and pro-mote minorities has gone beyond reason. To begin with, there are academic specialties that have become the official preserve of blacks. For all practical purposes, professorships in African-Amer-ican history or African studies, for example, are no longer open to whites.

At Berkeley, part of the new campaign for "diversity" is to make sure that only blacks teach black history, only Hispanics teach about Latin America, etc. White students feel "warned off" of majoring in ethnic studies because these are the preserve of ethnics. White instructors face open hostility from nonwhites if they presume to teach about the experiences of nonwhites. Today Berkeley still has two distinguished white scholars of African-American history, who date from the time when the department was still open to all. A colleague laments that "a [Leon] Litwack or [Lawrence] Levine couldn't happen now."[586]

In other departments, universities across the country are so ea-ger to hire blacks that they are making hiring promises they can-not keep. In 1988, the University of Wisconsin established a five-year plan to increase minority faculty by 75 percent.[587] The Uni-versity of Vermont promised to hire four to eleven minorities ev-ery four years, beginning in 1989. California state law requires that 30 percent of all new faculty at community colleges be non-white.[588] Yale University has set a ten-year goal of increasing its tenured minority faculty by 40 percent and its nontenured minor-ity faculty by 60 percent. President Benno Schmidt announced that Yale would raid other universities to make the appointments.[589] In 1988 Duke University promised to hire one black for every department by 1993.[590]

All of those colleges were going to have a hard time, especially Duke. In 1986 only 820 blacks earned Ph.D.s in the whole country, and half of those were in education. Not a single black got a Ph.D. in geology, aerospace engineering, astronomy, geometry, astrophysics, or theoretical chemistry. No black got a Ph.D. in European history, Russian, Spanish, German, architecture, or the classics. American universities gave out 8,000 Ph.D. degrees in physical sciences and engineering, but blacks earned only 39 of them.[591]

In 1987, of the 290 doctorates granted in electrical engineering, not one went to a black. Blacks earned 3 of the 281 doctorates in chemical engineering, 2 of the 240 doctorates in mechanical engineering, and 5 of the 698 doctorates in astronomy and physics. In subsequent years the total number of Ph.D.s granted to blacks bumped along at the same level: 813 in 1988 and 811 in 1989.[592] The first real increase in black Ph.D. degrees since 1977 did not come until 1991, when 933 were awarded.[593] What is more, many black Ph.D.s plan to work in industry, where they are diligently recruited and can make more money. In 1986 a survey of 547 blacks earning doctorates found that fewer than half expected to teach. And, of course, one of the reasons why there are so few black Ph.D. candidates is that private companies are wooing black college graduates so ardently.[594]

Where is Duke going to find a black for every department? Until 1988, Duke avoided raiding the black colleges, but it then decided that was a scruple it could no longer afford.[595] What possible good does it do for Duke to hire teachers away from Spellman College or Howard University?

And what of the University of Wisconsin's five-year plan to increase minority faculty by 75 percent? To do so, it had not only to add minority professors at a rate of more than twenty a year, but also keep all the ones it already had. That is not easy. In the first year of its five-year plan, it managed to hire eighteen new minority professors, but it *lost* even more than that to other universities.[596]

While Wisconsin's black faculty are poached by competitors, its law school does not hesitate to do its own poaching. When it set up four tenured positions specifically for minorities and women, the first people to fill them were hired away from tenured jobs at other universities. Nor is the law school alone in establishing jobs specifically for minorities. Northeastern has set aside money for exclusively minority slots throughout the university.[597]

Purdue University recently promised that the first five departments to hire minority faculty would be rewarded with funds for more positions. Williams College has set a quota of 20 percent for minority faculty, and aimed to fill it by the early 1990s. Fully half of Hampshire College's academic appointments over the past few years have been reserved for minorities.[598] Bucknell University recently set aside money for five minority hires—in *whatever field* qualified candidates could be found.[599]

Such zeal for hiring minorities means that many whites looking for a teaching job are likely to face discrimination. John H. Bunzel is the former president of San Jose State University and a past member of the U.S. Commission on Civil Rights. He has documented just a few of the deliberate acts of prejudice directed against white candidates. When an affirmative-action search was launched recently in a large department at San Francisco State University, the head of the hiring committee instructed its members to "save time and energy by not examining any applications from white males." In March 1989, the hiring committee in another department designated four candidates who were "persons of color" as "hirable" while designating six white candidates as "also well qualified but not hirable." They were disqualified because of their race. Over the winter of 1989–90, a white with a Ph.D. applied for an opening in Stanford University's required course in Culture, Ideas, and Values. He learned that "only racial minorities will be hired to fill the slots in the Europe and America 'track.' "

Often, whites know better than to apply at all. Ohio Wesleyan ran an advertisement that began with these words: "Ohio Wesleyan University seeks black applicants for a tenure-track position." A faculty member explained that his department had been given two years to find a black; otherwise the position would be taken away.

In the past, employers could make their intentions known with ads that said, "We are an equal opportunity employer." Some colleges even put the phrase on their official stationery. However, once everyone started using it, it no longer stood out. Now it is common to see ads for academic positions that say, "Minorities are encouraged to apply." The Political Science Department of the University of California at Los Angeles (UCLA) has run ads saying it "invites nominations and applications from outstanding minority and female candidates."

This makes it pretty clear that the employer is not interested in white men. It may be just as well to let them know that their applications are going to be a waste of time. When the provost of San Francisco State University approved the English Department's 1984 application for two additional slots, he wrote: "Candidates recommended to me [must] be nonwhite. Let me underscore that the stipulation is an absolute condition." In 1988 a dean of one of the university's schools got written approval for two positions "for the purposes of affirmative-action minority hiring only." In September 1989, the head of the faculty search committee for sociology at Wayne State University wrote a memo to the committee saying that both of the two newly authorized positions *"must* be filled by a minority person" [emphasis in the original]. At the law school of the same university, the provost authorized a new tenure-track appointment in an August 1989 memo in which he wrote, "the position must be filled by a minority faculty person."[600]

The casualties of this process are white people who may have no idea what is happening to them. One white academic wrote about a faculty search he participated in in which there were orders from the top that a nonwhite be hired. A white candidate who had been part of a series of interviews away from the campus wanted to know how he had done and whether he had a chance of being invited on campus for another interview. The author fobbed him off with generalities but later wrote:

I knew that when he got the standard rejection letter he would blame himself for not doing better in the interview, not getting that extra letter of recommendation. I don't know if he would have felt better if I had said, "You're not going to get an interview. You're white." But I would have.[601]

Since there is such desperation to hire black faculty, black professors are constantly being wooed from campus to campus with higher salary offers. Not surprisingly, blacks now make more money than whites with equivalent Ph.D.s.[602]

Neither this fact, nor the well-known shortage of black Ph.D.s, stops activists from complaining about the "systematic racism" that keeps blacks out of jobs. When white administrators point out how hard they are trying to find capable blacks, they are accused of deliberately setting false standards. Recently, when the political science department at the University of Tennessee at Knoxville hired a white woman to chair the department, the administration rejected her. She had a national reputation, but the university wanted a black. It took control of the selection committee away from the Political Science Department and put a black activist professor in charge. Now the department has a black chairman. Michael Harris, a black professor of religion, warned that whites could not be trusted to make fair hiring decisions. "[W]hen you see the word 'qualifications' used," he said, "remember this is the new code word for whites."[603]

Carolivia Herron, a black assistant professor of Afro-American Studies at Harvard, rejected the notion that professors should be judged by what they write. She accused the university of not recognizing that minorities think it is "boring" to write books. Even if Harvard was so stodgy as to require such boring evidence of scholarship as books, other colleges were not. Nine of them offered jobs to Professor Herron, and she accepted a tenured position at Mount Holyoke.[604]

The same racial preferences that help blacks get teaching jobs help them get into college in the first place. For more than twenty years, schools have been actively recruiting minorities and bending the admissions requirements to get them in. Even the National Merit Scholarship Corporation, which makes prestigious cash grants to the nation's most promising high school graduates, has

[603] William Hawkins, "Letter From the Volunteer State," *Chronicles* (November 1988), p. 46. In the art world, as well, ever since the 1960s, many blacks have dismissed the word "quality" as racist. They refuse to acknowledge such things as polish, technique, content, and finish; that they should be held to such "white" standards is a form a racial oppression. Michael Brenson, "Is 'Quality' an Idea Whose Time Has Come?," *The New York Times* (July 22, 1990), Sec. 2, p. 1.

an affirmative action program. Since there are almost no blacks among the six thousand students who win its regular scholarships, it sets aside seven hundred scholarships for "outstanding Negro students" who cannot meet the normal standards.[605] This, of course, has not stopped people from claiming that its tests are racially biased.[606]

The Scholastic Aptitude Test (SAT) is also routinely denounced as racist because the average white combined score is 200 points higher than the average black score.[607] Georgetown's black basketball coach, John Thompson, for example, talks of its "proven cultural bias." However, even the sharpest critics are hard pressed to produce examples of biased questions. Furthermore, although Asians consistently outscore whites on the math test, no one appears to think that the SAT has a pro-Asian bias.[608]

It is frequently pointed out that children of wealthy parents get better SAT scores than children of poor parents. The economic advantages of whites are said to give them better access to the culture that is embodied in the test. In fact, white children from families with incomes of $10,000 to $20,000 get better SAT scores than black children from families with incomes of $70,000 or more. Even Asians from poor families, many of whom are newcomers to the United States and are from genuinely different cultures, score slightly better than black children from the wealthiest families.[609] For thirty years, the test has been the best indicator we have of how well a high school student will do in his freshman year of college. For black students, the test predicts performance significantly better than high school grades do, whether they go to black or to mainly white colleges.[610] For whatever it may be worth, the head of the College Board, which devises and administers the test, is black.[611]

Nevertheless, blacks with low scores are routinely accepted at colleges in preference to whites with high scores. Admissions officers simply have no choice if they are to increase the number of black students. At the University of Virginia, for example, average combined SAT scores for blacks in 1988 were 246 points lower than for whites.[612] At UCLA in 1990, blacks and Hispanics had average scores 250 points below the average white score—and just

as one would expect from a differential of that magnitude, graduation rates for blacks were about half that of whites.[613]

At the best engineering schools, the average SAT math score is
700 or better. In 1983, only 205 blacks in the whole country scored
that high (0.28 percent of all test-takers), while 31,704 whites and
3,015 Asians did (3.3 percent and 8.6 percent, respectively, of all
test-takers).[614] Engineering schools are constantly criticized for
not admitting enough blacks, but what are they to do?

They lower standards. The black students at the Massachusetts
Institute of Technology (MIT) have SAT math scores that put
them in the top 10 percent for the country. That sounds promising, but they are still in the *bottom* 10 percent at MIT, since MIT
gets the nation's top *1* percent. Many blacks drop out, and those
who do not, get the worst grades.[615]

Admissions officers know that many blacks are unqualified and
will drop out; they are admitted anyway, in the name of "diversity." Practices like this are not without cost to society; people who
might well have stayed on and graduated must be denied admission.

The Medical College Admissions Test (MCAT) is the standard
entrance exam for medical schools. The top score is 7, and in 1979,
no whites who scored 4 or below got in. However, 15 percent of
the blacks who scored that low were admitted. Overall, black
scores were 1.5 standard deviations lower than white scores. In
most years, blacks who are admitted to medical school have lower
average scores than whites who are *rejected.* Blacks also have
much higher dropout rates.[616]

Scores on the Graduate Record Examination, which is the basis
for admission to graduate school, show an even greater disparity.
In 1983 the national average for the verbal part of the test was
499, while for blacks it was 370. For the quantitative test, the
figures were 516 and 363, and for the analytical test, 522 and
363.[617] The blacks who take this test are the educated elite—
college graduates who hope to get advanced degrees.

[614] Walter E. Williams, "Race, Scholarship, and Affirmative Action," *National Review*
(May 5, 1989) p. 36ff. Achievement on the verbal portion shows a similar gap, except that
the numbers are smaller and Asian leadership is not so pronounced. Blacks, 66 (.093
percent); whites, 9,024 (0.94 percent); Asians, 496 (1.4 percent).

Despite the yawning gaps in achievement, graduate departments all around the country are vowing to admit more blacks. Stanford University's recent promise to double the number of minority graduate students within five years[618] is likely to be impossible without lowering standards even farther.

The University of California at Berkeley requires that whites and Asians have at least a 3.7 grade point average even to be considered for admission. Blacks and Hispanics with much lower grades are automatically admitted, as long as they meet minimum requirements. Roughly one fifth of the applicants to Berkeley who are rejected have nearly perfect 4.0 averages. In 1989 that was twenty-five hundred people, none of whom was black. Once they are in, can it be a surprise that many blacks fail to graduate? Seventy-three percent of all blacks admitted to Berkeley drop out, while only 33 percent of whites and Asians do.[619] This is not considered a waste of taxpayers' money. If Berkeley admissions were conducted without regard to race, blacks and Hispanics would be no more than 4 percent of the student body.[620] Thanks to racial preferences, they are 22 percent.[621]

Clear bias against whites does not merely sound wrong to most people; it also sounds illegal. It sounds like the very opposite of the "equal opportunity" that America is presumably striving for. Very occasionally the government commits to paper the rules that are to govern "equal opportunity" in American schools. IRS Publication 557 explains how schools get tax-exempt status. The publication could not be more emphatic about explaining that schools *must not discriminate by race.* It goes into great detail about how important this is and even requires that schools advertise in local newspapers or on radio that they do not discriminate by race. The IRS kindly includes examples of what a print ad should say and gives specific instructions on how big it must be. It all sounds like the most rigorous possible antidiscrimination message. Then Publication 557 says this:

A policy of a school that favors *racial minority groups* with respect to admissions, facilities and programs, and financial assistance does not constitute discrimination on the basis of race when the purpose and effect of this policy is to promote establishing and maintain the school's nondiscrimination policy [emphasis in the original].[622]

Discrimination against nonwhites will not be tolerated. Discrimination against whites is fine—as long as the discrimination is done in the name of nondiscrimination. The IRS tortures the language as much as it does common sense. The publication also says, in effect, that it is perfectly all right for nondiscrimination ads—the ads the IRS requires a school to run—to be less than true.

One way to attract minority students is to set aside money for them that is not available to whites. Close to 90 percent of all private colleges offer scholarships that are off-limits to whites. The average award is $6,800 a year.[623]

Stanford University combs the nation's SAT results every year, looking for nonwhites who have gotten good scores. It then mails out fifteen thousand letters, inviting these people to apply for admission. Once an application has been coaxed out of a minority, it is routed to a minority admissions officer for special handling.[624]

The state of Pennsylvania recently set up what it calls the Pennsylvania Graduate Opportunities Tuition Waiver Program. Thirty of the state's 133 universities have agreed to offer complete, graduate-studies scholarships to blacks. Sixteen have made the offer to any qualified black, in any field of study he chooses. Fourteen will waive tuition only for certain numbers of blacks or in certain departments. Race, not financial need, is what makes students eligible. The state is raising $15 million to pay for the program, which is modeled on a similar scheme in Florida.[625]

The University of Chicago, along with twelve campuses of the Big Ten universities, has established something called the Summer Research Opportunities Program. It offers research experience under the one-on-one guidance of a professor, in the hope that this will encourage students to go on to graduate school. The program was started in 1986 and sponsored 571 students for the summer of 1990. Whites are not eligible.[626] Yale University has just announced a similar minorities-only summer research program.[627]

Eighty-nine American colleges participate in something called the Minority Engineering Program. Nonwhite engineering students get money, counseling, advice, tutoring, and other special services not available to whites. This program does not consider Asians to be minorities, and excludes them along with whites.[628] In the state of Utah, this program is supplemented with a similar effort, begun in 1985, to guide nonwhites in secondary schools into science and engineering careers.[629]

Many university systems have their own, smaller-scale programs. The state of Louisiana searches out promising nonwhite junior high school students and shepherds the most likely ones into special teaching tracks. The best go on to summer internships and get scholarships to university.[630]

The University of Michigan has what it calls a Minority Summer Institute. It pays all travel, living, and campus expenses for thirty nonwhites to come to the university for six weeks during the summer. There they work with representatives from thirty different business schools, who try to persuade them to enter doctoral programs in business. Every participant is paid a $2,500 "stipend" just for showing up.[631]

In 1990, the General Electric Foundation announced a ten-year, $20 million program designed to train nonwhites for teaching careers in business, science, and engineering. The program would fund graduate studies and would provide money to professors who wish to hire nonwhite assistants. None of the money was to be used to benefit whites.[632]

One of the reasons black teachers are wooed so fiercely by universities is that with the current rage for "role models" and "diversity" their presence on campus is considered indispensable. However, there can be no doubt that all the fellowships, courting, and pampering bring some blacks into the teaching business who do not have a real interest in it. Students who might have blossomed into first-rate teachers may never get the chance because they had the misfortune to be born white; the fellowships they might have won are available only to nonwhites.

At the undergraduate level as well, the principle of minorities-only scholarships is well established and has the same corrosive effect. Children of well-off blacks qualify for them, while the children of poor whites do not. At Harvard Graduate School, for example, all minorities get full scholarships whether they need them or not. Columbia University has a Malcolm X Scholarship

Fund.[633] General Motors has promised the NAACP to give $500,000 to five law schools, to be used to support nonwhite students only. Ford and Chrysler have signed similar agreements. Some of this earmarked money is being spent very questionably. At Penn State University, in the late 1980s, black students who managed a C average were getting cash rewards of $550. Blacks with a B average or better got $1,100.[634]

In late 1990, the injustice of programs like this came to the attention of Michael Williams, an assistant secretary of education who is black. He announced that it was illegal, under civil rights laws, for colleges that receive federal funds to grant scholarships on the basis of race. This brought down the wrath of the entire civil rights establishment. Benjamin Hooks, then head of the NAACP, called Mr. Williams "insensitive, callous, and illogical."[635] Carl Rowan wrote that the decision was nothing short of a deliberate effort to keep the underclass down.[636] Other blacks told Mr. Williams privately that if he stuck to his policy he would be drummed out of black society.[637]

A skittish White House ordered that the ruling be modified. Private money, it decided, could be earmarked by race—at least for nonwhites. Race could also be considered a factor in granting scholarship money so as to increase campus diversity. Race-exclusive scholarships would also be permitted when they were used to remedy proven discrimination.

Since it was nearly impossible for colleges to figure out what was legal and what was not, the administration announced a four-year moratorium on strict enforcement. Activists hoped, in the meantime, to overturn the ruling entirely and return to open racial preferences.[638]

Although race-exclusive scholarships were supposed to be legal if they made up for past discrimination, just what did that mean? Would an applicant be asked to show that he had suffered racial discrimination from that very university in the past? No first-time applicant could possibly show that. If discrimination against other blacks could be proven at *any* time in the past, would that make today's race-exclusive scholarships legal? This was similar to the problem faced by cities trying to revive set-aside contracts by proving past discrimination. Who had to have suffered discrimination? When?

Early in 1992, a federal appeals court pointed the way when it ruled that the University of Maryland could fund blacks-only scholarships only if it could show "a specific finding" that there was still discrimination at the university. What might appear to be an entirely reasonable ruling reportedly "stunned" education experts.[639] Of course, if a university has unearthed "a specific finding" of discrimination, the reasonable and obvious thing to do would be to stop discriminating.

Colleges that want to earmark public money for nonwhites will find ways to do it. They have already shown remarkable determination. For example, Florida Atlantic University in Boca Raton recently decided to increase the size of its freshmen class, and decided it must increase the number of blacks by the same proportion. The university was already struggling to get blacks on campus, and knew it could not get more in the usual ways. It therefore hit upon a plan that might work: To every black who meets admissions standards, it offered free tuition—whether he needs it or not.[640]

When this policy was criticized by the U.S. Education Department, the university's president, Anthony Catanese, wondered if he might not be a victim of "the neoracism of the 1990s." "This [the criticism] says that neoracists are not illiterate Southerners in hoods and sheets trying to burn crosses, but people who are well-educated . . . they are trying to say the same thing as old-time racism—that the economic and social problems of this country are due to giving minorities an even chance."[641] It is hard to see how offering automatic scholarships to blacks whether they need them or not is an "even chance," but this is the sort of incoherence to which affirmative action so often leads.

According to one survey, in just three years—from 1987 to 1990 —the number of colleges that give scholarship money to minorities *regardless of financial need* rose from 15 percent to 24 percent.[642] Most Americans still think that scholarships are granted to outstanding but needy students. To give money to black students simply because they are black is nothing more than a form of bribery that serves to increase the number of minorities on campus. Obviously it bids up their price.

The machinery of minority recruitment—admissions personnel, counselors, orientation, special scholarships, mentor programs—is far more expensive than most people realize. For example, in the early 1990s, Texas A & M University was spending *$5.5 million a year* on minority recruitment and retention. A report issued by the faculty senate in 1992 found this insufficient and recommended a 40 percent increase to $7.7 million a year.[643]

There can be serious troubles for colleges that do not make strong efforts in favor of minorities. At Baruch College in New York, only 36 percent of the students are white, the student body president is black, and there have been no reports of racial incidents. Nevertheless, the Middle States Association of Colleges and Schools delayed renewal of accreditation because there are not enough minorities on Baruch's teaching staff, and minorities drop out more often than whites do.[644] As usual, there was no suggestion that Baruch had done anything at all to hinder minorities; it risked losing accreditation because it had not taken enough specifically race-based measures to help them. It promptly drew up plans to lower its hiring qualifications for blacks and Hispanics.[645]

There was a disturbing subplot to this story. The accreditation review committee was chaired by a man named T. H. Bonaparte. He wrote that Baruch should "cease relying upon labor market availability [and recruit] additional Black and Latino administrators." Shortly thereafter, he offered himself for the job of provost. Since Mr. Bonaparte is black, he was presumably qualified to do the kind of recruiting he had recommended. It was not until Mr. Bonaparte's conflict of interest was publicly reported that the accrediting agency asked him to forgo the opportunity that his official functions may have brought his way.[646]

Another subplot to the story was that shortly after the Baruch accreditation controversy, one of its professors was awarded the Nobel Prize in economics. At least one newspaper did not fail to note that this was probably the first time in the history of American higher education that a university that was producing Nobel-quality research had been threatened with disaccreditation.[647]

Most people think that accreditation is the assessment of a school's academic standards. Over the years it has come to include a judgment on a school's preference policies for minorities. During the Baruch controversy, it came to light that at least fifteen other colleges had had their accreditation delayed that year for the same reason. Baruch was only the first to be identified publicly.[648] Increasingly, the reasoning is that "diversity" is a crucial ingredient of educational excellence and that any university without some unspecified level of it is defective.[649]

Not everyone thinks racial preferences should be a criterion for accreditation. Lamar Alexander, appointed as secretary of education in 1991 by President Bush, announced that he would look into the standards used by the Middle States Association.[650] Others pointed out that "diversity" requirements appear to apply only to colleges that are largely white; if they were applied objectively, the first and most obvious offenders would be historically black colleges.[651]

Of course, widespread racial preferences leave a bad smell that no one can fail to notice. At Cornell University, blacks operate in what one professor calls "a shadow of the university life":

. . . permanent quotas in admission, preference in financial assistance, racially motivated hiring of faculty, difficulty in giving blacks failing marks, and an organized system of grievance and feeling aggrieved. And everywhere hypocrisy, contempt-producing lies about what is going on and how the whole scheme is working.[652]

What possible good does it do to bend the admissions rules at Cornell or Berkeley and then pay blacks to jump in over their heads? Even under the best of circumstances, they must contend with an underlying suspicion—even among themselves—that they are not the intellectual equals of white students.[653] These are solid youngsters who would have gotten a sound education and a lot of self-confidence at good, second-tier colleges. Instead, they get failure and bitterness. The same failure and bitterness cascades down to all levels. The second-tier schools, which see their natural prospects wooed away by the Ivy League, have to raid the third-tier schools to meet their quotas. Blacks are in over their heads at every level. They fail, and their white classmates see them fail. Is it any wonder that blacks at majority-white universities are five times more likely than their white schoolmates to drop out of school?[654] This is a terrible waste, both for them and for the universities.

All the sensitivity training for whites and special treatment for blacks will change nothing if blacks are simply not prepared for the work. One black associate professor writes:

At the university where I currently teach, the dropout rate for black students is 72 percent, despite the presence of several academic-support programs; a counseling center with black counselors; an Afro-American studies department; black faculty, administrators, and staff; a general education curriculum that emphasizes "cultural pluralism"; an Educational Opportunities Program; a mentor program; a black faculty and staff association. . . .[655]

Blacks need not drop out. Mainly-black colleges enroll only 17 percent of all black freshmen, but they produce twice that many graduates.[656] Black colleges can hardly lower standards "only for blacks," so their students are not forced into classes they cannot handle.

This whole system is as unfair to whites as it is cruel to blacks. The headmaster of a college prep school describes how it works. One year, two of his graduates applied to Berkeley. B was accepted and W was rejected. B was in the bottom third of the class while W was in the top third. B had College Board scores of 890 while W scored 1,290. B broke major school rules and was expelled, while W was a good citizen. B, who was accepted, was black, while W had the misfortune to be white. The headmaster calls Berkeley "a scary model for the future" and wonders what kind of message this sends his students about the fairness of our society.[657]

Berkeley has been recruiting minorities so vigorously that although 65 percent of all California high school graduates that are eligible for Berkeley are white, they made up only 34 percent of the 1989 freshman class—a close to 50 percent *under*representation. Like most whites, they have accepted discrimination in silence. Asians are not intimidated, though. They have complained that their numbers, too, are held down to let in blacks and Hispanics, who are *over*represented by figures of 480 percent and 325 percent, respectively.[658] A black California assemblywoman, Teresa Hughes, has explained that the problem was that the university was discriminating against *all* minorities.[659] A nearly 50 percent white underrepresentation appears not to be enough for her.

In spite of the ruckus over discrimination against Asians, it happens that they are the only race that is admitted to Berkeley in close proportion to their number of high school graduates who meet admissions requirements. It is whites who have paid the price for increased black and Hispanic enrollment, but the federal Department of Education dutifully launched a review of Berkeley's admissions policies with respect to Asians.[660]

A professor at Berkeley points out that in 1987, the average combined SAT score for whites and Asians was 270 points higher than that for blacks and Hispanics. Differences in preparation and ability are clear to anyone who must teach. "What our recent admissions policies have really done," he writes, "is to give us two student populations whose academic levels barely overlap."[661] In the face of mounting criticism and obvious disparities in student performance, Berkeley reviewed its admissions policies and, in 1991, finally ended its decades-long policy of guaranteeing admission to all blacks and Hispanics who meet minimum entry requirements.[662]

Some admissions officers are surprisingly candid about what they do. James A. Blackburn is the dean of admissions at the University of Virginia, where combined SAT scores for blacks are 200 points lower than combined scores for whites. As he explains, "If you were looking at the academic credentials, you would say Virginia has it upside down. We take more in the groups with weaker credentials and make it harder for those with stronger credentials."[663]

Law school admissions are particularly easy to check for lowered standards. The Law School Admissions Service keeps track of the average undergraduate grades and score on the Law School Aptitude Test (LSAT) for every applicant who is admitted to law school. Thus one can tell at a glance that the 150 or so black students who are admitted to the top law schools—Yale, Harvard, Stanford, Chicago, Columbia—are admitted at ten times the rate one would expect if the process were color-blind.[664] With their natural prospects drawn to more prestigious schools, second-tier law schools must also admit less-qualified blacks. At the University of Texas Law School, LSAT scores for admitted students have been around the ninety-second percentile for whites and the fifty-fifth percentile for blacks. Many law schools ensure that about 10 percent of their students are black. They can do this only by admitting students who would probably be rejected if they were white.[665]

Timothy Maguire, a white student at Georgetown Law School, worked for a time in the admissions office. There he discovered what has become routine all over the country: Black students have markedly lower scores on qualifications tests than whites. When he pointed out this disparity in the student newspaper, the article stirred a huge controversy. Mr. Maguire was browbeaten into a public apology. Though he had named no names, the law school launched a formal prosecution against him for revealing "confidential" admissions data. The Black Law Student Association called for his law degree to be withheld. Many lawyers refused to defend Mr. Maguire against suits brought against him for fear of being tarred as racists.

Mr. Maguire need not have looked into anyone's records to reach his conclusions. The average student admitted to Georgetown Law at the time had a college grade-point average of 3.55 out of a possible 4.0 and a score on the Law School Aptitude Test (LSAT) of 42 out of 48. Data from the Law School Admissions Service shows exactly how many blacks had grades and LSAT scores that matched or exceeded the Georgetown average: 17. Even if every one of them went to Georgetown—which, of course, they did not—the seventy or so blacks that Georgetown admits every year must necessarily have qualifications lower than the white average.[666]

Underqualified blacks are not brought up to the level of whites while they are in law school. In New York State, for example, 78 percent of white law school graduates pass the bar exam on their first try; only 31 percent of blacks do.[667]

At the same time, law schools have been steadily jettisoning ability as the sole criterion for filling slots on their prestigious law reviews. Harvard, Cornell, New York University, the University of Illinois, and the University of Virginia all have formal programs specially designed for minorities. The *Columbia Law Review* broke new ground by setting aside five jobs, not only for minorities and women but also for homosexuals and handicapped students.[668] The plan is supposed to remedy some unproven past bias, but henceforth the bias will be deliberate and systematic.

Nonwhites are perfectly happy to see their numbers increase at the expense of whites, even if everyone knows that standards are being lowered. When the number of whites first sank below 50 percent on the Berkeley campus, black and Hispanic groups greeted the news with cheers.[669]

Whites, on the other hand, are expected to support, or at least remain silent about, a system that discriminates against them. The administration of Smith College, for example, has made it clear that it will ignore all criticism of racial quotas and preferences, no matter how thoughtful.[670]

On some campuses, people who dare point out what everyone knows to be true may be quickly punished. At Michigan State University, a student was kicked out of school for three semesters when he refused to take down a "racist" cartoon. It showed two white students painting themselves black, as one says to the other, "Who needs to work so hard to get a perfect GPA [grade point average] or money for tuition when ya have this stuff."[671] At least one university has considered a rule that would formally punish any student who questioned the qualifications of a nonwhite student.[672]

It must be something of a shock for university students to learn one of the great, unwritten rules of race relations in America today: Affirmative action has lowered employment and admissions standards for nonwhites all across America, but everyone must pretend not to have noticed. After they graduate, students discover that affirmative action is not limited to employment and student admissions.

5

Affirmative Action Spreads

*M*OST PEOPLE THINK THAT AFFIRMATIVE ACTION does not extend beyond school and employment. In fact, racial preferences for blacks appear in many unexpected areas.

For example, legislation of virtually any kind can have affirmative action provisions added to it. When the government established the Resolution Trust Company (RTC) to sort out the mess in the savings and loan industry, it set up racially segregated bidding rules to ensure that all bankrupt, minority-owned thrifts that went on the block would stay in minority hands. It has also offered minority companies a price advantage whenever they bid for any of the legal, accounting, or other work that the RTC does by contract.[673] When the RTC seizes the assets of defunct banks and places them under the control of independent managers, it is under orders to find minority and female managers "to the maximum extent possible." It must report annually on how many assets it has put in the custody of such managers.[674]

Some legislative measures turn into affirmative action despite their original intentions. In 1978 Congress passed a bill called the Community Reinvestment Act. It says that any bank applying for a merger has to show that it "serves the convenience and needs" of local communities. Minority activists use this provision to get favors from banks in exchange for the clean bill of health the banks need for permission to merge. The activists are not really concerned about the merger itself; it is an opportunity to put pressure on a bank.

What they usually demand is subsidized loans in declining neighborhoods and "affirmative action" lending. One activist says, "They must affirmatively market their loans [to minorities]."[675] Some banks refuse to earmark money for certain neighborhoods at giveaway rates, but others have promised millions in return for a chance to merge. One banker calls this "pure blackmail."[676]

As we saw in Chapter One, racism—not cash flow, credit history, or value of the collateral—is assumed to be the reason that blacks are turned down for loans more often than whites. Once again, an institution is guilty on purely circumstantial evidence. In 1991, when the Bank of America wished to merge with Security Pacific, permission was held up because blacks and Hispanics were approved for mortgages 61 percent of the time while the figure for whites was 74 percent. To be allowed to merge, the Bank of America promised to waive closing costs on certain mortgages in certain neighborhoods and to approve lower-than-usual down payments of 5 percent in black neighborhoods. The bank also promised to build in financial incentives for bank officers to make loans to blacks.[677]

When Manufacturers Hanover merged with Chemical Bank, their differential turndown rates were also used to extract favors for minorities. The newly-merged bank agreed to set aside $750 million for low-income housing loans, and $10 million for loans on which the usual credit requirements would be waived.[678]

When banks can make safe, profitable loans to minorities, they do. It is hardly fair to ask them to take risks with their depositors' money and then call them racist if they do not. As one black commentator points out, "[B]lack-owned banks that do not find the ghetto an attractive place to make loans are not called racist, and we should note that more black-owned banks invest more of their loan portfolio *outside* the community in which they are located than do white-owned banks."[679] As is so often the case, when "discrimination" is alleged on the basis of numbers alone, the "cure" requires that discrimination henceforth be deliberate.

Broadcasting stations are subject to similar shakedowns when they change hands or when their licenses come up for renewal. The law permits any citizen to challenge the racial bona fides of their hiring policies. This has resulted in a good living for Pluria Marshall, chairman of the National Black Media Coalition. Since there is no penalty for filing frivolous actions, he has filed *thousands* of formal complaints with the FCC, charging that television and radio stations have not hired enough blacks. At one time, Mr. Marshall's complaints reportedly accounted for 60 percent of the FCC's entire litigation work load. Even if the complaint is groundless, stations find it is cheaper and quicker to pay Mr. Marshall to withdraw his complaint rather than fight in court. Virtually all of Mr. Marshall's $500,000 annual budget comes from such payoffs, and in 1988 Mr. Marshall could afford to pay himself and his wife combined salaries of $158,000.

For years the FCC has known that Mr. Marshall was using its regulations to extort money from broadcasters, but it has been afraid to challenge him directly for fear it would be accused of racism. In the fall of 1990, the FCC tried to make it more difficult for Mr. Marshall to play his game by forbidding broadcasters to make cash settlements in exchange for a withdrawn complaint. Now Mr. Marshall bills broadcasters (in amounts equal to whatever a settlement might have been) for help in finding black potential employees.[680]

While the FCC struggles to contain Mr. Marshall, it must still enforce affirmative action laws passed in 1978 to encourage minority ownership of broadcasting stations. First, minorities get extra points when they apply to the Federal Communication Commission (FCC) for broadcast licenses. Second, if a broadcaster is challenged, and is in danger of losing his license, he may sell the broadcast rights at three quarters of their market value, as long as he sells to a minority; otherwise, he may lose everything. Finally, anyone who voluntarily sells a broadcasting business to even a partially minority-owned group gets a tax break from the IRS, which means that blacks can win the bid with a lower offer.

Recently The New York Times Company got a $50 million tax break because it sold a $420-million cable TV subsidiary to a group with 20 percent minority ownership. Was that really a good enough reason for our government to add $50 million to the budget deficit? Blacks who buy radio or television stations at bargain prices have no obligation to run them. If they choose to, they can almost immediately resell them at market rates for a quick profit.[681]

The breaks for minority buyers are so good that whites have recruited nonwhites to act as front men for them. In 1984 the FCC approved a cut-rate, distress sale to a "minority" firm. The Hispanic general partner, who had a "controlling interest," had put up only $210 of the $3.1 million purchase price.[682]

Affirmative action thinking can sometimes arise to thwart otherwise sound government policies. Student loan defaults can cost the taxpayer over $2 billion a year, and Congress has been trying to find ways to bring down the losses. One plan would have allowed the government to stop making loans to any school with a default rate of more than 25 percent. This idea ran into trouble when it was discovered that a number of historically black colleges are well above the 25 percent figure.[683]

Another little-noticed form of publicly funded affirmative action is the establishment of "enterprise zones" in blighted neighborhoods that governments want to revive. The usual method is to induce companies to move in by granting tax waivers and other benefits. So far, thirty-eight states have set up, or at least authorized, enterprise zones. Florida grants fifteen-year interest-free loans to businesses in target areas, and Maryland offers a "guarantee" against failure, which means that companies can operate indefinitely in the red.[684]

These programs are not cheap. By the end of 1988, enterprise zones had cost the state of New Jersey alone more than $50 million. The national price tag has run to hundreds of millions of dollars.[685] The neighborhoods that benefit from this kind of taxpayer largess are almost invariably black.[686]

Political parties, especially the Democrats, have been practicing affirmative action for years. Now Republicans are playing the same game. They are afraid of becoming known as the party of white people[687] and have decided to do something about it. When Ed Rollins was the director of the Republican Congressional Campaign Committee, he explained what the GOP would do when seats come open: "We'll back a black and a Hispanic in a district where no Republican can lose. That's how you get black Republicans in Congress."[688] When the Republicans put race before ability, they are at least candid about it.

Another new area for affirmative action is the management of pension fund assets. Private companies have been deliberately steering assets toward nonwhite asset managers, but the most vigorous affirmative action efforts have come from governments. New York City, Chicago, Washington, D.C., and the states of Maryland, Pennsylvania, and Washington have all established targets for minority participation in managing public pension fund assets. The effects have been felt throughout the industry. "[Being a minority] clearly offers me an opportunity to get business that I wouldn't get if I wasn't [sic] a minority," says J. D. Nelson of Rhumbline Advisors in Boston.[689]

Because it is so important that such funds be managed skillfully, governments have traditionally set high standards for the compa-

[686] In fact, many of America's ghetto neighborhoods have become pockets of socialism in an otherwise capitalist country. For example, 62 percent of East Harlem is owned by the New York City government, and almost two thirds of all residents live in public housing. About 30 percent get welfare or some other form of the dole. Mark Alpert, "The Ghetto's Hidden Wealth," *Fortune* (July 29, 1991), p. 167. East Harlem is, in effect, a socialist enclave in a market economy.

[687] Even in the traditionally Democratic South, whites are flocking to the Republican Party. In Alabama, 52 percent of whites say they are Republicans while only 33 percent describe themselves as Democrats. For white men between ages eighteen and twenty-four, the gap is a lopsided preference for the GOP of 68 percent to 14 percent. Thomas Edsall, "Racial Forces Battering Southern Democrats," *Washington Post* (June 25, 1989) p. A6. In the nation as a whole, 90 percent of blacks are registered Democrats, whereas only a third of whites are. A black senior adviser to the Republican National Committee, Joshua Smith, explains that "there's tremendous peer pressure among black people to not be a Republican." Robin Toner, "In Ratings of Bush, Omens for Democrats," *The New York Times* (February 26, 1990). Vernon Jordan, Jr., "Passages: 1989–2000," *Vital Speeches of the Day* (April 15, 1989) p. 406.

nies to which they entrust assets. Since minority-owned companies rarely meet those standards, qualifications have to be lowered. New York City, for example, used to place its assets with companies that were already managing at least $500 million and whose principal investors had had at least five years of experience at their own firms. To let in minority firms, the city has dropped its asset threshold to $20 million dollars and now counts training at other firms toward its experience requirement.[690]

The state of California has set a minority-management goal of 15 percent for its enormous pool of pension assets. For the white-owned firms it uses, it requires evidence of deliberate preference for nonwhite subcontractors. The state's Public Employee Retirement System recently declined even to consider four well-regarded asset managers, including Security Pacific Bank, because it decided they had not tried hard enough to find minority subcontractors.[691] Recently the state's teachers' retirement fund delayed a $1.5 billion investment in foreign stocks because the applicants to manage the money could not meet affirmative action quotas.[692]

Maintaining pension assets for public employees has always been considered something of a sacred trust, but here, too, competence now takes a backseat to race.

Manipulating the Housing Market

Since housing segregation has long been one of the clearest lines of racial cleavage, Congress passed a Fair Housing Act four years after it passed the Civil Rights Act of 1964. It prohibited all racial discrimination in the way that houses are sold, but this law has since been stood on its head, just as the Civil Rights Act has.

In Chicago, the South Suburban Housing Center fixed up some houses in a black part of town. It wanted to integrate the neighborhood, so it asked the realtor's board to market the houses only to whites. It even told the realtors not to put up "for sale" signs, for fear that blacks might see them. The realtors, who have for years been careful to avoid what is known as illegal racial steering, refused. They were sued *and lost.* In a 1988 decision, Judge Harry

Leinenweber ruled that "affirmative marketing" was not a "discriminatory housing practice." A lawyer for the Housing Center noted that the judge had declined to find the realtors guilty of discrimination in refusing the center's demand, but suspected that there would be no "leniency" the next time.[693]

The Fair Housing Act has joined the Civil Rights Act in never-never land. It has now been reinterpreted to mean that black buyers may be discriminated against after all, if it means that other blacks will thereby get white neighbors. Realtors who fail to discriminate in this way may be punished for . . . discrimination.

Shaker Heights, Ohio, a suburb of Cleveland, has been quietly practicing discrimination for thirty years. Blacks who move to neighborhoods thought to be excessively white get help with their mortgages. So do whites who move to black neighborhoods. The town manages housing the way a company manages inventory, and uses city money to ensure that as many sales as possible result in greater integration.[694]

Florida has likewise revamped the notion of fair housing. Palm Beach County schools were to be exempted from mandatory busing if enough blacks could be induced to move into white areas by 1995 and send their children to local schools. People dislike busing so much that towns were willing to rewrite housing codes to allow cheap apartments in million-dollar neighborhoods. Real-estate developers advertised heavily in black newspapers and offered rent subsidies and reduced-rate mortgages for blacks. They took up the slack by charging higher rates to whites.

William D. North, executive vice president of the National Association of realtors, admitted that "the plan creates a real question of legality," but the county was moving full speed ahead.[695] No one seemed to note the irony of breaking a law designed to prevent housing discrimination, in an attempt to conform to laws that are supposed to prevent discrimination in education.

Mr. North's worries about the law may have come to an end in early 1992. Late in January, the U.S. Supreme Court declined to overrule an "affirmative marketing" plan in Park Forest, Illinois, similar to the one practiced in Shaker Heights. Realtors had protested against being asked to steer buyers toward different neighborhoods on the basis of race, but the Court's decision effectively lifted the legal cloud that had hung over the practice for a decade.[696]

Real-estate advertising has resulted in an unanticipated form of quota hiring for black models. An organization called the Leadership Council for Metropolitan Open Communities has sued at least half a dozen Chicago-area developers for not running black models in their housing ads. Most cases have been settled out of court with cash and with pledges to use black models. The developer need not have discriminated in the slightest; his advertising was held to be discriminatory.[697]

Although it would never occur to most people that advertisements must show a certain number of black faces, this appears to be the law. The owner and agent of a New York property called North Shore Towers were ordered by a U.S. District Court to pay $245,000 to four blacks who claimed they were discouraged from trying to live there because the company's ads featured only white people. The owners were also ordered to run ninety-seven ads over the next four years, at an estimated cost of $200,000. Seventy-five percent of the ads had to have people in them, and one third of the people had to be black. The owners were made to pay, not for discrimination, but simply for inappropriate advertising.[698]

The situation is even more surprising than this. In 1991, the U.S. Court of Appeals for the Second Circuit ruled that *The New York Times* could be sued because it accepted real-estate ads that did not depict enough nonwhites. A black couple, along with a Manhattan fair housing organization, charged that since *The Times* so rarely featured black models in its real estate ads, it was violating the Fair Housing Act of 1968. The *Cincinnati Inquirer* has a similar case on appeal in the U.S. Court of Appeals for the Sixth Circuit.

The *Washington Post* has settled a 1986 lawsuit by promising to use black models 25 percent of the time in real-estate ads. Soon thereafter, twenty-two Washington-area real-estate developers, sales companies, and ad agencies agreed to use black models 33 percent of the time.[699]

It is hard enough to make the case that an advertiser should be punished because his models were of the wrong race. How can it possibly be fair to punish a newspaper? Newspapers do not choose what goes into ads. Will newspapers start having to count heads in their ads for clothing or automobiles? Will they have to feature a certain number of Hispanics, Asians, handicapped people, American Indians, and open homosexuals in them, too? In the meantime, in some parts of the country, blacks have a guaranteed percentage of the modeling work. Laws to end discrimination almost always seem to result in rigid, numerical discrimination.

The Voting Rights Act of 1965 has been tied into equally marvelous knots. It was originally passed to eliminate literacy tests, grandfather clauses, and other ways to keep blacks from voting. In 1982 Congress amended the act along "disparate impact" lines. Now nonwhites can claim they were denied the right "to elect representatives of their choice" if nonwhites are not voted into office in proportion to their numbers in the electorate.

At the time, the "at large" voting system was particularly decried as unfair because a large jurisdiction was more likely to have a white majority than a small jurisdiction formed around a black neighborhood. Thus, if a city council were elected at large rather than by district, a city that was 30 percent black might end up with blacks holding only 10 percent of the council seats. In 1986 the U.S. Supreme Court ruled on such a case. In arguments before the Court, defenders of the at-large system pointed out that in many such jurisdictions blacks were winning office despite the fact that the majority of voters were white. The NAACP conceded that, yes, this certainly was happening, but only when black candidates campaigned in such a way as to attract whites. The NAACP was clearly implying that if a black candidate had to appeal to white voters in order to be elected, blacks were suffering from "discrimination."[700] Such arguments prevailed; the Supreme Court mandated racial quotas for elections as well as for employment.

The established ways to ensure the election of black representatives are to get rid of at-large systems and to draw racially gerrymandered voting districts. All across the country, boundaries have been systematically redrawn so that a single minority will make up at least 65 percent of the voting population—the proportion that has generally been found to be necessary for a minority victory, since nonwhites do not vote as often as whites.[701] The nationwide redistricting that followed the 1990 census was required by law to produce safe, nonwhite seats and resulted in battles over whether minorities were getting enough districts. Since the law required that district boundaries follow residential patterns rather than natural town boundaries, many of the new districts are exotically shaped monstrosities with tentacles in every direction.[702] *The Wall Street Journal* called the new procedure, which officially carves the country up into racial voting blocs, the equivalent of South Africa's notorious Group Areas Act.[703] In early 1991, the Supreme Court upheld obligatory racial gerrymandering in a 9–0 ruling.[704]

The idea of official racial constituencies is odd on a number of counts. First, it flies in the face of the law itself, which explicitly disclaims any requirement that minorities be proportionately represented in election results. Second, it suggests that Americans can be represented properly only by people of their own race, and virtually guarantees that many voters will have no choice but to vote for candidates of their own race. Third, it gives blacks elected in such districts a reason to oppose residential integration because it would dilute racial bloc voting. Finally, it violates James Madison's rule that electoral districts should include a broad variety of people so that representatives will be less likely to speak for only a single faction.[705]

Just as disturbingly, the affirmative action interpretation of the Voting Rights Act has been invoked by whites, who are a minority in 57 percent-black Birmingham, Alabama. They recently got the city to abolish at-large voting and to institute racially segregated voting districts because they said the old system gave blacks too much power. Richard Arrington, the black mayor, sounded rather like Madison when he wondered whether voting by racial district would not put extremists into office.[706]

Congressman Craig Washington holds a black district in Houston, Texas. He worries that racially segregated districts will mean that white elected officials will think they no longer have to think about the needs of black voters.[707] He does not seem to worry that black representatives might not feel the need to think about the needs of white voters.

There have been fights between minorities over redistricting. A black Illinois congresswoman opposed the creation of a Hispanic congressional district because it would have removed sixteen thousand blacks from her district. "They did not want to be represented by anyone other than their like kind," she explained.[708] No one made much of this remark.

New York City recently adopted a new city charter that sets up racial guidelines for appointments to certain city commissions. The mayor no longer has the power to make appointments as he sees fit; he must choose people by race, in proportion to their numbers in the city. "For the first time, as far as I know," complained former mayor Ed Koch, "quotas have been written into law."[709] His successor, David Dinkins, has directed that the New York City school board reflect the races of the school system's students, 80 percent of whom are nonwhite. Ability and experience are to be subordinate to race.[710]

Voting districts for the New York City Council, recently expanded to fifty-one from thirty-five, are now required by law to ensure racial representation. The 1991 redistricting set off endless feuds among Asians, Hispanics, blacks, and even homosexuals, all of whom tried to carve out as many "safe" seats as possible.[711]

The New York Post, which opposed the plan, pointed out that if race was so important, the city should get rid of physical districts entirely. Blacks could vote for blacks, Hispanics for Hispanics, etc., and each race would be represented on the City Council in proportion to its population.[712]

The same argument could be made for congressional districts. Sensible geographical or municipal boundaries have been sacrificed to race. Towns, cities, counties, school districts, communities —the organic groupings without which regional representation means nothing—have been ruthlessly carved up to create racial voting blocs. Why not take the logical next step and eliminate regions altogether? Why not set aside 12 percent of congressional seats for blacks—their portion of the total population—and hold blacks-only elections for them?

Government, like the rest of society, refuses to admit it, but it is moving steadily toward a rigid racial quota system. In early 1992, Louisiana officials settled a civil rights lawsuit by agreeing to install twenty-five additional black judges.[713] What was this but clear acknowledgment of the priority of race over everything else?

The state of Michigan has forged ahead with an entirely new

kind of racial quota system. Black state legislators noticed that Detroit's overwhelmingly white symphony orchestra did not reflect the city's population, which is 70 percent black. It made no difference to the critics that the symphony has for years run "blind" auditions in which applicants play behind a screen so as to eliminate favoritism. In February 1989, black legislators threatened to withhold $1.3 million in state funding and to picket concerts. Within days, the orchestra hired a black without the audition. Blind auditions have a "disparate impact," so they had to be abandoned.

The people most outraged by this were black classical musicians who have won jobs across the country through pure talent. Like all affirmative action plans, the Detroit decision casts doubt on their achievements. Already two promising black musicians have refused to consider the Detroit Symphony because of the odium of favoritism. James DePriest, the acclaimed black conductor of the Oregon Symphony, also declined a job in Detroit. "[Y]ou fight for years to make race irrelevant, and now they are making race an issue," he said.[714]

"Disparate impact" theory also shows up in surprising places. Employers who must put people in charge of money sometimes examine a candidate's credit rating. The Equal Employment Opportunity Commission has found that since blacks generally have worse credit ratings than whites, this is a racially discriminatory standard and may be against the law.[715] Of course, a bad credit rating is a bad credit rating, regardless of race. However, this is one more piece of information, like test scores, that employers must forgo in the name of racial equality.

One of the sillier "disparate impact" cases had to do with residency in the town of Harrison, New Jersey. The town always had a policy of hiring only residents for public jobs. Municipalities like such policies because people are loyal to their towns and are likely to work hard for them. Also, if off-duty police or firemen must be suddenly called out for emergencies, they can respond quickly.

The NAACP decided this policy was discriminatory because only 1 percent of the population of Harrison is black, and only one black person had ever worked for the town. Both a federal district court and the U.S. Court of Appeals for the Third Circuit agreed with the NAACP. In 1991 Harrison was ordered to junk its residency requirement and to hire blacks by quota. It must hire blacks *in proportion to their population in the five surrounding counties.*[716] Once again, a policy that had been established for entirely innocent and defensible reasons was struck down because of a "disparate impact" on minorities.

In the classroom, affirmative action can take strange forms. Dr. Janet Schofield of the University of Pittsburgh offers a way for black children in integrated schools to overcome the disappointment of always being outperformed by white children. She suggests that teachers first teach a lesson only to the blacks and then let the black children teach it to white children.

Dr. Robert Slavin of Johns Hopkins University thinks that equal results are more important than democracy. He says that in order to get the right racial mix on the student council, minorities who can't get elected should be appointed. As he explains without a trace of irony, "You need to pay careful attention to issues of equity."[717]

Environmental groups such as the Sierra Club and the Wilderness Society have likewise been told they are racist because they do not have enough black staffers. No one has bothered to find out how many blacks are trained as environmentalists, are willing to work for nonprofit wages, or have even applied for jobs. Most "cause-oriented" blacks work for urban, race-based groups already, but none of this stopped one activist consortium from giving environmentalists sixty days to figure out how to make their staffs 30 to 40 percent nonwhite. This is a typical "civil rights" strategy of finding a niche—any niche—where blacks are underrepresented, and demanding that "discrimination" be cured with reverse discrimination.

Environmental groups have duly formed the Environmental Consortium for Minority Outreach.[718] John Cook of Boston has also launched what he hopes will be a $5 million effort to recruit minorities into environment-related careers. He has already raised $375,000 not only from private sources but also from the taxpayer, via the Environmental Protection Agency.[719]

Another unexpected locale for affirmative action is the "Men's Movement." Robert Bly is the acknowledged leader of this new exercise in male bonding, which involves woodsy encounters for men who seek to revive the savage within themselves. There are virtually no blacks among the thousands who have attended these gatherings, so Mr. Bly has helped set up a scholarship fund to attract more.[720]

The *Atlanta Constitution,* apparently in all seriousness, thinks that baseball tickets should be sold at a special discount to blacks. It reasons that whereas 72 percent of all professional basketball players and 61 percent of all professional football players are black, "only" 18 percent of professional baseball players are black. Worse still, only 6 percent of baseball fans are black. The newspaper proposes to increase that figure through affirmative action ticket sales and thinks that black baseball players should be paid more than whites of equal talent so as to raise their numbers above that apparently unsatisfactory 18 percent.[721]

A black sociology professor at Yale has proposed what is probably the craziest affirmative action plan so far. He has noted that past discrimination does not have to be proven to justify corrective action; numerical imbalance is all it takes. He points out that the prison system is therefore a perfect candidate for affirmative action, since blacks are eight times more likely to be in jail than whites. Since people can be hired and fired on the basis of race rather than qualifications, should it not be possible to throw people in jail on the same grounds? "More whites and middle- and upper-class persons must be sent to prison to correct the existing disproportionality," he writes, ". . . while members of groups now overrepresented in prison must be allowed to leave or be admitted at lower rates of entry."[722]

The professor's logic is flawless. If numbers alone prove bias, then our prisons are hopelessly biased. Why should this bias not be corrected by the same process that is so widely accepted elsewhere in society?

America already practices forms of affirmative action that are almost as preposterous. Most people do not know that recent immigrants may qualify for affirmative-action preferences over native-born whites—as long as they are nonwhite, as 90 percent of legal immigrants now are. Absurd as this may be, it is the logical outcome of a massive national undertaking to favor nonwhites.

What started out as compensation for black slavery and segregation has become automatic preference for *any* nonwhite and an automatic *handicap* for any white. What but an utterly mechanical search for nonwhite faces can explain that the California Highway Patrol has advertised job vacancies in *Mexico* in the hope of meeting affirmative action goals for Hispanics?[723] In its extreme manifestations, affirmative action seems nothing short of hysterical.

In the midst of strenuous affirmative action, the National Survey of Black Americans asked blacks whether they thought most whites wanted to give them a better break, hold them down, or just did not care. Forty-one percent said that whites want to hold them down, 36 percent said that whites do not care, and only 23 percent said whites want them to get a better break. Many other measures of black alienation increased from the 1960s to the 1980s.[724] Could it be that affirmative action, with its constant emphasis on race and racial grievances, has only added to feelings of alienation?

Special Treatment as a Right

Some blacks have become so accustomed to preferential treatment that they may be unhappy when others get a break. In January 1989, Miami blacks rioted and looted for two days after a Hispanic policeman shot and killed a black motorcyclist. Rioters burned down twenty-seven buildings, and six people died. The violence was clearly a reaction to the death of a black man, but many observers also saw in it resentment of Miami's then-current mobilization to accommodate a sudden new wave of Hispanic immigrants, mostly Nicaraguan. Blacks were angry at what they called "red-carpet treatment" for immigrants and charged that their own needs were being ignored.[725]

Ironically, many people did not think the Hispanic-run city was doing much for Nicaraguans at all. When one top official was asked why it did not offer them more help, he replied, "We don't want to make them into American blacks."[726] In Miami, repeated waves of immigrants have worked hard, gotten ahead, and leapfrogged blacks. Many of these immigrants have been blacks from Haiti and the West Indies who think American blacks have become dependent on handouts from whites.[727]

American blacks have been able to benefit from claims of victimhood for so long that they may be annoyed when others work the same ground. Kenneth Tollett, distinguished professor at Howard University, says this:

> A substantial sector of the black community is suffering because so much of the energy and driving force of the movement have been deflected toward Hispanic Americans, middle-class white women, homosexuals, the handicapped, the consumer, the children of the affluent [?], the aged, and the environment. . . . Don't forget, the civil rights movement started out with blacks . . . [and they are] losing ground at each displacing development."[728]

The University of Texas at Austin has a Minority Information Center, which works to keep nonwhites from dropping out of school. It distributes job and scholarship information, refers students to tutors and counselors, and holds workshops. In 1992 its director, Shuronda Robinson, rejected efforts to let American Indians use its services. She said that it was already busy enough serving blacks and Hispanics.[729]

On a different front, in public school districts across the country, concerned parents are raising money among themselves to pay for additional programs that schools cannot afford. These range from Latin classes to science laboratories. Predictably, some blacks have insisted that this is unfair. They do not want white parents to beef up their own children's schools if they will not give equal help to black schools. In Atlanta, voluntary busing lets black children attend predominantly white schools, where there has been a considerable amount of private enrichment. That is not good enough for Lillian Lewis, wife of a black Atlanta congressman. "Why should he [her son] have to get on a bus and cross town for these things?" she asks.

The Los Angeles school district discourages private fund-raising for individual schools, for fear that not all schools will benefit equally—this despite widespread recognition that parent involvement and commitment are key ingredients in the success of a school.[730] Ironically, one of the most highly touted methods to improve the school performances of black children is based on an extraordinary degree of parental involvement. It was devised by Dr. James P. Comer of Yale, who is black.[731]

Many blacks appear to believe that anything they ask for is fair and reasonable. Derrick Bell is a black professor at Harvard Law School. In 1990 he put himself on leave without his $100,000-a-year pay and promised to stay away until the law school gave tenure to a black woman. Of the sixty tenured faculty, three were black and five were women, but none was a black women. In the previous ten years, 45 percent of all faculty appointments had gone to minorities and women, but Professor Bell insisted on a black woman.

Less qualified blacks are already admitted to Harvard Law School as students, so as to keep their numbers at about 10 to 15 percent of the student body, but the dean of the law school has refused to be pressured into hiring a black woman. He says that Harvard must define its own standard of excellence. Jesse Jackson, who visited the campus in support of Professor Bell's demand, dismissed this as "cultural anemia" and said that the law school's "moral character" was on trial.[732] Black columnist Carl Rowan weighed in with the view that " 'merit' is the code word privileged whites use to protect their special hutches at Harvard and hundreds of other universities. . . ."[733] A group of Professor Bell's supporters filed a suit against the law school, claiming that even if its hiring practices are not discriminatory by design, they are discriminatory "by default."[734] Just how it is that an employer can discriminate "by default" was to be up to a court to decide. Professor Bell himself filed a complaint against Harvard with the federal Department of Education.

Leave of absence at Harvard Law School is strictly limited to two years. As the school's dean explains, "People should make a choice whether they are going to be at Harvard or not." As Professor Bell's leave of absence swung into its second year and the law school had still not given tenure to a black woman, Professor Bell said he would challenge the two-year limit because he thought it should not apply to "people who have walked away for reasons of conscience"[735]—perhaps with especially favorable consideration for people who have sued the school.

Harvard is not the only target of this form of protest. In 1990 a black federal judge refused to participate in a moot court at the University of Chicago because the law school did not have any black, tenured professors.[736] For the past three years at Berkeley Law School, students have boycotted classes and blocked access to classrooms, insisting that the school has failed to hire enough blacks and women. The facts appear not to matter. Of the eight professors hired in the past three years, six were minorities or women.[737]

There is something else that minority activists overlook. Since they have helped create a huge demand for black law professors, black lawyers are more than twice as likely as white lawyers to be hired to teach law. According to one law school administrator, the nation's top five law schools would have no more than two tenured or tenure-track blacks if race were not a hiring consideration. Harvard alone has five.[738]

Sometimes pressure from blacks is too great to resist. Essex County College serves a largely black student body in 58 percent-black Newark, New Jersey. In late 1990, a white man, Joseph Montuoro, was elected chairman of the college's board of trustees, narrowly defeating the incumbent black woman. At his first board meeting, Mr. Montuoro learned just how unwelcome he was because of his race. A mob of black students poured into the meeting hall, chanting "traitor, traitor," and demanded that he resign. Zachary Yamba, president of the college, took the microphone and agreed that the problem was a "black and white matter."

Mr. Montuoro soon did resign in the face of pressures he called "clearly racist." President Yamba denied any discriminatory pressure but said that it was important as a "symbol" that the board be run by a black person.[739]

Some blacks have carved out profitable niches for themselves as racial shakedown artists. For more than ten years, Mustafa Majeed of New York City has made a business of extorting money from moviemakers. When directors try to film a scene outdoors, Mr. Majeed shows up with a gang and demands that more blacks be hired for the crew. If he is refused, Mr. Majeed's recruits blow whistles and shoot off flashbulbs, making it impossible to film.

Mr. Majeed appears to be happy to accept money rather than more black employees. In 1991 he reportedly told film director Woody Allen that in return for $100,000 he would leave Mr. Allen's sets alone. Other filmmakers have hired private security guards to keep Mr. Majeed away. Mr. Majeed is the head of the Communications Industry Skills Center, an organization that is supposed to train blacks for jobs in the entertainment field. Until April 1990 it was financed by the city of New York.[740]

Pressure from blacks takes many forms. When Nelson Mandela toured Miami in 1990, Cuban-American officials criticized him because of his warm support for Fidel Castro. Miami blacks were incensed that their hero should be criticized, and formed a group to sabotage what is arguably Miami's most important industry: tourism. A year later, the group estimated that it had managed to keep $27 million of convention business out of the city. Its latest tactic was to make a video that was highly critical of Miami and send it free to any group that might hold a convention there. Although 12 to 25 percent of the people who work in the tourism industry are black, the group vowed that it would continue its campaign until it got an apology from city officials and agreement on a list of affirmative action demands.[741]

The city of Dallas, Texas, was searching for a new police chief in the fall of 1990. A black county commissioner promised mass violence if the new chief did not meet his standards for racial sensitivity. "If you try to bring a 'good old boy' in this system, we're going to be in the streets—physically, literally shooting folks," he said.[742]

In Milwaukee, a black alderman has taken the strong-arm approach even farther. In April 1990, Michael McGee threatened bloodshed and terrorism if the city did not set aside $100 million for black neighborhoods and take other measures to put blacks on the same economic level as whites. Mr. McGee gave the city until 1995 to act. Otherwise, he promised, there would be killing. "Our militia will be about violence," he said. "I'm talking actual fighting, bloodshed and urban guerrilla warfare." Six hundred blacks crowded into a grade school auditorium to sign up for training in Mr. McGee's militia.[743]

In 1992, after his district was redrawn in accordance with the 1990 census, there was a chance that Mr. McGee might not be reelected. He promised that if this should happen he would unleash "chaos" and guerrilla warfare—and not on the voters of his largely black district. "I've got people who've already committed violence—they've just been doing it against the wrong people," he explained.[744]

It has long been an accepted part of the racial dialogue in America that demands made by blacks in the name of race are legitimate and that any white who does not go along is "racist." The more fervently the demand is made, the more legitimate it must be. Now black demands will be pressed not just with civil disobedience but also with threats of mass violence.

School Desegregation

Though the thinking behind it is slightly different from that of affirmative action, school busing has had a similarly tortured history. In 1954, when the Supreme Court heard the case of *Brown* v. *Board of Education,* no one asked for or dreamed of forced integration, racial quotas, or busing. The main plaintiff in the case, Oliver Brown, was not an activist. All he wanted was to send his daughter, Linda, to the white school just seven blocks away, rather than across town to the "colored" school. Mr. Brown's lawyers repeatedly argued before the Court that the Constitution forbids classification by race and that the state should not have the power to discriminate.[745] These compelling arguments won the day.

Ten years later, the Civil Rights Act put this thinking into law; schools were not to discriminate by race. Just as it did in the case of hiring quotas, the law made it plain that it did not require schools to move students around to achieve racial balance. Once again, this did not stop the nation's courts from making school districts do exactly the opposite of what Congress intended.

The original idea behind school desegregation was that it was impossible for schools to be "separate but equal." Soon, however, the objective of busing became one of mixing children by race for its own sake. In 1967 federal appeals judge J. Skelly Wright defended busing by saying, "racially and socially homogeneous schools damage the minds and spirits of all children."[746] Does this mean that schoolchildren in Japan, for example, have damaged minds and spirits because all their classmates are Asian?

Exactly as with minority hiring, there was no need to prove that school districts had discriminated in the past. Even districts in the North, which had specifically forbidden assignment to schools by race, were given busing orders. The courts set out to eradicate any racial imbalance, whatever its cause. In their zeal, they lost sight of the ultimate objective—providing the best education for all children. Before long, busing advocates were behaving as if they thought black children simply could not learn unless they had white children sitting next to them.

In Los Angeles, Judge Paul V. Egley said it in almost as many words: He told the school district to get on with its busing program and to "make the most efficient use of increasingly scarce white students as possible." Thomas Sowell calls this a new version of the white man's burden.[747]

Unlike affirmative action, school busing stirred up a great deal of opposition. Neither whites nor blacks saw the point in shipping children across town just to get the numbers right. In 1972 President Richard Nixon urged Congress to pass a bill to limit the powers of the courts to order busing. A filibuster by northern liberals killed the bill. President Nixon, however, was acting on the will of the people. A Gallup Poll taken the next year showed that only 4 percent of whites and 9 percent of blacks approved of busing.[748]

Many white parents have given up on public school and now send their children to private, fee-charging schools. Many black parents do exactly the same thing. There are now more than three hundred private schools run by and for blacks, and fully half of the students in urban private and parochial schools are black.[749] Today only 3.3 percent of American white children are educated in the decaying urban school systems.[750]

What has been the ultimate effect of busing? One student of civil rights describes it this way:

[It] set into motion a perpetual, vicious cycle of doom and despair; the school district diverts scarce resources into social engineering at the expense of educational quality; individuals who can afford to do so leave, resulting in further racial imbalance; resulting in more judicial intervention; resulting in more efforts to attain numerical parity, resulting in yet additional defections. . . . [E]ducational opportunity is extinguished for everyone. In a perverse sense, the revisionists [who have abandoned the original goals of equal rights] can at this point in the process be said to have attained their elusive equality in result, for everyone is equally ravaged.[751]

This author could have been describing practically any big-city school system, but Boston's is a good example. It was integrated in 1975, with a court-ordered busing plan that stirred up great resentment. Thirteen years later, the school district was about ready to give up. Although it was spending more than $7,000 a year per pupil (the national average is $3,752),[752] 40 percent of all ninth-graders were dropping out before graduation. Middle-class students had steadily left the schools, and white attendance had dropped from 60 percent in 1972 to only 22 percent in 1990. With so few whites left, students had to be bused for crazy distances to achieve racial balance. So many children came from poor families that 80 percent of Boston grade-school students got free or cut-rate lunches.[753] The president of the Boston Schools Committee, who had been a supporter of busing, called it a process of "shuffling black children across the city to a mediocre school to attend a school with other black children."[754] Boston is finally considering giving up busing.

Curtis Wells, a black man who is a veteran of the Boston public schools system and who is now principal of Hyde Park High school, says this:

To go through such a traumatic process, to lose 40,000 students in the school system, to lose teaching staff, to lose the reputation of an education system that Boston has never regained, was it worth it? My judgment is no.[755]

As noted above, Florida has rolled busing and housing into a package deal. In Boca Raton, Florida, school officials and the owners of a proposed 160-unit apartment complex reached an agreement that would make the complex more attractive to whites. As long as at least 10 percent of the apartments were set aside for black tenants, the children of white tenants would be excused from busing and could attend the neighborhood schools. The owners of the complex figured they could attract black tenants by knocking $155 a month off of rents that would, for white people, be $600 to $1,000 per month.[756]

Of all American cities, it may be Kansas City, Missouri, that has taken the most contortionist approach to busing. According to a court-approved integration plan, magnet schools and voluntary busing are supposed to keep schools from being any more than 60 percent black and any less than 40 percent white. However, white students have been reluctant to take the bus to magnet schools in black neighborhoods. In June 1989 there were 3,436 black children waiting to get into these magnet schools, but to admit them would tip the ratio past the 60:40 limit. The school board virtually begged whites to enroll, but only 79 accepted. This meant a few more blacks could be taken, but it still left thousands out in the cold. There were places in magnet schools going begging, but since integration was seen as more important than education, black children could not have them.[757] *Just as Oliver Brown did in 1954,* black parents filed suit because they were being kept out of good neighborhood schools on account of their race.[758]

Federal judge Russel Clark decided that he would solve the problem single-handedly. He ordered the people of Kansas City to spend $500 million to $700 million to make the magnet schools the best in the entire country—so good that whites would have no choice but to attend. There would be courses in everything from cosmetology to robotics. There would be a twenty-five-acre farm and a twenty-five-acre wildlife preserve, and fifteen personal computers in every classroom. There would be broadcast-quality movie and television studios, and even a Model United Nations wired for simultaneous interpretation. There would be a two-thousand-square-foot planetarium, a thirty-five-hundred-square-foot, dust-free, diesel mechanics room, Olympic-size swimming pools, etc. Judge Clark even had a way to pay for all this: He ordered a doubling of property taxes.

Kansas City fought this ruling clear up to the U.S. Supreme Court. The citizens argued that it was their elected representatives, not an appointed judge, who had the power to levy taxes. In an astonishing, 5–4 decision, the Supreme Court upheld Judge Clark. If it was to foster racial integration, it ruled, a federal judge had the right to bypass the democratic process and raise revenues entirely on his own, like a medieval monarch.[759]

The great pity of school integration is that in spite of court orders, busing, and terrible dislocations, it has done very little to improve classroom performances of black children. In 1983, the research arm of the Department of Education could not find a single study that showed black children were learning appreciably better after the switch to integrated schools.[760] In Mecklenburg County, North Carolina, for example, schools were integrated by court-ordered busing. Just before busing, the black/white gap in reading achievement for sixth-graders was the equivalent of 1.6 school grades. In 1978–81, after ten years of busing, the gap was as high or higher, and the children had now attended integrated schools all their lives.[761]

Gary Orfield of Harvard, who is perhaps the nation's leading scholar of desegregation, has found that nothing, integration not excepted, has been found that significantly reduces the differences between black and white test scores.[762] In fact, when specially enriched instruction is used to raise the achievement level of *all* children in a class or school, the gap between white and black scores *widens*. Thus, to the extent that schools are under pressure to narrow the gap between black and white school performance, they actually have an interest in watering down school curricula. If little is taught and standards are low, the black/white gap is likely to be narrower.[763] This may be one of the reasons why the California Achievement Test has been gaining in popularity. It is not unusual for most of the whites and a good number of the blacks to get perfect scores. School administrators can then claim to have raised black performance closer to the white level.[764]

Thus the white children, whose presence was supposed to help black children get a better education, may have gotten worse educations than before, while the performances of black children scarcely changed. The 1970s, the period during which schools were most disrupted by busing, was also the time when school performances dropped sharply, while real spending on schools grew by more than 25 percent.[765]

But the greatest irony of all is that desegregation of schools was supposed to be about removing racial barriers. In 1954, Linda Brown won the right not to be excluded from a school because of her race. Now a child cannot *escape* from a school because of his race. What was meant to be a freedom is now a constraint. It was forgotten long ago that the 1954 decision explicitly rejected the idea of making children go to specific schools to correct a racial imbalance.[766]

A restaurant or movie theater is considered integrated when anyone, regardless of race, can go there if he wants. If movie theaters operated the way our schools do, moviegoers would be forcibly shipped all over town to make sure that all audiences had the right racial mix. People could be prevented from going to a theater that was just down the street.

Early in 1991, the Supreme Court finally decided that forced busing may be doing more harm than good. It ruled that formerly segregated school districts could be released from mandatory busing if they had "complied in good faith" with a court order and had done everything "practicable" to end segregation. The court recognized that if blacks and whites lived in different parts of town, there were limits to what a school district could do to bring the races together. At the time, some eight hundred school districts were still under court decrees,[767] and many were expected to bring mandatory busing to an end.[768]

However, the end of busing for students may not mark the end of a similar but less known practice. Teachers can be pushed around because of race, just like students. In Prince Georges County, Maryland, for example, teachers can be transferred invol-

[767] Few people realize how expensive busing has been. In 1990, the state of California alone was spending a staggering $500 million a year on integration; as a staffer at the state legislature put it, the state pays for "anything a judge will sign for." Tim Ferguson, "California Seen Wasting Away and Needing a Tax Gulp," *The Wall Street Journal* (May 29, 1990), p. A15. Many school districts spend a quarter or even more of their budgets on transportation. "Busing's Reality Recognized" *The Wall Street Journal* (January 21, 1991), p. A10.

untarily to ensure that each school has at least 35 percent but not more than 50 percent minority staff.[769]

The rationale for these transfers is that minority students need role models of the same race. Minority teachers, who have always been in short supply, are therefore wooed from school district to school district, just like minority college professors. In California, where more than half of all public-school children are nonwhite, the competition is particularly fierce. However, the state's Commission on Teacher Credentialing is not optimistic about getting more. It notes that minorities who have the qualifications to teach are "in great demand" for better-paying jobs in industry,[770] not exactly what one would expect from a racist society. School districts all over the country are not only fighting each other for minority teachers but also must compete with all the private companies that are trying to get more blacks on the payroll.[771]

But no matter how strenuously everyone denies it, race-based hiring inevitably means lower standards. As Americans begin to wake up to the poor quality of their schools, a few states have begun to test teachers to see if they are up to snuff. Teachers' unions resist this for obvious reasons, as do "civil rights" organizations. In the California teachers' examination in 1983, 76 percent of the white teachers passed, but only 26 percent of the black teachers did. In a Florida exam the same year, 90 percent of whites but only 35 percent of blacks passed.[772] In the case of the National Teachers' Examination, 84 percent of whites passed it but only 33 percent of blacks.[773] Are lower standards a legitimate price to pay for "role models"? Even if black children were somehow helped by this, it is difficult to see what good such role models can do for white children.

Of course, it is minority students who suffer the most at the hands of unqualified minority teachers. In New York City, where many schools have lost virtually all their white students, schools have scrambled to hire proper racial "role models," even if they are not competent. A study by Susanna Pflaum, the dean of Queens College School of Education, shows that as a result, New

[772] National Research Council, *A Common Destiny, Blacks in American Society* (Washington, D.C.: National Academy Press, 1989), p. 363. For pass rates by race in several other states, see Andrew Hacker, *Two Nations* (New York: Charles Scribner's Sons, 1992), p. 173.

York City school districts with the most minority students have the most uncertified and inexperienced teachers.[774]

From all the clamoring for role models, one would think someone had proven that black children cannot learn from white teachers. In fact, there is no hard evidence to suggest that students learn better from teachers of one race rather than another. Scholars can point to no conclusive studies. Yet, as Thomas Sowell writes, even to ask for evidence that students need teachers of their own race is to be branded as "insensitive." He points out that Japanese-American schoolchildren have done marvelously without an Asian teacher in sight and that Jewish immigrants to New York did brilliant work under Irish Catholic teachers.[775] School districts across the country are turning their staffs inside out, at great trouble and expense, in the name of an unproven theory that could well be wrong.

School systems in Detroit and Atlanta, for example, have switched their teaching staffs from almost all-white to almost all-nonwhite to match the racial shift of their students. Black student performance has not improved as a consequence. In New York City, School District 16 is in Bedford-Stuyvesant, one of the most blighted parts of Brooklyn. Almost all its students are nonwhite, as are three quarters of its teachers and principals. It ranks sixteenth among the city's thirty-two school districts. District 5, in Harlem, has almost an identical racial profile, yet ranks last.[776] What black students need is exactly what white students need: good teachers. Nevertheless, as recently as May 1990, federal judge Arthur Garrity ordered the Boston school system to increase the proportion of its black teachers every year.[777] No doubt he believed that this would help black children learn, even if it meant that they get less-qualified teachers.

It has begun to dawn on a few people that a logical extension of the role-model theory would be the reestablishment of "separate but equal" schools, segregated by race. Dr. Edmund Gordon, a professor of psychology at Yale, says that although there are no studies to prove it, many people insist that black people have some kind of special capacity to teach black children. Such people, says Dr. Gordon, point to segregated schools, which "had a reputation for doing a decent job with black kids." In Dr. Gordon's view, success was probably due not to race but to the close ties that rural black teachers developed with students' families.[778]

"Separate but equal" has become an awkward issue for the "historically black colleges." Plenty of blacks oppose integrating them, claiming that this would halt the special nurturing they give blacks. Unlike white colleges, they have therefore not been forced to integrate. The state of Louisiana appointed a commission to study the problem and came up with a plan for integration. Virtually all-black Southern University promptly went to court to fight the plan. It is not as though Southern was going to be swamped with whites; the plan required that it set aside *10 percent* of its openings for whites.[779] Another solution the commission has studied would be the merger of black colleges with nearby white colleges. One commission member, a black New Orleans lawyer named Norbert Simmons, says that black students would find the postmerger environment "devastating."[780]

The Failure of Affirmative Action

Though there is still much pressure on whites not to be open about their resentment of affirmative action, its manifest unfairness is moving more and more people to brave the accusations of "racism" and to denounce it. Even its proponents have begun to argue that it would be more palatable if it were less explicitly race-based. The latest theory is that programs should be recast as benefits for the poor; a disproportionate number of beneficiaries would still be black, and the abandonment of explicitly racial criteria would be welcomed by taxpaying whites.

For the most part, this is an empty distinction. Affirmative action comes on top of the hundreds of billions of dollars a year[781] that government *already* spends on poor people (see Chapter Eight). Furthermore, although to say so is to invite a mighty chorus of indignation, American society is already structured to help the poor in crucially important ways.

Public education is the most powerful engine of "affirmative action" ever devised. All across the country, the children of the poor attend schools that others pay for. The quality of schools differs enormously, but a child who applies himself will get a free education. Public, state-supported universities continue the ideal of free or virtually free education to the very highest levels. Even the most expensive and exclusive private universities pride themselves on seeking out talented but poor students and giving them scholarships. This, too, is "affirmative action."

The graduated income tax—first proposed by Karl Marx—is another form of "affirmative action" for the poor. Even with loopholes, the rich pay vastly more tax than do the poor, despite the fact that the rich usually consume far fewer public services. All of these mechanisms, which are so familiar that we take them for granted, are designed to equalize chances in life. They are part of what has kept America from developing rigid social classes.

Race-based preferences for minorities are yet another array of benefits, inducements, and advantages. Partly because they come on top of a system that is already designed to recognize and reward effort, affirmative action has made a real difference for only a small number of blacks. The majority of people who have benefited from it are well-qualified people who would have gotten good jobs anyway. The only difference is that they can now charge a premium for the fact that they help meet hiring targets. Other, less-qualified blacks have been thrown into positions for which they were not prepared and that they otherwise might not have reached.

Some blacks who were marginally employable may have gotten jobs because of affirmative action, but others have clearly been hurt by it. This is because affirmative action has made it very hard to fire minorities. The same guidelines that make bosses explain in detail any failure to hire a minority make them explain in equal detail why they fired one. Furthermore, blacks who are fired might sue their bosses for racism. This means that a company will be afraid to take a chance on hiring a doubtful black in the hope that he might work out. Employers have bid up the wages for smart, hardworking, sure-bet blacks, but they may be more hesitant than ever to risk hiring the marginal cases that affirmative action is presumably supposed to help.

Some of the most powerful critics of affirmative action are

thoughtful blacks. Thomas Sowell says this: "While doing little or nothing to advance the position of minorities and females, it creates the impression that hard-won *achievements* of these groups are *conferred* benefits. Especially in the case of blacks, this means *perpetuating* racism instead of allowing it to die a natural death. . . ."[782] Racism can hardly die a natural death when the policies that are supposed to end it are explicitly racial.

Mr. Sowell also points out that the whites who are the victims of affirmative action are likely to be struggling, recent immigrants who can hardly be blamed for the sins of the past. As he puts it, "those who have protested their losses all the way up to the Supreme Court have not been named Adams, Cabot, or Rockefeller, but DeFunis, Bakke, and Weber."[783] The people who have imposed affirmative action on the country—judges, legislators, university provosts, partisan editorialists—are middle-aged white men with established careers, who will never suffer from racial preferences. The people they are punishing are young white men who are trying to get a start in life—young whites who certainly never practiced the evils that affirmative action allegedly corrects.

Another black, Shelby Steele, argues that affirmative action encourages blacks to invest in their status as victims, because it is as victims that they reap the benefits of race-based preferences. Power comes from portraying oneself as "oppressed," not from work or achievement. "When power itself grows out of suffering," he writes, "blacks are encouraged to expand the boundaries of what qualifies as racial oppression, a situation that can lead us to paint our victimization in vivid colors even as we receive the benefits of preference."[784]

Of course, this is heresy to mainstream "civil rights" leaders whose understanding of the word "equality" is different from that of the rest of us. Benjamin Hooks, former head of the NAACP, calls people like Mr. Sowell and Mr. Steele "a new breed of Uncle Tom." He adds that they are "some of the biggest liars the world ever saw."[785]

Unlike such men as Mr. Hooks, who claim to speak in their names, most blacks understand perfectly well that reverse racism is still racism. According to one national survey, while 77 percent of black leaders favored special treatment in jobs and college admissions, 77 percent of all blacks were against it. In the same survey, 66 percent of all blacks thought they were making progress in society, but 61 percent of the leaders thought blacks were going backward. This is especially interesting, since 59 percent of the leaders had household incomes over $50,000 in 1984, while only 3 percent of the people whom they claim to speak for did.[786]

A tiny handful of fair-minded minorities has rejected affirmative action, even to their own hurt. When Shelby Steele was an English professor at San Jose State University, he decided not to apply for any more minority research grants. He wanted to make it on his own. Kirk Dunham, president of the Denver Black Police Officers Association, is incensed that blacks need not score as high as whites on examinations to be promoted. All questions of fairness aside, he fears for his life if he is made to serve with incompetent officers. Freddie Hernandez, a Hispanic fire fighter in Miami, turned down an affirmative action promotion to lieutenant and spent three extra years working to get the job on pure ability. "I will stick to merit," he says.[787] Eugene Allen owns a mini-conglomerate of three companies, but refuses to take advantage of special breaks for minority companies. "This set-aside stuff is a bunch of garbage," he says: "I'm not a minority vendor. I'm an entrepreneur who happens to be black."[788]

Alas, only a few lonely black voices are raised in the call for self-reliance. Newspaper columnist William Raspberry writes, "Enforcement of civil rights can ensure us only a place in the starting gate. What is required for victory is that we run like hell."[789] Clarence Pendleton of the U.S. Civil Rights Commission says that race-based privileges are demeaning to blacks and calls those who favor them "the new racists."[790] Of all genuinely prominent black leaders, the only one who seems to preach black self-reliance with any consistency and fervor is Louis Farrakhan, whose black nationalism and criticism of Jews have discredited him among most whites. Malcolm X had nothing but contempt for handouts from whites, and whatever one may think of the Black Muslims, they do a good job of helping people get a grip on their lives. Unarmed Muslim patrols have virtually eliminated drug dealing and drug violence from some of Washington, D.C.'s, most blighted housing projects.[791] We might learn something from the pride, respectability, and self-reliance the Muslims seem able to bring to the ghetto.

Quotas and special treatment were the last things that America's first black leaders expected. Frederick Douglass scorned the idea. At the turn of the century, some blacks even viewed Jim Crow laws as a challenge to work hard and surpass whites. The president of the Nashville Negro Business League, Rev. Richard Boyd, claimed that "[t]hese discriminations are only blessings in disguise. They stimulate and encourage rather than cower and humiliate the true, ambitious, self-determined Negro."[792]

Such a sentiment is almost shocking today. It fills us with a strange nostalgia for what one author calls "the vanishing Negro," the black for whom we stripped away legal barriers to success, the fine fellow we hoped to encourage when we passed civil rights laws.[793]

What would Rev. Boyd's true, ambitious, self-determined Negro have thought of minority set-asides, quotas, and reverse discrimination? Is it possible that they might have weakened his ambition and self-determination?

It is ironic that the very meaning of "civil rights" has been perverted. The term first appeared in American law in 1866, and referred to the rights of individuals that government must not be allowed to violate.[794] It was used during the campaign for racial equality to mean the rights denied to blacks but permitted to whites: employment, public accommodations, voter registration, housing, etc. These rights were established as soon as they ceased to be violated. To call the forcible redistribution of benefits along racial lines "civil rights" is a cruel mockery of the term for which so many worked so hard.

The real civil rights struggle led to decisive victory in 1964. As one black puts it, "[it's] over—for the same reason that World War II is over: we won it."[795] Now what pass for civil rights are what cynics call "snivel rights." Martin Luther King once said: "I have a dream that my four little children will one day live in a nation where they will not be judged by the color of their skin but by the content of their character." For a brief, glorious moment, it seemed that Dr. King's dream would come true.

Someday the entire edifice of race-based preferences will be torn down. On that day, someone will cite *Plessy* v. *Ferguson,* the 1896 U.S. Supreme Court ruling that first established the concept of separate but equal. In a dissent, Justice Harlan wrote:

> In respect of civil rights, common to all citizens, the Constitution of the United States does not, I think, permit any public authority to know the race of those entitled to be protected in the enjoyment of such rights. . . . Our constitution is color-blind, and neither knows nor tolerates classes among citizens.[796]

6

Double Standards

CIVIL RIGHTS LAWS AND AFFIRMATIVE ACTION WERE SUPPOSED TO narrow and eventually eliminate the gaps between black and white America. The great disappointment was that they did not work. Black crime, illegitimacy, and unemployment rose during the very period when the color bar was coming down. Since America was not prepared to abandon the whites-are-responsible theory of black problems, white racism now had to explain not just a lack of achievement but crime and social irresponsibility as well. If necessary, white racism could even excuse for blacks what, for whites, was the worst possible offense: racism itself. A host of double standards took root in America, with the result that blacks could be excused for a great deal, simply because they were black.

There are now many things that whites may not do but that are tolerated and even encouraged among blacks. We have double standards in politics, in school, at work, in the press, even in our speech. Many Americans are reluctant to acknowledge these double standards.

One of the simplest governs the language we use. Whites are held to a system of "sensitivity" requirements that do not apply to blacks. This concerns, first of all, the terms by which blacks are called. Over the years, they have asked that they be called various things: colored, Negro, black, now African-American. Most whites have been willing to abandon terms they may have used for years if that is what blacks want. That so many, including President George Bush, have dropped the monosyllabic "black" in favor of something seven times as long shows a remarkable willingness to please.[797]

The Methodist Church is just as worried about language. In its recently revised hymnal, goodness must no longer be represented by colors. Thus a line from "Nothing but the Blood of Jesus" has been changed to read, "make me as *bright* as snow."[798]

Whites are even willing to tinker with the past to avoid giving offense. In the 1938 edition of Bartlett's *Familiar Quotations,* there is a reference to an 1849 essay by Thomas Carlyle called "Occasional Discourse on the Nigger Question." In the 1955 and 1968 editions, Carlyle's essay is about "the Negro Question."[799] Perhaps later editions will update it further.

Some critics of the language seem to be working overtime. An Education Commission set up by the state of New York recommended in 1991 that the word "slave" in school textbooks be replaced with "enslaved person." Otherwise some readers might not realize that the status of a slave was involuntary and something different from that of a cook, say, or farmhand.[800]

Our speech has already been battered by the tortuous course of the struggle for equal treatment. "Civil rights" now means special treatment for blacks, the meaning of "equal opportunity" has been neatly reversed, and "affirmative action" is a euphemism for

[797] Not everyone is pleased with "African-American," which has been most strongly promoted by Jesse Jackson. Recent immigrants from Africa are surprised to discover that people who do not have relatives in Africa, speak no African language, and have never been to Africa wish to call themselves African-Americans. Perry Lang, "New Name Ties Blacks to Homeland," *San Francisco Chronicle* (September 27, 1990), p. A1. Nelson Mandela, leader of the African National Congress, must have been amused when a befuddled reporter referred to him during a trip to New York as an "African-American." Deborah Wright, "American, Not African-American," *The Wall Street Journal,* (October 30, 1990), p. 18. Curiously, a 1991 survey by a black organization, the Joint Center for Political and Economic Studies, found that only 15 percent of blacks wished to be called African-American, while 72 percent preferred to be called black. It concluded that the new term had caught on only among certain elite, outspoken blacks but that a large number of whites had adopted it out of deference to what they thought were the wishes of blacks. Associated Press, "Poll Says Most Blacks Prefer 'Black' to 'African-American,' " *The New York Times* (January 29, 1991.)

officially sanctioned racial discrimination. This kind of word fraud has gotten to the point where *Newsweek* can print the following sentence with no apparent irony: "Some employers have tried harder than others to make integration work by aggressively recruiting qualified blacks and by making the workplace as color-blind as possible."[801] Aggressive recruitment of blacks is, of course, the very opposite of a colorblind hiring policy.

The city of St. Paul, Minnesota, went farther than any other in America in regulating what lawyers call "symbolic speech." Until the U.S. Supreme Court struck down the city's ordinance in June 1992, it was against the law to burn a cross anywhere within the city limits.[802] Thus one could burn the flag on the steps of the St. Paul courthouse, but one could not burn a cross even in the privacy of one's own backyard.

Whites, especially publicly visible whites, must be constantly vigilant about what they say. On a 1988 television program, Robert Michel, the House minority leader, expressed regret that minstrel show humor and the television show *Amos 'n' Andy* were no longer acceptable in America. He also compared the removal of the word "nigger" from song lyrics to Soviet attempts to rewrite history. He was immediately attacked by Benjamin Hooks, who called his remarks "shocking."[803]

Congressman Michel apologized lavishly, but a few days later, *The New York Times* published an op-ed piece by a black congressman, Floyd Flake, who accused him of a "callous and dangerous philosophy" and said he should consider resigning so as to "demonstrate that there is no place for bigotry and racial insensitivity in our country."[804] Mr. Michel had been in Congress for thirty-two years without the slightest racial taint, yet he was suddenly "callous," "dangerous," and a symbol of "bigotry." Congressman Flake is not known to have called for Gus Savage's resignation from Congress for having repeatedly called people "white motherf——rs."

Whites can lose their jobs because of a single word. Dan Landes, a bureau chief in the Kings County, New York, district attorney's office, was fired after he complained to colleagues that his office was tied down with work because of a large number of "*schvartze* burglaries and robberies." *Schvartze* is a Yiddish word that means black and is considered derogatory.[805]

It is instructive to compare his fate with that of Hazel Dukes, a black friend of New York's mayor David Dinkins, and appointee to a $110,000-a-year job in his administration as head of the Off-Track Betting Corporation (OTB). One of the first things she did was to fire more than half a dozen executive-level whites and replace them all with blacks, but that caused hardly a ripple.[806] In the fall of 1990, she complained in a radio interview about hotel waiters "who not only aren't black, but can't even speak English." When it was suggested to her that this sounded anti-Latino, Miss Dukes replied that she wasn't referring to Latinos. "I'm talking about another nationality," she said. "Latinos can speak English." Asked what nationality she had in mind, Miss Dukes thought for a moment and said, "Ecuadorans. I don't know what they are [but] I know they're not Hispanic."

There was considerable hooting from New York's Hispanics, but Miss Dukes remained securely in her job,[807] thanks to protective coloring. Any white city official who said anything so "insensitive" on the radio, and then replied to questions with such colossal ignorance, would be very quickly gone. Later Miss Dukes went on to give raises only to certain black employees of OTB, despite a citywide wage freeze. She claimed, without substantiation, that they had suffered racial discrimination under the previous administration—which had already been out of office for more than a year.[808]

In this age of heightened sensitivity, newspapers must also be careful about how they write about blacks. The School of Journalism at the University of Missouri has published a dictionary of terms to be avoided if a writer does not wish to offend. Along with the derogatory expressions that no journalist would ever use, here are some of the words that are out of favor.

Burly: "An adjective too often associated with large black men, implying ignorance, and considered offensive in context."

Lazy: "Use advisedly, especially when describing nonwhites."

Shiftless: "As a description for blacks, highly objectionable." Whites, presumably, may be described as shiftless.

Fried Chicken: "A loaded phrase when used carelessly and as a stereotype, referring to the cuisine of black people. Also applies to 'watermelon.' "

The journalism school did not bother to include pejorative expressions for white people.[809]

Another compilation, known as the *Dictionary of Cautionary Words and Phrases,* was compiled in 1989 by a group of professional journalists. It urges writers not to call blacks "articulate," because to do so implies that they usually are not.[810]

Meanwhile, as whites worry about whether they are using the socially acceptable race words, blacks can call whites anything they like. No one has ever been reported to have gotten into trouble for talking about whitey, crackers, rednecks, honkies, buckra, or white trash. The same double standard has emerged in the fact that many familiar ethnic jokes that were once told about nonwhites have been recirculated as jokes about blonds. They can be insulted with impunity.[811]

Occasionally black parents have books such as *Huckleberry Finn,* which uses the word "nigger," removed from libraries or reading lists.[812] Any whites who wanted to take a violently antiwhite writer such as LeRoi Jones off the shelves would be accused at least of censorship, if not of racism.

What, on the other hand, is to be made of the fact that many blacks refer only to each other as "brothers" and "sisters"? Is it not the current theory that in America brotherhood is supposed to cross racial lines? Any group of whites that called only other whites brothers and sisters would surely be called racists.

T-shirt slogans hew to their own double standard. "Black is Beautiful" and "Black Power" have been replaced by the perhaps more ominous "Fight the Power" and "By Any Means Necessary." "Black by Popular Demand," "Too Black and Too Strong," and "It's a Black Thing . . . You Wouldn't Understand" are also popular. A T-shirt that extolled the virtues of being white would be thought, at the very least, to be in bad taste.

Some blacks take it for granted that whites should adjust to them rather than vice versa. The young black film director Mario Van Peebles suggests that it is racist for whites to want blacks to sit quietly during a movie. Whites must "get hip to the extroverted reactions by black audiences to what they are seeing on the screen," he explains.[813]

In 1979 and 1980, the National Survey of Black Americans asked blacks whether they felt closer to black people in Africa or to white people in America. Fifty-six percent said they felt closer to Africans, 20 percent said neither or both, and only 24 percent said they felt closer to white Americans.[814] This means that more than twice as many blacks say they feel closer to people they have never met and with whom they have nothing in common but race, than they do to their fellow American citizens. This does not seem to bother anyone, but it is not hard to imagine the hand-wringing over any poll showing that a majority of American whites felt closer to Danes or South African whites, say, than to American blacks.

Perhaps this is all part of what is known as "black pride." But just what is black pride? Are blacks supposed to be proud of their color or of their accomplishments? Jimmy "the Greek" Snyder lost his television job for saying that blacks were, by nature, better athletes than whites, and that some may have been bred for size and strength during slavery. Whites are not supposed to speculate about a possible black superiority in athletics because to do so could be construed as a suggestion that blacks may also have a natural inferiority in other areas. The tennis champion Arthur Ashe, however, is allowed to think blacks may be specially talented at running[815] because he, himself, is black.

Brooks Johnson, a black who coached the U.S. women's Olympic track team, disagrees with Ashe. He thinks that white racism, not biology, makes blacks such good sprinters. He says that instant gratification appeals "to a people who are subjugated or oppressed."[816]

Except for the occasional lost job or public humiliation, these black/white double standards probably do not do much harm. Language conventions are a practically unnoticed part of American life. However, there is a point at which double standards begin to reflect self-deception, and to ignore them is to hide the truth.

Congressman Michel was not far off the mark when he compared the bowdlerizing of song lyrics to the rewriting of history. The Jefferson Memorial in Washington, for example, falsifies the third President's views of blacks. Inscribed on one of the interior walls are these words: "Nothing is more certainly written in the book of fate than that these people [the Negroes] shall be free." When Jefferson wrote those words, he did not end them with a period, but with a semicolon, after which he wrote: "nor is it less certain that the two races, equally free, cannot live under the same government."[817] Thomas Jefferson believed that slavery was wrong, but he did not believe in racial equality. He wanted to send blacks back to Africa.

President Abraham Lincoln is likewise falsely portrayed, presumably to salve white consciences and to mollify blacks. He is extolled as the Great Emancipator who wanted to set up the freed slave as the equal of his master. He was certainly opposed to slavery, but he did not want free blacks living in the same society as whites. As President he asked Congress several times to appropriate money to send them to Africa, and even argued for a Constitutional amendment for this purpose.[818]

Slanting the News

Today, our media present a deliberately slanted picture of race in America. The eighty-eight daily newspapers of the Gannett chain are under strict orders to look for articles and photographs that show minorities in a favorable light. In stories that are not specifically about minorities, editors are under orders to include them in photographs and quote them as sources. Editors who do not practice "affirmative action" journalism feel it in their paychecks,[819] and they get points for hiring and promoting minorities.

USA Today is one of the best-known Gannett papers. Every day it runs four photographs on the top half of page one. At least one photograph must be of an ethnic minority. Al Neuharth, who established the rule, had a standard reply to anyone who objected that the news was being forced to fit an ideology: "Don't tell me the f——ing news of the day doesn't justify that 'cause that's the formula." Over one two-month period, about a third of the time there were two or more nonwhites on the front page. According to

Gannett's policy, minorities are essentially black; in that two-month period they accounted for 92 percent of the front-page nonwhites. One result is that *USA Today* puts a great many sports stories on the front page that other newspapers would put in the sports section.[820]

Other papers may not have such specific policies but are still selective in their reporting. *The New York Times,* for example, recently ran a front-page, thirty-column-inch story about how rival drug gangs, the Bloods and the Crips, have branched out from their home territory in Los Angeles to places like Nebraska, Missouri, and Kansas. Although they might stand out in a place like Nebraska because of their race, the *Times* only hinted that all members of these drug gangs are black.[821]

In another thirty-inch story, *The Times* wrote about Washington, D.C.'s, losing battle against drugs. It mentioned that the city has the highest drug-related arrest rate of any major American city, that its crime rates have increased five times as quickly as those in other cities, that the number of murders has doubled in the past two years, and that our national capital has proportionately more people in prison than virtually any other part of the country.[822] In this welter of statistics, not once did *The Times* mention that at over 65 percent, Washington also has a larger proportion of blacks than nearly any other major American city.

Recently, the *San Francisco Chronicle* ran a special report on crack cocaine, which filled several pages. It was full of terrifying facts and statistics, but not once did it mention that crack use is an overwhelmingly black problem. In fact, the paper gave the opposite impression by its choice of photographs of crack victims: one baby of indeterminate race and several white children.[823]

However, one of the most striking—and destructive—examples of the way the media handle news about race was the Rodney King affair. It is not an exaggeration to say that the coverage of this incident was so slanted as to be a major cause of the riots that later rocked Los Angeles.

Rodney King is a convicted felon with a long criminal record. On March 3, 1991, he was out of jail on parole, and driving recklessly and at great speed through residential streets of Los Angeles. It was later determined that despite parole conditions that forbade him to use alcohol, he was thoroughly drunk—there was two and a half times the legal limit of alcohol in his blood, and he had marijuana in his system. An officer saw him driving recklessly and flagged him, but he refused to stop. He then led police on a chase at speeds up to 115 miles per hour, running through stop signs and red lights.

When he was finally forced to a stop, police approached his car with great caution. There is no telling what a man may do if he has just put his own life in danger by trying to outrun the police. A policewoman approached Mr. King when he got out of the car, but he grabbed his right buttock and shook it at her. He would not let himself be frisked, spat at the police, laughed maniacally, and danced about when told to stand still. Mr. King is six feet, three inches tall, weighs 250 pounds, and was acting dangerously crazy.[824] He refused to lie face-down on the ground so that police could safely handcuff him, and when police approached him, he started flailing his arms wildly, hitting one officer in the chest. The police decided to force him down.

Their first attempt was with a twenty-five-thousand-volt electronic stun gun. One shot of this device will knock a person down 80 to 90 percent of the time. The officers hit Mr. King twice with the gun but he still resisted arrest, and managed to knock one officer off his feet. The police began to think that he was on PCP, a drug that can cause psychotic behavior and give a person almost superhuman strength.[825] The best way to take Mr. King down might have been with a choke hold, but the city of Los Angeles banned choke holds in 1982 after a few drug users died from the hold.[826]

The only way to tackle Mr. King was with nightsticks, and the police clubbed him repeatedly.[827] They later testified that this was because they were afraid Mr. King would attack them and try to grab a gun. Mr. King refused to stay on the ground, and every time he tried to get up, he was clubbed again. An amateur video cameraman recorded the lengthy beating, which was later broadcast on television.

The video is eighty-one seconds long. It shows Mr. King resisting arrest, lunging at an officer, and repeatedly attempting to get to his feet after he was told to stay down. Virtually all television stations chose to show only the last twenty seconds, in which Mr. King was on the ground and was being pounded in a way that appeared—and may very well have been—excessive. A careful study of the *entire* tape suggests that the beating was provoked by Mr. King's resistance, and stopped when Mr. King did as he was told and kept still.[828]

Three of the policemen who clubbed Mr. King were white and one was Hispanic. The media consistently described them as all white and immediately concluded that the beating was an unjustified racial attack. Television stations showed the tape so often that there must be scarcely anyone in America who has not seen it. As it happens, Mr. King was not badly hurt. The paramedic who treated him said she saw only minor injuries, the worst of which was a cut on his face. She said there was gravel in the cut, which suggested to her that he had gotten it from rolling on the ground, not from being beaten. On the way to the hospital, he laughed, used obscenities, and struggled with the medics when they tried to take his pulse and blood pressure.[829]

What would have been different if Mr. King had been white? For one thing, the media would have taken the trouble to look into the reasons for the beating. However, since Mr. King is black, the media had a ready-made explanation for it: racism. They scarcely mentioned that Mr. King was drunk and that he had resisted arrest. They ignored the fact that Mr. King had two companions with him in the car, both of whom were black, both of whom did what the police told them to do, both of whom were unharmed (though months later one claimed he had been roughed up).[830] Both Mr. King and the police department's largest black organization said they did not think race had anything to do with the beating, but the media brushed this aside. (Later, Mr. King changed his story and claimed that the police shouted racial epithets as they beat him.)[831] Thus the media took an ambiguous case of police brutality and blew it into a coast-to-coast case of white racism.

The policemen were charged with assault and their trial opened a year after the beating. The defense methodically analyzed the entire videotape, described the dangers the officers faced, and convinced the jury that three of them were not guilty on all counts, and the fourth not guilty on all but one count. The jury could not agree about the officer who had struck the most blows, and he was to be retried. Members of the jury later explained they did not think the Rodney King arrest was ideal police work, but they were not convinced that the officers were guilty of the serious crimes of assault with a deadly weapon and assault under color of authority.[832]

By the time of the verdict, the media were so committed to a "racist" version of events that they had little choice but to call the jurors—none of whom was black—"racist." Jurors themselves explained that they did not think about race, nor did they believe the police did, either. As one said, "Had the man been white, had he been . . . Oriental . . . , had he been anything and acted as Rodney King did, he would have been given the same treatment."[833]

The jury heard twenty-nine days of testimony[834] and deliberated for seven days.[835] The nation saw twenty seconds of videotape. The nation, misled by slanted news reports, convinced itself the officers were guilty long before the jury reached its verdict. This presumption of guilt, combined with the constant messages blacks receive about white racism and social injustice, primed them to act exactly as they did when the verdict was announced.

Had the media reported the full circumstances of the beating, it is possible that the violence would have been much less severe or might not even have occurred. Instead, in Los Angeles, rioters burned more than 5,300 buildings and caused the deaths of 58 people. More than 2,300 people were injured—227 of them critically—and property damage was estimated at more than $750 million.[836] There were smaller-scale outbreaks of violence in San Francisco, Las Vegas, Atlanta, and many other cities.[837]

Although white racism, both by the police and by the jury, was said to be the sin that prompted the riots, the media were remarkably restrained about the many acts of racist violence committed by blacks against whites. The best known was an attack on a truck driver, Reginald Denny, who was pulled from his tractor-trailer by blacks, who beat him mercilessly and smashed his face with a fire extinguisher. Other blacks ran up to kick the barely breathing Mr. Denny and dance little jigs of glee. Doctors said the man's injuries were like those of someone who had been in a sixty-mile-per-hour car crash without seat belts. The only reason Mr. Denny is well known is that a helicopter TV crew happened to tape the attack.[838]

Few people heard about Matt Haines, a thirty-two-year-old white man who, with his nephew, was riding through South-Central Los Angeles. A gang of about fifteen blacks knocked them off their motorcycle and beat them. One of the blacks shot Mr. Haines in the head and shot his nephew three times in the arm. When the gunman held the pistol to the nephew's face, the weapon did not fire. Mr. Haines died; his nephew survived.[839]

Howard Epstein was driving to his South-Central Los Angeles machine shop to protect it and its employees when three black men shot him. After his car crashed to a stop, looters stripped him of valuables and ransacked the car.[840]

A gang of blacks smashed the car windows of Jeff Kramer, a white reporter for the *Boston Globe*. They tried to drag him out onto the street, but his seat belt held him in. One youngster then pulled out a gun and shot him three times. Mr. Kramer had the wit to pretend to be dead, and this probably saved his life.[841]

Blacks attacked whites in Richmond, California; San Jose, California; Atlanta; Las Vegas; New York City, and elsewhere.[842] A careful search of news reports did not reveal a *single* instance of retaliatory violence by whites against blacks for any of these attacks.

How many of the whites who died in the riots—nine men and one woman—were killed simply because they were white? How many of the badly injured were, like the truck driver and the reporter, attacked simply because they were white? We will probably never know. The media, which made a national incident of it when a black criminal was beaten with nightsticks, have an entirely different perspective on racial murder of whites by blacks. It would be hard to think of a more spectacular example than the Rodney King affair and the Los Angeles riots of the slant the media give to news about race.

A Skewed Picture

Black reporters come under particular pressure to slant the news about blacks. Juan Williams has been attacked for what he thought were honest, factual stories about Jesse Jackson, Coretta King, and Spike Lee in the *Washington Post*. As he says of one critic who called in to a live television show, "It seems to me that caller knew what he wanted from black journalists; he wanted them to lie."[843]

School textbooks present a skewed picture of America. Guidelines from publishers practically forbid illustrations of blacks as janitors or waiters; they must be shown in responsible, white-collar jobs. Black contributions to every field must be sought out and recognized, even if it takes some straining to find any. Here is what the rules from the Macmillan Publishing Company say about how to write science texts: "Because of the societal roles that have been traditionally assigned in our culture to women and minority people, white males are *credited with* most of the significant achievements in science." Nevertheless, illustrations in science texts "should depict women and minority people at least 50 percent of the time, avoiding sexual and racial stereotypes."[844] Instruction in our schools is rigorously "inclusive" and "multicultural"; the correct image is more important than accuracy.

Television dramas commonly present a carefully race-sanitized version of America. ABC's vice president for motion pictures and television, Bruce Sallan, explains that blacks are almost never chosen as bad guys. Instead, it is white businessmen who commit the on-screen wickedness because they never complain about stereotypes. "Almost every villain you see is a WASP," says Mr. Sallan. "I think we should be able to show that there are bad blacks as well as good blacks." In a typical casting decision, Mr. Sallan notes that although the vast majority of people on death row are black, a white was made the subject of a movie about a man awaiting execution. "In their desire to avoid stereotyping, I think broadcast standards and practices sometimes go to an absurd extreme," he says.[845]

Blacks have long complained about "negative stereotypes," but movies bend over backward to give them a positive image, both in the present and in the past. *Glory,* which claimed to be a historically accurate account of the formation of a black regiment that fought in the Union Army, is a good example. Most of the black soldiers were recruited in the North and had always been free men, but in the movie they are escaped slaves who bravely go into battle against their former masters. Their white regimental commander demanded that they be paid as much as white Union soldiers, but in the movie it is blacks themselves who agitate for "civil rights." Other elements that demean whites or glorify blacks are purely fictional: a racist quartermaster refuses to issue shoes to the black soldiers, a black who goes AWOL is brutally flogged, a learned black soldier quotes Emerson.[846]

Anyone who has read the Tom Clancy novel *Hunt for Red October* and seen the movie version will notice a difference. In the book, the brilliant sonar operator who saves the day for the U.S. Navy is white. In the movie he is black. A similar change has been made in the movie version of Tom Wolfe's *Bonfire of the Vanities.* At the last minute, the script was rewritten so that a major, sympathetic character could be played by a black rather than a white[847] —in spite of the fact that Mr. Wolfe deliberately set out to make his characters into realistic racial portraits.

When real events are made into "docudramas," it is common to make changes that improve the images of blacks. Marla Hanson was an aspiring model living in New York in 1986. She got into a dispute with her landlord, Steve Roth, over a security deposit and because Mr. Roth wanted to have sex with her. Mr. Roth hired two black men to slash Miss Hanson's face with razor blades so as to ruin her modeling career. He and the thugs were caught and went to jail. In real life, the man who defended the blacks was Alton Maddox, a black lawyer who was later barred from practicing law because of his role in promoting the Tawana Brawley hoax. Although no one had made race an issue in the case, Mr. Maddox submitted Miss Hanson to an insulting cross-examination in which he tried to portray her as a slut and as a racist who had pinned the crime on his clients only because they were black.

In the television version, the lawyer behaves almost as offensively as Mr. Maddox did, but he was made into a white. Other race changes include a white policeman who played an important role in catching the thugs; he is now black. Likewise, the sympathetic prosecutor on whom Miss Hanson depends was changed from a white Hispanic to a black. The changes are consistent: An unattractive character is changed to a white, and attractive characters become black.[848]

The Howard Beach killing (see Chapter Two) was made into a two-hour television docudrama that twisted the facts at every turn to discredit whites. In its depiction of the original face-off between the whites and blacks, the blacks do not walk in front of the car, do not flash a knife, do not spit in anyone's face, do not say "F— — you, honky"; in fact, they do not do anything at all. The whites deliberately try to run them down, and shout "Get out of the neighborhood, niggers," a line invented purely for television.

White brutality is deliberately exaggerated. For example, in real life, the black who was beaten needed five stitches; on television he gets a concussion and needs sixty-seven stitches. The thesis of the TV version is that blacks merely had to find themselves in the Howard Beach neighborhood in order to be attacked. In fact, the bowling alley across the street from where the attack took place has a black bowling league.

One of the white defendants has an ex-girlfriend who is black. She is furious about what she calls the TV version's "horrendous" distortions. Apparently scriptwriter Steve Ballo and producer Ken Kaufman were not even trying to be truthful. They were making propaganda about racist white people.[849] No one, of course, is planning a film about the death of Danny Gilmore, the white man who was run over with his own truck, even though the story has all the elements of high drama: a brutal killing, a big-city newspaper that covers up the facts, a brave black reporter who fights for truth, a streetwise detective who sees through the lies. If only whites had killed a black man, this would be the perfect Hollywood plot.

A recent television "docudrama" of the 1965 Los Angeles Watts riots strikes the same themes of white wickedness and black heroics. *The Wall Street Journal* described the program as "unremittingly silly, when it is not vicious, in its stereotyping of whites." Its reviewer went on to conclude: "It is also guilty, in its treatment of whites, of something normally called racism when such stuff is directed at blacks."

Alan Parker directed the recent film *Mississippi Burning,* which is based on the murder of three civil rights workers in 1964. Not even *The New York Times*'s reviewer, who says the film "literally crackles with racial hate," was comfortable with the film's exaggerated and fictionalized white perfidy. Mr. Parker explained that he wanted his treatment to "cause them [the viewers] to react to it viscerally, emotionally, because of the racism that's around them now. And that's enough of a reason, a justification, for the fictionalizing."[850] Today's racism apparently justifies an exaggeration of yesterday's racism. Perhaps since he is British, Mr. Parker knows more about American racism than we do. No white, much less a foreigner, would think of making a movie that exaggerated black racism.

None of this stops one white writer from bemoaning the "incredibly deft racism" of today's movie industry,[851] apparently because all the heroes are not yet black nor all the villains white. Perhaps "incredibly deft" racism is as damaging to blacks as the "unconscious" racism that zealots have detected in the laboratory (see Chapter One).

A determinedly favorable presentation of blacks in newspapers, on television, and in movies may have contributed to some curious voting patterns during Jesse Jackson's campaign for the Democratic nomination. Mr. Jackson got the highest proportion of white votes precisely in those states with the smallest numbers of blacks.[852]

It should not be surprising that whites who get their impressions about blacks only from television should be more favorably disposed toward them. A study conducted in 1980 showed that at 10 to 12 percent, there are about as many black characters in television dramas as there are in the American population. However, instead of committing 46 percent of the violent crime, as they do in real life, they commit only 10 percent. That is to say that they are 4.6 times *less* likely to commit murder, rape, or assault than in real life.[853]

In real life, less than half of the people arrested for murder in the United States are white. In television dramas, 90 percent of the people arrested for murder are white.[854] Jesse Jackson himself must not watch television. He says that it stirs up "antiblack fervor." When whites watch television, he said recently, "[they] see us projected as less hardworking than we are. . . . They see us as more violent than we are."[855]

Some blacks, of course, will be dissatisfied no matter how they are portrayed. In a long article in *The New York Times*, a black professor at Cornell complains that when blacks are portrayed as different from white people, that is stereotyping. When they are portrayed as successfully middle class it suggests, dangerously, that racism might not be such a horrible obstacle to them after all.[856]

Unacknowledged Double Standards

The less obvious double standards are rarely pointed out, and we have grown so used to others that we hardly notice them. A widespread one was on display when a black comedian, Eddie Murphy, was a guest on a talk show hosted by a black woman, Oprah Winfrey. Miss Winfrey asked Mr. Murphy if there was a particular kind of woman he especially liked to date. Mr. Murphy replied that, yes, he preferred to date black women. Miss Winfrey applauded and the studio audience applauded. If a white actor had told Miss Winfrey he preferred to date white women, there would surely have been much clucking about white bigotry.

Over the years, Al Campanis, Jimmy "the Greek" Snyder, and Andy Rooney have been publicly humiliated, and punished by their employers for saying (or allegedly saying) things their employers thought might be unflattering to blacks. With just a few words, all three men became national news. In 1985, black trumpeter Miles Davis said, "If somebody told me I only had an hour to live, I'd spend it choking a white man. I'd do it nice and slow."[857] It caused hardly a ripple. John Singleton is a successful black movie director who keeps an albino cat as a pet. The cat's name is White Boy, so when Mr. Singleton wants his cat, he presumably says, "Come here, White Boy." *The New York Times* reported the name without comment;[858] it is not hard to imagine how it would have reported the news of a prominent white person with a black cat named Black Boy.

By the same token, membership in certain white groups, such as the Ku Klux Klan or the skinheads, has, in some cases, been considered sufficient reason to fire otherwise capable employees.[859] If anyone has ever been fired for being a member of the Nation of Islam or for advocating black supremacy or black nationalism, it has never been widely reported—and black groups would see to it that it was.

A peculiar form of double standard was on painful display when it became known in late 1990 that Martin Luther King had plagiarized large chunks of his doctoral dissertation. Clayborne Carson, the chief editor of Mr. King's papers, as well as more than twenty colleagues, knew about the plagiarism for more than three years but chose to suppress the story. The National Endowment for the Humanities had known about the plagiarism for a year, as had editors at *The New Republic,* the *Washington Post, The New York Times,* and the *Atlanta Journal and Constitution.* All kept silent.[860] It is difficult to think of a single white person, dead or alive, whose reputation is so holy that it would have been protected so diligently against taint.

The same hagiographic thinking is behind the myths that circulate about Malcolm X (Little), who has lately enjoyed a revival among young blacks. The usual story is that his parents' house was burned down by a white hate group. In fact, it was probably set on fire by the elder Mr. Little because the family was about to be evicted. Nor was Malcolm X's father killed by whites. These are stories that appear to have been invented by the mother to conceal the fact that Mr. Little was an adulterer, wife-beater, and poor provider.[861]

One of the most deeply rooted double standards that no one notices is the existence of explicitly race-based black organizations. Some of these are holdovers from the civil rights era: the National Urban League, the National Association for the Advancement of Colored People (NAACP), the Southern Christian Leadership Conference (SCLC), and the Congress of Racial Equality (CORE).

The older groups, such as the NAACP, were founded with the help of whites and often had white executives. Their goals were the legal abolition of segregation and discrimination. After these goals had been attained and the focus shifted to special treatment for blacks, whites felt—and were—unwelcome. As late as 1961, the Congress of Racial Equality had a membership that was two thirds white and a national leadership that was almost entirely white. Only a few years later, its leaders were all black, and in 1965 it amended its constitution to limit the positions that whites could hold—a curious decision for an organization with the phrase "racial equality" in its name.[862] It was a clear sign that the goal of the organization was changing from equality to privilege.

Today's "civil rights" groups now have umbrella organizations, such as the National Black Leadership Forum, to further their specifically racial goals. They receive national attention and are wooed by politicians from presidents on down. They continue to exist long after the passage of civil rights laws because their members think that the interests of blacks are not the same as those of other Americans.

Some of the most suspect black groupings are the "caucuses" that spring up as subgroups within practically every organization in America. The Congressional Black Caucus is probably the best known. It has a $2 million war chest, raised mainly from corporations, that it plans to spend promoting black candidates.[863] State legislatures have their own black caucuses, the U.S. State Department has Concerned Black Foreign Service Officers, and the Republican Party has a National Black Republican Council. Every major Protestant denomination has its chapter of the National Committee of Black Churchmen. Virtually every university has an association of black faculty and staff. The American Anthropological Association, the American Bar Association, the Catholic Church, and advocacy groups for the aging have well-established black subgroups. Even the American Museum Association has, within it, the Afro-American Museums Association. The National Coalition on Black Voter Participation is devoted exclusively to persuading black people to register and vote. There is the National Association of Black Journalists and the National Conference of Black Mayors, the Council of Black Elected Democrats, the Negro Dance Ensemble, and the Negro Ensemble Company. In nearly every good-sized police and fire department, there is a Black Officers' (or Fire Fighters') Union, and black government workers have established Blacks in Government.

There are so many blacks-only organizations that they need organizations just to stay organized. Recently a coalition of a hundred such groups formed the National Association of Black Organizations.[864]

Some middle-class blacks who have been admitted to mainly white clubs find that they prefer the society of other blacks. This has led to a revival of black Jack and Jill clubs, which whites are not invited to join. There is even a Miss Black America beauty contest, even though four blacks have won the Miss America contest—and twice in a row, in 1989 and 1990.[865]

Far from criticizing black groups for their racial exclusiveness, American society encourages them. It was, for example, the Ford Foundation that paid to establish the Joint Center for Political Studies. Its job is to create networks and caucuses of black elected officials.[866]

It is ironic that after having joined groups from which they may have been excluded in the past, blacks invariably set up subgroups in which whites are not welcome. They maintain a separate set of racial priorities that are explicitly different from the goals of the other members of the larger organization. Of course, any subgroup that had the word "White" in its name would be ostracized, if not expelled.

The Black and Hispanic Alumni Association of Baruch College is an interesting example of the dynamic of racial caucuses. In 1983, black and Hispanic graduates asked for official approval of a racially segregated alumni association. They wanted campus office space, secretarial help, and all the other services that were provided to the general alumni association. The president of Baruch refused, saying that such an organization would run counter to his goals of integration.

The black and Hispanic group then filed suit, saying that the college's refusal was racist. Seven years later, the parties reached an agreement. All the demands for the new association were met, and the college agreed to pay $15,000 in court costs and $22,000 of the other side's legal fees. Baruch College now has two alumni associations, one open to all students and the other open only to certain races.

The only unusual aspect of this race-based subgroup is that together, Hispanics and blacks outnumber whites at Baruch.[867] They cannot even pretend to be doughty minorities struggling against an indifferent and oppressive white majority. They are, themselves, excluding a minority that happens to be white.

It is generally argued that whites do not need race-based organizations of this kind because society is set up automatically to put them into positions of privilege and power. In effect, it is said, whites have been playing the race game all along. This completely misunderstands the difference between black and white expectations and behavior. Among the many reasons for which whites are in positions of power—better education, more experience, greater numbers, past exclusionary practices—white racial solidarity today plays practically no role. Whites are forbidden to think in terms of racial identity unless it is to think of ways to promote the interests of *other* races. When whites act in their own interests, they are to act strictly as individuals rather than as conscious members of a racial group.

Black behavior is the very opposite of this. Blacks are encouraged to identify with their racial "brothers," to promote "black consciousness," and to see themselves as a group defined clearly by race. They need not be concerned with what is fair for whites. They are to work openly for the advancement of people of their *own* race, and if advancement comes through the exclusion or dispossession of whites, so be it. Blacks, therefore, use racial solidarity as a tool to win advantages for themselves, while whites are to smother their sense of their own racial cohesion. Affirmative action requires that whites go even farther and deliberately sacrifice their own interests to the interests of blacks.

To some extent black racial solidarity is inevitable. Blacks were discriminated against as a race, and it was natural that they seek justice as a race. However, the terms on which justice was sought foresaw the ultimate disappearance of race as a relevant category in America. This was Martin Luther King's vision, and it was the vision that whites embraced. They set about dismantling their own racial identity in the expectation that America would become a nation of individuals rather than an uneasy assembly of races.

But while all but a handful of whites renounced an explicitly racial consciousness, blacks continued to develop an ever more explicitly racial identity. To the extent that it gave direction to their struggle against segregation, exclusion, and all the other curses of second-class citizenship, it was good and probably necessary. But when it became the guiding light of a movement to carve out special privileges based on race, it was a rejection of the color-blind vision of Martin Luther King, and a violation of the tacit agreement under which whites were abandoning their own racial identity. At the same time, since race and racial consciousness had become the ways to extract benefits from whites, they became ever more attractive, even essential to blacks. Thus the great irony of the "civil rights" movement was that as whites dutifully tried to strip away their own consciousness as members of a racial group and tried to think of all Americans as individuals, blacks defined themselves ever more distinctly as a group and made race consciousness a central part of their identities.

The histories of organizations like CORE and the NAACP reflect this irony. Whites and blacks, working together, intended not only to stamp out racial prejudice but also to eliminate the very relevance of race. The elimination of whites, not only from the leadership but from the rank and file of the civil rights groups, marked the change in the civil rights movement from one in which blacks and whites could work together for equality to one in which blacks worked openly for their own advantage.

These two opposite processes—waning white consciousness and ever stronger black consciousness—explain a great deal that is otherwise incomprehensible. They explain why the death of a black at the hands of a white unleashes torrents of black indignation, whereas a white death at the hands of blacks passes in silence. They explain why any black who is criticized by whites—for whatever reason—will always find a deep reservoir of support among other blacks. They explain why blacks work the racial spoils system while whites remain silent as other whites are penalized. They explain why blacks instinctively form racially exclusive solidarity groups while whites are expected to act as individuals without racial consciousness. They explain why some black juries can no longer be counted on to convict black defendants no matter how convincing the evidence.

It is likewise the waning of white racial consciousness that accounts for the absurdity of affirmative action for Hispanics, Asians, and other nonwhite immigrants. Whites might have been persuaded that they owed blacks something because of slavery and Jim Crow, but what could they possibly owe an immigrant from Guatemala or Trinidad? The case for preferences for resident Hispanics is flimsy enough; Hispanics were not enslaved, and were subject to nothing like the systematic legal exclusion that was common for blacks. But not even a Rube Goldberg case can be made for affirmative action for immigrants.

Something so obviously indefensible came about only because white racial consciousness has been forced underground. Black preferences at the expense of whites were instituted with scarcely any resistance. Preferences were extended to Hispanics with no more than a murmur of opposition. Immigrants just off the boat get preferential treatment, and no one even thinks about it. If whites had even the faintest sense that injustice to one was injustice to all, affirmative action for immigrants would be unthinkable. The near-total disappearance of white racial consciousness is one of the most remarkable but unremarked phenomena in recent times.[868]

[868] Samuel Elliot Morison was regarded as America's foremost historian. In a widely used textbook published in 1930 called *The Growth of the American Republic,* he argued that of all the different social groups of the antebellum South, it might have been blacks who suffered the least from slavery. Robert Fikes, "Racist Quotes from Persons of Note," *The Journal of Ethnic Studies* (Fall 1987), p. 141. Harry Truman wrote privately, "I am strongly of the opinion Negroes ought to be in Africa, yellow men in Asia, and white men in Europe and America." He also said that Northerners who went south to help in the civil rights movement were "meddlers" and he called Martin Luther King a "troublemaker." Rich Hampson, "Private Letters Reveal Truman's Racist Attitudes," *Washington Times,* (October 25, 1991.) After a lifetime of service to Africans, Dr. Albert Schweitzer said, in 1961, "They [Africans] have neither the intellectual, mental, or emotional abilities to equate [*sic*] or to share equally with white men in any of the functions of our civilization." "On the Negro Race," Reedy (W. Va): Liberty Bell Publications (undated), p. 1. Public expression of such sentiments by prominent men was common until a few decades ago. Likewise, until 1967, it was still a crime in twenty states for people of different races to

This disappearance has other strange consequences. White men who have suffered on account of affirmative action—and one expert has estimated that as many as one in ten may have[869]—are victims of an injustice that officially does not exist. Affirmative action is the law, it is practiced by America's most prestigious institutions, and it is praised by a chorus of media partisans. Therefore it cannot be wrong. Whites who are discriminated against know perfectly well that it is not only wrong but a cynical denial of the "equal opportunity" that America so proudly proclaims.

Nothing is more demoralizing than to be wronged and then to be told that one's injury is an illusion. To be betrayed by the central pillars of society—government, employer, university—leaves a lasting bitterness and alienation. Furthermore, unlike nonwhites, who have well-funded organizations that spring to the defense of alleged victims, the disappearance of white solidarity means that a white man is entirely on his own.[870]

Thus the rule in America today is that blacks may make race the centerpiece of their identities, while whites ignore their own race as they work to benefit other races. White racial solidarity is punished by being labeled as bigotry and hatred, while black racial solidarity is promoted as a healthy expression of pride. This is a double standard that has been hammered deep into our national consciousness, but it is giving rise to very dangerous resentments. White consciousness might have died a quiet death had it not been for the continuous development of a black consciousness that has often been openly hostile to whites. White consciousness, never entirely absent, now lies dangerously like a coiled spring that could lash out with sudden and surprising strength.

---

marry; these laws were not repealed by new legislation but were struck down by the U.S. Supreme Court. Tracey Eaton, "Interracial Couples Built Happy Lives Despite Hostility," *Orange County* (Calif.) *Register* (June 27, 1991), p. E1.

[870] See Frederick Lynch, *Invisible Victims* (New York: Praeger Publishers, 1991) for a full-length sociological study of the psychological effects on whites of official discrimination.

Rising White Resentment

The occasional acts of demented violence that whites commit against blacks have deep roots that go back to the lynching, segregationist mentality of the past, but they also have more shallow roots in the very real sense of grievance that many whites feel in the present. There is now a different kind of white reaction that is sure to become more common and that reflects today's injustices rather than yesterday's.

In the fall of 1988, a white senior at Temple University founded the first White Student Union, because he was frankly angry at the racial privileges that were accorded to blacks. Temple put up every possible resistance but could find no way to deny whites their own student union when other races had theirs. Michael Spletzer, the union's president, rejected the inevitable charges of white supremacy. "White people are being discriminated against by affirmative action," he said. "We feel that giving scholarships, jobs, or anything else because of race is wrong and they should be given on merit alone." In January 1989, when the union tried to recruit members, clusters of black students shouted obscenities and threatened violence.[871] Any whites who so disrupted a black organization would, of course, be immediately disciplined.

A similar organization has been established at the University of Florida at Gainsville and has met with the same shrill opposition. The group's founder, Mark Wright, has been called a racist for his opposition to race-based preferences. Mr. Wright argues that it is his opponents who are bigoted. "They prejudged us," he says; "they stereotyped us when they said, 'Whites can't form a group without being racist,' and they weren't open to new ideas."[872] "One of our main premises," he explains, "is that white students are treated differently. Because they are trying to stop us [from meeting] they are proving our point."[873]

White student unions have sprung up at the Universities of Nebraska and New Orleans as well.[874] Given the long history of open, systematic preferences for blacks on campuses, it is surprising that white student unions have appeared only now. Unless campus policies change, there will certainly be more of them.

The move to establish white subgroups is spreading to younger students. When whites at Lowell High School in San Francisco found themselves to be a minority, they applied to form a whites-only club, just like all the other racially exclusive clubs at the school. The administration turned them down flat.[875] In the San Jose area of California, where whites are often minorities in high schools, six different groups that wanted to start "European-American" clubs were turned down in just one twelve-month period.[876] Nevertheless, high schools will eventually give in to the relentless logic of deliberate race consciousness that they, themselves, have helped foster.

Not all whites in the labor force are submitting cheerfully to nonwhite preference either. Although they get no public support and virtually no publicity, white men have started filing discrimination cases with the U.S. Equal Employment Opportunity Commission. Every year the number rises, even though the overall number of filings is dropping. In 1990, white men filed 2,195 cases,[877] more than a tenth of all cases filed with the EEOC.[878] More and more have begun to win their cases.[879]

Other whites have begun to organize against systematic discrimination. A group of white men at the Southern New England Telephone Company has founded what they call the White American Management Association. "If you are a white male, the chances for promotion are nil," says Wayne Bennett, the chief organizer.[880] In Houston, Texas, white police officers have formed the Caucasian-American Police Group to fight discrimination against whites. Although blacks and Mexicans have long had their own racial subgroups, the white group's formation was met with widespread calls that it be banned.[881]

Regrettable as white-rights organizations may be, they are the natural consequence of America's racial policies. And although whites who organize along racial lines will be called the foulest names in the contemporary lexicon, it will not stop them from opposing what is, to them, blatant racial discrimination. It is important to note that not a single one of these groups advocates racial preferences for whites. What they call for is exactly what Martin Luther King called for: equal treatment for all races.

If anything is surprising, it is that whites have remained so quiet in the face of discrimination. This is partly because white victims of discrimination are simply not recognized as victims. When the media raise the subject of affirmative action, it is usually to describe it as the *equal* treatment of people of all races. Those who oppose it are invariably portrayed as incompetent, bigoted whites who are dismayed to find that they cannot advance on the strength of skin color alone. This caricature survives unchallenged because whites have stripped themselves of collective racial consciousness. They do not see themselves as a distinct class and do not organize themselves along racial lines. Thus any challenge to affirmative action is a lonely, solitary action, unlike the broadly based class-action suits that minorities frequently bring.[882]

In fact, there has been a deliberate attempt to squelch discussion of the morality of affirmative action and to discredit it even as a subject of debate. Both Senator John Danforth—who is unlikely ever to suffer from affirmative action—and the U.S. Civil Rights Commission have argued that open debate on affirmative action and of other racial policies should be avoided because it is unhealthy and divisive.[883] The Civil Rights Commission is essentially appealing for a gag rule that would shield the absurdities of affirmative action from view.[884] No one seems to find this reprehensible, though it is easy to imagine the uproar that would meet a request by the Pentagon, for example, that the cost of weapons *not* be raised as a campaign issue.

It was only a matter of time before something like the National Association for the Advancement of White People (NAAWP) be established. It is opposed to affirmative action and its slogan is "equal rights, even for white people." Although its name is an imitation of a respected organization that is openly dedicated to the advancement of a particular race, it is consistently attacked as bigoted and racist.

The NAAWP's founder, David Duke, is a former grand wizard of the Knights of the Ku Klux Klan. In February 1989 he came to national attention when he was elected to the Louisiana state legislature. In November 1990 he astonished commentators by winning 60 percent of the white vote in a failed bid for a U.S. Senate seat from Louisiana. A year later, he won 55 percent of the white vote in an unsuccessful campaign for governor of Louisiana. His relative success was all the more remarkable, since not only was the national and local press united against him, even the Democratic and Republican parties joined forces to defeat him. Mr. Duke claimed, in all his campaigns, to have repudiated white supremacy, and he built a platform of lower taxes and abolition of affirmative action. It was a message that many whites thought was long overdue.[885]

Many commentators linked Mr. Duke's appeal to opposition by Republican presidents to affirmative action and other special treatment for blacks. Campus officials have likewise attributed the formation of white student unions to Republican policies.[886]

These people are dead wrong. Legitimate white resentment against special treatment for blacks would be far *greater* if Presidents Ronald Reagan and George Bush had preached affirmative action and pushed it ever farther into people's lives. There would probably be a dozen David Dukes in office by now if they had. Eighty percent of whites think that race-based privileges are just plain wrong,[887] and it should be no surprise if they vote for men who promise to do away with them.

In the same election season that saw Mr. Duke's failed bid to become governor of Louisiana, the race in a different state went to a man who was saying almost exactly the same things as Mr. Duke. Kirk Fordice, a passionate opponent of affirmative action, glided into the Mississippi governor's mansion on the back of overwhelming white support.[888] If Mr. Duke had never worn a Nazi armband or a Klan hood, he might well have become governor as well.

White racial solidarity, the very thing that America has been doing its best to eliminate, was always a likely consequence of black racial solidarity. Affirmative action made it inevitable. White consciousness is still an insignificant movement, but the best way to make it grow would be to expand affirmative action. To call vocal white opposition to affirmative action "racism," as so many do, is either perversity or deliberate blindness.

The Asymmetry of Daily Life

Black solidarity is so taken for granted in America that almost no one ever points out that what is entirely acceptable for blacks would be considered hopelessly racist if done by whites. Brigette Rouson is a lobbyist for the American Newspaper Publishers Association, and she lives in Washington, D.C. At one time she lived in the Virginia suburbs, but moved back to the capital. One of her reasons: "I really have a commitment to D.C. I really love the fact that the local government is run by African-Americans."[889] Such a comment is considered perfectly normal; yet any white woman who moved from Washington to a white suburb because she liked being governed by white people would be considered a racist.

One black writer says that he has a friend who speaks of "white folks overload," or excessive exposure to white people. This person chose a home in a black neighborhood as a refuge.[890] If the corresponding sentiment were expressed by whites it would, of course, be called racism.

There are eight nationally recognized black fraternities and sororities. Their members make no bones about preferring the company of blacks. "I'm more comfortable in a black fraternity," says a typical member.[891] Blacks demand admission to any organization established by whites but see no contradiction in setting up their own, racially exclusive organizations. What is more, while decrying color consciousness in society at large, there are even black fraternities that judge their members according to the lightness or darkness of their skin.[892]

There are other forms of perfectly respectable black consciousness whose counterparts among whites would be considered sure signs of bigotry. Kwanzaa is a seven-day holiday that was invented in 1966 by a black professor as a direct competitor with Christmas. It is an eclectic borrowing of bits and pieces from African harvest festivals, liberally spiced with East African Swahili words. It even includes a black equivalent of Santa Claus. The increasing numbers of middle-class blacks who celebrate Kwanzaa[893] have no connection with any of this other than race. Most American blacks were from West Africa and never had ancestors who spoke Swahili.

Every year the NAACP hosts a gala evening at which it makes Image Awards. This is a kind of separate, black Oscar night at which the black organization honors entertainers, shows, and films that boost the image of blacks.[894] There could never be an equivalent ceremony for whites, even though blacks participate as full equals in the Oscar ceremonies.

George C. Fraser has founded a line of reference books that he calls *SuccessGuide.* They list organizations, entrepreneurs, professionals, charities—all black. Different volumes cover different cities, and they make it easy for blacks to do business and make connections with other blacks. *SuccessGuide* was licensed to seven cities in 1991, and Mr. Fraser expected to add more cities in coming years.[895] Whites are supposed to be making a point of seeking out blacks with whom to do business; blacks are entirely candid about wishing to do business with each other.

In book publishing, the shift toward the explicitly black is even clearer. New publishers with names like Black Classic Press, Just Us Books, and Black Butterfly have no reservations about establishing exclusive racial identities. There is now an African-American Publishers and Booksellers Association, and a regularly published list of black best-sellers, called Blackboard. In the past decade, the number of bookstores specializing in black books has grown from a few dozen to more than two hundred. There is even a chain of bookstores called Pyramid that carries only black-related titles.[896]

One of the main areas of growth has been children's books for blacks—by blacks and about blacks. Titles such as *Jamal's Busy Day* and *Afro-Bets Book of Black Heroes from A to Z* do the very thing that books for white children are now forbidden to do: paint all the characters one color. The all-white world of Dick and Jane went out of print twenty years ago, and now scarcely a new title for white children comes out without friendly Hispanic neighbors and black authority figures.

Many blacks are not interested in friendly Hispanic neighbors or white authority figures. They want stories about black people, set in black neighborhoods, and they do not want to have to look through shelves of carefully integrated books to find them. One seller of books for blacks says, "People of color want these books separated out [for display in stores] because they are looking for something very specific."[897]

American society takes these many expressions of an explicitly racial identity entirely in stride. As white society makes every effort to open itself to blacks—sometimes painfully, sometimes reluctantly—the boundaries drawn by the black racial identity become ever clearer. These boundaries are porous to blacks but impermeable to whites. Blacks glide from a world of black identity into integrated society and back again as they choose; the black identity is firmly closed to whites, who are, at the same time, forbidden to establish an explicitly racial identity of their own.

The world of black identity can be demanding, and those who set its standards may mete out harsh punishment to those who dissent. As we saw earlier, the black assistant secretary of education, Michael Williams, who criticized race-exclusive scholarships, was threatened with expulsion from black society and has since been ostracized by black leaders.[898] Blacks who criticize affirmative action are called names. To some blacks, Justice Clarence Thomas is "a white man in a black skin." Other blacks who simply embrace the hardworking values of American society may be called Afropeans, Afrosaxons, or Incognegros.[899]

At the 1990 convention of the National Association of Black Journalists, there was a workshop called "What's Black, Who's Black, What's Not." Roger Wilkins, who is a professor at George Mason University, puts the issue very clearly: "[T]here is some political and intellectual behavior in which you engage that keeps you from being a black person."[900] It is enormously significant that blacks are saying such things, and it demonstrates the extent to which race, for some, determines virtually everything. It is difficult to imagine a white intellectual talking about behavior that disqualifies a person from whiteness.

Congressman Gary Franks, who represents a district that is 96 percent white, reports that when he first attended a meeting of the Congressional Black Caucus, the general view was that he was "not really black."[901] Julius Lester of the University of Massachusetts writes about the pressure on black students to unite along racial lines against "that amorphous white 'they'. . . ." He describes the code that requires that blacks have only black friends, sit at black tables in the dining halls, and always close ranks if criticized by whites. "Thinking black took precedence over thinking intelligently," he writes.[902]

Many black dissenters are understandably bitter. Professor Lester was asked by colleagues to leave the African-American Studies Department after he criticized the black novelist James Baldwin. He finds the rigidity of the orthodox black identity intolerable. As he put it to a newspaper reporter, "Having been involved in the civil rights movement, I didn't fight against whites trying to limit and define me to turn around and have blacks try to limit and define me."[903] When Howard University tried to make its curriculum more Afrocentric, not all the blacks on the faculty thought this was a good idea. However, according to the *Washington Post*, they kept silent because they "feared retribution from peers, students, or administrators."[904]

Casualties of Black Consciousness

The solidarity that blacks feel for each other can go to entirely inappropriate lengths. In May 1992, a rap singer named Sister Souljah was quoted in a newspaper interview as saying, "if black people kill black people every day, why not have a week and kill white people?" She also observed that there might be some good white people, but she had never met one. Her remarks reflected not uncommon attitudes among blacks, which have been encouraged by constant media portrayals of whites as racists. Her views caused no stir until they attracted the attention of Democratic presidential candidate, Bill Clinton.

The month after Sister Souljah's interview appeared, Mr. Clinton gave an address at a conference held by Jesse Jackson's political organization, the Rainbow Coalition. The group is ostensibly devoted to racial harmony, and Mr. Clinton questioned the wisdom of inviting Sister Souljah to speak at the conference. Mr. Jackson reacted by all but accusing Mr. Clinton of racism. He claimed that Mr. Clinton had "exposed a character flaw" and demanded that the Democratic candidate apologize to Sister Souljah.

Congressman Charles Rangel of Manhattan called Mr. Clinton's behavior "insulting" and several other members of the Congressional Black Caucus sided with the rap singer. Bryant Gumbel, co-anchor of NBC's *Today* show accused Mr. Clinton of "trying to appeal to white voters at the expense of African-American voters."[905]

It was not especially surprising that a rap singer should urge blacks to kill whites. It was far more significant that black leaders and spokesmen should defend her and try to explain away her anti-white animus.

There was more misplaced black solidarity the same year when black former heavyweight boxing champion Mike Tyson was convicted of raping a contestant in a black beauty pageant. A common reaction among blacks was that after having done away with Martin Luther King, Malcolm X, and other "strong black men," the government had turned on Mike Tyson. Far sadder than this was the reaction among black clergy. Many insisted that Mr. Tyson was an important "role model" for young blacks and should therefore not be jailed.

Ministers in Indianapolis gathered ten thousand signatures from local churchgoers asking for clemency. "We ask the court," said the petition, "to consider that Mr. Tyson is one of a very few in number of modern-day African-American heroes."[906] Surely black ministers can think of better role models than a street-fighting thug and convicted rapist.

Black consciousness has other regrettable consequences. There are many black but hardly any white children available for adoption. Plenty of childless white couples would be happy to adopt a black child, but this is almost always prohibited because blacks insist that white families cannot give black children the proper racial identity. A professor of social work at Howard University has even advocated the reestablishment of orphanages[907] for the thousands of children whom blacks won't adopt, but whom whites would adopt if they could.[908]

Many frustrated whites have gone overseas to adopt Hispanic and Asian children. Some whites have been permitted to adopt black children only after submitting to a court order that they seek education in black culture.[909]

The plight of San Francisco's black children is typical. The city's Department of Social Services has scores of abandoned and court-protected babies for whom it cannot find black foster parents. Some have been sent "temporarily" to white families, where they may stay for several years. Many of the families have come to love their black foster children and have applied to adopt them. Although there is plenty of research to show that transracial adoption does no harm to a black child's identity,[910] San Francisco does not permit whites to adopt blacks.

Instead, parents must attend Black Adoption Fairs, where they display their foster children to prospective parents of the correct race. Many of the black children are terrified of leaving the only homes they have known. Many are forced to leave anyway, though a few whites have proven in court that snatching a child away from the only parents it has ever known would cause psychological damage. The Department of Social Services has permitted a few adoptions, but a black employee of the department complains, "We're losing a generation of children not only to crack but to white families."[911] One wonders which he thinks is worse.

In Detroit, black babies who have been abandoned by their mothers may be kept in hospitals for $365 a day rather than be given to white foster parents at a cost of $10 a day. In that city, a single, black woman on welfare with four of her own children is more likely to be given a black baby for adoption than a married white couple.[912] Who is more likely to give the child a better start in life? It is hard to see rules against transracial adoption as anything but a capitulation to black activist demands that are based

---

[908] One black adoption official explains that it is biased adoption standards that account for the excess of black babies. "Adoption is white-middle-class-oriented," he says; "it was never created with black people in mind." Mackenzie Carpenter, "Adoptions Across Racial Lines Can Cost Cultural Identity," *Milwaukee Post Gazette* (September 15, 1990).

purely on separatist consciousness rather than on an interest in the welfare of blacks.

In charitable giving as well, black solidarity gives rise to a double standard. Most black giving goes to explicitly racial organizations: the Black United Fund, Associated Black Charities, the NAACP, the National Urban League,[913] and the United Negro College Fund. There are no equivalent white organizations; a specifically white charity could probably not get tax-exempt status. Moreover, many broad-based charities make a strong effort to help blacks. Even the United Negro College Fund, for example, is heavily dependent on white contributors.[914]

Double Standards at the University

Of the thousands of colleges and universities in this country, only the black colleges receive grants of federal money for operating expenses. Although other colleges do contract research and other services for which they receive government money, the 107 black colleges come under what is called the White House Initiative on Historically Black Colleges, which requires the twenty-seven major federal agencies and departments to support black institutions with special grants and loans. In 1990, black colleges got more than $800 million in federal aid.[915]

Howard University gets the most of this federal money—more than $1.5 billion over the past ten years, or about two thirds of its annual academic budget. This gives Howard one of the highest per-student expenditures in the country but hardly the best scholarship. Waste and mismanagement have been so bad that some of Howard's schools and colleges have been threatened with disaccreditation.[916] A recent internal report suggested that the entire

[913] In 1985 the Urban League's receipts were $23,573,000 and the NAACP's were $7,686,000. Today the NAACP's primary program is its "Fair Share" program, which threatens boycotts of organizations that, in its opinion, do not have enough black employees or use enough black-owned contractors. National Research Council, *A Common Destiny, Blacks and American Society* (Washington, D.C.: National Academy Press, 1989), p. 186. Peter Applebome, "New Agendas Face Civil-Rights Drive," *The New York Times* (April 2, 1990).

tenured faculty at the medical school be asked to take early retirement and recommended that five other schools be shut down or consolidated.[917]

When they go to largely white universities, many blacks gravitate toward black student newspapers, with names such as *Black Ink* (University of North Carolina); *Black World* (State University of New York at Stony Brook); or, of all things, *The Black Explosion* (University of Maryland). Many black papers contain puerile, antiwhite sentiments of the sort that would never be permitted if expressed by whites about blacks. Obviously there is no such thing as a "white" student newspaper, even on campuses where whites are a minority.

At the same time, it is common to find racially exclusive student organizations for nearly every conceivable different group—law students, architects, homosexuals, history majors, etc. At many universities it has become difficult to keep track of all the student groups that have the words "black" or "African-American" in their names.[918] As we saw above, it is exceedingly difficult to get permission to form a white group of any kind.

At U.C. Berkeley, there are certain floors in the library where whites do not feel welcome. The university guarantees on-campus housing for blacks but not for whites. At both Harvard and Yale, there are all-black fraternities.[919] At the University of Illinois, blacks hold a separate, informal commencement ceremony, with their own speakers.[920]

Likewise, Vassar has recognized a breakaway Black Commencement Committee that plans graduation activities appropriate for blacks. Blacks had complained that the senior class activities did not meet their social and cultural needs.[921] Dartmouth also allows separate graduation ceremonies for minorities, as does Northern Illinois University. Even high schools may have separate ceremonies. In 1991, black and white students at Chicago's Brother Rice School held separate senior proms.[922]

The University of Pennsylvania pays for a special black yearbook, even though blacks are only 6 percent of the student body. California State University at Sacramento has formally recognized the separatist nature of minority aspirations by establishing a "college within a college," just for blacks.[923]

These are double standards of the starkest kind. As one black educator complains, "Administrators would never give white students a racial theme house where they could be 'more comfortable with people of their own kind,' yet more and more universities are doing this for black students, thus fostering a kind of voluntary segregation."[924]

Of course, whites may not have the same need to stick together. As one college professor puts it:

Those [blacks] who are not good students, but have the same advantages as those who are, want to protect their position but are haunted by the sense of not deserving it. This gives them a powerful incentive to avoid close associations with whites, who might be better qualified than they are and who might be looking down on them. Better to stick together, so these subtle but painful difficulties will not arise.[925]

The same author adds: "Affirmative action (quotas), at least in universities, is the source of what I fear is a long-term deterioration of the relations between the races in America."[926]

Colleges that are largely black are under no pressure at all to "celebrate diversity," as largely white institutions are straining to do. Medgar Evers College in Brooklyn has a student body that is approximately 95 percent black. Its administrators endorse Afrocentrism and do not hesitate to promote the college as a black institution. Nearly all conferences, special observances, and arts performances have unabashedly black themes.[927] There is no university in America that is so actively and explicitly white, nor could there be.

As we have seen, universities—largely white universities, at any rate—have begun to restrict free speech, for fear that it might offend minorities. These restrictions are applied unequally. At the University of California at Los Angeles (UCLA) there was a campus newspaper comic strip about a rooster that was attending the university. When a character in the strip asked how he had been admitted, the rooster replied, "affirmative action." The editor of the paper was promptly suspended for racial insensitivity. However, when a UCLA minority student newspaper said that Europeans "do not possess the qualities of rational thought, generosity and magnanimity," nothing happened.[928]

At the University of Wisconsin at Parkside, a white was suspended for addressing a black as "Shaka Zulu," the name of an African tribal ruler,[929] but when three white students complained of being called "rednecks," they were told that the word was not on the forbidden list and that no offense could be taken.[930]

Campus speaking programs likewise hew to double standards. Steven Cokely of Chicago has made something of a name for himself by claiming that Jewish doctors inject black babies with the AIDS virus. In 1991 he was a guest of a black student group at the University of Michigan.[931] It is unlikely that a Klansman would have been permitted to speak.

In January of the same year, Minister Dr. Khalid Abdul Muhammad of the Nation of Islam gave a talk at Columbia University sponsored by the Black Students Organization. He spoke of "Columbia Jewniversity" and "Jew York City" and argued that the blacks who attacked the Central Park jogger were in jail because of a "no-good, low-down, nasty white woman." He said that the government had killed Malcolm X and Martin Luther King, and that blacks were the fathers of civilization. Whites, on the other hand, had produced nothing but "murder, bloodshed, destruction, misery, slavery, colonialism, racism, sexism, Zionism, and all forms of madness." Minister Khalid's visit was paid for out of the university's mandatory student activities fee, and his remarks were reportedly met with great enthusiasm.[932] His speech was certainly a tour de force exercise of free speech, but it is difficult to imagine a neo-Nazi ever being allowed to address a Columbia audience, much less as part of campus-funded activities.

Some college officials have tried to justify speech double standards by distinguishing the speech of "insiders" from that of "outsiders." White males are "insiders" and must govern their tongues. Everyone else is an "outsider" and need not exercise the same care.[933] Professor Charles Lawrence of Stanford argues that speech codes should protect only members of "historical victim groups"—that is, everyone but white males.[934]

California's public grade schools have quietly instituted a different double standard: no IQ tests for black children. Some years ago, activists sued the school system because blacks were three times more likely to be in remedial classes than anyone else. IQ tests helped teachers decide whom to put in those classes, but blacks claimed the tests were culturally biased. After years of fighting the case, the school district gave up and exempted blacks from the tests.[935]

A double standard was boldly displayed on the bulletin board of Balboa High School in San Francisco in March 1990. An assistant principal posted the following notice: "Essay Contest: African-American students who earned a D, F, or Incomplete on the final report for the fall semester or on the first report of the spring semester are eligible to enter an essay contest. The topic is 'What I would Do with a Million Dollars.' . . . The first prize will be a $100 U.S. savings bond."[936] One wonders, first, why only blacks could enter the contest and, second, whether it is wise to reward poor schoolwork with a chance to win $100.

The latest educational double standard—promoted almost exclusively by blacks—is that the public schools should be resegregated. Black boys, it is said, will be better off if they are taught in schools that are segregated by both race and sex, and if their educations are centered on Africa. Separatist schools of this kind have been promoted in New York, Milwaukee, Detroit, and Baltimore, and have even won the endorsement of President George Bush and Mayor David Dinkins of New York.[937] By 1991, several cities had made all the preparations for such "African Immersion" schools, only to be forbidden by courts from excluding girls and students of other races.[938]

Detroit, in particular, had gone full speed ahead. It had given several schools new names—Malcolm X Academy, Marcus Garvey Academy, Paul Robeson Academy—and established a curriculum that would make Africa the center of nearly every subject.

Nearly two thirds of Detroit's black boys fail to graduate from high school, twice the rate for black girls. In some neighborhoods, 70 to 80 percent of schoolchildren are reared by single mothers, so the thinking was that all-male schools with male teachers would give black boys a better start on education.[939] When a court ruled that separate public schools for boys would discriminate against girls, three hundred Detroit protesters gathered in front of Detroit's Federal Building to complain that the ruling was "racist." Since Detroit public schools are virtually all-black, racial segregation was not even an issue.[940]

Because of court orders, what were to be Detroit's all-male schools have accepted a handful of girls.[941] This does not change the Afrocentric character of their curricula, which may be academically dubious. Pat Browne, a black woman who is in charge of multicultural education for the Indianapolis school system, tells high-school students that Africans had sailed to America "two thousand years before anyone had ever heard of Columbus."[942]

Claims like this are the mainstay of the model Afrocentric program that was developed for the Portland, Oregon, schools and is now being introduced in Pittsburgh, Atlanta, and Washington, D.C., as well as Indianapolis. The underlying theme is that every cultural advance of any worth was the work of Africans but that non-Africans have stolen the glory. "Eurocentric" history credits the Greeks with achievements that are due to the Egyptians who are claimed to be black. Even mathematics can be made African. As the principal of what had become Malcolm X Academy in Detroit explains, "My approach is, don't turn in a lesson plan in math unless you show the pyramids and how black people were involved."[943]

Basir Mchawi, who was hired by a New York City school district to produce an "Africa-centered" curriculum, had little to say about biology in his proposal, but what he did say was out of the ordinary: "Attention will be given to great biological scientists from the African world, such as Imhotep, Charles Drew, and Daniel Hale Williams." Likewise, students would be taught about the effects of "certain behaviors on their bodies," such as living on potato chips and Pepsi during pregnancy, and smoking crack cocaine.[944]

Afrocentrists are eager to teach young black Americans hieroglyphics, Egyptian cleansing rituals, and numerology—not things that employers are likely to care very much about. Wade Nobles, who runs the Manhood Development and Training Program for black high-school students in Oakland, explains the reasons for this approach: "When we educate a black man, we're not educating him for a job; we're educating him for eternity."[945]

That this folly should have gotten as far as it has is due, in part, to the timidity of whites. When John Leo of *U.S. News & World Report* telephoned seven different Egyptologists to ask whether the ancient Egyptians were black, every one told him they were not, but *none would agree to be quoted.* As one explained, the subject is "politically too hot" to be talked about openly.[946]

Since even some experts dare not say what everyone knows to be true, falsehoods circulate freely. If radical black educators have their way, black children will be hauled off by themselves to be taught nonsense rather than the knowledge necessary to become productive citizens. Any educators who proposed segregated schools in which white children were taught that Hammurabi and Confucius were white would be treated like the cranks they would clearly be.

The only reason Afrocentric teaching has gotten the attention it has is because it is making such headway in public schools. There are many private, all-black schools that have been teaching an African, even separatist curriculum for years. Every morning, the students of Shule Mandela Academy in East Palo Alto, California, pledge to "think black, act black, speak black, buy black, pray black, love black, and live black."[947] At Visions for Children in a Cleveland suburb, the Fourth of July is not a holiday but Emancipation Proclamation day is. Halloween has been replaced by Africa Day. In many Afrocentric schools, children recite a Pledge to African People rather than the Pledge of Allegiance. There are now scores of black, Afrocentric schools all across the country, with names like Nyerere Education Institute, Afrikan People's Action School, and Timbuktu Academy.[948]

Whites cannot, by law, set up all-white schools. As it is, they are criticized if they take their children out of integrated public schools and send them to private schools that are largely white. None of these schools teaches a deliberate racial consciousness the way many black private schools do. Blacks, on the other hand, are increasingly demanding that *publicly funded* schools teach black racialism—with only a murmur of criticism from whites.

The very idea of Afrocentric education marks an important shift in the way black academic difficulties are to be explained. In the 1960s, programs like Head Start were designed to make up for the fact that poor black children did not get early instruction at home that would prepare them for school. They were said to be culturally deprived. This notion has gone completely out of favor. The current thinking is that blacks are not culturally deprived but culturally *different.* This is why no one any longer explains racial differences in test scores by saying that blacks are ill prepared. Instead, it is the tests that are culturally biased (see Chapter Four).

This is an important change in thinking, but it has gone almost completely unnoticed. It marks a rejection by many blacks of the original goals of racial integration. It suggests that blacks are no longer to be seen as striving to enter the mainstream by mastering mainstream abilities. Their race destines them to a separate, African culture. The white mainstream is an alien imposition to which they owe no allegiance. Therefore it makes no more sense to think of blacks as culturally deprived than it would to call Japanese culturally deprived because they do not speak English. Just as their culture requires that Japanese learn *kanji* characters, so African-American culture could require that young blacks learn hieroglyphics and Egyptian cleansing rituals. By hewing to their own culture rather than that of the alien mainstream, blacks will rise to meet their challenges.

Of course, this is a hoax. Japanese-American children do not learn *kanji;* they learn English. If we are to judge by SAT results, they learn it better than white people do. If they wish to learn *kanji* as well, that comes after having mastered the mainstream. The creation of an artificial African-American culture is yet another double standard. Though other ethnic groups do not claim to be victims of the application of "culturally biased" mainstream standards, Afrocentrism would give blacks a ready-made excuse. They would be culturally different, and the standards that everyone else accepts would not apply to them.

Another double standard in education that is beginning to draw attention is something called "black learning style." According to Asa Hillard of Georgia State University, black children are supposed to prefer inference rather than deductive or inductive reasoning. He says they also show "a tendency to approximate space, number, and time, instead of aiming for complete accuracy."[949] Does Mr. Hillard expect teachers to encourage this "difference"?

Dr. Janice Hale-Benson, a black associate professor at Cleveland State University, has a slightly different theory:

[B]lack children require instructions that deal more with people than with symbols or abstractions. . . .
[B]lack pupils need more chances for expressive talking rather than writing. Black children also require more freedom to move around the classroom without being rebuked. . . .[950]

That sort of thing used to be called bad conduct or poor self-control.

Perhaps it was Dr. Hale-Benson's style of instruction that black organizations were demanding when they sued Florida's Orlando County school district for failing to educate black students properly. They have demanded that all black children in grades six through eight be given an individualized education plan, with special monitoring of each student's progress and careful planning for the future. With no apparent concern for the symbolism of their demands, they have sued the school to give all black children the same individualized care it gives to students who are handicapped, retarded, or emotionally disturbed. One element of the special education plans for black students would be consideration of "black English" as the language of instruction.[951]

Black English, the dialect spoken in the ghetto, got official notice in 1979, when a Detroit court ordered schools to recognize it as a "distinct, definable version of English"[952]—this in spite of increasing evidence that constructions such as "twice as less" keep children from understanding the quantitative relations that are essential in science and math.[953] No one claims that the incorrect speech of uneducated whites is a distinct and valid form of English.

A prominent champion of black English was recently welcomed to the U.C. Berkeley English Department. One of June Jordan's slogans is, "If it's wrong in standard English, it's probably right in black English." This, in effect, means that it is all right for blacks to speak incorrectly. When Miss Jordan was hired, she was reported to be looking forward to liberating freshmen students of all races from the tyranny of standard, white English.[954]

Whatever idiom they speak, blacks are often given a polite hearing simply because they are black. Adelaide Sanford, a black member of New York State's educational policy-setting board, has a fanciful explanation for black drug addiction: "The melanin in the skin of children of African descent bonds with narcotics and causes addiction." A white spokesman for the state Education Department smoothed over her remarks by saying, "She was just making the point that there ought to be more research and I don't think anyone disagrees with that view."[955]

In March 1991, the African-American Institute of the State University of New York released a report on racism. It explained that former mayor of New York Ed Koch is a racist, as are journalists at *The New York Times,* New York's *Daily News,* and the *New York Post.* It found that Republicans were "connoisseurs of subtle racism" and that New York's Jews had refused to vote for Mayor David Dinkins only because he was black. This completely undocumented "study" was funded by an annual New York State grant of $500,000 to the African-American Institute.[956]

Rather more comical was an issue that came up in Dallas during an exhibit of Egyptian art called "Ramses the Great." Since few dare tell them otherwise, more and more blacks are insisting that Ramses was a black man. A local activist group insisted that the exhibit's posters so portray him. Dallas authorities dutifully called on Egypt's cultural attaché to settle the question. To his great surprise, Abdel-Latif Aboul-Ela found himself explaining that Ramses was not black but Egyptian. "I wish people would not involve us in this kind of mess," he added.[957] Mr. Aboul-Ela, at least, recognizes a mess when he sees one.

Double standards are perfectly acceptable in the fight for market share. The National Survey of Black Americans reported in 1979–80 that 63 percent of all blacks thought that blacks should patronize black-owned stores whenever possible,[958] and black businessmen make openly racial appeals.

Blacks spend $1 billion a year on special hair products: sheens, straighteners, and the like. Black-owned companies used to have the market to themselves, but white companies have recently moved in strongly. Black manufacturers have put together a trade association and agreed to put the same "Proud Lady" logo on all their products so they can easily be identified. The association has launched a campaign to get blacks to boycott products from white-owned companies, especially Revlon. Lafayette Jones, executive director of the association, says, "We must learn to marshal our dollars like we do our votes." White manufacturers would be fiercely denounced for even hinting about a boycott of black-owned companies. Jesse Jackson supported the Revlon boycott; he says the company is "insensitive" to the needs of blacks. Black customers seem to disagree; Revlon's market share keeps on growing.[959]

Malt liquor is a kind of fortified beer that may contain more than 5 percent alcohol, as opposed to the usual 3.5 percent. It is far more popular among blacks than among whites, but brewers that specifically advertise to blacks are accused of "exploitation." The G. Heilman Brewing Company gave up on its PowerMaster malt after intense criticism from black groups and problems with regulatory agencies. R. J. Reynolds killed its plans to test-market a brand of cigarettes aimed at blacks after it, too, was criticized for "exploitation."[960]

It is understandable that black groups might oppose campaigns that could encourage more blacks to drink and smoke. Nevertheless, malt liquor and cigarettes are legal products, and there is no clear reason why their manufacturers should be allowed to market their products to whites but not to blacks. Even the manufacturers of entirely harmless products may be attacked. Just as Revlon has faced boycotts simply because it has successfully sold hair products to blacks, so Maybelline Company had to face opposition from black activists when it launched a line of cosmetics for blacks. Blacks have more different skin colors that whites, so makeup in a large number of darker shades was an obvious area for cosmetics companies to explore. Corporations larger than Maybelline had stayed out of the market because they were reportedly nervous about charges of "exploitation" if they had tried to get in.[961]

Making things that blacks want to buy hardly seems like exploitation. Perhaps some activists are simply opposed to the idea of white-owned companies making a profit from any product that is oriented toward blacks.

Similar reasoning seems to have been behind Operation PUSH's boycott of the shoe company Nike. PUSH officials claimed that 30 percent of Nike's revenues came from the sale of shoes to blacks (Nike said the correct figure was 14 percent). PUSH therefore demanded that Nike keep 30 percent of its money with black banks, do 30 percent of its business with black suppliers, make 30 percent of its board members black, etc. "We want 30 percent of everything," explained Tyrone Cirder, national executive director of PUSH. PUSH loudly called for a black boycott of Nike products until these demands were met.

In theory, this was no idle threat. In 1984 the brewers of Coors beer promised to invest 8 percent of their profits in the black community after PUSH threatened a national boycott. In 1986 PUSH strong-armed Burger King into an agreement that it would buy 15 percent of its supplies from black-owned businesses and give 35 percent of its charitable contributions to minority causes. However, the PUSH glory days, when it was led by Jesse Jackson, seem to be over. Nike refused to submit to extortion, and months after the boycott was announced, sales appeared to be unaffected.[962]

The South DeKalb Mall near Atlanta practices a different kind of commercial double standard. As the population around it has changed, it has completely revamped its image and now styles itself an "Afrocentric retail center." Its ads specifically and almost exclusively target blacks and feature black models. It has deliberately boosted the number of black store managers; now 85 percent are black. The goods for sale in the mall, from clothes, to books, to recorded music, are all geared toward blacks.[963] There seems to be nothing wrong with turning away from "inclusiveness" and making openly racial appeals to a racially distinct clientele—as long as it is not whites who are doing it.

Racial Politics

Mr. Jackson himself was the beneficiary of double standards for black political candidates. The press treated him with great care and "sensitivity"; it made light of the malodorous record of Operation PUSH and barely whispered the reports that when the young Mr. Jackson worked in a restaurant he would spit in the food he served white people.[964] There would be quick retirement for any white politician who admitted spitting in the food of black customers.

After the presidential election, Mr. Jackson thumbed his nose at the Democrats and backed a third-party candidate in the Chicago mayoral election against the Democrat. Why? The Democrat, Richard M. Daley, was white, and the third-party candidate was black.[965] Any white Democrat who broke ranks for a racial "brother" would probably be drummed out of the party.

When Mr. Daley ran for reelection in 1991, one of his opponents ran under the banner of the Harold Washington Party, which was named after Chicago's first black mayor.[966] The party was essentially formed to field black candidates and appeal to black voters.

Ron Brown, the black chairman of the Democratic Party, braved black criticism to support a white fellow Democrat in Chicago, but others were not so principled. John Johnson, the publisher of *Ebony* and *Jet,* is one of the richest men in Chicago. When word leaked out that he planned to support white candidate Richard M. Daley against his black opponent, the black community rose up against him. Black radio stations, one of which he owns, accused him of treachery and called for a boycott of his magazines. A black editorialized in the *Chicago Tribune* about "the nerve of this man to play around with Daley when he has become a millionaire off black people." Black City Council members called for a black mayor "not as a matter of fairness but of divine right." Despite an estimated net worth of $200 million,[967] Mr.

Johnson was shaken by the furor. He promptly broke with Daley and contributed $25,000 to the black candidate.[968]

Hazel Dukes, chair of the NAACP board of directors and a Dinkins appointee to a high New York City job, routinely supports candidates on the basis of race rather than political principle. Although she is a Democrat, she supports Republicans as long as they are black. "You have to separate the roles," she explains. "When I'm doing NAACP business I'm doing the people's business. That's separate and apart from my politics."[969]

Miss Dukes is simply sticking to another common double standard. When blacks vote overwhelmingly for a black candidate, they are only exercising their civil rights. When whites vote for the white opponent, they are racist. This double standard was in full force during the 1989 election for mayor of New York City. The Democratic primary pitted the incumbent, Ed Koch, against a black challenger, David Dinkins. Mario Cuomo, the Democratic governor of New York, vowed not to play favorites with either of his fellow Democrats in the primary race, but he did express the hope that Mr. Dinkins would get a lot of white votes.[970] In racially tense New York City, that was not considered an endorsement, but an attempt to encourage racial harmony. Mr. Dinkins won, with 97 percent of the black vote and about a third of the white vote.[971]

One wonders, however, why Governor Cuomo's contribution to racial harmony was to urge that whites should vote for a black but not vice versa. He probably knew that it would be futile, even ridiculous, to ask blacks to vote for a white in the name of racial harmony. When blacks vote near-unanimously for a black candidate, "racial harmony" is maintained as long as a good portion of whites vote for him, too. Good race relations are strictly a white responsibility.

Whites were reminded rather forcefully of their one-sided responsibility. Many were uneasy over the fact that twenty years earlier, Mr. Dinkins had failed to file income taxes for four years in a row. The *Village Voice* dismissed this uneasiness as "bullshit" and explained that "anybody voting for Koch because of Dinkins's late tax payments is a dishonest bigot."[972] Blacks, of course, did not have to have any reason to vote for Mr. Dinkins other than the fact that he was black. Did this make them honest bigots?

The same double standard was at work—even endorsed—during the partisan election, which Mr. Dinkins won over a white Republican, Rudolph Giuliani. Neither candidate inspired much enthusiasm, but one white columnist, Ken Auletta, wrote that although he thought Mr. Giuliani the better candidate, he was going to vote for Mr. Dinkins because he was black. His reasoning? "Reject Dinkins, and the 98% of black New Yorkers who polls say are for Dinkins will blame racism. . . . Reject Dinkins and we license haters like Sonny Carson, who proclaim whites will never accept blacks."[973]

Mr. Auletta was voting against his better political judgment so as not even to *appear* racist, and was urging other whites to do the same. And who was this Sonny Carson, to whom Mr. Auletta was afraid of appearing racist? He was a convicted kidnapper who had played a brief, murky role in Mr. Dinkins's campaign. In a well-reported press conference just one month before Mr. Auletta's column appeared, Mr. Carson had announced that rumors of his anti-Semitism were absurd. "I'm antiwhite," he said, "I don't limit my 'anti' to just one group of people."[974] As early as 1964, his Brooklyn chapter of the Congress of Racial Equality (CORE) was not recognized by the national organization because it was considered a front for extortion.[975]

Is it possible to imagine a black columnist urging blacks to vote for a less-qualified white candidate simply because a bloc vote for a black would be just what the KKK was predicting? Whether or not they were taking Mr. Auletta's advice, one third of all white voters joined nearly 100 percent of black voters in giving Mr. Dinkins the election. Since blacks are only 25 percent of the city's population, white support was crucial.[976]

On the very same day, white Virginians likewise demonstrated that they can elect blacks. In the heart of the old Confederacy, 40 percent of the whites and nearly all of the blacks made Douglas Wilder the first elected black governor of a state. Only 15 percent of the electorate is black.[977] Also on the same election day, black candidate Norm Rice won 58 percent of the vote for mayor of Seattle, even though the city is only 10 percent black.[978]

In the elections of November 1990, blacks voted, as usual, by racial bloc, but whites were criticized because not enough of them voted for blacks. Jesse Helms, the conservative white senator from North Carolina, was decried, first of all, for criticizing the enthusiasm of his black opponent, Harvey Gantt, for affirmative action. Mr. Gantt had reason to be enthusiastic about it. He had made a profit of several hundred thousand dollars by taking advantage of FCC preferences for blacks who wish to buy broadcast stations. Rather than operate the station, Mr. Gantt was part of a group that immediately resold it to whites, who paid full tariff. Senator Helms was called a racist for bringing this transaction to the attention of the public. When Senator Helms got 65 percent of the white vote and Mr. Gantt 93 percent of the black vote, it was, of course, the white voters who were accused of letting race dictate their choice.[979]

Mr. Auletta and the journalists who wrote disparagingly of North Carolinians seem not to know it, but whites have been electing blacks to office for a long time. When Mr. Gantt lost his bid to unseat Senator Helms, few people bothered to recall that Mr. Gantt's debut in serious politics was his 1983 election as mayor of Charlotte—a city that is 75 percent white.[980] Fewer still pointed out that in the South, 62 of the region's 215 black mayors represent towns and cities that are *more than* 50 percent white.[981] In the nation as a whole, between 1970 and 1987 the number of black elected officials more than quadrupled, from 1,479 to 6,384.[982]

This could not have happened without white votes. Unlike older black politicians who trumpeted an openly racial message to a monolithic black electorate, a new generation of black "crossover" candidates has discovered that real power lies in representing all the people, not just black people. Kurt Schmoke, the mayor of Baltimore, and Richard Austin, the secretary of state of Michigan, did not get where they are by preaching race; they worked hard for all voters.

Black Kansas City congressman Alan Wheat gets 65 percent of the white vote in his majority-white district.[983] Tom Bradley was elected mayor of Los Angeles in 1973, and has been reelected four times, even though only 17 percent of the city is black.[984] Georgians elected Andrew Young to Congress in 1972—twenty years ago—from a majority-white district.[985] A black Republican, Edward Brooke, was senator from Massachusetts from 1967 to 1979, at a time when blacks were only 3 percent of the state's population.[986]

Even in Mississippi, whites vote for capable blacks. Mike Espy's district is not only rural, it is also the poorest district in the nation's poorest state. The majority of the population is white,[987] and if one expected to find bigotry, this would be the place. How does one reconcile the notion of an America seething with white racism with poor, rural Mississippi whites voting for a black man?

In March 1991, Kansas City, Missouri, elected a black mayor, even though the city is only 26 percent black.[988] In 1991, Denver, Colorado, with a population that is only 12 percent black, elected a black mayor. The president of the board of education and the superintendent of schools are also black. Other mostly white cities that have recently elected black mayors are Roanoke, Virginia; Rockford, Illinois; Dayton, Ohio; and Tallahassee, Florida.[989] Gary Franks, a black Republican, was elected to Congress from Connecticut in 1990. Only 4 percent of the voters in his district are black.[990] Would it be possible for a white to be elected to any office at all in a jurisdiction that was heavily black, much less one that was 96 percent black?

Blacks, themselves, rarely cross racial lines to vote for a white. *Every single* congressional district in the country that has a black majority has a black representative. Also, with the sole exception of Richmond, Virginia, *every* city of over two hundred thousand with a majority-black population has a black mayor.[991] Yet the doctrine of white racism holds that it is white voters who are prejudiced against black candidates and not the other way around.

Many blacks are unwilling to live by the political standards they demand of whites: They expect special favors from black officials but insist that whites serve all the people. A black man, Alex Williams, was elected chief prosecutor of Prince Georges County,

[989] Dirk Johnson, "Denver Elects Mayor as Personal Touch Prevails," *The New York Times* (June 20, 1991). Other cities that have black minorities but have elected black mayors are Cleveland, Oakland, Dayton, Philadelphia, Chicago, Hartford, New Haven, Newport News, and Charlotte. Andrew Hacker, *Two Nations* (New York: Charles Scribner's Sons, 1992), p. 208.

Maryland. He had to win a lot of white support to beat the white incumbent. After his victory, Mr. Williams refused to play godfather to blacks and served the entire county instead. Predictably, blacks who were counting on patronage were disappointed. Tommie Broadwater, a former state senator says, "If whites think he's okay, then we [blacks] have a problem."[992]

All during 1988, the city of Yonkers in New York State was a prominent victim of double standards. It was in the news because of its fierce resistance to court-ordered construction of low-income housing that would attract poor blacks. The white suburbanites claimed that their main concerns were quality of life and property values, but they were repeatedly accused of racism.[993]

No one seemed to recall that in 1970 there was a similar fight against federally subsidized housing in the Long Island town of North Hempstead. Opponents argued that "neighborhood deterioration would take place and quality of life would change."[994] That time there was no hint of racism; the middle-class opponents were black. On at least three different occasions, blacks have brought suit to stop housing projects that were to go up in their neighborhoods.[995]

The Yonkers housing controversy had an unsavory footnote that highlights current racial attitudes. At one open meeting of the Yonkers City Council, Laurie Recht was the only resident to argue in favor of the project. She said that by disobeying the court order, the Council was "doing something illegal, immoral, and unethical," and immediately became a hero in the media. Later, after continued support for the project, she claimed that she had received death threats and that someone had spray-painted a swastika outside her apartment. Miss Recht was promptly granted an Honorary Doctor of Humane Letters degree from the College of New Rochelle, where the president said that people who fight inequity are "far too few in number yet they are deserving of the highest recognition from society." Miss Recht got a standing ovation from faculty and students.

After the degree was awarded, a police investigation discovered that it was Miss Recht herself who recorded the death threats on her answering machine and who probably painted the swastika. The police concluded that her speech at the City Council was designed primarily to call attention to herself. The College of New Rochelle fell for her posturing because it, like everyone else, is prepared to think the worst of white people and to honor those who denounce them.[996]

Typical double standards surrounded the establishment of the Imani Temple, a breakaway group of black Catholics under the leadership of a black priest, George Stallings. Arguing that the Catholic Church was not sufficiently sensitive to the needs of blacks, Rev. Stallings introduced a new kind of service with soul music, shouts from the congregation, and all the elements of a tent revival meeting. Church government reacted by forbidding him to celebrate Mass or administer sacraments, but no one seems to have accused the Imani Temple of racism.[997] Any white priest who started an all-white breakaway church would be mercilessly attacked as racist, even if he left the liturgy scrupulously intact. Rev. Stallings has, of course, called the Catholic Church racist.[998]

In late 1989, a black artist painted a giant picture of Jesse Jackson, but with blond hair, blue eyes, and pink cheeks. Across the bottom were the words "How Ya Like Me Now." The message of this painting was that if Mr. Jackson had been white, he would have been elected president. The city of Washington, D.C., decided to display this artwork publicly. Before three white arts workers could even finish putting it up, a group of black passersby decided that it was an insult to Mr. Jackson. They grabbed a sledgehammer the arts workers had used and destroyed the painting. Some of the attackers shouted that whites had no right to put up such a thing.

This incident and its aftermath were interesting on several counts. The painting was a standing insult to whites, in that it suggested they were so blinded by prejudice that they voted the wrong man into office. Nevertheless, it was blacks who took offense and attacked the painting. They were not prosecuted, pursued, or denounced in any way. A spokesman for Mr. Jackson publicly sympathized with the "pain" that led them to wreck the painting. Of course, if white passersby had understood the message, felt insulted, and torn down the painting, they would have been charged with vandalism, assault, disorderly conduct, and racism. If black workers had been putting it up, and the white vandals had shouted that blacks had no right to put up such a thing, it would have been a national incident.

As it was, the city of Washington decided not to replace the painting but to insult whites anyway. It set up a sign at the same spot explaining the message the painting was meant to convey.[999]

Sometimes blacks drop all pretense and preach the double standard with embarrassing frankness. Recently, a group called the Assembly of American Cultures asked for money from the National Endowment for the Arts. The ironically named "Assembly" deliberately excludes whites. Its representatives pointed out that in thirty years "people of color" will be a majority in America. They said the Endowment had better get ready for the future now, and stop making grants to white people.[1000] As noted earlier, that is exactly what some of our richest foundations plan to do.[1001]

Carolyn Pitts, a black, was the affirmative action officer of the State Insurance Fund of New York. In 1987 she wrote a training manual on affirmative action that explained how racism works: "In the United States at present, only whites can be racists since whites dominate and control the institutions that create and enforce American cultural values." She went on to conclude that "all white individuals in our society are racist," whether or not they are conscious of it.[1002]

This is not an unusual point of view among blacks. Coleman Young, the black mayor of Detroit, says, "I don't consider that blacks are capable of racism."[1003] Harry Allen is "minister of information" for Public Enemy, one of the country's most popular rap groups, with considerable political influence among young blacks. When it was pointed out that his virulent antiwhite statements were racist, he replied, "It's impossible. Only white people can be racist, and I am not white. The only form of racism is white supremacy." He urges that the word "racism" be expunged from the language and be replaced with "white supremacy," since the two are equivalent and the latter is more precise.[1004]

Miss Pitts, Mayor Young, and Mr. Allen certainly reflect what a great many blacks believe. Whether or not whites believe the same thing, many write and act as if they did. That is why they no more than raise an eyebrow when blacks do what would immediately be denounced as racism were they white. In Miami, a black city commissioner explained why he had shelved the nomination of a Harvard-trained candidate for a city job: "He's Hispanic, he's not black."[1005] Scarcely anyone noticed or cared.

Race and Crime

Another obvious double standard governs the way in which the media and the nation react to "hate" crimes. In New York City, during the first month or so of 1992, the double standard was in full swing. On January 6, a fourteen-year-old black boy and his twelve-year-old sister reported that four whites had roughed them up, stolen their lunch money, and shouted "You'll be white today," as they smeared white sneaker polish on the young blacks' faces. The city went into an uproar over the incident. A visibly angry Mayor David Dinkins held a tearful press conference and called the assault "truly heinous." One hundred extra police were sent to patrol the area where the incident took place. A delegation of City Council members, borough presidents, and professional psychologists descended on the junior high school that the young blacks attended, to give comfort and calm fears. There was vast, even national publicity over the incident, and Mayor Dinkins offered a reward for information leading to an arrest. New York State's criminal justice officials raised a call for new laws that would mete out harsher punishment for "hate" crimes.[1006]

Within the same ten-day period, a number of black-on-white crimes took place: A fifteen-year-old and a thirteen-year-old were arrested for the shooting death of a Russian immigrant during a mugging; fifty young Brooklynites went on a rampage in lower Manhattan, slashing people with knives and taking their coats; near Columbia University, nine young blacks—five ten-year-olds, two eleven-year-olds, a fourteen-year-old, and a fifteen-year-old—likewise rampaged through the streets, viciously beating and kicking people. None of these crimes rated more than a brief notice.[1007]

The sneaker-polish attack, however, brought not just media attention but also immediate retaliation. A half-dozen racially motivated beatings, stabbings, and robberies of whites quickly ensued. Retaliation reached a culmination when two black men abducted and raped a fifteen-year-old white girl. None of these crimes, not even the rape, resulted in extra police patrols, nationwide coverage, or schoolwide counseling sessions. Mayor Dinkins did, however, attempt to console the girl's father, and posted a reward for the capture of the rapists.[1008]

The rape had other consequences. Three days later, a black man reported he was beaten by five white men with a pipe, who told him that this was revenge for the rape. High-ranking police officers rushed to his bedside, and Mayor Dinkins immediately issued a statement calling the attack an "absolutely appalling act of bias violence." Fortunately, the very day of the attack, the man confessed that it was a hoax he had perpetrated to get attention from his family.[1009]

What might have happened had he not confessed? The preceding few paragraphs are a good indication. By February, investigators at work on the original sneaker-polish attack had concluded that *it was a fraud.* It was thought that the mother of the two children had staged the incident so she could persuade school authorities to transfer her children to a school in a better neighborhood.[1010] The temptation to claim a bias attack is great, of course, because of the enormous attention and sympathy that blacks can count on receiving as a consequence. Whites are far less likely to make fraudulent claims because relatively little is made of legitimate ones.

By February, New York City was back to its usual ways. A bus carrying sixty six- to twelve-year-old Jewish children came under attack in Brooklyn from a gang of black teenagers. The blacks shouted racial insults, stoned the bus, and smashed its windows. Inside, the children screamed in terror, and some were injured by flying glass. The media and the city largely looked the other way. The contrast to the reaction to the phony sneaker-polish attack was spectacular.[1011]

"Hate" crimes essentially provoke the same reaction that interracial crime of all kinds provokes. As we saw earlier, whereas whites choose black victims for their violent crimes less than 2.5 percent of the time, blacks attack whites more than half the time.

If these numbers were reversed, everyone in America would have heard them often enough to know them by heart. As it is, the true proportions of interracial crime are passed over in squeamish silence. Charles Silberman explains, "Whites of good will have shied away from acknowledging this fact for fear of hurting black sensibilities, and both they and blacks have avoided talking about the problem lest they provide ammunition to bigots."[1012] A nation that is afraid of the truth about itself is in serious trouble.

Even when they learn the statistics on interracial crime, many Americans refuse to impute a racial motive to black criminals. They argue that blacks murder and assault whites to steal from them and that this is reasonable because whites have more money. Mr. Silberman has a different view:

After 350 years of fearing whites, black Americans have discovered that the fear runs the other way, that whites are intimidated by their very presence; it would be hard to overestimate what an extraordinarily liberating force this discovery is. The taboo against expression of antiwhite anger is breaking down, and 350 years of festering hatred has come spilling out.

The expression of anger is turning out to be cumulative rather than cathartic. Instead of being dissipated, the anger appears to be feeding on itself. . . .[1013]

Even if interracial murder could be explained by greed, black rape of white women—many, many times more likely than white rape of black women—cannot. Former Black Panther Eldridge Cleaver once explained why he raped white women: "Rape was an insurrectionary act. It delighted me that I was defying and trampling upon the white man's law, upon his system of values, and that I was defiling his women. . . ."[1014] Mr. Cleaver goes on to quote a poem by LeRoi Jones:

Come up, black dada nihilismus. Rape the white girls. Rape their fathers. Cut the mothers' throats.

I have lived those lines and I know that if I had not been apprehended I would have slit some white throats. There are, of course, many young blacks out there right now who are slitting white throats and raping the white girl. They are not doing this because they read LeRoi Jones' poetry, as some of his critics seem to believe. Rather, LeRoi is expressing the funky facts of life.[1015]

Prisons, where blacks and whites live on close terms, have their own funky facts of life. Rape is one of them. As it is on the outside, the overwhelming majority of interracial rapes are of whites by blacks:

A young offender, particularly a white offender, is likely to be subjected to gang rape his first night in jail. In a number of large cities, jail officials automatically place young whites in protective custody for their own safety. Sometimes the move comes too late; young offenders are often raped in the van transporting men to jail.[1016]

Men who submit to anal sex are called punks while their rapists are called wolves:

[O]ne man's defeat is another's triumph; the ultimate triumph is to destroy another man's manhood—to break his will, defile his body, and make him feel totally (and often permanently) degraded. Indeed, the triumph may be a double one: a wolf may convert a punk into a possession, to be offered to other inmates in exchange for favors of one sort or another. And when the wolf is black and the punk is white (the most frequent arrangement, by far), the wolf's demonstration of power is infinitely sweeter. . . .[1017]

Some whites fight back. Nearly one fifth of all murders in prison are by white rape victims who kill their black tormentors. Others retreat to protective custody, where they may spend as much as twenty-three hours a day.[1018] In one Florida prison, black-on-white rape was so common that white inmates sued the state for failing to prevent it.[1019]

Not even prison authorities are willing to face the ugly truth.

One white inmate describes how the orientation program at Attica prison in New York State skirts the entire subject of rape: "We have lectures on getting mail and sending mail out and getting packages, and what the procedures are on getting a haircut, but nothing on the biggest number one problem in the institution itself. Nothing at all."[1020]

Rape is not the only violence white inmates fear. According to one study, in North Carolina, seventy-seven of every hundred prisoners is assaulted every year. Forty percent of those assaults are interracial, and of these, *80 percent* are black assaults on whites. As one author puts it, "This pattern of victimization is quite common. Indeed, in some institutions, blacks seem to dominate whites totally."[1021] Can it be a mystery why white convicts are much more likely to be depressive or suicidal than black convicts?

If our nation were not so obsessed with white racism or so diligent about excusing blacks, these "funky facts of life" would be a national scandal. Instead, America continues to search for unconscious white racism in the laboratory and submit quietly to outlandish charges of genocide.

One of the most spectacular examples of our racial double standards is the way we treat Africa. Denouncing Pretoria's apartheid government has been one of America's favorite exercises in righteousness, but we hardly notice the far worse abuses of black governments. Even Archbishop Tutu has acknowledged that most Africans were freer under white colonial rule than they are under their own leaders today,[1022] but no white would dare say such a thing.

Probably the most notorious incident in South African history is what is known as the Sharpeville Massacre. In 1960 a few young white policemen, surrounded by an angry black crowd, opened fire and killed sixty-nine people. All students of African history, and many other people as well, know about this incident.

Burundi, on the other hand, is a small African nation of which most Americans have never heard. A 15 percent minority of Tutsi tribesmen dominates the other 85 percent, who are Hutu. Like blacks in South Africa, the Hutu have tried to throw off minority rule. The Tutsi do not take kindly to this. In 1972 the Tutsi army crushed a rebellion and then went on to massacre an astonishing one hundred thousand Hutu. In 1988 the army went on another rampage, after which it admitted having killed five thousand Hutu. Independent witnesses think they may have killed as many as fifty thousand. Most of the dead Hutu were unarmed peasants, killed with modern weapons such as helicopters and machine guns. In the Hutu town of Marangara, Tutsi stopped killing Hutu only when there were no more left to kill.[1023]

Did the media wring its hands over the horrors of tribal violence? Did America impose sanctions against the murderous minority regime of Burundi? Did the Congressional Black Caucus denounce the oppression of its "Hutu brothers"? Did Hollywood stars organize a sit-in at the Burundi embassy? No. Whites must be denounced when they behave like brutes, but there is nothing that can be done about it when blacks do.

When whites kill sixty-nine blacks, we call it the Sharpeville Massacre and make it a symbol of white wickedness. Twelve years later, when blacks murder a hundred thousand people, we do not even have a name for it. Africa, too, is part of our system of white guilt and black innocence.

The Danger of Double Standards

That our double standards can be both so glaring and so little noticed is a sign of America's terrible confusion about race. Americans are hypnotized by the specters of white racism and white guilt. We try to explain every black failing in terms of white guilt— even failings that cannot possibly be explained by it. If we cannot find racist people to denounce, we talk darkly of institutional racism.

We have built up a colossal myth about the power and pervasiveness of white racism. Since there is so much black failure that the myth must explain, we keep up a constant, frantic search for the horrible white sin that causes so much grief. That is why whites give themselves up to such self-flagellation when they find The Real Thing, no matter how marginal or uncharacteristic.

This is why every time some white semi-moron burns a cross he becomes a news celebrity. Such people are inevitably from the dregs of society, and whites denounce them just as earnestly as blacks do. Yet they somehow become symbols of impregnable, monolithic, white racism.

When the Klan marched in Washington, D.C., in the fall of 1990, it had to be protected by 2,000 city police in riot gear, 800 U.S. Capitol police, and 325 U.S. Park police. Eight officers were injured trying to protect 27 very nervous Klansmen from thousands of screaming opponents.[1024]

A look beneath the white sheets of the Ku Klux Klan does not reveal college professors and bank presidents but high-school dropouts and gas station attendants. Is this minuscule band of losers supposed to be capable of oppressing an entire race? Are they the people who set the tone for America? Their sole effect is to increase sympathy for blacks.

If the only thing the myth of monolithic racism did was tar whites, it would not do much harm. But the damage it does blacks is far worse. It tends to exempt them from responsibility, from autonomy, ultimately from America itself. It implies that they can achieve only what white society allows them and no more. It denies their capacity to follow the obvious routes to success that other minorities have taken in America.

The insidious logic of the myth is therefore a huge insult to blacks. Blacks are victims of white society, so must be forgiven. But what about the whites whose alleged racism causes all this horror? Are they not just as much the victims of a society that has taught them to be racist? No. No "root cause" excuses for them. We hold them fully accountable for their abominations. We punish them like responsible men because they are white. We excuse blacks and treat them like children because they are black. What could more clearly suggest the moral inferiority of blacks? What more destructive double standard could a society erect?

Affirmative action is the crowning, debilitating insult. Blacks must be helped at every stage in life, from Head Start to college recruitment, to job quotas, to race-based promotions. How can this help but sap the efforts of even the most hardworking? How can it help but insult real achievements?

Affirmative action also gives whites a genuine grievance. Maybe the generation of judges who turned the Civil Rights Act upside down felt guilty. Maybe they were guilty. But the young white men they are now punishing for the sins of their ancestors are not guilty —though if they object to an unjust system that discriminates against them, they will be pelted with charges of racism.

What if there really were something to the reported rise of racism among white college students? Perhaps eighteen-year-old minds cannot be expected to grasp the high logic that requires that they be punished for sins they did not commit. Perhaps they are confused by all-black fraternities, or do not enjoy finding they are not welcome on certain floors of the library. Perhaps they resent it when they see black classmates get race-based preferences for jobs and college admissions.

American colleges are like parents who reserve all of their love, gifts, and favors for only one of their two children. They profess astonishment when the slighted child takes an occasional swipe at the favorite, and salve the hurt by lavishing even more care on the one they love. What would be stupid and unfair at home is just as stupid and unfair at school. How can anyone be surprised at white student unions?

There may be grim prophecy in the race relations in our prisons. Here, whites are already in the minority that demographers predict for the entire nation. Black prisoners often form groups that are openly hostile to whites. The whites who survive best, who keep their dignity and morale, are the ones who join white solidarity and even white supremacy groups.[1025]

The black leaders of this generation have much to answer for. They have perpetuated the myth that salvation comes only from whites. They have made careers out of shaking down a guilt-ridden society and dispensing the booty as patronage. In Thomas Sowell's words, these are men "whose own employment and visibility depend upon maintaining an adequate flow of injustices. . . ."[1026] Their very livelihoods depend on finding enough white wickedness to denounce.

Benjamin Hooks is an educated man and was executive director of the NAACP. If he can claim, as he did in 1989, that if it were not for racism he would be President of the United States,[1027] how easy must it be for blacks who have ruined their lives to say that if it were not for racism they would have nice houses in the suburbs?

Many whites are just as blameworthy. Their minds are trapped in the language of the past. They thunder against the faintest trace of white racism while they ignore the blatant racial excesses of blacks. They have convinced themselves that blacks cannot get ahead without handouts and special treatment. By exempting blacks from individual responsibility, they treat them as vassals. Somehow they have tricked themselves into thinking that this is noble and compassionate rather than degrading.

The greatest horror of this largely well-intentioned folly is the terrible damage it has done to the very people it was meant to serve. Blacks were freed from slavery over 125 years ago. But the chains that fell from their bodies will never fall from their minds as long as they believe that their destiny lies not in their own hands but in the hands of whites. No people that does not believe itself to be free can ever be free. By telling them that they are not free, America has done blacks a monumental, a criminal disservice. A mind in shackles is as tragic as a body in chains.

7

The Underclass

MERICAN BLACKS FACE TWO DIFFERENT KINDS OF problems—those that are common to the human condition and those that particularly affect blacks. At the same time, there are essentially two black Americas. One, a growing middle class, lives by the norms of the larger society. The other, the underclass, flouts them. No serious analysis can ignore the widening gap between the two.

Black and white alike are beset by woes that no society has ever eliminated. Crime, poverty, imperfect justice, greed, envy—these affect all peoples at all times. T. E. Lawrence's opening sentence in *Seven Pillars of Wisdom* is sadly universal: "Some of the evil in my tale may have been inherent in our circumstances."[1028]

Some people believe that the fundamental circumstances of society can be altered to reduce the evil that may be inherent in them. Others are more willing to accept that even the best human societies harbor irreducible evils. The former view is certainly more appealing, but the latter seems to be borne out by history.

Different conceptions of human nature have driven American social policy at different periods. To the extent that it actually is possible for society or government to attack such things as crime and poverty head on, blacks will be the greatest beneficiaries be-

281

cause they suffer from them the most. Any "program" that eliminated crime or drug addiction would help American race relations more than all the seminars on racism that will ever be given. If, someday, social engineers were to invent an equivalent of the philosophers' stone, whose touch would galvanize the lazy, inspire the irresponsible, and reform the criminal, blacks would rise with everyone else.

However, no matter how reluctant Americans may be to acknowledge this, social problems are not exclusively scientific or political or economic problems. They are largely moral problems, and morals are rarely improved by "programs." Some governments exhort their people to behave morally, but no American politician since John Kennedy has been able to preach to us and be taken seriously. When President Jimmy Carter urged Americans to launch an energy program that was "the moral equivalent of war," America laughed at him.

There is only one exception to America's wholesale rejection of morality as a solution to social problems. There is still one form of moral exhortation that is repeated and insistent, and to which Americans do not react with the yawn or smirk that would otherwise be fashionable. That is the exhortation to "tolerance," especially of blacks.

Judging from the torrent of moral energy that America invests in "tolerance," one would conclude that "intolerance" was the most dangerous problem in America today—and that is precisely the implicit reasoning that governs so much of what is said and written about what obviously *are* dangerous problems. According to this reasoning, if only white "intolerance" of blacks could be eliminated, then the worst of crime, poverty, welfare dependence, illegitimacy, etc., would go away.

Practically no one is any longer in the business of urging Americans to be self-reliant, honest, hardworking, civic-minded, and faithful to their spouses. It is as if "tolerance" is the only virtue that matters, and the rest are quaint, outdated concerns of Boy Scouts and nineteenth-century novelists. There are, of course, a great many things of which a healthy society should be vehemently *intolerant,* yet the massive campaign to make Americans tolerant of other people has merged imperceptibly into one to make them tolerant of intolerable behavior.

At the same time, the moral fabric of our society is woven at a level not easily accessible to government—primarily in the home, but also in the minds of novelists, clergymen, scriptwriters, journalists, teachers, advertisers, politicians, and songwriters. Government can shuffle resources from rich to poor, from productive to unproductive, but this does not strengthen the moral fabric.

There are, nevertheless, obstacles that blacks face in America because of race. Most have little to do with the common notion of racism—that is, efforts by whites to hold them down. The two most important obstacles are both internal. The first is the conviction that whites, not blacks, are responsible for what happens to them. The second is the belief that blacks need and deserve special treatment to succeed. To the extent that any black of whatever class believes these things, he is a prisoner of his own illusions.

Who, then, is responsible for what happens to blacks? Our nation has invested more moral energy in improving race relations than in anything else since the fight to win the Second World War. This process has had an undeniable effect on white Americans. The vast majority profess to believe in equal treatment for all races, and in their daily lives they generally act in accordance with that belief. They may not live in mixed neighborhoods and they may not even particularly like blacks, but they certainly do not oppress or hinder them. It will never be possible entirely to eliminate antiblack sentiment and behavior, but the prevailing mood in this nation does not countenance overt white racism. Today's America is vastly different from that of forty or even twenty years ago. It would be hard to find a national majority anywhere in the world that is as rigorously, even agonizingly "fair" in its treatment of a national minority as white Americans are in their treatment of blacks.

White racism persists, and wherever it does it should be combated. However, if this book has shown anything, it is that there are more irresponsible, unfounded charges of racism than there are serious acts of racism. The reasoning behind these charges is the simpleminded syllogism that governs virtually all thinking on black/white relations in America today: Blacks who fail do so be-

cause of white racism. Some blacks are failing very badly. Therefore there must be an enormous amount of white racism. Those
blacks will not stop failing until white racism is eliminated, and
whites must therefore transform themselves before blacks can be
expected to succeed. This is to misdiagnose the problem, and without correct diagnosis there can be no cure.

This misdiagnosis is so widely accepted that white Americans
listen politely to the most improbable charges of racism and accept any that seem plausible. Blacks, of course, seize upon this
false syllogism because it is so difficult to admit fault. To admit
fault is to accept the need for work, effort, action, and responsibility. It is far easier to blame someone else for one's own failings,
and much more satisfying. Blacks who preach the gospel of white
guilt are vastly encouraged when they find that so many whites
embrace it.

The Minority Black View

Only a few blacks have publicly attacked this dangerous and
patronizing view. Joe Clark, the black high-school principal who
won notoriety by disciplining his students with bullhorn and baseball bat, put it this way:

> The white liberal philosophy cheats them [blacks and His-
> panics] by making allowances for their deviant behavior, as
> though normal behavior patterns were alien to them. It fos-
> ters a concept of indolence that keeps them on welfare,
> keeps them emotionally, academically, and economically dis-
> enfranchised. It's the antithesis of what this country is about:
> The door of opportunity is open to all. But you have to be
> willing to work hard.[1029]

Newspaper columnist William Raspberry was saying the same
thing when he denounced the excuse-making mentality as "a false
focus on race when we ought to be looking at effort. It communi-
cates to our children the crippling notion that their fate is not in

their own hands but in the hands of people who don't love them."[1030] Mr. Raspberry is right. The denial of black responsibility is nothing short of crippling. Why should poor blacks try to help themselves when, as they are constantly told, whites are responsible for everything that goes wrong?

Walter Williams, another black, noting that many major cities have black mayors, black city councilmen, black school teachers, and black principals, says, "It is high time that responsible black people stop worrying about what whites are doing to blacks and begin to focus on what blacks are doing to blacks."[1031]

Shelby Steele, also black, has put his finger on why it is so hard for blacks to do just that:

> If conditions have worsened for most of us as racism has receded, then much of the problem must be of our own making. But to fully admit this would cause us to lose the innocence we derive from our victimization. And we would jeopardize the entitlement we've always had to challenge society.[1032]

In other words, it is by trading on their status as victims of white racism that blacks have intimidated whites and won favors. With responsibility comes the end of innocence and the end of easy favors.

Mr. Steele goes on:

> So we have a hidden investment in victimization and poverty. These distressing conditions have been the source of our only real power, and there is an unconscious sort of gravitation toward them, a complaining celebration of them. One sees evidence of this in the near happiness with which certain black leaders recount the horror of Howard Beach and other recent (and I think overcelebrated) instances of racial tension.[1033]

Since poverty, violence, and ignorance are supposed to be indisputable evidence of victimization, and since it is through victimization that "civil rights" leaders wield power, their continued influence depends on the continued misery of their people.

Glen Loury of Harvard, who is also black, points out that this preoccupation with victimization means that black success becomes almost a guilty secret. "It leads to a situation where the celebration among blacks of individual success and of the personal traits associated with it comes to be seen, quite literally, as a betrayal of the black poor, because such celebration undermines the legitimacy of what has proven to be their most valuable political asset—their supposed helplessness."[1034] By the logic of helplessness, blacks who succeed are not an inspiration but a reproach.

Roy Innis, chairman of the Congress of Racial Equality (CORE), denounces the many black leaders who still blame whites for all the woes that befall blacks:

> With few exceptions, these leaders have failed to recognize or do not accept that the major impediments to black progress have been removed. . . .
> The major remaining impediments to the progress of black people today are the evils indigenous to the black community. This is the new civil-rights battleground. . . .[1035]

With the exception of Mr. Innis, none of these men who consistently preach black self-reliance—Mr. Clark, Mr. Raspberry, Mr. Williams, Mr. Steele, Mr. Loury, not to mention Thomas Sowell—is the leader of a black organization. None is a politician. All have been denounced by black leaders and politicians because what they say cuts straight to the heart of the matter.

The power of the conventional black view was evident in the visceral attacks by the black establishment against the nomination of Clarence Thomas to the Supreme Court. Some commentators noted that black opponents were particularly vicious in their remarks about the nominee precisely because he was black; they would have been much more accommodating toward a white man.[1036] Judge Thomas challenged the monopoly of a relentlessly affirmative-action view of America, a monopoly so strong that one dissenting black calls it "intellectual fascism."[1037]

If the conventional view among blacks verges on "intellectual fascism," its effect is perhaps even stronger among whites. Is there even one prominent white person in the entire country who calls consistently for black self-reliance? Whites may be delighted when a few brave blacks argue that white people are not the root of all evil, but they dare not say so themselves. Whites who do speak out on black/white relations must mouth the old, patronizing, guilt-ridden lines about white wrongdoing.

Therefore, the first step in halting black decline is to throw out the deadly equation of Black Failure = White Guilt. Black shakedown artists and white guiltmongers alike must be exposed as the dangerous frauds they are. The misspent energy that goes into constant charges of white racism must be redirected as exhortations to black responsibility. As millions of successful blacks have shown, opportunities are abundant in America for anyone who will take responsibility for his own life. The millions who have not yet succeeded must not shirk that responsibility.

A change of this kind could be spearheaded only by private effort. It would be a moral change, not an economic or political change. It is the public weavers of the nation's moral fabric who must cleanse their minds of the deadly equation. What they say and think matters a great deal, and until that changes, we will not make progress. The most important moral development goes on in the home, but every home is swayed by the moral climate that surrounds it.

The Underclass

Previous chapters have made the case that to blame whites for what happens to blacks is to treat blacks less well than they deserve. It is to suggest that they are incapable of responsible behavior. This is certainly true of the many hardworking blacks who seized the opportunities that arose as racial barriers fell. Unfortunately, it is not true of all blacks—or of all whites, for that matter. For many in the underclass, an appeal to self-reliance will not be enough. America now has a growing segment of the population that has been so thoroughly exempted from responsibility that it is probably impervious even to the strongest exhortations. Who is the underclass, and what must be done for it?

It is worth noting that the term "underclass" did not even exist before the civil rights movement. There were poor people, of course, and criminals, but they were the *lower* class. The implication was that although they were at the bottom, they were on the same social scale as everyone else. By contrast, the underclass is a group that has veered so far from conventional, responsible behavior that its members seem to have dropped completely off the social scales that measure class. Definitions of the underclass are vague, but it is a class among whom crime, poverty, ignorance, and illegitimacy all combine to produce more of the same. Its members seem to flout the conventions to which all other classes show at least nominal allegiance, and to live outside the bounds of middle-class morality.

The emergence of this new class in the wake of the civil rights movement and the social programs of the same period was not a coincidence. A strong case can be made for the view that the underclass is a direct consequence of the best of intentions gone tragically wrong.

Estimates of the size of the underclass range from two million to eight million.[1038] Another estimate is that it is about 15 percent of the black population. Many observers believe that the number is growing rapidly, not only in absolute terms but also as a proportion of the black population. According to one estimate, the underclass tripled in size between 1970 and 1980.[1039]

This is not necessarily because middle-class blacks are tumbling into it. Birth rates for middle-class blacks have dropped close to the figure for whites, but birth rates for poor blacks are still high. In a recent twelve-month period, married black women with incomes over $15,000 had fewer than 165,000 babies, while single black women with incomes of less than $10,000 (counting welfare) had 177,000 babies.[1040] On average, a poor black woman has twice

[1039] Spencer Rich, "The Underclass: Beyond Just Poor," *Washington Post* (June 26, 1989), p. A9. For a well-researched dissent from the view that the underclass is growing rapidly, see Christopher Jencks, "Is the Underclass Growing?," Christopher Jencks, Ed., *The Urban Underclass* (Washington, D.C.: The Brookings Institution, 1990), pp. 28–100. Mr. Jencks argues that the underclass may be too vague a concept to be useful and that by several measures it appears not to be growing. He offers no estimate of its size.

as many children as a black woman with a household income of more than $35,000.[1041]

No one knows exactly what made the underclass take root and grow, but one important cause was the exemption from responsibility, not only of blacks, but of deviants and failures of all kinds. Affirmative action was explicitly based on the assumption that blacks were not responsible for their condition and that "fairness" required special treatment. However, public policies that were not specifically race-based have also made assumptions about why people fail. Since failure in America has been disproportionately black, the impulse to find excuses for blacks got tangled up with the impulse to find excuses for everyone who was failing.

If it turned out that poverty was a largely black problem, and blacks were not responsible for their poverty, then it made sense to treat all poor people as though they were not responsible for their poverty.

During the 1960s and 1970s it was fashionable to talk about society's inadequacies rather than personal inadequacies. To hold people responsible for their failures was to commit the sin of "blaming the victim." William Ryan wrote a best-selling book of that name in which he made the classic case for excusing failure. After discussing social ills, he wrote, "It is highly unlikely that any of the major issues I have covered . . . could have their causes rooted in the personal qualities or the individual characteristics of those who are suffering from the problem." He went on to propose a social analysis that will "focus, not on problem families, but on family problems; not on motivation, but on opportunity; not on symptoms, but on causes; not on deficiencies, but on resources; not on adjustment, but on change."[1042]

On reflection, this was no less than a wholesale rejection of the most basic rules of human society. Every society in every age has made demands on its citizens. Men and women must overcome their deficiencies, sustain their motivation, and adjust to the requirements of responsible citizenship. In one breathtaking sentence, Mr. Ryan completely rewrote the contract between society and individual. It was society that was to "change" so that people would not have to "adjust." Failure and deviance were forgiven. The very concept of an individual's responsibility for his own failure was replaced with notions such as "underprivilege" and "victimization." People ceased to be lazy or stupid or degenerate or improvident. They became victims.[1043]

This was an irresistible analysis for compassionate and generous people. It loosened the purse strings for what turned out to be *trillions* of dollars in spending programs and supplied the vocabulary of social welfare. Unfortunately, it was a misreading of human nature that made problems worse. For the least capable, least motivated blacks, it made problems much worse. Since they wore the badges of failure most conspicuously, they were the most obvious "victims" of society and therefore most assiduously exempted from blame or responsibility. The people who should have made the greatest effort were asked to make the least. The best of intentions resulted in policies that were cruel and destructive.

Poverty

One problem people in the underclass have in common is poverty. Thirteen percent of all Americans are officially counted as poor.[1044] However, an American has a less than 1 percent chance

---

[1043] This thinking is still common. America used to have bums, derelicts, hoboes, winos, and drifters. Sometime in the late 1980s they all got a promotion and became "homeless." All the earlier words suggested some degree of responsibility. A bum or a derelict presumably got that way because there was something wrong with him. The word "homeless," on the other hand, used to be reserved for people whose houses were destroyed by fire, earthquake, or tornado—that is, victims of circumstances beyond their control. Calling bums and winos "the homeless" suggests that they, too, are victims and therefore not responsible for their condition.

[1044] Although everyone quotes poverty figures, no one knows what they mean. Currently, a family of four with a cash income of less than $12,100 is considered poor. This figure applies throughout the country; a rural Mississippi family is thought to need as much cash income as one that lives in Manhattan. Moreover, the poverty threshold ignores noncash income, which is not just garden vegetables and barter of services. Difficult though it may be to believe, of the $184 billion that the nation spent on welfare in 1988, only $27 billion was actually counted as "income" for the poor. Noncash programs such as food stamps, subsidized housing, and Medicaid, and even some cash payments do not count as income. We could therefore double the spending on these programs, and the poverty figures would not budge. Not surprisingly, the Census Bureau found that in 1988, poor families spent $1.94 in cash for every $1.00 in "income" they reported.

It would not be hard to devise a much more accurate measure of poverty, but politics gets in the way. Conservatives want a measure that minimizes poverty, while liberals want one that maximizes it. In the meantime, we have one that simply distorts it. Katherine

of being poor if he manages to do just three things: finish high school, get and stay married, and stick with a job—even a minimum-wage job—for at least a year.[1045] These are symptoms as much as they are causes. A job, marriage, and a little education are all good for cash flow, but they also reflect a certain state of mind. Is this state of mind—are these three things—too much to ask of the population of a wealthy, late-twentieth-century, industrialized nation? Surely not. They are minimal demands, and anyone who can manage them has a more than 99 percent chance of not being poor. Why are 13 percent of our people poor instead of less than 1 percent?

It would be hard to argue that society maliciously thwarts millions of doughty young people—black or white—who are fighting to stay in school or to keep a job at McDonald's or to stay married. But far more ominous is the fact that if American young people don't have the will to do these three things, there is virtually nothing that government can do to give it to them. Let us examine each in turn.

A good education is one of the most obvious requirements for a good job. In manufacturing, a college graduate makes 2.4 times as much money as a high-school dropout. But in services, where many of the new jobs are, a college graduate makes 3.5 times as much. In both sectors, the differential is getting wider, not narrower.[1046] This helps explain why fully 62 percent of black female high-school dropouts, according to one authority, live below the poverty line. For black male dropouts, the figure is 37 percent.[1047] And there is worse than poverty. In New York State, fully 82 percent of the black men in prison are high-school dropouts.[1048]

Why do people drop out of high school? It is not because they need an income and can't afford to stay in school. In Washington, D.C., where 44 percent of the students fail to graduate, and 80

Barrett and Richard Greene, "Half Truth," *Financial World* (October 3, 1989), p. 25. Robert Recter, "Poverty in U.S. is Exaggerated by Census," *The Wall Street Journal* (September 25, 1990), p. A22.

[1045] "Politics Without Economics," *The Economist* (August 6, 1988), p. 8. Black economist Walter Williams makes essentially the same point when he says, "If people would wait until they're married to have children and work when they have children, there would not be a poverty problem." Dorothy Gaiter, "Diversity of Leaders Reflects the Changes in Black Community," *The Wall Street Journal* (May 6, 1992), p. A6.

percent of these leave before they finish tenth grade, a study showed that only one third of the dropouts even had jobs. Seventy-five percent of these dropouts had lived with only one parent, almost always a mother or grandmother.[1049] Whatever family pressure they may have felt to stay in school was not enough. Some girls drop out because they have had a baby. But many drop out simply because they do not like school and nothing is keeping them there.

Some studies suggest that some children either see no connection between education and a good job or just do not care. In Boston, private employers tried to encourage students to stay in school with what was called the Boston Compact, which *guaranteed* a job to anyone who graduated from high school. The dropout rate *rose* after the compact was announced,[1050] suggesting that what little interest students had in a job was not enough to keep them in school.

It is often argued that in spite of court-ordered integration, blacks are still more likely to attend bad schools, and this explains their poor performance. However, even in the best high schools there is a persistent difference in black/white dropout rates. In the majority-white suburbs, where Philadelphia's middle-class blacks live, their children still drop out two and a half times as often as those of whites.[1051]

Although calls for more education money are so frequent one might think we have been starving our schools, the opposite is true. During the 1970s, while academic performance was plummeting, the nation increased its education spending more than 25 percent in real terms. During the 1980s, real expenditures were up *40* percent. Real spending *per pupil* rose 16 and 24 percent in the 1970s and 1980s. There has been a real increase every decade since the 1930s. From 1930 to 1987, real, per pupil spending has increased by 500 percent. Pupil/teacher ratios have also decreased steadily. In 1959, the average class size was 26. By 1988 it was down to 17.6.[1052] From 1970 to 1985, education spending as a percentage of the GNP grew from 2.8 percent to 6.8 percent.[1053] In no way can the United States be considered to have stinted on education.

Money does not seem to be the key to a good education. America spends more money on every primary and secondary student than any other country in the world except Switzerland.[1054] We spend 83 percent more money per pupil than Japan does, but Japanese consistently beat us in international student competitions. Recently, even Koreans have started beating us.[1055] In domestic comparisons, New Hampshire is outranked in per-pupil spending by more than half the other states, but its students get the highest SAT scores in the country. Alaska and the District of Columbia are first and third in spending, but twentieth and forty-sixth in performance.[1056]

Comparisons of public schools with Catholic schools invariably highlight how much can be done with only a little money if students and teachers are motivated. In Scranton, Pennsylvania, for example, parochial schools consistently give a better education than the public schools. Yet the Scranton Diocese spends less than one third the amount per student as the public system ($1,740 vs. $5,800), and each teacher in the Diocese must handle more students (nineteen vs. thirteen).[1057]

People so wish to believe that more money can solve school problems that they ignore consistent evidence to the contrary. More than thirty years ago, after a massive study of how school spending and program enrichment affect student performance, the Office of Education concluded:

> [S]chools bring little influence to bear on a child's achievement that is independent of his background and general social context; and . . . this very lack of an independent effect means that the inequalities imposed on children by their home, neighborhood, and peer environment are carried along to become the inequalities with which they confront adult life at the end of school.[1058]

Subsequent studies have confirmed this finding. Eric Hanushek of the University of Rochester has surveyed sixty-five case studies

[1055] John Hood, "Money Isn't Everything," *The Wall Street Journal*, (February 9, 1990), p. A10. Interestingly, in international competitions American students often assume they will be the best even when they finish dead last. Henrik Bering-Jensen, "America's Smarts Weapon," *Insight* (July 1, 1991), p. 33. Their "self-esteem" has been well cared for in school, but their education has not been.

on the effect of more money on school performance. He found no effect at all in 75 percent of the studies, a positive effect in only 20 percent, and a negative effect in 5 percent.[1059] If black children do not get a good start at home, their schools will not make up the difference.

Moreover, black children face a problem that no educator would have anticipated: In both largely black and in integrated schools, there is fierce peer pressure on blacks *not* to do well. Those who study hard are taunted for "acting white," and some stop studying rather than be picked on.[1060] According to a black anthropologist who spent two years studying the attitudes of black high-school students, studying is not the only thing they despise because it is "white." Speaking standard English, being on time, camping, doing volunteer work, and studying in the library are just as contemptible.[1061] Even at university, blacks who get A's in such things as physics or calculus may be reviled as traitors.[1062]

Even the smartest, most motivated children from the most concerned families often wish they could leave school. If it were not for pressure from their parents, many of them would. Teachers can hardly carry the burden of motivation all by themselves if students' families and friends are indifferent to education. Government is even less capable of changing a student's mind.

Much the same is true of marriage. People often say that black families are breaking up, but the fact is that they are not forming in the first place. Why should a teenage boy marry a girl just because he has made her pregnant? In the past, the girl's father might have marched him down the aisle with a shotgun. It might not have been a marriage made in heaven, but at least the child would have had a claim on a man's income and a couple's care. Today the girl's father may well be nowhere to be found. Government cannot make him reappear or hand him a shotgun. Nor can it keep the girl from getting pregnant in the first place.

Furthermore, the whole country now winks at unwed motherhood. Our society has moved steadily from self-control to self-expression, and many people dismiss old-fashioned values as repressive. As one writer puts it, beginning in the 1960s, "instead of feeling morally superior to anyone who had a baby without marrying, the young began to feel morally superior to anyone who disapproved of unwed mothers."[1063] With movie stars and middle-class white people having illegitimate babies, it was much harder for society to frown on it.

The drop in black marriages has had gruesome results. The percentage of black children born out of wedlock has climbed steadily upward, and now two thirds are illegitimate. The rate for whites has likewise surged and is now 21.6 percent.[1064] In Harlem, 80 percent of the babies are illegitimate.[1065] Only 38 percent of black children now live with both parents, while 79 percent of white children do.[1066] In the 1950s, black children had a 52 percent chance of living with both of their biological parents until age seventeen. In the 1980s, they had only a 6 percent chance.[1067] Put differently, in 1959, only 2 percent of black children were reared in households in which the mother never married.[1068] Today that figure must be close to 60 percent.

In many black communities today, the absence of fathers is taken for granted. They are either dead, in jail, on drugs, or just not interested. Many of the forms used in foster care programs in New York City *do not even have a space for the name of the father.*[1069]

Part of the problem is due to sexual behavior that differs by race. Black girls, on average, start having sex when they are two full years younger than white girls, and the age at which a girl starts having sex is one of the best predictors of teenage pregnancy.[1070] Black teenagers are twice as likely to have babies as white teenagers, and fully one third of the daughters of girls who had children as teenagers become teenage mothers themselves.[1071]

The teenage birth rate had been declining ever since the late 1960s, but started climbing sharply again in the late 1980s, about the time that crack cocaine hit the nation. Of all the fifteen- to seventeen-year-olds living in America in 1988, more than one in thirty had a baby that year. *One in every twelve* babies in America that year was born to an unmarried teenager. And unlike the 1970s, when two thirds of the teenage mothers were married, in 1988, two thirds of the teenage mothers were single.[1072] Whereas in Sweden, Japan, and Germany the proportion of single-parent families has fallen since 1960, in the United States it has almost doubled.[1073] This has enormous consequences for children.

A single black mother is dooming her child to poverty—or worse—with near certainty. In 1987, black families headed by women had a median income of $9,710 a year, or little more than one third of the median family income of black couples.[1074] This helps explain why more than two thirds of all black children in homes without a father are poor[1075] and are more than five times as likely to be poor as children who live with a mother and father.[1076] In New York City, 70 percent of teenage mothers are on welfare within eighteen months of giving birth.[1077]

A large part of the increase in child poverty can be traced directly to single parenthood. According to demographers David Eggebeen and Daniel Lichter, there would have been one third fewer poor children in 1988 if Americans had continued to marry and stay together at the rates that prevailed in 1960—and that without a single additional penny in welfare or GNP.[1078] Because the rise in illegitimacy was so great among black children during that period, its poverty-inducing effect was much greater on them than on the nation as a whole.

All signs indicate that birth out of wedlock is the best predictor for any number of problems: bad nutrition, poor school performance, delinquency, crime—and more welfare.[1079] To begin with, children of single parents have a higher infant mortality rate, and this is true without regard to race or education. That is to say, children of black women with little education have a better prospect of making it through the first year than children of white women with more education—if the black woman is married and the white woman is not.[1080] As Thomas Sowell puts it, "The difference between being married and unmarried reflects differences in attitudes, and attitude differences have consequences which can be literally fatal to infants."[1081]

Then there is the prospect of abuse. One study describes the profile of potential child abusers as "poor, single, got pregnant at an early age, and had chaotic households,"[1082] the very description of many welfare mothers. Children whose parents are on welfare are four times more likely to be reported as abused or neglected than other children.[1083]

One major study of single-parent children found that they were twice as likely to drop out of school as children with two parents. The Bureau of Justice recently reported that 70 percent of the young people in state reform institutions grew up with only one parent or no parents at all.[1084] A 1988 study found that if anyone wants to predict whether boys will later become violent criminals, the clearest warning sign is that they are growing up without fathers. Not having a father in the house is a much more reliable sign of future criminality than either race or poverty.[1085]

The disappearance of families is probably the most crucially important element in the emergence of a black underclass, but most middle-class people have no idea that they live next door to a society in which marriage has virtually gone extinct. Only occasionally can they glimpse the texture of life in such a society, and then only from a distance.

In 1988, after a series of murders at a Chicago housing project, the authorities clamped down on security and refused to let anyone who was not a leaseholder or spouse stay overnight. Since most of the apartments were in the names of welfare mothers, this meant that a large number of live-in boyfriends suddenly found themselves out on the street at midnight. Some of these men had had children by leaseholders, but since they were not legal spouses, they were only "visitors" in their children's homes.

Eight of the men were shocked into matrimony, in a group ceremony that was funded and feted by local merchants. As she described the merriment, a reporter caught something of the novelty of the occasion:

> Most of the brides and grooms said they had never been to a wedding before. A few said they were the first in their families to get married. Several said they did not even know any married people.[1086]

It is hard for most whites to imagine a world in which people may not even know one married person. From 1890 to as late as 1950, black women were *more* likely than white women to be married.[1087]

In Atlanta, another housing project was in the news. A mailman got caught in a gun battle, and the post office stopped delivering mail. This was more than an inconvenience for the five-hundred-apartment complex, since only forty-two of the seventeen hundred residents held jobs. Welfare checks come by mail. In passing, the news story noted that 98 percent of the households in the complex were headed by women and that the average age at which they became grandmothers was *thirty-two.*[1088]

There is a rapidly growing problem in the underclass that is even worse than not having a father: not having parents at all. Poor blacks have long been reconciled to fathers who run out on their children, but now crack-addicted mothers are also dumping their children like so much unwanted baggage. Some leave them at Grandmother's and never return. Others drop them off in day care centers and disappear.

In 1990, some six and a half million American children were not living with either parent. From 1970 to 1990, the chances of being an orphan went from one in fifteen to nearly one in ten. In inner-city neighborhoods, the proportion is vastly greater. For example, at Frick Junior High School in Oakland, California, *more than two-thirds* of the 750 students are orphans.[1089]

Across the country, foster parents, relatives, and grandparents are increasingly the only people left to look after the waifs. "Long as I can recall," says one San Francisco grandmother, "there have been no real fathers in this community, but I never thought I'd live to see the day when mothers were so irresponsible."[1090]

Social workers point out that many of these grandmothers are themselves on drugs or alcohol and have made a terrible mess of rearing their own children. Even worse, the grandmothers are afraid to adopt their grandchildren officially and thereby receive welfare payments, because this would cut off payments to the mothers. Some grandmothers fear that their addicted daughters, who spend their welfare money on drugs, would hurt them if the checks stopped coming.[1091]

It is the daughters of the underclass—mothers at age sixteen, grandmothers at thirty-two—who bear the next generation. It is their sons who get the sixteen-year-olds pregnant. It is the sons who also account for the fact that the leading cause of death for young black men is murder by another young black.[1092] They are the one in four of all black men in their twenties who are in prison, on probation, or on parole.[1093] The disappearance of marriage and normal family life is the *single best guarantor* of a self-perpetuating underclass.

What about a minimum-wage job? The numbers of young men who are not working have risen along with the numbers of unmarried mothers, but not because there are no jobs. During the 1980s, the economy was in one of the longest booms in history. In the heavily black Washington, D.C., area, employers were so desperate for workers that they were hiring recovering addicts, welfare mothers, former prison inmates, and even mentally ill street people. Giant Food, the Marriott hotel chain, and American Security Bank were not hiring these people out of charity. They could not get anyone else. Fannie May Candies was hiring women right off the welfare line to work in its D.C. administration offices. In Atlanta, the Days Inn hotel chain was recruiting workers at homeless shelters.

Companies like these have spent millions of dollars, not just on job training but also on detoxification, counseling, and temporary shelter. In the country as a whole, private employers spend $25 billion on *remedial* education for employees. In one plant in Suffolk, Virginia, the Planters Company uses rap songs to teach the alphabet to illiterate workers.[1094] Until the recession of the early 1990s, businesses were starved for even minimally competent workers.

Even in 1992, during the depths of the recession, companies were spending enormous sums to teach their employees to read. At that time, Simon & Schuster figured that the remedial-reading textbook market for employers was worth $500 million a year and was bound to grow.[1095] In a country that, even during a recession, spends half a billion dollars a year just on textbooks for illiterate employees, there is not likely to be a cruel shortage of jobs for someone who really wants one.

Likewise, even during the recession of the early 1990s, the U.S. Border Patrol made over one million apprehensions a year of illegal aliens trying to enter the United States from Mexico. For every person they catch, one or two get through. This means that millions of people who are in the country illegally, *many of whom do not even speak English,* are able to find jobs.

Why are there still so many unemployed blacks? A spokesperson for blacks was asked on the *McNeil/Lehrer News Hour* why so many black men committed crimes rather than work, especially when jobs were plentiful. She explained that since blacks have already "passed through the work cycle," they should not be expected to take low-paying jobs. Her meaningless explanation went unchallenged.[1096]

During the late 1980s, the National Bureau of Economic Research asked unemployed sixteen- to twenty-four-year-old ghetto blacks in Boston, Chicago, and Philadelphia how easy it would be to get a minimum-wage job. Forty-six percent said it would be "very easy" and 25 percent said it would be "somewhat easy."[1097] These men did not have minimum-wage jobs because they did not want them. In Chicago's ghetto neighborhood of Oakland, there are only nineteen employed young black men for every hundred employed young black women.[1098] Many more men than women are in jail, but many more women than men are on welfare. A difference in employment rates of this magnitude can only reflect a difference in the desire to work.

Researchers have found that some inner-city blacks think that "straight" jobs are for "suckers," that an arrest record is a sign of toughness, and that taking a conventional job is a kind of defeat.[1099] Some studies have shown that black teenagers hold out for higher wages than unemployed white teenagers—that is, they refuse to work at the wages young whites will accept.[1100] For these black teenagers, $5.00 or $6.00 an hour is "chump change."[1101]

It is attitudes like this that help explain why, in 1954, the proportion of blacks in the work force (58 percent) was not only higher than it was in 1987 (56.8 percent) but also higher than the 1954 figure *for whites* (55.2 percent). By 1987, the traditional preponderance of black participation in the labor market had been decisively reversed, and 5.5 percent *fewer* blacks than whites were working.[1102] It would certainly be hard to blame this switch on racism.

Generally, men who refuse to work fit the profile of the underclass perfectly. They grew up in public housing as the illegitimate children of poor, uneducated teenagers.[1103] Women who do not work are often single parents on welfare. The burdens of making a living, running a household, and rearing children are too heavy for many to bear alone. However, an astonishing number of single women with children do work, and whether they do often depends on how easy it is to get welfare in their state. In Wisconsin, 78.7 percent of all single mothers are on welfare, whereas in New Hampshire, only 21.6 percent are. In Ohio the figure is 73.3 percent and in Idaho 28.6 percent. It is difficult not to conclude that if some of the welfare recipients in Wisconsin or Ohio had been living in Idaho or New Hampshire, they would have found jobs.[1104]

The disagreeable truth is that many underclass blacks simply refuse to work at low-paying jobs. There is enough welfare money and untaxed income in their communities to maintain them. There is no doubt that underclass blacks live in areas where good jobs are not plentiful. However, when the unemployed spurn the jobs that are available, there is little that government can do about it.

Finish high school, get married, get a job. Black teachers, Afrocentric curricula, black pride, busing, Jesse Jackson, black learning style, Bill Cosby, affirmative action—none of this seems to help. To persist in blaming problems on racism is deliberate blindness.

The Shackles of Welfare

Over the tragedy of the underclass, the welfare system casts a long, dark shadow. It is difficult not to conclude that, well-intentioned though it may have been, welfare has only made things worse.

The elimination of poverty was one of the goals of President Lyndon Johnson's Great Society. The analysis of poverty was extremely simple: What made poor people different from the rest of us was that they had less money; give them more and they would become like us. Money would give them dignity, motivation, and values. John Conyers, a Democratic congressman, perhaps best

302 ● *Paved With Good Intentions*

expressed the contradictions of this magic-touch approach: With a guaranteed income, the poor would be "free to feel that they are directing their own lives."[1105] Presumably they would direct them toward getting a job.

Killjoys grumbled that a guaranteed income would have the very opposite effect, that the last thing free money would do is put poor people in the mood for a job. To justify their programs, the poverty fighters in the Johnson administration therefore conducted a major social experiment designed to show that the killjoys were wrong. Over a ten-year period beginning in 1968, and with a sample of eighty-seven hundred people, they set out to show that welfare does *not* make people work less.

The results were a big disappointment to the idealists. People with guaranteed incomes worked significantly less than people without them. This wrecked the assumptions of the welfare advocates, but it did not stop them—or the country—from pouring money into public assistance.[1106]

The primary welfare program in America is Aid to Families with Dependent Children (AFDC). It was started under President Franklin Roosevelt, as temporary help for widows with small children—that is, married women whose husbands had died. AFDC was to make up for bad luck. Divorce, illegitimacy, and single motherhood did not get society's sympathy. They were considered deviance. Also, AFDC did not last forever. The government tided families over until they could support themselves. Consequently, in the 1950s, fewer than 1.5 percent of American families got AFDC. During the 1960s, when deviance was replaced by victimization, the rules changed. The husband need not be dead but simply absent. Eventually, men had nothing to do with AFDC at all. Any woman with a child and no income was eligible, and payments could go on for years. Not surprisingly, by 1980 the proportion of families on welfare had more than quadrupled, to over 6.5

[1106] Charles Murray, *Losing Ground* (New York: Basic Books, 1984), p. 148ff. A similar program for recently released prisoners showed the same results. In the late 1970s, ex-cons were randomly assigned to two groups. One got small weekly unemployment checks and the other did not. The group that got the checks "took much longer to find a job, were much less likely to get a job at all, and when employed worked for many fewer weeks and earned less money. . . ." P. Rossi, R. Berk, and K. Lenihan, *Money, Work, and Crime* (New York: Academic Press, 1980), p. 192. Cited in J. Wilson and R. Herrnstein, *Crime and Human Nature* (New York: Simon & Schuster, 1985), p. 322.

percent of all families.[1107] In just ten years—from 1961 to 1971—while the number of single mothers on welfare living in Washington, D.C., tripled, the number of single black *teenage* mothers on welfare increased *eightfold*.[1108] For the nation as a whole, *real* spending on welfare shot up 540 percent between 1960 and 1982.[1109]

Today there are 13 million Americans[1110]—4.42 million families[1111]—on welfare. That is 1 in every 19 Americans. Of the women on welfare, about 56 percent have been on the rolls for more than ten years.[1112] Seventy-two percent of all black children born in the late 1960s were on welfare at some point before age eighteen; the figure for all children was 22 percent.[1113] The number of food stamp recipients, 23.1 million,[1114] is even greater.

Some areas have worse dependency problems than others. During the 1980s, while California's population was growing by 24 percent, the number of welfare recipients grew 49 percent, to 2.1 million.[1115] Every 14 Californians—every 6 taxpayers[1116]—now support a welfare recipient. New York City, with a population of 7.3 million, staggers on with a welfare population of 940,000—nearly 13 percent of its population. Columnist Pete Hamill suspects that something close to half of the city's $29 *billion* budget is spent on services, including fire and police protection, for people who do not pay taxes.[1117] In twenty-three of the fifty states, welfare and other benefits now give a mother with two children a better standard of living than a full-time, minimum-wage job would.[1118]

The most common way to get off the dole is to get married; only one fifth of welfare recipients leave the system because they start making enough money on their own. Women who have been married before but are divorced, separated, or widowed have some chance of remarrying and getting off welfare. The hardest, most chronic cases are women who were never married, but went on welfare after they had an illegitimate child.[1119] An astonishing 80 percent of mothers who have never been married get a government check of some kind[1120]—yet another indication of how single parenthood can wreck lives and eventually whole societies.

Governments are now less confident that free money buys motivation and values, though black and white elected officials differ sharply on the role of government. In one 1976 poll, 76 percent of the blacks thought that government owes every citizen a home, an income, and leisure. Only 30 percent of the white elected officials thought so.[1121] Black voters are more tough-minded than black officials. In a 1988 poll, fully half said they thought welfare makes people dependent and keeps them poor. Sixty-six percent of whites thought so, too.[1122]

Welfare seems to have a curious effect on a pregnant teenager's decision whether to keep a child or put it up for adoption. Girls on public assistance are three times more likely to keep the child, no doubt because they know they have means to do so and probably because their milieu is one in which this is acceptable. Teenagers with the most education and from the wealthiest families are most likely to *give up* children rather than keep them. White teenagers who become pregnant are four times more likely than black teenagers to give their children up for adoption,[1123] presumably because whites are better aware of the economic challenges of single motherhood and may still feel the sting of opprobrium.

It has long been argued that despite their generous intentions, welfare programs are a perverse incentive to irresponsibility. If an illiterate sixteen-year-old girl drops out of high school to have a baby, the government will give her her own apartment, Medicaid, and an independent income. She can quit school, which she probably hates, and set up house. She suddenly becomes an adult, with all the trappings and none of the responsibilities of one. This is probably a far more attractive life than her eighteen-year-old boyfriend could give her, even if he wanted to. Arline Geronimus of the University of Michigan at Ann Arbor concludes that for a poor teenager, having a baby is a "sensible response" to poverty,[1124] despite the fact that prospects for her and for her child are exceedingly bleak.

Welfare does not *make* people get pregnant, drop out of school, or fail to get a job. It simply removes the penalties for doing so. Single mothers know they will not starve. Their families know they will not starve and that *somebody else* will pay for rent and groceries. The men who fathered the children know this, too. Why shouldn't the girl go on welfare? Who can deny the appeal of a guaranteed income and an apartment of one's own? Who is going to tell a pregnant youngster that she is about to doom herself and her child?

The stigma against single motherhood has collapsed. So has the ironclad rule that men must support their children. Sex is fun. Babies are cute. Women want to be mothers. This is perfectly natural, and when there is no middle-class morality—or wolf at the door—to stand in nature's way, babies are the inevitable result. Welfare payments are the comfortable safety net into which the single mother lands when she walks off the edge of middle-class morality. Welfare makes it that much more likely that she will take that walk. The answer to the question of why black families (and white families) are disintegrating is brutally simple. The family is no longer biologically necessary. Any woman with a child knows that she can count on a check in the mail. She needs no husband, and her child needs no father. The government is their family.

Our grandparents would not have dreamed of having children until they were married, and they did not marry until they had the means to support a family. In social terms, therefore, the crucial difference between America of today and America of fifty years ago is the millions of unmarried people who have children they cannot support. This is likewise the crucial social difference between the middle class and the underclass. If there is a single statistic that underlies the crime, poverty, and failure that beset blacks in America today, it is an illegitimacy rate of 66 percent. No people naturally loses the foresight to forgo children it cannot support. That happens only when a people has the misfortune to live under unnatural conditions in which the penalties for reckless childbearing are artificially removed.

Anyone who resists the idea that welfare promotes irresponsible childbearing should consider the example of recently reunited Germany. Despite the relative poverty in the East, its women could count on free child care, guaranteed employment, and subsidies for single mothers. It can hardly be a coincidence that the illegitimacy rate, at over a third, was three times higher than in the West.[1125]

[1125] "New 'Miracle': Germans Stimulate Their Economy, Avoid Recession Through Heavy Spending on East," *The Wall Street Journal* (June 11, 1991), p. A11. Some people

At the same time as it removes the penalties of illegitimacy, welfare takes the sting out of unemployment. Many people on the dole are probably not qualified for a job that pays much more than the minimum wage. Why on earth should they work, when they can have the same income without working? Anyone whose alternatives are a drudge job or a welfare check would have to have extraordinary ambitions to take the job. It takes confidence and vision to see that there is no such thing as a dead-end job and that even the lowliest levels of competence and experience are rungs on the ladder.

For people who work, life is a series of exchanges. They understand that groceries and an apartment are not free and that work is necessary, even if it is sometimes unpleasant. Ever since Adam and Eve were chased out of the Garden of Eden, man has had to live by the sweat of his brow. Welfare rewrites this most ancient rule of human existence. It creates a false world in which money—at least enough to live on—grows on trees. Unfortunately, the people it affects the most are children. Charles Murray's oft-quoted description of the welfare dilemma is worth quoting again:

> Let us suppose that you, a parent, could know that tomorrow your own child would be made an orphan. You have a choice. You may put your child with an extremely poor family, so poor that your child will be badly clothed and will indeed sometimes be hungry. But you also know that the parents have worked hard all their lives, will make sure your child goes to school and studies, and will teach your child that independence is a primary value. Or you may put your child with a family with parents who have never worked, who will

have tried to deny the link between welfare and illegitimacy by pointing out that the American underclass has grown steadily even when the real value of welfare payments was declining. See, for example, Paul Peterson, "The Urban Underclass and the Poverty Paradox" in Christopher Jencks and Paul Peterson, eds., *The Urban Underclass* (Washington, D.C.: The Brookings Institution, 1991), p. 14ff. It is not the real value of payments that matters nearly so much as the fact that they can be counted on and are enough to live on. A fifteen-year-old will not know or care that the payments she can anticipate will be 8 percent less, adjusted for inflation, than those her mother received. What matters most is that if she has a baby she can be sure to get a check and all the other benefits that come with it. Small adjustments in payments are not likely to change behavior. It is the presence or absence of welfare that is decisive.

be incapable of overseeing your child's education—but who have plenty of food and good clothes provided by others.[1126]

No sane parent would make the second choice, yet our misguided benevolence has dragged more and more children into just that kind of home.

And what about Mr. Murray's hardworking family that is barely getting by? Welfare makes it easy for the parents to let go and have the government clean up the mess. Government programs have the same perverse effect on their children. Robert Woodson, president of the National Center for Neighborhood Enterprise, puts it this way:

> If you are poor and you are pregnant, there's a program for you. If you are poor and you are a drug addict, there's a program for you. If you're a truant, there's a program. . . . [Y]ou get more of what you reward and less of what you punish. As long as we keep rewarding pathological behavior, we will get more of it.[1127]

We pounce upon the poor and apply goodwill to them so thickly that they forget how to help themselves.

James Meredith, who, with the help of sixteen thousand federal troops, was the first black to attend the University of Mississippi, in 1962, also thinks that government programs have turned blacks into dependent, "second-class citizens." He calls busing, affirmative action, and welfare "the worst thing that has happened to the black race in thirty years."[1128]

As we saw earlier, one prominent pollster reports that the greatest difference in black and white opinion is that blacks think that government can solve all problems. This does not only mean that blacks are likely to vote Democratic; it also means that their view of personal responsibility is different from that of whites. If government can solve all problems, why should individuals bother about them? Surely this thinking is not just another version of the whites-are-responsible theory but a warped consequence of social programs that appear at every turn.

Welfare agencies are slowly waking up to how debilitating it is always to receive and never to give. "Workfare," or making recipients work for their welfare, is now the fashionable thing. Oklahoma has had work rules since 1975. It puts recipients through training and finds them jobs and child care. Even so, by no means do all recipients get to the point where they are offered a job, and of those who are actually hired, three quarters end up back on the welfare rolls. Even this modest success rate is the envy of the nation.[1129]

Obviously, the way to enforce workfare is to cut off payments to people who will not work. No state is brave enough to do this. A legislator who helped draft a workfare law for California says, "The number of people forced off the welfare rolls for failure to comply is essentially zero."[1130] In practice, since workfare programs have no teeth, they degenerate into cajoling and pleading. If the recipient refuses to take a job or is soon back on the dole, workfare actually becomes more expensive than plain old welfare: It costs money to arrange child care, transportation, job training, and job interviews. One author concludes that the idea of putting welfare recipients to work "must be seen at present largely as an exercise in symbolic politics, as homage to a widely held value that government cannot actually achieve."[1131]

The unhappy fact of the matter is that many welfare recipients can do nothing that an employer is willing to pay for. When the state of California began to think seriously about trying to make them work, it found that most cannot read and write well enough to take even a simple job.[1132]

If not work, the state of Wisconsin has tried to get something else in return for welfare. It threatens to cut off assistance if the children of recipients do not go to school. As caseworkers have discovered, this means that children can now shake their parents down for expensive sneakers or stereo sets by threatening to play hooky.[1133] In March 1990, a study in Milwaukee County by the University of Wisconsin declared the program a failure.[1134]

Even if welfare makes problems worse, Charles Murray has very wisely pointed out that it is our consciences that most require it:

It seems that those who legislate and administer and write about social policy can tolerate any increase in actual suffering as long as the system in place does not explicitly permit it. It is better, by the logic we have been living with, that we try to take care of 100 percent of the problem and make matters worse than that we solve 75 percent of the problem with a solution that does not try to do anything about the rest.[1135]

Drugs

As if conditions were not grim enough, the underclass has been assailed by a plague that no one anticipated: crack cocaine. *The New York Times* has wondered in an editorial whether crack might not be to the 1980s and 1990s what the Depression was to the 1930s.[1136] Crack is worse than heroin on virtually every count. It is much cheaper and more addictive. Laboratory animals that have been trained to press a lever for a shot of cocaine do not stop even to eat or sleep. They press the lever until they drop. Animals addicted to heroin at least stop to eat and sleep.[1137] Cocaine is also a stimulant rather than a sedative. Heroin users nod out and are not even interested in sex, but crack hops people up and can make them run wild. Also, unlike heroin, there is no known chemical substitute, like methadone. An addict must have cocaine and nothing else.[1138] The United States consumes 85 percent of the world's refined cocaine.[1139]

Perhaps the worst thing about crack is that it is popular with women in a way that heroin never was. In 1989, more women than men were being arrested for crack in New York City, Kansas City, Portland, and Washington, D.C., and teenage girls were forming drug gangs for the first time in American history.[1140] In Detroit, female gang members carry guns and do not hesitate to use them. "We carry our guns so if there is a confrontation with somebody, we spray [shoot] 'em and go on about our business," explains one.[1141]

Girls under age eighteen are committing crimes at unprecedented rates. In New York City, between 1986 and 1990, the number of girls arrested for felonies increased by 48 percent. In New Jersey, during the decade of the 1980s, the number of girls arrested for violent offenses such as robbery and assault leapt by 67 percent.[1142]

Women are pouring into jails as never before. While the number of male convicts in the New York State prison system has increased by 30 percent since 1986, the number of women there has increased by 82 percent.[1143] In the country as a whole, the number of women in jail has doubled in the past five years.[1144]

Welfare is the prime source of drug money for many women. At Langston Terrace, a housing project in Washington, D.C., the first of every month is called mother's day. That is the day when welfare checks come in the mail, and the mothers throng the streets looking for crack dealers.[1145] Using welfare to buy drugs is called "smoking the check."

The desire for crack is so strong that mothers often abandon their children in the search for the next high, or offer them as sex toys in exchange for drugs. San Francisco social workers have found growing numbers of infants and toddlers suffering from venereal disease after they have been bartered in drug deals.[1146]

Unborn children often suffer terrible damage when their mothers use crack. Some actually have strokes while still in the womb. Crack babies are often premature and need intensive hospital care. Some weigh less than two pounds and can be kept alive only by extraordinary means. As one San Francisco doctor explains, "a baby like this will cost $1,500 a day, with the total bill ranging from $100,000 to $200,000 for a baby that when it's all over wasn't wanted in this world and may have lasting health problems." Those who survive are likely to have damaged brains.[1147] One commentator calls them a "bio-underclass, a generation . . . whose biological inferiority is stamped at birth."[1148]

The first wave of crack babies is now old enough to start attending school. They have a baffling array of psychological and physical ailments and are very difficult to teach. Most of them will need both special education classes, which, in New York City, cost $15,000 a year, and foster care, which costs nearly $17,000 a year.[1149] In 1990 New York City saw a sharp rise in the number of five-year-olds that had to be referred to special classes. The real surge of crack babies came after 1985, so the majority had not yet begun to attend school.[1150] In the five years since 1985, New York

State had produced 467,000 children of crack-addicted parents, a number just lower than the population of Seattle.[1151] Dr. Judy Howard of UCLA estimates that 40 to 60 percent of the students in some inner-city classrooms will eventually be crack children.[1152]

San Francisco now spends three times as much money fighting crack as it does on AIDS. In New York City the number of newborns who tested positive for drugs—usually cocaine—went from 1,325 in 1986 to 5,088 just two years later. Ten percent of the babies born in San Francisco start life on drugs, as do 20 percent of the babies delivered at Oakland's Highland Hospital. According to one estimate, 375,000 drug-exposed babies were born in America in 1989, and of that number, perhaps 50,000 were born as addicts. In 1989 one New York City social worker reported a crack mother who was in her fifth pregnancy; her four other children were in foster care.[1153]

Child care services all across the country have been overwhelmed. In New York City the number of children in foster care had dropped every year from 1980 to 1985. In the four years from 1986 to 1990—the years when crack cocaine took hold—the number leapt 265 percent.[1154] Not even the best-run services were prepared for such an onslaught.

Doctors and social workers are astonished at how indifferent crack mothers are to their children. One woman who was told that her just-delivered baby was dying, only wanted to know when breakfast would be served. Crack mothers often care so little about their babies that they cannot be bothered to name them— nurses find names for them. Some pregnant crack users deliberately smoke more of the drug during the last months of pregnancy because they know it will cause premature birth and get the inconvenience over with.

Some mothers just dump the baby as soon as they can get up and walk. In New York City more than four hundred newborns a month are either abandoned by drug-addicted mothers or taken away from them by health authorities.[1155] In the summer of 1989, Howard University Hospital in Washington had to devote hospital beds to twenty-one "boarder" babies, whose mothers had vanished.[1156]

The babies are, themselves, a kind of crack by-product. Addicted women do not hesitate to peddle their bodies for money or drugs. Crack houses have become squalid brothels. In 1989 the going rate for oral sex in one Harlem crack house had reportedly dropped to 25 cents.[1157] In their desperation for the drug, women are hardly going to worry about pregnancy or disease.

It is these sex-for-drugs transactions that have produced the flood of crack babies. They have also caused an upsurge in venereal disease. In Washington, D.C., for example, syphilis cases increased by more than 90 percent between 1985 and 1988, while cases of penicillin-resistant gonorrhea leapt from only 34 to 1,371.[1158] In the state of Massachusetts, the Department of Public Health found that in 1989, black men were 61 times more likely than white men to have syphilis and 102 times more likely to have gonorrhea.[1159]

Between 1985 and 1990 the rate of syphilis infection among blacks, nationwide, shot up by more than 150 percent, while it *fell by half* among white men. Across the country, blacks are more than fifty times as likely as whites to have the disease. Drug-related sex is thought to be the cause of the increase among blacks.[1160] The rise of syphilis has been so remarkable that in 1991 the nation had the highest infection rate in forty years.[1161]

In the current outbreak, it is impossible to control the disease through the usual method of contact tracing. Dr. Don Williamson, who is responsible for monitoring communicable diseases in the state of Alabama, explains why: "It's not at all unusual for somebody to come in for treatment who can't even remember how many people he or she has had sex with in a week's time. And if they can remember, they don't know their names."[1162] Crack-related cases of congenital syphilis have increased so rapidly in New York State that in 1989 the Health Department established mandatory VD tests for all *newborns*.[1163] As recently as 1986, the state of Michigan did not report a single case of congenital syphilis, but by 1991, cases were in three figures and on the rise. The overwhelming majority of them were in Detroit.[1164]

Even more ominously, sex-for-crack is helping spread AIDS. Bleeding venereal sores are thought to be transmitting the virus; blacks are 50 times more likely than whites to get AIDS heterosexually. Eighty-five percent of the women in New York State who have AIDS are black or Hispanic, as are 90 percent of the children who have it.[1165] The virus has now pulled ahead of heart disease, cancer, and accidents, and AIDS is the leading killer of black women of childbearing age in the states of New York and New Jersey. They suffer from the disease at the same rate as women in Ivory Coast, in West Africa.[1166]

This portends tragedy for thousands of children, since virtually the only way they can get AIDS is from infected mothers. For the nation at large, 55 percent of the children with AIDS are black; each infected baby costs the Medicaid system $18,000 to $42,000 every year.[1167] By late 1990, congenital AIDS cases were so common that 45 states were testing all newborn babies for AIDS.[1168] It can take years before a person infected with the AIDS virus actually gets the disease.

AIDS is becoming an increasingly black and Hispanic disease. Between the end of 1989 and the end of 1991, blacks were 3.6 times more likely than whites to be diagnosed as having full-blown cases of AIDS, and Hispanics were 2.9 times more likely.[1169] Black leaders have been almost uniformly silent about exhorting their people to take the precautions that are virtually guaranteed to keep a person from getting the disease. Black AIDS activists are extremely rare, and even they do not reproach black leaders for their silence. Alexander Robinson, head of the Inner City Aids Network in Washington, D.C., says that to ask prominent blacks to combat AIDS is "adding another burden to an already overburdened people."[1170]

Crime

The crack epidemic has brought a huge wave of drug-related crimes. In New York State they went from 17,541 in 1979 to 87,679 in 1988,[1171] a 500 percent increase. In New York City, where 1,500 felonies a month are reported in the subways alone,[1172] in late 1989, a shocking 83 percent of arrested criminals were testing positive for drugs.[1173]

For the country as a whole, violent crime, which had held steady or even drifted down slightly from record levels in the early 1980s, appears to have gotten an important boost from the crack epidemic. Murder was at record-breaking levels in 1990, with about 23,400 killings. The year 1991 broke that record again, by another 300.[1174] More informative than the raw numbers themselves are comparisons with other countries. American males between ages fifteen and twenty-four—the most likely ages for mayhem—are 15 times more likely to be murdered than Frenchmen, Dutchmen, or Greeks of the same age. Americans are 44 times more likely to be murdered than Japanese and 73 times more likely to be murdered than Austrians.[1175]

Black men of the most dangerous ages are eight to ten times more likely to be killed than white men of those ages.[1176] In Michigan, whose statistics are skewed by the very violent city of Detroit, black men are *35* times more likely to be murdered. To draw what is perhaps the most extreme comparison possible, a young black man in Michigan is therefore *770 times* more likely to be murdered than a young man living in Austria.[1177]

From 1984 to 1988, the rate of gunshot deaths for black teenagers doubled.[1178] Increased murder rates and a rising AIDS toll lowered life expectancy for black men in 1989 *for the fifth year in a row,* while life expectancy for whites rose or held steady. On average, whites can now expect to live nearly seven years longer than blacks.[1179]

In the District of Columbia, where people murder each other more briskly than in any other American city,[1180] residents in 1988 and 1989 were more likely to be killed than were people living in El Salvador, Northern Ireland, the Punjab, or even Lebanon.[1181] In 1989, District residents were estimated to spend more money on cocaine than on food and drink.[1182] Seventy percent of all people arrested for crimes there in 1988 were on cocaine; nearly all the rest were on other drugs.[1183] Unsolved murders are so common in Washington, D.C., that in 1989 the police chief announced rewards of up to $10,000 for tips leading to arrests of suspects.[1184]

The city has one of the toughest gun control laws in the country, but anyone who needs a pistol for the weekend can rent one for a few dollars.[1185] In just three years, from 1987 to 1990, Washington's murder rate doubled.[1186] In 1991 the city set a new record for murder for the fourth year in a row.[1187] Harried homicide detectives may have no more than ten minutes to spend at a murder scene,[1188] even though the city has a policeman for every 126 residents—more than three times the rate of Los Angeles, for example.[1189] Eighty-five percent of black men in Washington are arrested at some point in their lives and on any given day, 42 percent of black men between the ages of eighteen and thirty-five are caught up in the criminal justice system: in jail, on probation or parole, awaiting trial, or wanted by the police.[1190]

In New York City, whose residents kill each other at a rate of about 2,200 a year, a freak five hours without a single murder during the most dangerous time of day—midnight to 5:00 A.M.—had the police shaking their heads in disbelief. The next day's headline in the *New York Post* read, "Eerie Calm Spooks Police as Death Takes a Holiday."[1191] In some New York City housing projects, people do not say "Have a nice day" or "See you later." They say "Be safe."[1192]

New York City would have set its fourth straight murder record in 1991 had it not been for an arson case in 1990 that killed 87 people and kept that year's total about ten higher than the figure for 1991.[1193] Dallas, Los Angeles, Chicago, and Detroit also had more murders in 1991 than in the previous year,[1194] and San Diego, Milwaukee, and Phoenix set new all-time records.[1195] Chicago's murder rate was twice as high as during the "Roaring Twenties," when the city was notorious for gangsters and bootleggers.[1196] More disturbing for Americans who live outside the big cities, the migration of crack cocaine into middle America pushed up crime in the hinterlands. Smaller cities that had record murder rates in 1991 included Albuquerque, New Mexico; Birmingham, Alabama; Norfolk, Virginia; Youngstown, Ohio; Anchorage, Alaska; and Rochester, New York.[1197]

In late 1991, the city of St. Paul was so concerned about crime that it was considering writing crime-deterrence standards into its building code. These would require certain kinds of locks and lighting, and would forbid construction that offered hiding places for robbers. Seattle and Los Angeles were also studying similar changes to their building codes.[1198] If there was any comfort to be taken from the crime trends in America today, it is that violent crime, though certainly rising, is not rising at as rapid a rate as it did when crack cocaine first appeared, in the mid-1980s.[1199]

In the big cities, lawlessness is seeping into every corner of life. Homeowners in New York City find that they must plant shrubs under heavy metal screens and even chain six-foot trees to underground cinder blocks because thieves have discovered a market for them.[1200] Crime changes the very face of a city. A decade or two ago, there were hardly any shuttered storefronts in Manhattan. Now an unprotected glass display window stands out as an inviting target.[1201]

New York City has steadily been closing off lightly traveled subway passageways and entrances because people are robbed, raped, and murdered in them.[1202] In other words, facilities that New Yorkers could once be trusted to use safely and civilly have become too dangerous to leave open. Most public toilets were closed long ago. Although the subway and the city had nearly seventeen hundred of them in the 1930s,[1203] nearly every one has now been closed. New Yorkers cannot be trusted not to copulate, murder each other, shoot up drugs, or simply take up residence in them.

On weekdays, an estimated 180,000 New Yorkers beat the fare and ride free on the subway. In April 1990, 38 percent of the people who got on trains in one Harlem subway station were fare-beaters. The Transit Authority, which was expected to run a $55 million deficit in 1990, loses $100 million every year because of fare-beaters.[1204]

The crime wave has even washed over people who, in the past, had no reason to fear. In some Brooklyn parishes, nuns and priests now carry at least ten dollars at all times. Robbers who get less than that punish their victims by thrashing them; if they get ten dollars they can buy two doses of crack, so they go away satisfied.[1205]

Ministers in some black New York neighborhoods have taken to carrying guns to protect themselves and their congregations.

[1204] Calvin Sims, "As Token Lines Lengthen . . . ," *The New York Times* (June 23, 1990), Margie Feinberg, "Subway Riders Go Down the Tubes," *New York Post* (September 25, 1990), p. 3. Much of the operating deficit of the New York City subway system is covered by grants from the federal Urban Mass Transportation Administration. This means that fare-beating is subsidized by taxpayers in the rest of the country.

Those who are not able to get legal permits are arming themselves illegally. After his entire congregation was held up and robbed one Sunday, Rev. Milton Corbin of Brooklyn asked all members with legal firearms to start bringing them to worship services. Black preachers were particularly shaken in October 1989 when Rev. Irving Wilson was gunned down in his church on Malcolm X Boulevard. His killers dragged Rev. Wilson to the front of the altar and left him lying in a posture that made him look like Jesus nailed to the cross.[1206]

The texture of life is just as thick with fear on the other side of the country. In black neighborhoods in Oakland and San Francisco, residents of some housing projects have taken to sleeping on the floor, where they are less likely to be hit by stray bullets. In East Oakland, where children once played freely outdoors, gunfire is now so common that worried parents forbid their children to leave home. Some churches have stopped having evening services because members dare not leave their houses in the evening. In some neighborhoods, bullets whine through the air so often that residents fear even to tend their yards.[1207] One Los Angeles shopkeeper who sells the Rolex watches popular among gang members has shot five would-be robbers to death on four different occasions during the past two and a half years.[1208]

There are horror stories from all across the country. In 1991, when gangs sacked and burned the office building of a Miami construction company, the owners decided to rebuild rather than move away. The new building sits atop a three-and-a-half-foot-high, solid concrete base so no one can smash a car through the wall. The windows are made of six-inch-thick bulletproof glass. The owners decided that the only way they could stay in the neighborhood was to turn their office into a fortress.[1209]

In virtually every major city, young blacks have been stealing each others' fashionable clothes off their backs, often committing murder in the process. In Philadelphia the problem became so bad that the city health commissioner issued a public health warning that urged young people not to wear earrings or expensive leather coats. Milwaukee also has a campaign to urge people not to wear the clothes that are the rage. The city has put up billboards showing a chalk outline of a body and the message "Dress Smart and Stay Alive."[1210]

Clogging the System

As crime sweeps the nation, arrests are clogging the courts and jails. More than three times as many Americans *per capita*—426 per 100,000 population—are now in jail than just ten years ago, an appalling increase. In California, prison operating costs have quadrupled in the same period, and women's prisons are at 270 percent of capacity. The United States recently overtook South Africa and the Soviet Union and now has a larger proportion of its population behind bars than any other country. Incarceration rates are three to five times higher than in other industrialized countries.[1211]

It is sometimes argued that if incarceration rates are increasing but crime keeps going up anyway, it is proof that putting people in jail does not work. In fact, there would probably be a great deal more crime if people were not going to jail and staying there longer. People who commit serious crimes usually have a long record of lesser offenses. For example, between 1980 and 1986, 87 percent of the murders in the city of Chicago were accounted for by people who already had records of criminal violence.[1212] If those people had been in jail rather than at large, they could not have killed anyone.

During 1989 and 1990, the United States spent $6.7 billion on new prisons, 73 percent more than in 1987 and 1988.[1213] It was not enough. Federal guidelines set crowding limits on state prisons, and wardens are forced to send convicts home in order to stay within those limits. In Houston, Texas, felons are back on the street after serving about one thirteenth of their sentence. Sales of guns and burglar alarms have been booming in the wake of forced prisoner releases.[1214]

In Philadelphia, the prisons are so crowded that pretrial detention is virtually unheard of. As a result, thousands of accused criminals, whom the police have arrested at great effort, go free and do not show up for trial. In 1990 the city had 32,880 outstanding warrants for fugitives who had failed to appear in court. It had only 30 investigators trying to catch them. In Detroit, in 1987, overcrowded prisons had to send home 2,700 felony convicts and pretrial felony defendants.[1215]

Criminals who cannot be jammed into jail go on probation instead. In the past, this was reserved for minor offenders, but now rapists and other felons are commonly put on probation. This makes a mockery of the way the system is supposed to work. Probation officers are expected to counsel and help rehabilitate their charges. But when one probation officer must handle as many as 1,000 criminals, as is common in Los Angeles, he becomes a kind of auxiliary policeman who does nothing but collar parole violators. In the past decade, while the number of criminals in jail has shot up, the number on probation has grown 67 percent faster.[1216]

The country is going broke paying for law enforcement. In 1988, governments at all levels spent $61 billion for courts and police protection, or $218 for every man, woman, and child in America. In the District of Columbia the cost was $859 per person.[1217] From 1980 to 1989, state and local spending on prisons leapt by 229 percent.[1218] First-degree murder is a particularly expensive crime. By the time each capital case has been appealed endlessly, it costs an average of $8 million in taxpayers' money.[1219] New York City is so strapped for money to pay for policemen that its legislators are trying to divert hundreds of millions of dollars in federal transportation aid to pay for more officers.[1220] As the murder rate climbs, the infrastructure crumbles.[1221]

The cost for police protection is actually much higher than government figures suggest; there are now nearly twice as many *pri-*

[1221] It is crumbling quite literally. In 1991 the city closed the lower deck of the Manhattan Bridge, a major link between Manhattan and Brooklyn. After years of neglect, an engineer finally decided there was a good chance a truck would fall through it. Calvin Sims, "Truck Ban Is Announced for a Bridge," *The New York Times* (January 4, 1991), p. B1. A subway line that used to cross the bridge has also been closed. Of all the bridges in the city, 56 percent are "structurally deficient" and 70 percent can no longer bear the weight for which they were originally designed. George Will, "Manhattan Dreams and Nightmares," *Los Angeles Times* (May 26, 1991). The city recently had to close several that were built in the 1930s and had *never been repainted*. Stephanie Strom, "New York City Names a New Chief of Bridges," *The New York Times* (May 8, 1991). It would be hard to think of a clearer indictment of a city. Today's New Yorkers cannot even maintain what yesterday's New Yorkers had the wit and energy to build.

vate security guards as there are uniformed police officers. People who can afford it pay for additional protection when the public force is overwhelmed. In 1970 there were about equal numbers, with each at about 400,000. The number of private guards has since jumped to 1.2 million, while the number of police officers has risen to 675,000.[1222]

Many policemen moonlight as private guards for clients who are not satisfied with the level of protection the public force can offer. In downtown San Jose, California, for example, there are 40 moonlighting officers—wearing guns and uniforms—on any week-end night, hired mainly by nightclub owners. That is ten times as many as the city can afford to pay for on weekends. "I think frankly we'd lose control of downtown if we didn't have pay-job officers down there," says the San Jose deputy police chief. Dozens of other cities are letting their officers do double duty for the same reasons.[1223]

In Miami, police estimate that every third car on the road has a gun in it.[1224] In some middle-class neighborhoods, people are so afraid of rampant crime that they are setting up checkpoints and barricades on public streets. They get approval from the County Commission and set up a special taxing district to pay for the checkpoints. Even Miami's top police officers have admitted that crime is out of control, and now support the barricades. Local criminologists suspect that the rest of the country could follow this trend.[1225]

The rise in crime is coming just when police were expecting relief. The eruption of lawlessness during the 1970s was explained in terms of the number of young men in the population, and demographers told us their number would fall. Crime specialists confidently predicted that crime would fall along with it. The demographers were right, but the crime specialists were wrong. From 1983 to 1988, as the baby-boom generation grew up, the number of twelve- to seventeen-year-olds in America decreased by 8 percent. Nevertheless, over the same period the number of minors arrested each year for murder rose 31 percent, to 1,765.[1226] From 1983 to 1987 there was an increase of 15 percent in rape arrests for boys under eighteen.[1227] In New York City, crimes in schools against schoolteachers were up 25 percent during the first half of the 1989 school year. The younger the children, the more rapid the rise. Violent crimes against elementary school teachers were up 54 percent.[1228] Teachers all over the country are now taking seminars to learn how to defend themselves and how best to handle brawling students.[1229]

The more crime there is, the harder it is to catch and jail the criminals. Between 1962 and 1979, the chances of an Index crime (one of the FBI's categories of serious crimes such as murder, rape, assault, and larceny) resulting in an arrest dropped from 32 percent to 18 percent. At the same time, the chances of someone who was arrested for an Index crime going to jail fell from 32 percent to 14 percent. That means the chances of someone actually going to jail when an Index crime was reported dropped from one in ten to one in forty.[1230] Even when people are *convicted* of serious crimes, fewer than one third go to jail.[1231]

Even murder, the most serious of crimes, is increasingly likely to go unsolved. In the early 1960s, 95 percent of all murders led to an arrest; thirty years later that number was 70 percent and dropping. Part of the problem is that more and more murders are random or drug-related killings committed by complete strangers. These cases are much more difficult to solve than those involving family members or acquaintances.[1232]

Some ghetto children start carrying guns at age ten. In Detroit, which is 74 percent black, 365 children under age sixteen were shot by other children in 1986—an average of one child every day.[1233] This helps explain why homicide is the leading cause of death for Detroit children between ages ten and fourteen. Yes, homicide. Between 1980 and 1988, the homicide rate in that age group *nearly tripled.*[1234] In Washington, D.C., as well, homicide is the leading killer in the same age group. In 1985 it came ahead of traffic accidents and house fires, and, at 22 percent, was twice the rate in neighboring Maryland and Virginia.[1235] Nationwide in 1986, black children were about five times more likely to be killed than white children.[1236] The year 1985 was the start of the crack epidemic; no doubt the child homicide rate is worse today.

Drug wars have filled big-city hospitals with so many shot-up drug dealers that they have started using field-medicine techniques perfected in Vietnam. High-velocity assault rifle bullets make especially vicious wounds, and thirty- and forty-round clips pack enormous firepower. "We sometimes spend fifteen minutes just counting the holes," says the director of the trauma unit at an Oakland hospital.[1237] The U.S. Army now assigns young military doctors to the Martin Luther King-Drew Medical Center in the black section of Los Angeles because they can get such realistic training in combat medicine.[1238]

They can also get realistic training in combat. Gang members like to follow wounded rivals into hospitals to finish them off. In recent years there have been hospital killings in Los Angeles, New York, Washington, D.C., and San Diego. Los Angeles has installed closed-circuit surveillance cameras and metal detectors in nearly all of its public hospitals. At Martin Luther King-Drew Medical Center, wounded gang members are called "John Doe" on patient lists so enemies will not be able to track them down. A beefed-up staff of security officers has managed to intercept a number of hit squads that had come to the hospital to polish off wounded rivals.[1239]

Treating shot-up drug dealers is expensive. In San Francisco the average bullet wound costs $7,000 and takes six hospital days. For the nation as a whole, gunshot wounds cost about $1 billion a year. Although the federal government pays 53 percent of the cost of all hospital expenses in America, it pays 85 percent in gunshot cases. Why? "If you look at who gets shot, you find that it's generally indigent inner-city people who do not have insurance," explains a San Francisco doctor.[1240] Wealthy drug dealers have come in with as much as $15,000 in cash stuffed into their pockets, but they do not have health insurance either.[1241]

Crack patients are a terrible strain on emergency rooms, and blacks are reportedly ten times more likely than whites to get emergency-room treatment for cocaine.[1242] At Highland Hospital

[1241] Gonzales and Cooper, "Carnage of Drugs Burdens Hospitals," *Washington Times* (February 27, 1989), p. A1. Jane Gross, "Emergency Room: A Crack Nightmare," *The New York Times* (August 6, 1989), p. A1. When they go to court, these same drug dealers get free legal help intended for poor people. At least one criminal judge in the Bronx has complained publicly about defendants in mink coats and gold jewelry who demand public defenders, but since their incomes cannot be proven there is no way to make them pay. In New York City, only about 10 percent of each year's three hundred thousand criminal defendants pay for their own lawyers. Charles Sennott and Mike Pearl, "Drug Dealers Cashing in on Legal Aid," *New York Post* (November 27, 1989), p. 5.

in Oakland, which is nearly 50 percent black, every emergency patient in a twelve-hour period in 1989 tested positive for cocaine. The staff has started conducting initial patient interviews in the hallways because doctors and nurses were being beaten up in their offices by crack users. Staff are trained in self-defense but still get concussions and broken noses. Often they see the same crack-crazed patients on the first and fifteenth of every month—just when the welfare checks arrive. Doctors and nurses have lost sympathy for these "frequent fliers," whom they sometimes refer to as "dirtballs."[1243]

This parade of horrors has had one good result. At least in Los Angeles, the NAACP has finally changed its view on crime. Until 1989, it stuck to the heroic assumption that since black criminals were only reacting to white racism, all the NAACP had to do to stop crime was to fight racism. At about the time black gang killings hit the rate of one every seventeen hours,[1244] the Los Angeles chapter officially changed its tune. In doing so, the newly elected president frankly admitted that black leaders have been wrong for years. "When we constantly talk about excuses for this kind of behavior, we simply make it worse," said Joseph Duff.[1245] It took record-breaking mayhem for the chapter to come around.

Like all plagues, crack will eventually recede. The most violent, impulsive users are already dead, and police have jailed many of the rest. After several years of increase, the last quarter of 1989 marked a small drop in the number of cocaine-related medical emergencies.[1246] In Washington, D.C., the percentage of people arrested who test positive for cocaine peaked at 70 percent in 1989 but had dropped to about 55 percent by mid-1990.[1247] In New York City the figure peaked at 80 percent in 1986, and was down to 70 percent by 1990 (though another 10 to 15 percent still tested positive for other drugs).[1248] The number of babies either abandoned by addict mothers or taken away from them by hospital officials dropped from an average of 484 a month in 1989 to 423 a month in the first half of 1990.[1249]

On the other hand, waves of stimulant addiction are generally followed by epidemics of sedative use. Deaths and emergency-room visits due to heroin, which had held steady in the 1970s, grew by more than 25 percent during the 1980s.[1250]

Schools for Scandal

Drugs, and the rising barbarity of the surrounding communities, have swept into America's urban schools. Some face such overwhelming problems that it is a wonder they manage to impart any learning at all.

More than fifty school districts, including those in Houston, Miami, and Philadelphia, have had to ban telephone beepers because they were so frequently used by children for making drug deals.[1251] Students have so often assaulted and murdered each other to steal fancy clothes that dress codes have been enforced in schools in Detroit, Baltimore, Chicago, Los Angeles, New York, and New Haven.[1252] Close to 300,000 American high-school students are physically attacked *each month.* In 1987, 338,000 American students admitted that they carried a handgun to school at least once. One third of those admitted that they carried one *every day.*[1253] New York City has assigned police officers to ride in designated subway cars so that students will know where they can ride without being attacked.[1254]

The New York City school system spends $60 million every year on *security guards*—$60 million that is not spent on laboratory equipment, band instruments, or field trips.[1255] In 1988 the city began a weapons-detection program that, by 1990, had been extended to fourteen high schools and one junior high school.[1256] In 1992 Mayor Dinkins announced he would try to find another $28 million to pay for metal detectors and X-ray machines at another thirty-five schools.[1257] Student activities coordinators, who used to organize dances and other good times, now see their main job as trying to prevent violence.[1258]

In the five years to 1992, fifty students at Thomas Jefferson High School in Brooklyn died, most of them violently. The school maintains a "burial fund" to help indigent parents inter their children, and a classroom has been permanently set aside for use by grieving friends.[1259] It was hardly a surprise when a black state assemblyman from Brooklyn, Roger Green, decided to send his teenage son to live in Georgia, where he hoped to go to school without being shot at.[1260]

Besides the constant fear of violence, New York City's poorer children are surrounded by other abominations. At Public School 40 in the Bronx, there is so much prostitution in the streets that children must sometimes be held late while they wait for the fornications to finish. Drug dealing creates so much traffic that the police have put up barricades to try to stop the flow. Even so, every morning the children are treated to the spectacle of addicts lining up to buy drugs.[1261]

At Public School 43 in the Bronx, the sun never shines into many of the classrooms. Teachers keep the shades drawn and push students' desks away from the windows. This is because an abandoned lot across from the school has become an open-air market for drugs and sex. If the children could look out the windows they would see addicts pushing needles into their arms and crack users copulating.[1262]

Some New York City nursery schools are in such violent neighborhoods that children barely old enough to talk are trained to hit the floor whenever they hear shots ring out.[1263] There is no telling who might be doing the shooting. Late in 1990, Brooklyn nursery-school teachers found that one of their three-year-olds had come to class with a loaded pistol. Police said he was probably the youngest such offender on record.[1264]

The West Coast is well on its way in the same direction. One junior high school in Long Beach, California, spent $160,000 on a concrete wall to stop stray bullets from a neighboring housing project from flying into the playground.[1265] At eighteen-hundred-student Jordan High School in the black section of Los Angeles, there are no less than thirteen security guards, two police officers, one parole officer, and several administrators who patrol the place with walkie-talkies. Every day a workman checks the school's walls and paints over provocative graffiti that could start a gang battle. Violence is so bad that the school has opened classrooms in a nearby housing project so students need not risk their lives by coming to school.[1266]

All across the country, schools are practicing the same "drop drills" and "bullet drills" as in New York, so students will know how to react to gunfire—though school officials are reluctant to talk about these drills for fear of alarming parents. School districts in at least twenty-three different cities use metal detectors to search for weapons.[1267] In 1991, school security guards in Chicago alone made nearly ten thousand arrests.[1268]

Crime and violence have prompted new thinking in the way schools are designed and built. Bathrooms are no longer put at the end of hallways, but in the center, because crime breeds on the periphery. Halls are laid out in straight lines so guards can sweep them with their eyes. Grounds are designed so that all entrances can be surveyed from a central administration office. School architects have found that much of the design work has already been done for them; they need only adapt many of the features that prison architects have used for years.[1269]

Festering Sores

The United States, the greatest accumulation of wealth and power the planet has ever known, now has pockets of degeneracy as horrible as anything found in the poorest nations of the world. From the interstices of our twenty-first-century cities there oozes a hideous misery.

Drug users, AIDS carriers, vagrants, and Third World immigrants, have brought back a disease that was considered essentially eradicated in the 1960s: tuberculosis. Until recently, doctors and nurses never saw a single case in all their clinical training. Now, if they work in big cities, they see plenty of them. The populations who get the disease do not come in for treatment until they are thoroughly sick and extremely infectious. Many do not have the discipline to stick to the six-month treatment necessary for a cure. By 1990 the disease was spreading so rapidly that in some parts of the city it was as prevalent as in Third World countries. Even healthy people living ordinary lives were beginning to catch it, and editorial writers were muttering about quarantine.[1270] By 1992, experts at the Centers for Disease Control called the disease "out of control" in at least two dozen American cities.[1271]

Occasionally, underclass behavior bubbles up into what always used to be oases of civility—public libraries. In one elegant, high-ceilinged Washington, D.C., library, a prostitute was practicing her trade in the basement bathroom, and a child found an unconscious woman slumped on the floor with a needle in her arm. In the main downtown library, workers plastered over stairwell openings because people were copulating in them. At the Martin Luther King Library, twenty-two "repeat offenders" were banned from the building for copulating in the bathrooms. At the West End branch library, a patron checked out a handful of books, walked out on the sidewalk, and started hawking them. Drug deals among the stacks are routine.[1272]

Derelicts who live under Interstate 395 in Miami steal the copper wiring out of the freeway light poles faster than the state Department of Transportation can replace it. In early 1992, after having seen hundreds of thousands of dollars' worth of copper disappear, the department gave up. Motorists had to drive in the dark.[1273]

In all our once-great cities there are stories like these to sicken and shame us. Our country is rotting. It is sick with a disease so shocking that we turn our faces from it in dread. Increasingly, it is home to a class of citizens for whom the most basic rules of social organization have come unraveled. No other advanced nation has such a class living in its midst; indeed, there may never have been a society or subculture that has ever suffered such a catastrophic collapse of values.

The Tragedy to Come

Throughout recorded history, human society has expected men to take honest jobs rather than live by theft and violence. It has expected them to support their wives and children. It has expected women not to get pregnant until they had a man they could count on. In America these minimum expectations go under the old-fashioned name of "family values." They are an easy target for scoffers who laugh at tradition or who fancy themselves superior to anything so stuffy and middle-class.

And yet these stuffy, middle-class "family values" must be built securely into a society or that society *will not survive*. They are taught by religion, custom, and example. Perhaps more important, they are part of a hard reality. Under natural conditions, men who do not support themselves starve. Pregnant women whose men run out on them starve. Their children starve. Any society that kept this up would quickly become extinct.

This is why every society has built up such elaborate traditions, customs, laws, and taboos around sex and marriage. Any society that let its adolescents bring forth generations of fatherless children would collapse. Before the invention of reliable contraceptives, Western societies enforced responsible reproduction through a fierce condemnation of sex outside of marriage.

It takes work to support oneself, foresight to take a spouse, dedication to stay with one, and patience to rear children. None of this comes naturally to anyone, and certainly not to teenagers. To have established stable families at all was one of man's first great victories over his animal nature.

It takes years of instruction to turn young humans into responsible adults. Societies must teach values to their children and limit their sex lives. What we have seen in the underclass is a spectacular collapse of the forces that teach values to children and limit their sex lives. It is families that must do this. If families do not form, they cannot do the job, and if they cannot do the job, it will not be done.

One of the few blacks who have studied the underclass firsthand writes that the only force that can reliably keep a girl from the culture of the street is a strong family. Without the love and discipline of people who know that life does not end at age thirty, girls slide relentlessly into pregnancy, welfare, and membership in the "baby club."[1274] This is a good description of the process among ghetto blacks, both male and female, that underlies the near-disappearance of normal family life in the underclass.

The children of the underclass are growing up without rules and controls. They are doing what children naturally do if they do not have parents, teachers, friends, and grandparents to nag, praise, blame, punish, love, and worry about them. Government cannot act in place of those people.

This collapse in values can only get worse. The percentage of black homes headed by a single parent has grown from 9 percent in 1950 to 28 percent in 1965 to 33 percent in 1970 to fully one half today.[1275] In the 1950s, black children had a 52 percent chance of living with both of their biological parents until age seventeen. In the 1980s they had only a 6 percent chance.[1276] Can we rationally expect the children of poor, disorganized, single parents to grow up and become wise, loving parents? Can we expect them to teach their children values?

If there is anything that will make today's generation of ghetto black children better parents than the ones they have, there is no sign of what that might be. The American government is not in the business of rearing children, nor can it be. There are certain things that only parents can do. When millions of parents refuse to do them, government looks on helplessly.

Endless talk about enriched curricula, Head Start, empowerment, Afrocentrism, victimization, special education, dysfunctionality, self-esteem, social justice, role models, etc., fails to recognize the most important fact of all: All too often, the children of indigent, unmarried fifteen-year-olds start life with problems *we cannot fix.* Government programs cannot take the place of loving, responsible parents.

To make the same point in a different way, is there a single social problem in this country that would *not* be well on its way toward a solution if every child had loving, responsible parents? The tragedy of welfare is that when reckless childbearing is rewarded with a government check, many more children are likely to start life with anything but loving, responsible parents.

Some blacks still refuse to see the tragedy staring them in the face. Toni Morrison is a Pulitzer Prize winner and, arguably, America's best-known black woman author. Besides blaming white racism for the problems that beset blacks, she thinks that teenage pregnancy and the high-school dropout rate are just fine. "Schools must stop being holding pens to keep energetic young people off the job market and off the streets," she says. "What is this business that you have to finish school at 18?" she wants to know. "The body is ready to have babies, that's why they are in a passion to do it. Nature wants it done then, when the body can handle it, not after 40, when the income can handle it." Miss Morrison sees no problems ahead for these dropouts and their children:

> They can be teachers. They can be brain surgeons. We have to help them become brain surgeons. That's my job. I want to take them all in my arms and say "Your baby is beautiful and so are you and, honey, you can do it. And when you want to be a brain surgeon call me—I will take care of your baby."[1277]

This is pure nuttiness, of course, but it is nothing more than an extreme form of the 1960s view that society can accommodate all forms of self-expression. In *Blaming the Victim,* William Ryan urged America to focus on change rather than adjustment. This meant that we were to change society rather than ask people to adjust to it. That is exactly what we have done, and now we are reaping the consequences.

8

What Is to Be Done?

*W*HAT IS AMERICA TO DO ABOUT THE RISING TIDE OF HOR-
ror? Visitors from Europe or Japan shake their
heads in wonder at the squalor and barbarity of
America's cities. They could be forgiven for thinking that the country had viciously and deliberately neglected its
poor and its blacks. Of course, it has not.

Since the 1960s, the United States has poured a staggering
amount of money into education, housing, welfare, Medicaid, and
uplift programs of every kind. Government now spends $240 bil-
lion a year to fight poverty,[1278] and despite the widespread notion
that spending was curtailed during Republican administrations, it
has actually gone up steadily, at a rate that would have astonished
the architects of the Great Society. Federal spending on the poor,
in real 1989 dollars, quadrupled from 1965 to 1975, and has nearly
doubled since then.[1279]

As the economist Walter Williams has pointed out, with all the
money spent on poverty since the 1960s, the government could
have bought every company on the *Fortune* 500 list and nearly all

the farmland in America.[1280] What do we have to show for three decades and $2.5 trillion worth of war on poverty? The truth is that these programs have not worked. The truth that America refuses to see is that these programs have made things worse.

How can we help the underclass? It is interesting to note that although the Los Angeles riots have revived the decades-old cry for more "programs," no one seems to have much real faith in them.[1281] The one exception is Head Start. Of all the social programs from the 1960s, it has the best reputation. The theory is that a year or two of intensive help for three- to five-year-olds will make up for the bad childhood environment that afflicts many poor people. The notion that Head Start was a great success has sunk deeply into popular consciousness despite the fact that the early gains reported by Head Start children are soon lost.

One of the most thorough, long-term studies was the Milwaukee Project, undertaken in the 1980s at a cost of millions of dollars. A group of infants was selected soon after birth to spend five days a week in "infant stimulation centers." The leader of the project claimed that the enrichment given these children made the early environments of such famous child prodigies as John Stuart Mill and Francis Galton seem impoverished. The children were kept in the program for *six years* and then sent to regular public schools.

The media reported delightedly that, on leaving the program, the children scored 30 points higher on IQ tests than did a control group. It was scarcely reported to the public at all when, three years later, the "enriched" children were found to be performing at the same academic level as the controls—that is to say, at a level commensurate to an IQ of 80.[1282]

A more recent study has produced similar results. J.S. Fuerst of Loyola University has tracked 684 black children who attended specially funded programs that were so intensive and far-reaching

[1281] Documents from the 1960s, such as the Kerner Commission report, are written with an almost touching faith in the powers of government. In addition to detailed recommendations on police procedures, riot control tactics, and the use of troops in emergencies, the report devotes seventy pages to the education, housing, job training, and welfare programs that the authors think will bring blacks into the national mainstream. The only real obstacle the commissioners foresaw was some resistance to raising the necessary taxes. If the money were available, the problems could be solved. Otto Kerner et al., *Report of the National Advisory Commission on Civil Disorders* (New York: Bantam Books, 1968), p. 23.

that Mr. Fuerst calls them "Head Start to the fourth power." The children stayed in these programs for two to seven years and had significantly better test scores than a control group. However, ten years later, after the children had returned to regular schools, their performances were practically indistinguishable from those of children who had not gotten the special instruction.[1283]

The earnestness with which people propose ways to help the poor and the underachiever suggests they believe that no one has ever seriously tried to help them before. In fact, vast resources have been poured into such attempts but with disappointing results. For example, from 1985 to 1989, New York City spent more than $120 million on a special program to keep the most likely truants from dropping out of school. Guidance counselors gave career and family advice, and social workers visited homes. Services costing *$8,000 per pupil* were lavished on specially chosen participants—but to no discernible effect. They dropped out at the same rates as everyone else. Program administrators concluded that by the time students got to high school there was nothing that could be done to help them.[1284]

Another enormous attempt to help the less well off has been New York City's "special education" program. This program is protected from funding cuts by state law and court rulings. One in eight of all public school students is now found to be "handicapped"—double the number of 12 years ago—and thus entitled to special handling. Screening alone costs $3,000 per child for a total of $240 million a year, and the 119,000 "specials" cost $16,746 a year to teach—more than twice the $7,107 for regular students. They get classes of no more than a dozen students and the services of an army of therapists. The results? Only 5 percent of "specials" ever rejoin the mainstream, and only 17 percent manage to graduate. This costs the city a remarkable $2 billion a year.[1285]

There is an understandable reluctance on the part of Americans to give up the idea that government intervention helps people. Americans are not inclined to sit by idly while others suffer. Nevertheless, even if government intervention worked, the problems that must now be solved are so great that we may no longer have the resources to make it work.

"Programs" are not going to help addicted women who rent their children out to be raped, nor will they help the men who pay to rape them. Charles Murray has suggested that crime, crack, and AIDS will so discourage America that it gives up on solutions and settles for containment. He predicts that slums could become like Indian reservations—supplied from without and shunned.[1286] Conventional welfare thinking would continue to supply subsistence means to increasingly unproductive and dangerous inner cities. The writ of law would gradually recede, leaving behind even greater anarchy and misery.

Such an end would be horrible, but it is not unrealistic. In fact, by any civilized standards, and even by American standards of only a few decades ago, *it has already happened.* Our nation endures unspeakable Third World squalor because it has crept upon us gradually, because the middle class can live beyond its reach, and because it is largely a product of good intentions.

The Tough Approach

A dawning realization that traditional remedies are failing has prompted a number of more hard-nosed proposals. Editorial writers are floating ideas that, twenty years ago, would probably never have gotten an airing.

Irving Kristol, for example, points out that in places such as Washington, D.C., Detroit, and South Los Angeles, black people are in greater danger from each other than Wild West settlers ever were from desperadoes. Mr. Kristol calls for a return to a kind of frontier justice. A mayor could call a state of emergency, or even declare martial law. The authorities would stop and search anyone, anytime, if they thought he might be carrying drugs. He points out that fifty years ago the police had just that kind of authority, and ghettos were much more habitable than they are today.[1287]

Crackdowns like that would have some effect, and the near certainty of punishment would keep at least some people from trying crime in the first place. The many law-abiding people in black neighborhoods would probably be delighted if something like martial law were declared. It will not be. White people who live in drug-free suburbs would say that it was an invasion of privacy. Black people who live in drug-free suburbs would say that it was racism, since most of the people rounded up would be black.

It has been pointed out that Japan has a simple, effective treatment for drug addicts. It throws them in jail and lets them go cold turkey. That is so unpleasant that very few drug users risk having to go through it again.[1288] We are unlikely to try this because it does not sound "compassionate."

Something else that might do some good—but will not be tried —is mandatory, no-appeal death sentences for drug dealers. A number of Middle Eastern countries have kept drugs out of their countries by quickly executing anyone who sells them. In America, law-abiding blacks who have seen their children and their neighborhoods blasted by drugs would probably be happy if we did that. We will not, because many people who do not suffer directly from the problem think the death penalty is inhumane.

In 1989, a Delaware state senator introduced a bill that would bring back the public whipping post for drug dealers. Thomas B. Sharp, the Democratic leader, proposed five to forty lashes, "well laid on," for convicted offenders.[1289] America is not going to reintroduce public flogging, but proposals like this show how desperately we are casting about for solutions.

Mike Royko of the *Chicago Tribune* is fed up with drug crime and assaults on women. He thinks that gun laws should be changed to let women carry concealed weapons. He knows this will not happen, so his advice to women is, "Get a gun and carry it in your purse anyway. To hell with the concealed weapon law."[1290]

Even the chief justice of the Supreme Court of West Virginia thinks that the threat to the social order is so great that conventional means of law enforcement can no longer do the job. Justice Richard Neely thinks that citizens should be organized into crime-fighting units, just like volunteer fire departments. He has no illusions about what he is proposing. "This is modern-day vigilantism," he says.[1291]

When its crime rate tripled in a single year, the city of Dermott, Arkansas, passed a special ordinance to deal with gangs and drug violence. Since juveniles are often beyond the reach of the law, the city decided to punish their parents instead—by putting them in a public stockade. Mom and Dad would spend up to six hours a day on display inside a portable chain link fence in front of the firehouse. They might also have their pictures printed in the local paper over the caption "Irresponsible Parents." Parents who admitted they could not control their children could sign custody over to the court for a fee of $100 per child. They would then have to put bumper stickers on their cars that said, "My children are not my responsibility. They are yours."[1292]

Can Schools Save America?

One of the latest theories is that help must come from the schools. There are two different views of what role the schools have played and how they can solve our problems. One is that they have somehow "failed" America's children and are partially to blame for our plight. The other is a frank admission that America's parents are failing to rear their children properly and that schools must take over.

Schools may be wasteful or poorly run, but it is hard to believe that they somehow give rise to the horrors detailed in the previous chapter. No other nation in the world asks children to learn under such shameful circumstances, but the schools did not create those circumstances.

American schools do not hire armed guards and install metal detectors because they are "bad" schools. Something went wrong at home long before students ever got to those schools. Samuel Sava, executive director of the National Association of Elementary School Principals, is one of the few people who dare say so. "It's not better teachers, texts, or curricula that our children need most," he says; "it's better childhoods, and we will never see lasting school reform until we first see parent reform."[1293]

It is scarcely the fault of New York City's public school system that more than 60 percent of its students live in homes with only one parent.[1294] Nearly two thirds of the city's high-school students failed at least one course during the fall semester in 1989, and one third failed *three or more* courses.[1295] It is hardly fanciful to think there might be a connection between illegitimacy and bad grades.

In 1982, a survey of educators found that the major discipline problems were "assaults on students," "assaults on teachers," and "bringing weapons to school." What were the major discipline problems that teachers faced forty years earlier? "Talking," "chewing gum," and "running in the halls."[1296] We hardly recognize our own past. It is surely a tour de force effort in refraining from blaming the victim to conclude that the schools have somehow caused children to start assaulting each other.

Nevertheless, some white educators seem able to manage it. Thomas Sobol, the New York State commissioner of education, recently sponsored a report that claimed black students fail and misbehave because they are the victims of intellectual and educational oppression. They are oppressed because the school system does not teach them that black culture was just as important in building America as European culture. One of the suggested remedies is that Indians and Puerto Ricans be given equal credit with Englishmen in the development of the nation and that European explorers be portrayed as greedy racists.[1297] Donald H. Smith, dean of the School of Education of New York's City University, thinks that a more culturally appropriate curriculum will "save" the black child.[1298]

Do even Mr. Smith and Mr. Sobol believe what they are saying? Do they really think that yet another new curriculum will keep underclass children off drugs, out of gangs, and in school? Will it keep girls from getting pregnant or persuade boys to marry them? The "Eurocentric" education that is supposed to be doing such damage to blacks today seems to have caused no harm to Booker T. Washington, W.E.B. Du Bois, Martin Luther King, Ralph Bunche, Julian Bond, and millions of unsung black men and women who led responsible, upright lives even in the teeth of Jim Crow and segregation.

In any case, our schools have certainly been changing to accommodate students rather than vice versa. One common change is that many administrators no longer expect students to do the

338 ● *Paved With Good Intentions*

things that students have always done—unless they are bribed to do them.

As we saw earlier, one Detroit school held a lottery with a $100 prize, to try to get students to hand in class registrations. At Thomas Johnson High School in Frederick, Maryland, any student who has missed fewer than four days of school in one year is entered in a lottery for $1,000. Maryland now requires all school districts to come up with such reward plans to boost attendance.[1299] Other schools have instituted systems whereby students who get good grades or have good attendance records get special parking privileges, free admission to school dances, and even discounts in local stores.[1300]

Some schools have started treating parents the same way. It is well known that parent participation in schooling is important if students are to succeed. Some schools have therefore decided that if parents will not get involved voluntarily, the schools should pay them to do so. Public School 85 in the South Bronx gives mothers cash every time they attend workshops at the school.[1301] In Milwaukee as well, officials at Benjamin Franklin Elementary School could not get some black parents to come to school meetings, so they started paying them to attend.[1302]

This is completely topsy-turvy thinking. It is like giving indigent people money and expecting that money will give them the attitudes—diligence, reliability, readiness to work—that result in money. If someone has noticed that students do well at schools to which parents often come for meetings, it is foolish to think that paying parents to come to meetings will have the same effect. Parents spend time at schools if they care about education and about their children. *Paying* parents to show up for meetings may not change their thinking at all. It is like paying people to do "volunteer" work, or forcing people to contribute to charity.

Nevertheless, bribing students and paying parents at least acknowledges an important new fact of life in America. Our country now has a class of people who will not behave in even minimally responsible ways unless they are paid to do so. This realization has begun to seep into the thinking that governs welfare. Officials are willing to try virtually anything that might forestall the harvest of catastrophe that awaits future generations of underclass babies.

For example, the state of Rhode Island has concluded that it is both humane and thrifty to offer free prenatal care to pregnant indigent women. Infant disorders can often be corrected most effectively and at least cost while the child is still in the womb. Nevertheless, the state has discovered that poor women will not come in for medical care even if it is free. The authorities decided to tempt them into clinics by entering them in lotteries. Any woman who keeps all her appointments through the first trimester is eligible for a $500 prize.[1303]

Washington, D.C., also offers free prenatal care for any woman whose annual family income is less than $20,000. There are convenient evening hours, and child care is available. The city has launched a "Better Babies" campaign to advertise health services through billboards, television, and radio. There is even a MOM (Maternity Outreach Mobile) van that makes the rounds of poor neighborhoods, hunting down pregnant women, reminding them of their appointments, and taking them to clinics if they do not have transportation. This is not enough. Washington has the highest infant mortality rate in the nation, and a black baby born in the District of Columbia is more likely to die before age one than a baby born in North Korea or Bulgaria.[1304] Despite free medical service for the poor and increased public education about the importance of prenatal care, the proportion of American babies who get no prenatal care or care only in the last trimester has *increased* slightly since the mid-1970s.[1305]

Lawton Chiles, the governor of Florida, thinks it is asking too much to expect poor, disorganized, pregnant women to come to clinics for free checkups. He suggests that it would be less intimidating for the mothers if health officials made house calls. "In their home, it's a very natural atmosphere," he explains.[1306]

The private group Planned Parenthood has started paying teenage girls a dollar for every day they avoid getting pregnant. Such programs are operating in Rocky Ford, Colorado, and in San Mateo, California. More are being planned elsewhere.[1307]

In Caroline County, Maryland, an official has suggested that public money be used to pay teenage girls not to get pregnant. The program would be directed at girls who already have had one child and who are therefore most likely to have another. In 1989, 14 percent of the teenage girls attending schools in Caroline County were pregnant. More than two thirds of these were pregnant with their second child.[1308] Maryland is the same state that has ordered its schools to develop rewards—such as lotteries—to keep students in school.

Isabel Sawhill of the Urban Institute has a proposal that combines both objectives. She says that children in underclass areas should be given a $5,000 reward if they manage to graduate from high school without bearing or fathering a child. The $5,000 would be in the form of a voucher that could be spent only on college or vocational training.[1309] LeMoyne-Owen College in Memphis, Tennessee, offers tuition-free admission to young black men who attend fourteen Saturday afternoon sessions on campus, get a C average in high school, and graduate without becoming fathers.[1310] The state of Rhode Island has just started a $10 million program to offer free college tuition to any of today's third-graders who manage to graduate from high school without getting on drugs or having a child.[1311]

What is significant about ideas like this is not that they would necessarily be great successes. It is that they do not flinch from two unpleasant truths. The first is that an increasing number of American children may not behave responsibly unless society takes extraordinary measures. The second is that whatever else we do for the underclass, it will not be more than a finger in the dike as long as the underclass keeps on having more babies.

The legal system is gingerly moving toward this realization. When Melody Baldwin got a twenty-year sentence for murdering her four-year-old son, a Superior Court judge offered to reduce her sentence if she agreed to be sterilized. Debra Forsterm, convicted of criminal child abuse, was sentenced to using birth control for her remaining childbearing years. Feminists and civil libertarians have yelped at these sentences, and they have a Supreme Court decision on their side. In 1942 the Court struck down an Oklahoma law that called for sterilization of certain criminals. The Court said that procreation is "one of the basic civil rights of man."[1312]

In 1987 the state of Wisconsin tried something else. It passed a law to make grandparents pay support when their minor children have babies. This is an appealing idea, but it has not had the slightest effect on the teenage pregnancy rate, since poor people— the very ones whose children are the most likely to get pregnant— are not required to pay.[1313]

A few courts have started punishing mothers for turning their unborn babies into drug addicts.[1314] Between 1987 and 1991, some sixty different cases had been brought against pregnant drug takers. The charges ran from criminal child abuse, to assault with a deadly weapon, and manslaughter.[1315] There is a certain logic to these charges, but what good do they do the baby?

The ghastly realities of underclass life have started people muttering about forced abortion and sterilization. Not least are members of the underclass themselves. Ghetto grandmothers who find themselves saddled with their crack-addicted daughters' unwanted babies talk openly of sterilization.[1316]

It is not only ghetto grandmothers who think that crack-addicted women should have no more children. It is likely that whatever they may say in public, a majority of Americans think that society may have the right to prevent such women from having any more children.

Reproductive Responsibility

Though sterilization and forced abortion are the options many people suggest when they know they will not be quoted, they are not solutions that America will adopt. Nevertheless, they approach the problem in the proper terms—those of reproductive responsibility. If you, the reader, do not think these are the proper terms, you might play the following mental game: Let us say that you have a brother named George who did not finish high school and who just can not hold a job. He is a well-meaning fellow, but over the years it has become clear that if your family did not support him, he would be sleeping under a bridge. He accepts help from all of his relatives, but since you are the most responsible, hardworking person he knows, you are the one he comes to when it is time to pay the rent.

Last month's rent is now past due, and George shows up all smiles. "I've got great news," he says. "My girlfriend Peggy's pregnant. And since she loves children, we're thinking we'll maybe have three or four. The studio apartment will be too small, of course, but if you could manage another $300 a month we could get a nice two-bedroom place where the kids could play and . . ."

If you are like most people, George would never get this far in his little speech. Since you are supporting George, you might think you had something to say about his plans for having children. You might think that George had no business bringing more mouths into the world for you to feed. You might have *a lot* to say about his plans if you happened to know that girlfriend Peggy had just discovered the joys of crack cocaine.

People do not willingly foot the bill for the children of indigents, even if they are their *own flesh and blood.* Yet our society is set up so that all of us—willingly or unwillingly—pay for complete strangers to have children they cannot support. Nothing stops a welfare mother from having as many babies as she likes. No one tells her she can not have any more, even if she has been a terrible mother to the ones she already has. In most states her welfare payments rise along with the size of her family.[1317]

If she spends her welfare money on drugs and starves her children, some overloaded social worker may be able to persuade a court to take away the children and place them in a foster home. But the woman is still free to have as many more children as she likes.

This system is wrong on all counts. It is wrong to make society pay for children whose parents cannot look after them. It is wrong to burden grandparents and foster parents with children who were not wanted. And it is wrong for the children, who are born into misery that is not of their own making and from which they are unlikely to escape.

It is all very well to talk about reproductive rights, but rights are

[1317] In 1992, New Jersey stopped paying increased benefits for women who have babies while on welfare. California, where about a third of welfare recipients have more children after they go on the dole, was likely to do the same. Jason DeParle, "Why Marginal Changes Don't Rescue the Welfare System," *The New York Times* (March 1, 1992), p. 3. Debra Saunders, "Welfare Reform, California Style" *The Wall Street Journal* (February 25, 1992).

not unilateral. If the indigent have an absolute, inalienable right to produce children they cannot support, then do not the self-sufficient have the reciprocal right to let the indigent fend for themselves? Or must the self-sufficient be *forced* to support them? Who should have more rights—people on the dole or the people who support them?

The Principle of Obligatory Charity

These questions are central to the very idea of welfare, but they are almost never asked. It is worth attempting to answer them, if only to gain a firmer understanding of what welfare programs really are and to grasp the extent to which they violate ancient, widely held, but seldom voiced assumptions about man and society.

A careful analysis of government welfare programs reveals that they rest on doubtful moral foundations. This may seem a surprising position to take, since the proponents of such programs often speak as though welfare were society's highest moral achievement. They can do this only because the morality of welfare is never challenged; the current intellectual climate treats the words "welfare" and "compassion" almost as if they were synonyms. In fact, they have virtually nothing in common.

What is the purpose of welfare? It is to help those in need. An old and honorable word for helping those in need is "charity." Welfare derives much of its moral status from the high esteem in which all societies hold charity. Shakespeare, writing of mercy, called it twice blessed: "It blesseth him that gives and him that takes." The giver is blessed by a grateful recipient, an admiring society, and the giver's own joy in a gift freely given. The blessings to the taker come both from what he receives and from the gratitude and inspiration of witnessing generosity in his fellow man.

Nevertheless, welfare and charity differ in crucially important ways. The more closely they are examined, the more different they are found to be. Welfare is not just a form of charity undertaken by government. It is not just a form of charity that has been stripped of every blessing. It is cursed—twice cursed—for it curses him that gives and him that takes.

Charity stems from compassion and generosity. The proof of this is that *it is freely given.* Contributions to welfare, on the other hand, are coerced. Everyone understands the difference between what we are made to do and what we choose voluntarily to do. Welfare is a form of obligatory charity to which all taxpayers are forced to contribute. It is fundamentally different from taxes that pay for the *common* good: roads, soldiers, diplomats, policemen, etc. In effect, our government says to its citizens, "You will give part of your money to poor people or you will go to jail for tax evasion." Obligatory charity is thus a contradiction—not charity at all.

If a beggar forces a citizen, under threat of violence, to hand over his money, this is robbery. If government forces the same citizen, under threat of jail, to give money to beggars, the same transfer is called welfare. As far as the citizen is concerned, the outcome is the same: He has been parted from his property against his will. In real life, obstreperous beggars are less of a threat than government, for they can be avoided or fought. Government cannot be avoided, and it is much more difficult to fight.

Everyone understands the difference between paying taxes and doing volunteer work. One is coerced and disagreeable; the other is voluntary and joyful. When charity is coerced, it is closer to extortion. Thus does welfare curse the giver.

What about the taker? Just as welfare is obligatory charity for the giver, so it is an automatic benefit for the taker. The very word we use for welfare programs—"entitlements"—describes them perfectly. They are benefits to which people feel *entitled.* No one was ever *entitled* to charity, to a stranger's generosity. And yet that is how welfare recipients feel and how they are told to feel.

Freely given charity can be tuned to circumstances—cut back, increased, or ended as appropriate. Government charity grinds along impersonally, according to regulations, whether it does good or harm.

Moreover, people feel no gratitude for something to which they are *entitled.* The very notion of grateful welfare recipients is almost comical. Many of them do not even realize that what is given to them had to be taken from someone else. They are left with the literally *de*moralizing notion that food stamps and welfare checks drop from the sky and are theirs by right. This warped, unhealthy view is easily passed on to children.

Finally, as we saw earlier, the knowledge that welfare will cushion the fall from middle-class morality makes it all the more likely that some people will fall. And once they develop a taste for the fruits of obligatory charity, some can never give it up. They become slaves to the welfare bureaucracy. They become addicted to a caricature of charity, which the givers themselves increasingly resent. Thus does welfare curse the taker, but malediction does not end there.

Welfare curses society at large, because it weakens the natural ties that bind people together. When a government check is *not* the solution to every crisis, people turn to family, friends, church, and community. These are the people who care the most about a person's misfortunes, who know best when help is needed and when it is not. The very notion of community is based on calls for help and offers of assistance. It is common to decry the thinning ties of family and community, but welfare is a powerful solvent of those ties. A pregnant woman needs no husband, no family, no community, nor even friends if the government will give her an apartment and pay for her groceries. In turn, she need not be friend or family when someone else is in need. Welfare severs the ties of mutual obligation that are vital to any community.

From a different point of view, welfare raises a fundamental question that deserves an answer. By what moral principle does government take money from one citizen and give it to another? The only answer ever proposed is the pseudo-Marxist notion that if some people have money it is only because they have wrested it immorally from people who do not. This economically illiterate idea crumbles at first contact with reality, but in fact no one is ever made to explain why government has the right to redistribute wealth. The only fact that matters is that there is an imbalance: Some citizens have more money than others. That is justification enough to force those with money to hand it over to those without.

What government is doing becomes clearer if we imagine what

it might do if it were possible to subtract intelligence from those who are smart and hand it over to those who are dull. There is an obvious imbalance in intelligence. Should government force smart people to turn over part of their wit to the witless? If anything, government might have *more* justification for redistributing intelligence than for redistributing wealth. Intelligence is largely an accident of genetics, for which an individual can take little credit, whereas someone may have worked very hard for his money.

Although it would be difficult to prove, the pervading view of wealth—that it should be forcibly taken from those who have it—probably has an effect on crime. If, as they are told over and over, the poor are entitled to money earned by others, why should they not simply take it themselves and cut out the middleman? Crime is, in fact, a much more efficient way to spread wealth. Of every dollar spent by Congress for welfare, only thirty cents actually reach recipients. Administration and bureaucrat salaries eat up the rest.[1318] New York City spends an incredible $18,000 a year per person to accommodate drifters on cots laid out by the hundreds on the floors of armories.[1319]

The idea that welfare and compassion are yoked concepts is easily exploded. "Entitlements" and the dependence they engender are a favor to no one. There is nothing compassionate about designing society so that it tempts a woman—a woman who might have gone to school, worked, married, and had a family—to have an illegitimate child and become a public charge.

Nor is there any compassion in assuming, as obligatory charity programs do, that Americans are mean-spirited people who will spurn the needy if only given a chance. Those who talk about welfare as essential to a "compassionate society" are not making sense. A nation that forces its people to give to the poor has written off compassion and has turned to coercion. Can such a people claim to be free or generous?

Despite coercion, Americans are freely generous. They are quick to aid victims of misfortune, and prodigal in their gifts to social causes. In 1990 Americans gave more than *$120 billion* to charities, and only 10.5 percent of this came from corporations or foundations. Individuals gave this money.[1320] They also did millions of hours of volunteer work and gave millions of pints of blood.

From a historical perspective, one might have expected them to do none of this. In 1948, a married couple with the median income and two children paid *only 2 percent* of its income in state, federal, and social security taxes. In 1991 they paid 30 percent.[1321] In return, today's couple does not get correspondingly better roads, schools, parks, libraries, and police. However, it does get a growing army of doletakers, and a growing army of bureaucrats, policemen, and social workers to process, supervise, and uplift them.

The generosity of Americans goes beyond their contributions to obligatory, government-run charities and makes it all the more remarkable. Or perhaps it makes it all the more understandable. The impulse to help others, which is always alive in the hearts of men, is *not satisfied* by the knowledge that taxes are spent on welfare. Welfare programs have little effect on what people will do, voluntarily, to help others. As long as the tax man leaves a few dollars behind, as long as someone has a little spare time, there will be charity and there will be volunteer work.

The dole in all its forms is now so common and has worked its way so deeply into society that it is difficult to believe it is only a few decades old. Franklin Roosevelt, under whose aegis it found its modern beginnings, would be astonished at its profusion. It is not likely to be coincidence that an industry that saps the morals of its presumed beneficiaries, taxes the patience of its contributors, and undermines the natural ties of community should have arisen in perfect parallel with the terrible problems that now bedevil America and its underclass.

A loss of faith in the idea of welfare, even outright contempt for it, is increasingly common. Welfare is one of those subjects about which public opinion and published opinion diverge sharply. Though they may not be able to explain why, a great many Americans feel in their bones that it is wrong for the government to take their money and give it away to other people—especially to people who have broken one of the most fundamental rules of the social order by having children they cannot support.

Can public faith in welfare be restored? Probably not. First, it has failed to rid society of the ills it was supposed to combat and has probably made them worse. Second, however well intentioned, it violates widely held views of what is right and wrong.[1322]

Ending Reckless Procreation

One could argue that the best and fairest way to bring down the number of irresponsible births would be gradually to bring back the penalties that, for thousands of years, have always held them down. If the government slowly phased out welfare, many in the underclass would reform their habits. Charity would return to where it should begin: the home. People who needed help—and people who gave it—would rediscover the importance of family and community.

Will America do away with welfare? Not until it is willing, once more, to embrace the sturdy virtues of the men and women who founded this country and made it great. These virtues are not alien to our spirit nor so far in the past as to be only memories. Nevertheless, the moral and intellectual momentum of American life would have to be reversed before welfare were abandoned.

What might be an alternative solution or a first step toward a return to greater reliance on family and community rather than on government? To the extent that America is finally prepared to recognize that reckless procreation lies at the heart of the rot, there is an approach that, sooner or later, the nation will accept.

Late in 1990, the FDA approved a five-year, implantable contra-

---

[1322] It is common to defend welfare by comparing it to other government programs that take money from some citizens and give it to others. Some, like Social Security and subsidies to farmers, do this directly. Others, like the tax deduction for mortgage interest, do it indirectly. Taken together, such payments consume more tax revenues than welfare does, and most beneficiaries are middle-class white people.

Powerful moral arguments can be made against all these transfer payments. Social Security, for example, is a coercive form of retirement planning that seems to assume that Americans cannot be trusted to save for their old age. Moreover, today's Social Security recipients are getting much more out of the system than they paid into it, while those who are paying today have no guarantee that they will get a fair return on their money.

Still, there is a crucial difference between middle-class transfers and welfare. It is preposterous to pay farmers not to grow crops, but farm payments do not directly subsidize or indirectly encourage reckless procreation and single motherhood. Middle-class transfers may be unfair, but they do not directly contribute to the illegitimacy and hereditary poverty from which our most intractable social problems spring.

ceptive known as Norplant. At the time, it was already being used by more than a million people all around the world,[1323] and it could be a great benefit to the underclass.

Welfare recipients are already being monitored by welfare agencies. The majority of Americans believe that people who are already living at public expense have no right to bring yet more people into the world whom we must feed, house, clothe, medicate, and try to educate.[1324] Welfare recipients could be required to use Norplant when they started receiving payments, and to continue using it for as long as they were on the dole. As soon as they could support themselves, the implant could be removed if the recipient wished. Kerry Patrick, a Kansas state representative, has already proposed paying welfare mothers $500 if they would agree to use Norplant.[1325]

Everyone would benefit from combining welfare with Norplant. Welfare mothers would not be tied down by more small children and would be available for training or work. The children they already had would get more attention from their mothers, and society would be spared the prospect of yet more children who have little going for them. Welfare recipients, whose likelihood of marriage decreases with every new illegitimate child, would have a better chance of establishing a conventional, two-parent home for their children.

Unfortunately, such a program would not help the people who have the most to lose from a pregnancy: girls who have not had children and who are not already on welfare. In our current moral climate, telling them not to have sex will not work. King Canute had about as much luck telling the tide not to come in.[1326] Students should get sex education, free contraceptives, and free abortions. If contraception and abortion did not work, high schools in

---

[1324] According to a poll by the *Los Angeles Times*, 61 percent of respondents were in favor of obligatory Norplant for women who use drugs. A poll by *Glamour* magazine found that 60 percent of its readers favored mandatory Norplant for women who abuse children. Charlotte Allen, "Norplant—Birth Control or Coercion?," *The Wall Street Journal* (September 13, 1991), p. A10.

[1326] In 1989, a Maryland organization called Campaign for Our Children was planning to spend $7 million on a media campaign with the message "You don't need to have sex." Leah Latimer, "Effort Aims to Shock Youngsters into Abstinence," *Washington Post* (August 7, 1989), p. E3. It was not likely to have a chance against the steady din of movies, billboards, TV shows, and magazines that tell us we *do* need to have sex.

some areas could institute implant programs. These could be voluntary, or with cash bonuses for girls who got implants. In any case, it must become the rule in America that people do *not* have the right to bear children they cannot support. Teenage pregnancy, the disappearance of marriage, and single parenthood are sure guarantors that the underclass will perpetuate itself.

It is not easy to say what should be done about the boys who get girls pregnant with no intention of marrying them. They are, if anything, the most irresponsible group of all. They cannot be forced to marry, nor are they likely to have an income that could be diverted to support a child. It probably would not have much effect, but they should be told repeatedly that if they make a girl have a baby, they are probably dooming that girl and her child to a life of poverty.

Those who would object to a Norplant policy should bear in mind that ever since the founding of this nation, and up until only about thirty years ago, our ancestors—black and white—took strong measures to see to it that teenagers did not have children they could not support. They used religion, custom, the law, social pressure, even shotguns and horsewhips. They used every means at their disposal because they knew that irresponsibility of so basic a kind destroys the social order. We can now see how right they were.

The old methods no longer work. They revolved around vehement condemnation of fornication, and it would take a transformation of not just the underclass but of the entire society to revive old strictures. But just because the old ways do not work, there is no reason to give up. We must find new ways that do work. The genie of the adolescent libido probably cannot be stuffed back into the lamp, but we can reduce irresponsible reproduction.

Indeed, when it comes to their own families, many Americans are as unalterably opposed to illegitimacy as their grandparents were. Though the means available to them are constantly shrinking, middle-class parents go to great lengths to try to keep their daughters from getting pregnant before they marry.

It would be foolish for whites to think that the problem of family collapse touches only blacks. They would do well to recall the circumstances that prompted what came to be called the Moynihan Report,[1327] which was published in 1965. In it, Daniel P. Moynihan called attention to the disintegration of black families and to the vicious cycle of poverty that this sets in motion. Though he was roundly condemned for poking into the sexual and conjugal habits of blacks, Mr. Moynihan's predictions have been largely borne out. What, though, were the signs of family collapse that so alarmed Mr. Moynihan? Illegitimacy and divorce rates among blacks of nearly 25 percent.[1328] Rates of divorce and illegitimacy for whites are today approaching these levels. People of all races would benefit from measures that reduce illegitimacy.

Nevertheless, some would complain that a Norplant policy would be racist, because a disproportionate number of the births that would be prevented, at least initially, would be black. When a December 12, 1990, editorial in the *Philadelphia Inquirer* called for incentives to encourage welfare mothers to accept Norplant, it was denounced as racist. The commotion was so great that the *Inquirer* took the unusual step of publishing a second editorial apologizing for the first.[1329] The furor over this editorial was as senseless as it was inevitable. There are laws against murder and robbery in this country, and blacks run afoul of them in disproportionate numbers. They then go to jail in disproportionate numbers. This does not make the laws racist.

There is nothing at all racist about insisting that people of all races support their children. If anything, it is the obvious and humane thing to do. Almost as many black women would have children as they do now, only they would have them at age twenty-five instead of age sixteen—after they had educations and husbands, not while they were still children themselves.

An end to the vicious cycle of reckless procreation is the *only* solution to the problems of the underclass. Anything else—Head Start, job training, enterprise zones, workfare—may do a little good here and there, but ultimately it is a distraction. If our country is to do something more than spend money and salve its conscience, it must recognize that single parenthood and welfare are not just an "alternative life-style" but a fatal violation of the social contract.

[1327] The official title of this document was *The Negro Family: The Case for National Action*, and it was written when the author was assistant secretary of labor.

A Norplant program will seem obvious to many, radical to some. Those who would find it radical should bear in mind that it would be a return to one of the simplest and most obvious rules by which healthy societies have always lived: People should not have children they cannot support. There is scarcely a social problem that would not recede dramatically if Americans once more began to live by this rule.

A sharp reduction in illegitimacy would not only bring about a reduction in crime, illiteracy, and unemployment. It would also reduce the need for welfare, which is the medium in which these problems breed. Even if welfare cannot be eliminated in the short term, its ultimate elimination should be our goal. Norplant can speed us toward that goal.

The Underclass Must Shrink

A smaller and shrinking underclass should be a goal for all Americans, especially for black Americans. The misbehavior and outright evil of some underclass blacks is so spectacular that all blacks risk being implicated. This is unfair, but little can be done about it. Increasing numbers of whites are being mugged, raped, murdered, or even just insulted by underclass blacks. This is why practically every middle-class black man has a wry story to tell about the white woman who gasped and clutched her purse when he stopped to ask her the time.

When New Yorkers read that the city transit police brace themselves for a wave of marauding youths every afternoon when school lets out,[1330] do those New Yorkers wonder for a moment what race the "youths" are? When the people of Detroit read that hundreds of houses in their city are burned down in arson attacks in the annual "Devil's Night" madness just before Halloween,[1331] do they imagine whites and Asians setting fire to those buildings?[1332] When gangs of teenage girls are reported to be running

[1332] The population of Detroit has dropped to 55 percent of its 1950 level, and the city issued only two building permits for single-family houses in 1987. There are twelve thousand abandoned buildings in Detroit, and the number grows by twelve hundred every year.

cocaine in Kansas City,[1333] what race are they likely to be? When the opening night of a movie is repeatedly interrupted by fistfights and finally called off because the patrons start shooting each other,[1334] is anyone surprised to learn that the movie is called *Harlem Nights?*

Even more hair-raising stories than this are beginning to drift up from the depths of the underclass. When whites read gruesome news about gang rapes and crack babies, they assume they are reading about black people. All too often, they are. If anything, whites exaggerate the size of the black underclass. This does no good for race relations. Nor does it improve them when middle-class blacks defend underclass deviants simply because they are black. The old complaints about how racism causes all this ring more false with every passing year. If only for their own reputations, for their own good name, blacks should be at the forefront of any effort to shrink the underclass. The ones who stand to lose are those who advocate and administer "programs" and whose jobs and reputations would dry up if America found real solutions.

The underclass is, of course, almost a separate world for most Americans. Middle-class people in quiet neighborhoods can lead their lives almost as if the underclass did not exist. It is nearly as remote from them as Indian reservations are. However, we cannot let our inner cities become reservations. They are too important, they are too close by; and above all, to turn them into reservations would be the starkest sort of cruelty. And yet that is precisely the direction in which our policies are pushing them.

Horrifying problems require extraordinary solutions, and anyone who thinks we do not have horrifying problems is blind. Americans have a reputation for waiting until the crisis strikes before they spit on their hands and get to work. Pearl Harbor is the most famous example. Though we refuse to hear them, the bombs are already falling.

The city spends $15 million every year tearing down buildings that have become drug dens and fire hazards. "Abandoned Buildings Litter Dying Detroit," *Omaha Sunday World-Herald* (January 7, 1990).

Middle-Class Solutions

Fortunately, despite their urgency, the problems of the under-class affect only a minority of blacks. In the other black America, what is needed is the realization that the bounty of this nation is not wrung from the reluctant, racist bosom of the white man but is won through individual responsibility and hard work. A recent book on the psychology of successful blacks includes a list of the ingredients of what the black authors call the psychology of black success. At the top of the list is personal responsibility. Another characteristic the authors found in successful blacks was that "they neither expect the Man to save them, nor blame the Man for all the problems and injustices of society."[1335]

Seminars on racism and mandatory college courses in ethnic studies are precisely what we do not need. Their ostensible purpose is to "sensitize" whites to the needs of minorities, but their real effect is to hammer at the old theme that whites are responsible for everything that goes wrong for blacks. This does nothing to help blacks, and whites have been so thoroughly "sensitized" that they are sick of it. College-age whites, especially, who have had no hand in shaping society, are increasingly confused and angry about constant harping on guilt they do not feel. What are they to make of the preposterous idea, propounded with the blessings of the university, that the Ivy League may be a subtle form of genocide? Ultimately, the very notion that Americans must be "sensitized" to race flies in the face of what we are presumably trying to achieve: a society in which race does not matter.

Moreover, there are limits to the patience with which whites will listen to appeals to a guilt they no longer feel. In the past, the best way to get whites to help blacks may have been to try to make them feel guilty. Increasingly, that will only make them angry. Blacks who seek the help and genuine goodwill of whites will not get it by dwelling on white racism and white guilt.

Something else that does no good is the constant proliferation of black subgroups. As soon as blacks join an organization, they band together into a racially exclusive subgroup. The doors of mainly white organizations are open to them, but their organizations are closed to whites. By any definition, this is racial discrimination.

There is a certain logic to this that few acknowledge. Mainly-white colleges must be integrated, but black colleges must stay black because they provide role models. Mainly-white fraternities must be integrated, but exclusively black fraternities will nurture the "black identity." The Miss America contest must be open to blacks, but blacks must have their own, racially exclusive beauty contest. There is black English and a black learning style, and they must be recognized. Job preferences for blacks are a civil right, but job preferences for whites are racism. "Black pride" is healthy and necessary, but "white pride" is bigotry. Standardized tests work for other races, but they are biased against blacks. All-black interest groups must be established to fight the racism within every American organization. Blacks should patronize black-owned stores and vote for black candidates. Blacks feel closer to Africans than to white Americans. Black students must have black teachers or they will not learn properly.

One man who understands where all this leads is Louis Farrakhan, leader of the Nation of Islam. The logic of black pride, black caucuses, and black role models leads straight to black nationhood. That, of course, is Mr. Farrakhan's stated objective. For him, whites are "devils" and "evil by nature." Blacks can expect nothing from them, and should carve out an independent black nation for themselves. He already has a national anthem for them.[1336] Citizens of a black nation would certainly escape the "racism" they claim to find at every turn in the United States.

Is Mr. Farrakhan's whites-are-devils theory any different from that of the equal employment officer who wrote that in America all whites are racist and only whites can be racist? Is it any different from the whites-are-always-responsible theory of black failure? Is the black nation that Mr. Farrakhan would carve out for himself so very different from the black caucuses that blacks so frequently carve out for themselves?

Whether they mean to or not, when blacks set up racially exclusive groups, when they demand special privileges, when they state black goals that are different from America's goals, they are widening the racial fault lines that divide this country. They cannot go on forever demanding special treatment in the name of equality, or practicing racism in the name of ethnic pride, or rebuilding segregation in the name of black identity. The "black agenda" all too often means nothing more than patronage, handouts, double standards, and open hostility to whites.

White Americans will eventually lose patience. The White Student Union at Temple University, the National Association for the Advancement of White People, the popularity in Louisiana of former Klansman David Duke—these are all disquieting signs that whites are tired of double standards. Only for so long will whites watch blacks use race as a weapon before they forge racial weapons of their own.

Of course, race matters in America. It may always matter. But if we really are trying to build a color-blind society, our methods are not merely wrong but perverse. The entire apparatus of government, industry, and education is painfully conscious of race and treats the races differently at every turn. Blacks now demand special treatment as a matter of course. In its befuddled way, society is trying to do what is right. But to favor blacks systematically and then call this sorry charade "equal opportunity" is self-delusion of the worst kind.

If anything brings down the American experiment, it will be the notion that deliberate race consciousness can lead to racial harmony, that reverse racism can eliminate racism. Affirmative action, minority set-asides, and double standards are well-meant folly. If America really were boiling with white racism and the nation's most urgent task were to stamp it out, what more insanely inflammatory policy could one invent than to discriminate against whites because of their race? When the occasional ragtag band of placard-waving Ku Kluxers is outnumbered, not only by hecklers but also by police sent to protect them from outraged citizens, can white racism really be the crippling evil it is made out to be?

Racial distinctions replace the principle of individual merit with that of group rewards. If blacks get favors simply because they are black, it encourages them to think of themselves neither as individuals nor as Americans, but as blacks. How can blacks help but think of themselves as a separate people when society, at every turn, treats them as a separate people? In turn, how can we expect whites not to respond in kind to "ethnic aggressivity"? And finally, how can blacks be expected to believe in ability and hard work when society rewards them for being black instead? They must listen to the words of Booker T. Washington, the former slave who went on to found Tuskeegee Institute:

> No greater injury can be done to any youth than to let him feel that because he belongs to this or that race he will be advanced regardless of his own merit or efforts.[1337]

Unlike the problems of the underclass, the folly of affirmative action could quickly be cured. We need only to interpret the laws on our books exactly as they were written. Nothing could be clearer than a prohibition against discrimination by race, creed, color, or national origin. The layman's understanding of these laws is precisely what their authors meant. Future generations will shake their heads in wonder at the mental acrobatics of our most learned judges, who have stood justice on its head.

Of course, judges cannot, by themselves, change the way America thinks. Even if all race-based preferences were thrown out tomorrow, the job would be only half done until the double standards that first justified them were discredited. For that, all Americans will have to believe that blacks can and must take hold of their own destinies. They must realize that America will cease to be America if race becomes more important than nation. Only then can we begin to heal the hidden wound.

De Tocqueville feared that white America's relations with its freed slaves would be the greatest social crisis the young democracy would face.[1338] He was right. Many great Americans—Abraham Lincoln, Thomas Jefferson, James Madison, John Marshall, Henry Clay, and Daniel Webster, to name just a few—did not believe that black and white could live peaceably in the same society.[1339]

We have not yet proven that they can. But if we do, it will be because we faced the truth unflinchingly. We will have to shun the shakedown artists and guiltmongers. Whites will have to turn their backs on cowardly, dishonest behavior designed solely to escape charges of "racism." They must reject wholesale, off-the-shelf accusations and search for explanations that go deeper than the sloganeering, grandstanding, and buffoonery that now control the field.

The men who founded this country and established the first modern democracy believed that in the marketplace of ideas, the truth would always prevail. It was a belief that the common man would have the courage of his convictions and that society would always honor the truth that made "the land of the free and the home of the brave" something more than an empty slogan. When whites submit to accusations they know are untrue, they are the silent accomplices of falsehood. They must have the courage to say what they know to be true.

Blacks have the harder but more inspiring task of shucking the old excuses and finally taking possession of their lives. They must learn, just as Asians have, that whites can thwart them only if they permit themselves to be thwarted, and that society can help them only if they are able to help themselves. They must recognize that the weapon of race consciousness, which they are so tempted to wield, is a sword that cuts in every direction. Blacks who understand this, and say so publicly, will be reviled by other blacks who are still looking for excuses and handouts. Brave, clear-sighted black men and women carry a heavy burden, for no one else can even hope to touch the desolated generations that are ravaging our cities.

One hundred thirty years ago, this nation very nearly tore itself apart because of race. It could do so again. Policies based on white guilt and reverse racism have failed. Policies based on the denial of individual responsibility have failed. We must have the courage to admit that they have failed, and forge new policies that will succeed.

Notes

1. Seth Mydans, "Homicide Rate up for Young Blacks," *The New York Times* (December 7, 1990), p. A26.
2. "AIDS, Homicides Increase Gap in Black, White Life Expectancy," *Detroit News* (January 8, 1992), p. 3A. Hilary Stout, "Life Expectancy of U.S. Blacks Declined in 1988," *The Wall Street Journal* (April 9, 1991), p. B1.
3. Don Colburn, "The Risky Lives of Young Black Men," *Washington Post Health* (December 18–25, 1990).
4. David Savage, "1 of 4 Young Black Men are in Jail or on Parole, Study Says," *San Francisco Chronicle* (February 27, 1990), p. A1.
5. Elaine Rivera, "High Jail Rate for Minorities," *Newsday* (New York) (October 4, 1990), p. 8.
6. Mortimer Zuckerman, "Meltdown in Our Cities," *U.S. News & World Report* (May 29, 1989), p. 74.
7. Detroit News Wire Service, "U.S. Syphilis Cases at Highest Level Since '49," *Detroit News* (May 17, 1991).
8. Associated Press, "Death Rates for Minority Infants Were Underestimated, Study Says," *The New York Times* (January 8, 1992).
9. Don Rosen, "Poverty Rate for Hispanic Children Rises 29% in 1980s," *Orange County* (Calif.) *Register* (August 27, 1991), p. A15.
10. "Race: Lingering Gaps," *Los Angeles Times* (August 13, 1991), p. A10.
11. National Center for Health Statistics, *Monthly Vital Statistics Report*, Vol. 40, No. 8(s), Dec. 12, 1991, p. 31.
12. Christopher Jencks, "Deadly Neighborhoods," *The New Republic* (June 13, 1988), p. 24.
13. "The American Dream, the American Nightmare," *The Economist* (October 7, 1989), p. 19.
14. Isabel Wilkerson, "Middle-Class Blacks Try to Grip a Ladder While Lending a Hand," *The New York Times* (November 29, 1990), p. A1.
15. National Research Council, *A Common Destiny: Blacks in American Society* (Washington, D.C.: National Academy Press, 1989), p. 289.
16. Robert Pear, "U.S. Pensions Found to Lift Many of Poor," *The New York Times* (December 23, 1988), p. 1.
17. Otto Kerner et al., *Report of the National Advisory Commission on Civil Disorders* (Kerner Commission Report) (New York: Bantam Books, 1968), p. 1.
18. Wendell Berry, *The Hidden Wound* (San Francisco: North Point Press, 1989).
19. Kerner et al., *Report of the National Advisory Commission on Civil Disorders,* p. 203.
20. "The Call to Service," *Yale Alumni Magazine* (Summer, 1989), p. 69.

21. Susan Estrich, "The Hidden Politics of Race," *The Washington Post Magazine* (April 23, 1989), p. 25.

22. Jesse Jackson, "Racism Made a Killer Believable in Boston," *Newsday* (New York) (January 15, 1990), p. 42.

23. Associated Press, "United Church of Christ Urges Fight Against Rising Racism," *The New York Times* (January 15, 1991).

24. *The Wall Street Journal* (December 23, 1987), p. 1.

25. Andrew Hacker, *Two Nations* (New York: Charles Scribner's Sons, 1992), p. 218.

26. See Charles Murray, *Losing Ground* (New York: Basic Books, 1984), p. 222.

27. John Leo, "Straight Talk About Race," *U.S. News & World Report* (April 20, 1992), p. 27.

28. Eddie Borges and Dick Sheridan, "Death Crush," *New York Daily News* (December 29, 1991), p. 3.

29. Robert McFadden, "Survivors of Tragedy Describe the Chaos in Which 8 Died," *The New York Times* (December 30, 1991), p. A1.

30. Vera Haller, "8 Killed, 28 Hurt in Crush to see Rap Stars in N.Y.," *San Francisco Chronicle and Examiner* (December 29, 1991), p. A2. Eddie Borges and Dick Sheridan, "Death Crush," New York *Daily News* (December 29, 1991), p. 3.

31. Rick Hampson, Associated Press, "Real 'Beast' in Deadly N.Y. Crush: Wild Crowd," *San Francisco Sunday Examiner* (January 5, 1992), p. A3.

32. Barry Walters, "Death Rides the Concert Rails," *San Francisco Examiner* (January 12, 1992), p. D1.

33. Lynda Richardson, "Outdoor Memorial Service Becomes Emotional Rally," *The New York Times* (January 13, 1992), p. B4.

34. Richard Hofstadter, *The Paranoid Style in American Politics and Other Essays* (New York: Vintage Books, 1967).

35. Richard Freeman, *Black Elite* (New York: McGraw-Hill, 1976), Chap 4.

36. Freeman, *Black Elite*, p. xx.

37. Freeman, *Black Elite*, p. 216.

38. Freeman, *Black Elite*, p. 21.

39. Walter E. Williams, *The State Against Blacks* (New York: McGraw-Hill, 1982), p. 56.

40. National Research Council, *A Common Destiny*, p. 147.

41. Thomas Sowell, *Civil Rights: Rhetoric or Reality?* (New York: William Morrow & Company, 1984), p. 101.

42. Williams, *The State Against Blacks*, p. 55.

43. Leah Krakinowski, "Black Women Miss Chances for That Mrs.," *Detroit Free Press* (August 19, 1991).

44. Hacker, *Two Nations*, p. 115.

45. Sowell, *Civil Rights*, p. 82.

46. Thomas Sowell, *The Economics and Politics of Race* (New York: William Morrow & Company, 1983), p. 107.

47. Clarence Page, "Foreign-Born Vendors of Success," *San Jose Mercury News* (August 10, 1989), p. 7B.

48. William Beer, "Real-Life Costs of Affirmative Action," *The Wall Street Journal* (August 7, 1989), p. A18.

49. Sowell, *Civil Rights*, pp. 80–81.

50. Freeman, *Black Elite*, p. 208ff.

51. Associated Press, "Study Finds Gains for Black Middle Class," *The New York Times* (August 10, 1991).

52. Department of Commerce, *Statistical Abstract of the United States* (Washington, D.C.: U.S. Government Printing Office, 1991), p. 38.

53. "The Minorities Decade," *The Wall Street Journal* (August 13, 1991), p. A16.

54. "Top Black-Owned Firms' Sales Rise 10%," *Los Angeles Times* (May 7, 1992), p. D4.

55. Dorothy Gaiter, "Diversity of Leaders Reflects the Changes in Black Communities," *The Wall Street Journal* (May 6, 1992), p. 1.

56. Thomas Edsall and Mary Edsall, "Race," *The Atlantic Monthly* (May 1991), p. 55.

57. Joan Rigdon, "For Black Men, Success Resolves Few Problems," *The Wall Street Journal* (May 8, 1992), p. B1.

58. Gregory A. Patterson, "A Delicate Balance," *The Wall Street Journal* (April 3, 1992), p. R5.

59. Thomas Sowell, " 'Affirmative Action:' A Worldwide Disaster," *Commentary* (December 1989), p. 26.

60. Gordon Green and Edward Welniak, "Measuring the Effects of Changing Family Composition during the 1970s in Black-White Differences in Income," manuscript (Washington, D.C.: Bureau of the Census, Department of Commerce, 1982), cited in Michael Levin, *Feminism and Freedom* (New Brunswick, N.V.: Transaction Books, 1987), p. 279. Warren T. Brookes, "Why Income Gap Between White and Black Has Widened," *San Francisco Chronicle* (December 25, 1990), p. C3.

61. Quoted in Scott Alan Hodge, "Davis-Bacon: Racist Then, Racist Now," *The Wall Street Journal* (June 25, 1990).

62. Thomas Sowell, " 'Affirmative Action': A Worldwide Disaster," *Commentary* (December 1989), p. 38.

63. David Wessel, "Racial Bias Against Black Job-Seekers Remains Pervasive, Broad Study Finds," *The Wall Street Journal* (May 15, 1991), p. A8. Frederick Lynch, "Tales from an Oppressed Class," *The Wall Street Journal* (November 11, 1991), p. A12.

64. Yelena Hanga, "What a Black Soviet Found Out About American Blacks," *The Christian Science Monitor* (February 24, 1988), p. 5.

65. James Jones, *Prejudice and Racism* (Reading, Mass.: Addison-Wesley Publishing Company, 1972), p. 131 [emphasis in the original].

66. Lawrence Auster, *The Path to National Suicide* (Monterey, Va.: American Immigration Control Foundation, 1990), p. 68.

67. See page 31.

68. Richard Schaefer, "Racial Prejudice in a Capitalist State," *Phylon* (September 1986), p. 193.

69. George Gallup and Larry Hugick, "Racial Tolerance Increasing, Most Americans Believe," *San Jose Mercury News* (June 13, 1990), p. 4A.

70. Pettigrew and Martin, "Shaping the Organizational Context for Black American Inclusion," *Journal of Social Issues,* Vol. 43, No. 1 (1987), p. 47.

71. Isabel Wilkerson, "Black-White Marriages Rise, but Couples Still Face Scorn," *The New York Times* (December 2, 1991), p. 1.

72. Daniel Goleman, "Black Child's Self-View Is Still Low, Study Finds," *The New York Times* (August 31, 1987), p. A13.

73. Pettigrew and Martin, "Shaping the Organizational context for Black American Inclusion," p. 48.

74. Pettigrew and Martin, "Shaping the Organizational Context for Black American Inclusion," p. 50.

75. William T. Bielby, "Modern Prejudice and Institutional Barriers to Equal Employment Opportunity for Minorities," *Journal of Social Issues,* Vol. 43, No. 1 (1987), p. 79 [emphasis in the original].

76. Pettigrew and Martin, "Shaping the Organizational Context for Black American Inclusion," p. 67ff.

77. Reported in Joe R. Feagin, "Changing Black Americans to Fit a Racist System?" *Journal of Social Issues,* Vol. 43, No. 1 (1987), p. 88.

78. William Julius Wilson, *The Declining Significance of Race* (Chicago: The University of Chicago Press, 1980), p. 151.

79. Nanine Alexander, "Black Executives Are Blazing Trail to the Top," *San Jose Mercury News* (February 26, 1989), p. 1 PC.

80. Audrey Edwards and Craig Polite, *Children of the Dream* (New York: Doubleday, 1992), p. 19ff.

81. R. L. Woodson, ed., *Black Perspectives on Crime and the Criminal Justice System* (Boston: G. K. Hall & Company, 1977), p. 164.

82. Wendell Bell, "Bias, Probability, and Prison Populations: A Future for Affirmative Actions?" *Futurics,* Vol. 7, No. 1 (1983), p. 19.

83. James F. Fyfe, "Race and Extreme Police-Citizen Violence," in R. L. McNeely and C. E. Pope, eds., *Race, Crime, and Criminal Justice* (Beverly Hills, Calif.: Sage Publications, 1981), p. 90.

84. Elaine Rivera, "Many Officials See One Cause: Racism," *Newsday* (New York) (October 4, 1990), p. 8.

85. Andrew Hacker, *Two Nations* (New York: Charles Scribner's Sons, 1992), p. 188.

86. Sam Roberts, "For Some Blacks, Justice Is Not Blind to Color," *The New York Times* (September 9, 1990), p. 5.

87. Clinton Cox, "Racism: the Hole in America's Heart," *City Sun* (Brooklyn) (July 18–24, 1990), p. 10.

88. D. Georges-Abeyie, "The Criminal Justice System and Minorities" in D. Georges-Abeyie, ed., *The Criminal Justice System and Blacks,* pp. 125–50.

89. James F. Fyfe, "Race and Extreme Police-Citizen Violence" in R. L. McNeely and C. E. Pope, eds., *Race, Crime, and Criminal Justice* (Beverly Hills, Calif.: Sage Publications, 1981), pp. 90–105.

90. William Wilbanks, *The Myth of a Racist Criminal Justice System* (Monterey, Calif.: Brooks/Cole Publishing Company, 1987), p. 78.

91. Andrew Hacker, *Two Nations,* p. 181. James Wilson and Richard Herrnstein, *Crime and Human Nature* (New York: Simon & Schuster, 1985), p. 462.

92. See page 37.

93. Wilson and Herrnstein, pp. 36, 463.

94. William Wilbanks, *The Myth of a Racist Criminal Justice System* (Monterey, Calif.: Brooks/Cole Publishing Company, 1987), p. 65ff.

95. National Research Council, *A Common Destiny: Blacks in American Society* (Washington, D.C.: National Academy Press, 1989), p. 476.

96. See page 38.

97. John F. Burns, "Shootings Jolt Toronto Race Relations," *The New York Times,* p. A3.

98. Wilbanks, *The Myth of a Racist Criminal Justice System,* p. 146.

99. Wilbanks, *The Myth of a Racist Criminal Justice System,* p. 146.

100. Wilbanks, *The Myth of a Racist Criminal Justice System,* p. 16ff.

101. Wilbanks, *The Myth of a Racist Criminal Justice System,* p. 79.

102. National Research Council, *A Common Destiny,* p. 496ff.

103. Wilbanks, *The Myth of a Racist Criminal Justice System,* p. 120.

104. National Research Council, *A Common Destiny,* p. 497.

105. David Tuller, "Prison Term Study Finds No Race Link," *San Francisco Chronicle* (February 16, 1990), p. 2.

106. See page 41.

107. *Dallas Times Herald* (November 17, 1985), p. 1, cited in Wilbanks, *The Myth of a Racist Criminal Justice System,* p. 17ff.

108. Tracy Thompson, "Blacks Sent to Jail More Than Whites for Same Crimes," *Atlanta Journal and Constitution* (April 30, 1989), p. 1A.

109. Curtis Taylor, "Black Convention's Agenda: Political Power," *Newsday* (New York) (August 15, 1989), p. 21.

110. See page 42.

111. Bell, "Bias, Probability, and Prison Populations," p. 21.

112. Jane Mayer, "In the War on Drugs, Toughest Foe May Be the Alienated Youth," *The Wall Street Journal* (September 8, 1989), p. A7.

113. Wilson and Herrnstein, *Crime and Human Nature,* p. 59.

114. A. Harris and M. Lewis, "Race and Criminal Deviance: A Study of Youthful Offenders," paper presented at the 1974 annual meeting of the American Sociological Association. Cited in Wilson and Herrnstein, *Crime and Human Nature,* p. 483.

115. Richard Reeves, "Addressing 'Comfortable People in Tight Houses,'" *International Herald Tribune* (August 16, 1990).

116. Quoted in Anne Wortham, *The Other Side of Racism* (Columbus: Ohio State University Press, 1981), p. 257. Originally in *The Black Poets,* ed. Dudley Randall, p. 226.

117. "Judge Removes Juror After Racial Remarks," *San Jose Mercury News* (January 18, 1989), p. 4B.

118. Barton Gellman and Sari Horwitz, "Letter Stirs Debate After Acquittal," *Washington Post* (April 22, 1990), p. A1.

119. John Kifner, "Bronx Juries Growing Suspicious of the Police," *The New York Times* (December 5, 1988), p. A16.

120. Gail Collins, "The Curse That Tries Patience," *Newsday* (New York) (February 4, 1991), p. 8.

121. William Blair, "Larry Davis Receives 5 to 15 Years on Gun Charge," *The New York Times* (December 16, 1988), p. A20.

122. "Black Texas Ranger Shies from Publicity Over Race," *The New York Times* (December 18, 1988), p. 18.

123. "4 Arizona Football Players Jailed in Racial Incidents," *Omaha World-Herald* (March 11, 1989).

124. "Brown May Seek Federal Help After Attacks," *The New York Times* (October 19, 1989), p. B18.

125. Sheila Wissner, "Beating Case Causes Concern," *The Tennessean* (December 15, 1990).

126. "3 Bias Incidents Provide Lessons for Class on Race," *The New York Times* (May 6, 1990), p. 53.

127. "Take Care," *The Economist* (February 10, 1990), p. 20.

128. Andrew Zappia, "Free Speech Violations: A Sampling," *Campus* (Fall 1990), p. 6.

129. Marilyn Soltis, "Sensitivity Training 101," *ABA Journal* (July 1990), p. 47.

130. Joseph Berger, "Campus Racial Strains Show 2 Perspectives on Inequality," *The New York Times* (May 22, 1989), p. 1.

131. Peter Applebome, "Woman's Claim of Racial Crime Is Called a Hoax," (June 1, 1990), p. A14. "Campus Racism: Seeking the Real Victim," *Newsweek* (May 21, 1990), p. 33.

132. Lewis Lapham, "Notebook," *Harper's Magazine* (December 1990), p. 10.

133. John Leo, "Bias by Any Other Name," *Newsday* (New York) (September 20, 1991), p. 64.

134. "Michigan U. Is Sued Over Anti-Bias Policy," *The New York Times* (May 27, 1989), p. 8. Connie Leslie, "Lessons from Bigotry 101," *Newsweek* (September 25, 1989), p. 49. Rogers Worthington, "U. of Wisconsin Regents Move to Rein in Racism," *Chicago Tribune* (April 12, 1989), p. 1. Alan Kors, "It's Speech, Not Sex, the Dean Bans Now," *The Wall Street Journal* (October 12, 1989). Felicity Barringer, "Campus Debate Pits Freedom of Speech Against Ugly Words," *The New York Times* (April 25, 1989), p. 1. "Racist Graffiti Leads to a Ban on Harassment," *The New York Times* (June 17, 1990), p. 38.

135. "Judge Voids University's Rule Against Hate Speech," *Orange County* (Calif.) *Register* (October 13, 1991).

136. Stephen Goode, "Efforts to Deal with Diversity Can Go Astray," *Insight* (September 10, 1990), pp. 16–17. Jon Marcus, "Court Ruling May Trip Up Campus Speech Codes," *Louisville Courier-Journal* (June 28, 1992), p. A6.

137. Lisa Foderaro, "In SUNY Student Election, Charges Fly and the Ballot Box Is Chained," *The New York Times* (December 17, 1991).

138. "Student at Brown Is Expelled Under a Rule Barring 'Hate Speech,'" *The New*

364 ⊛ *Paved With Good Intentions*

York Times (February 12, 1991). Nat Hentoff, "Newspeak from a University President," *Washington Post* (February 26, 1991).

139. David Savage, "Have Universities' Restrictive Conduct Codes Gone Too Far?" *Los Angeles Times* (May 14, 1991), p. A5.

140. "Thought Control in the Classrooms," *New York Post* (October 18, 1991), p. 26.

141. John Taylor, "Are You Politically Correct?" p. 37.

142. Christine Haynes, *Chronicles* (October 1990), p. 9.

143. "Time to Merge SUNY and CUNY," *New York Post* (March 4, 1992), p. 18.

144. "UC-Berkeley to Make Ethnic Studies a Required Course," *San Jose Mercury News* (April 27, 1989), p. 1B.

145. "Required Program Conceived in Conflict," *Insight* (October 9, 1989), p. 10.

146. Denise Magner, "Difficult Questions Face Colleges That Require Students to Take Courses That Explore Issues Relating to Race," *Chronicle of Higher Education* (March 28, 1990), p. A19. Joseph Berger, "Campus Racial Strains Show 2 Perspectives on Inequality," *The New York Times* (May 22, 1989), p. 1. James Tobin, "U-M Becomes First to Require Course on Racial Intolerance," *Detroit News* (October 9, 1990), p. 1.

147. Edward Alexander, "Race Fever," *Commentary* (November 1990), p. 45.

148. F. W. Brownlow, *Chronicles* (December 1990), p. 7.

149. William Celis, "Grants Given to Address Campus Race Issues," *The New York Times* (September 13, 1990).

150. "For Study of Race, All-White School Calls on an Actress," *The New York Times* (January 21, 1990), p. 36K.

151. "Trustees Approve Adding Faculty from Minorities," *The New York Times* (January 7, 1990), p. 35.

152. Robert Detlefsen, "White Like Me," *The New Republic* (April 10, 1989), pp. 18–20.

153. Isabel Wilkerson, "U. of Michigan Fights the Taint of Racial Trouble," *The New York Times* (January 15, 1990), p. A12.

154. James W. Lyons, *Final Report on Recent Incidents at Ujamaa House,* repr. *The Stanford Daily* (January 18, 1989), pp. 7–10.

155. Bill Workman, "Study Finds Racial Tension at Stanford," *San Francisco Chronicle* (April 5, 1989), p. 1. Don Kazak, "Stanford's Melting Pot," *Palo Alto Weekly* (June 7, 1989), p. 15ff.

156. Tracie Reynolds, "Group Accuses Stanford Administrators of Being Racist," *Palo Alto Times* (October 17, 1989), p. 8.

157. Lee Dembart, "At Stanford, Leftists Become Censors," *The New York Times* (May 5, 1989), p. A19.

158. Shelby Steele, "The Recoloring of Campus Life," *Harper's* (February 1989), p. 47.

159. Marcus Mabry, "Black and Blue, Class of '89," *Newsweek* (September 25, 1989), p. 50.

160. "University Panel Votes to Prohibit Harassing Words," *The New York Times* (May 27, 1990), p. 41.

161. Steve France, "Hate Goes to College," *ABA Journal* (July 1990), p. 44.

162. Carnegie Foundation for the Advancement of Teaching, *Campus Life: In Search of Community,* summarized in Francis Mancini, "Evidence Doesn't Support Charges of Campus Bigotry," *San Jose Mercury News* (May 9, 1990), p. 7B.

163. Spencer Rich, "Blacks in Baltimore, 9 Other Cities Hypersegregated," *Washington Post* (August 5, 1989), p. A3.

164. Associated Press, "Bias Against Black Renters up in Western Kentucky," *Louisville Courier Journal* (March 4, 1990).

165. Thomas Leucer, "New York Ranks High in Housing Bias," *The New York Times* (November 3, 1991), Sec. 10, p. 1.

166. Robert Slayton, "Time to Recognize Role of Bias in County Housing," *Los Angeles Times* (October 9, 1991), p. B11.

167. Sam Fulwood, "Blacks Find Bias Amid Affluence," *Los Angeles Times* (November 20, 1991), p. A1.

168. Sam Fulwood, "The Rage of the Black Middle Class," *Los Angeles Times Magazine* (November 3, 1991), p. 52.

169. James Farmer, "Freedom—When?" in Leon Friedman, ed., *The Civil Rights Reader* (New York: Walker & Company, 1968), p. 129.

170. Bill Dedman, "Home Loans for Blacks Twice as Likely to Be Rejected," *Louisville Courier-Journal* (January 22, 1989), p. 1.

171. Paul Duke, "U.S. Data Show Thrifts Reject Blacks for Mortgages Twice as Often as Whites," *The Wall Street Journal* (October 25, 1989), p. A16.

172. Jesse Jackson, "Racism Is the Bottom Line in Home Loans," *Los Angeles Times* (October 28, 1991).

173. "Unloved by Banks," *The Economist* (October 26, 1991), p. 29.

174. Dee Gill, "Loan Rejections Raise a Tangle of Racial Issues," *Houston Chronicle* (November 10, 1991), p. 1F.

175. Williams, *The State Against Blacks,* p. 30.

176. J. R. Green, "Cabbies Practice Passenger Selectivity to Protect Themselves," *The New York Times* (March 22, 1990), p. A26.

177. "The Strange Ways of Cab Bias," *Washington Post* (October 31, 1990).

178. Gabriel Escobar, "Rash of Violence Prompts Cabdrivers to Bypass Law," *Washington Post* (March 1, 1991), p. D1.

179. See, e.g., ". . . And from Doctors," *Louisville Courier-Journal* (January 25, 1989), editorial page.

180. Sandra Blakeslee, "Race and Sex Are Found to Affect Access to Kidney Transplants," *The New York Times* (January 24, 1989), p. B7. Shawn Hubler, "Blacks Less Likely to Get Operation, Study Reports," *Los Angeles Times* (January 31, 1991).

181. Tracie Reddick, "Blacks Spurred on Organ Donations," *Washington Times* (October 25, 1991).

182. Shawn Hubler, "Blacks Less Likely to Get Operation."

183. Sue Hutchison, "Group Urges Blacks to Donate Organs, Save Lives," *San Jose Mercury News* (Peninsula Extra) (November 13, 1991), p. 1C.

184. Walter Updegrove, "Race and Money," *Money* (December 1989), p. 165ff.

185. Jesse Jackson, "America Needs the Voter Registration Act," *Newsday* (New York) (August 13, 1990), p. 40.

186. Hacker, *Two Nations,* p. 92.

187. Keith Schneider, "Minorities Join to Fight Polluting of Neighborhoods," *The New York Times* (October 25, 1991).

188. Matthew Rees, "Black and Green," *New Republic* (March 2, 1991), p. 15.

189. "Hate-Crime Incidents This Year in OC," *Orange County (Calif.) Register* (July 22, 1991), p. A14.

190. Frank Messina, "Outrage Grows Toward Racial Hate Crimes," *Los Angeles Times* (August 13, 1991), p. B1.

191. Weston Kosova, "Savage Gus," *The New Republic* (January 29, 1990), p. 21.

192. Michael McQueen, "Rep. Gus Savage's Controversial Style, Values Face Critical Test in Tough Democratic Race," *The Wall Street Journal* (March 15, 1990), p. A16.

193. "Topics of the Times," *The New York Times* (April 4, 1990).

194. "He's No Martin Luther King," *Washington Post* (August 9, 1989), p. A20. Jim McGee, "Peace Corps Worker Alleges Rep. Savage Assaulted Her," *Washington Post* (July 19, 1989), p. A1.

195. Helen Dewar, "Ethics Panel Reportedly Faults Rep. Savage," *Washington Post* (February 2, 1990), p. A1.

196. Marilyn Rauber, "Reporter Says Black Rep Hurled Racial Slurs," *New York Post* (June 27, 1991), p. 18.

197. Salim Muwakkil, "Illinois Voters Prefer Savage Tactics," *In These Times* (March 28–April 3, 1990), p. 8.

198. Dirk Johnson, "Challenge at Home for Adept Player of Racial Politics," *The New York Times* (March 10, 1990).

199. Mary McGrory, "Profiles in Courage," *Louisville Courier-Journal* (March 30, 1990).

200. McQueen, "Rep. Gus Savage's Controversial Style, Values," p. A16.

201. Deborah Orin, "Gunmen Ambush Chicago Candidate," *New York Post* (March 14, 1992), p. 7. "End of the Line for a Bigot," *New York Post* (March 20, 1992).

202. " 'Al the Pal' Departs," *The Wall Street Journal* (March 12, 1992), p. A14.

203. *Los Angeles Times,* "11 Years Later, Atlantic City Waits for Gambling to Pay Off," *Omaha World-Herald* (August 28, 1989), p. 12.

204. Wayne King, "Issue of Race Rules Contest for Mayor," *The New York Times* (June 9, 1990), p. 25.

205. "Emperor Young," *The Economist* (April 14, 1990), p. 26. Robert Blau, "Corruption Charges Jeopardize Career of Detroit Police Chief," *Houston Chronicle* (February 9, 1992), p. 6A.

206. Ronald Smothers, "Birmingham Mayor Cited for Contempt," *The New York Times* (January 18, 1992), p. 6. Ronald Smothers, "Charge Against Mayor Strikes Chord in Birmingham," *The New York Times* (January 26, 1992), p. A12. "With 700 Supporters Rallying Round, Birmingham Mayor Goes to Prison," *The New York Times* (January 24, 1992).

207. Mark Mooney, "Black Leaders Charge Bias in Probe of Dinkins Stock," *New York Post* (December 18, 1989).

208. Mark Mooney, "Black Leaders Blame Racism for Criticism of Dinkins," *New York Post* (October 17, 1990).

209. Andy Logan, "Around City Hall," *The New Yorker* (March 2, 1992), p. 82ff.

210. "Now That's Housing!" *Newsday* (New York) (February 26, 1992), p. 1. Terry Golway, "Pink Sofa Politics, Racial Solidarity," *New York Observer* (March 2, 1992), p. 1.

211. Terry Golway, "Pink Sofa Politics," p. 1.

212. Alex Michelini, "Ex-Sen. Jenkins Gets Jail," *New York Daily News* (July 27, 1990), p. 20.

213. "Not so Colour-Blind," *The Economist* (October 28, 1989), p. 29.

214. Associated Press, "Federal Judge Is First to Be Convicted of Bribery," *Indianapolis Star* (June 30, 1991), p. A9.

215. Felicity Barringer, "Two Worlds of Washington: Turmoil and Growth," *The New York Times* (July 12, 1990), p. A16.

216. Bella Stumbo, "Barry: He Keeps D.C. Guessing," *Los Angeles Times* (January 7, 1990), p. A1.

217. David Whitman, "Marion Barry's Untold Legacy," *U.S. News & World Report* (July 30, 1990), p. 22ff.

218. Juan Williams, "D.C.: Divided We Fall," *Washington Post* (March 26, 1989), p. D1.

219. Richard Cohen, "Barry's Latest Outrage," *Washington Post* (January 1, 1989), p. B7.

220. Bella Stumbo, "Barry: He Keeps D.C. Guessing," p. A1.

221. Ann Devroy, " 'Selective Enforcement' Issue Raised by NAACP," *Washington Post* (January 23, 1990), p. A8.

222. Michael York and Elsa Walsh, "Barry Indicted on Cocaine, Perjury Charges; Mayor Calls Process a 'Political Lynching,' " *Washington Post* (February 16, 1990), p. A1. Mike McAlary, "Easy to Crack Jokes but Harder to Laugh," *New York Daily News* (June 10, 1990).

223. Barbara Reynolds, "Sought: Black Knight Who Respects Women," *USA Today* (July 27, 1990), p. 11A.

224. "Barry's Free Ride," *The New Republic* (May 7, 1990), p. 7.

225. Liza Mundy, "The Enigma of Mary Cox," *City Paper* (Washington, D.C.) (July 20, 1990), p. 14.

226. "Mayor Barry and the Guv'ment,"*Amsterdam News* (New York) (June 9, 1990), p. 14.

227. Roger Simon, "The Mayor Understood," *Newsweek* (August 27, 1990), p. 8.

228. Charles Krauthammer, "The Black Rejectionists," *Time* (July 23, 1990), p. 80.

229. "Barry's Free Ride," *The New Republic* (May 7, 1990), p. 7.

230. Mike Royko, "Short Takes," *New York Daily News* (April 24, 1990), p. 30.

231. R. H. Melton and Michael York, "Barry Acknowledges Using Crack at Hotel," *Washington Post* (May 30, 1990), p. 1.

232. Mary McGrory, "Jesse Jackson's Unholy Alliance with Barry," *Newsday* (New York) (June 20, 1990), p. 60.

233. Christopher B. Daly, "Barry Judge Castigates Four Jurors," *Washington Post* (October 31, 1990), p. 1.

234. Elsa Walsh and Barton Gellman, "Chasm Divided Jurors in Barry Trial," *Washington Post* (August 23, 1990), p. A1.

235. Carl Rowan, "The Barry Verdict: A Victory for No One," *Washington Post* (August 15, 1990), p. A21.

236. See, e.g., Juan Williams, "D.C.: Divided We Fall," *Washington Post* (March 26, 1989), p. D1.

237. Jennifer Allen, "The Black Conspiracy Establishment," *7 Days* (January 17, 1990), p. 16.

238. Richard Reeves, "Racism is Tipping the Scales of Justice," *New York Daily News* (September 12, 1990), p. 40.

239. Hastings Wyman, "What Jesse Jackson's Up To," *The Wall Street Journal* (August 21, 1990).

240. Andy Logan, "Around City Hall," *The New Yorker* (March 2, 1992), p. 82.

241. Patrick May, "Cultural Bias May Have Influenced Murder Trials," *Miami Herald* (June 30, 1991), p. 1B.

242. "Suspect in Reporter's Killing Free After 3 Mistrials," *Star-Ledger* (Newark) (March 7, 1991), p. 57.

243. Ellis Henican, "A Textbook Case in Patronage 101," *Newsday* (New York) (November 19, 1991), p. 8.

244. Joseph Berger, "Inertia of New York's School System: Shaky Tenure of Matthew Barnwell," *The New York Times* (December 27, 1988).

245. Blumenthal and Verhovek, "Patronage and Profit in Schools: A Tale of a Bronx District School," *The New York Times* (December 16, 1988), p. A1.

246. "Bitter Lessons in N.Y. Schools," *San Jose Mercury News* (June 22, 1989), p. 8A.

247. Joseph White, "Failures of Detroit Schools Spur Revolt as Three Longtime Officials Are Ousted," *The Wall Street Journal* (November 11, 1988), p. A16.

248. Ronald Smothers, "In School Conflict, Selma Discovers Old Racial Tensions Are Unresolved," *The New York Times* (February 20, 1990), p. A12.

249. Fox Butterfield, "Racial Dispute Erupts in Boston Over Dismissal of Schools' Chief," *The New York Times* (February 20, 1990), p. A16.

250. See page 75.

251. Maureen Dowd, "In an Ugly Atmosphere, the Accusations Fly," *The New York Times* (October 12, 1991), p. A1.

252. Richard Berke, "Thomas Accuser Tells Hearing of Obscene Talk and Advances; Judge Complains of 'Lynching,' " *The New York Times* (October 12, 1992), p. A1.

253. "On and About," *Washington Post* (October 25, 1990).

254. Paul Robeson Jr., and Mel Williamson, "Democrats Dare Not Deny Jackson," *The New York Times* (December 13, 1988), p. A19.

255. Don Feder, *Chronicles* (September 1989), p. 6.

256. Walt Karwicki, "Under the Influence," *New York Post* (January 13, 1991).

257. "New Orleans Votes for Term Limits," *The Wall Street Journal* (October 22, 1991).

258. Kevin Sack, "Officials from Minorities Angered by Cuomo's Budget," *The New York Times* (February 25, 1991), p. B1.
259. Robert Hanley, "Black Poet Says Faculty 'Nazis' Blocked Tenure," *The New York Times* (March 15, 1990).
260. John Taylor, "Don't Blame Me!" *New York* (June 3, 1991), p. 33ff.
261. Taylor, "Don't Blame Me!" p. 33.
262. Felicia Lee, "Doctors See Gap in Blacks' Health Having a Link to Low Self-Esteem," *The New York Times* (July 17, 1989).
263. J. A. Jahannes, "Towards a Saner View of Health," *Vital Speeches of the Day* (October 1, 1986), pp. 749–751.
264. Frederick Dicker, "Pol Admits She Nixed Hispanic for Job," *New York Post* (January 10, 1990).
265. Michael Cottman, "Hit 'Em Where It Hertz," *Newsday* (New York) (January 18, 1992), p. 3. Matthew Wald, "Politicians Assail Hertz for New York Surcharge," *The New York Times* (January 4, 1992), p. 23.
266. Marcus Mabry, "Bias Begins at Home," *Newsweek* (August 5, 1991), p. 33.
267. "Would-Be Flag Burner Abandons Incendiary Idea," *San Jose Mercury News* (July 9, 1989), p. 21A.
268. Mark Starr, "Miracle Workers Wanted," *Newsweek* (January 14, 1991), p. 42.
269. "Panel to Examine Remarks by Judge on Homosexuals," *The New York Times* (December 21, 1988), p. A12.
270. Russell Baker, " 'Warm Bath and a Bromide,' " *Omaha World-Herald* (February 21, 1990).
271. Associated Press, " 'KKK' Killing Draws Charges," *Omaha World-Herald* (July 18, 1988).
272. See page 79.
273. "Symbol v. System," *The Economist* (October 15, 1988), p. 37. *The New York Times* (November 1987–October 1988), *passim*.
274. Alan Dershowitz, "Racial Hoax with a Sour Echo," *Washington Times* (June 26, 1990).
275. Quoted in Jim Sleeper, "New York Stories," *The New Republic* (September 10, 1990), p. 21.
276. U.S. Department of Justice, Bureau of Justice Statistics, *Criminal Victimization in the United States, 1988* (Washington, D.C., 1989), p. 50.
277. Michael Macdonald, "Crying Race, Crying Wolf," *New York Daily News* (October 5, 1990), p. 82.
278. Perry Lang, "Angry Black Protest Stalls AIDS Poster," *San Francisco Chronicle* (September 25, 1990), p. A5.
279. Miguel Garcilazo, "New Anti-Smoking Ad Targets Blacks," *New York Post* (January 6, 1992).
280. William Schmidt, "Study Links Male Unemployment and Single Mothers in Chicago," *The New York Times* (January 10, 1989), p. 16.
281. See, e.g., *Report of the National Advisory Commission on Civil Disorders*, p. 280.
282. Sowell, *Civil Rights*, p. 75.
283. Carolyn Lochead, "Poor Neighborhoods Fall to a Widening Decay," *Insight* (April 3, 1989), p. 11.
284. Morton Kondracke, "The Two Black Americas," *The New Republic* (February 6, 1989), p. 17. Cheryl Laird, "Teen-Age Moms," *Houston Chronicle* (January 8, 1992), p. 1D.
285. National Research Council, *A Common Destiny*, p. 527ff.
286. Wayne Lutton, *The Myth of Open Borders* (Monterey [Va.]: American Immigration Control Foundation, 1988), pp. 4–12.
287. Kenneth Stampp, *The Peculiar Institution* (New York: Random House, 1956), p. 16.
288. Clarence Johnson, "Group Declares 'State of Emergency' for Blacks in S.F.," *San Francisco Chronicle* (September 26, 1990).

289. Dennis Hevesi, "Panel Finds New York Blacks in 'Crisis' and Lists Remedies," *The New York Times* (December 10, 1988), p. 1. Don Wycliff, "For Black New Yorkers, a Bleak Picture is Put into Words," *The New York Times* (December 18, 1988), p. E6.

290. Joe Klein, "Race," *New York* (May 29, 1989), p. 38.

291. Chris Olert et al., "Dinkins and Brown Huddle Over Police Killing," *New York Post* (March 3, 1990), p. 5.

292. William Raspberry, ". . . to Here," *Washington Post* (March 19, 1989), p. A19.

293. Lorrin Anderson, "Race, Lies, and Videotape," *National Review* (January 22, 1990), p. 40ff.

294. Joseph Sobran, "Howard Beach," *National Review* (March 27, 1987), p. 29ff.

295. Bob Drury, "Waylaid by Whites 'Out for a Fight,' " *Newsday* (New York) (August 25, 1989), p. 5.

296. Lorrin Anderson, "Cracks in the Mosaic," *National Review* (June 25, 1990), p. 37.

297. William Glaberson, "Bensonhurst Case Ends, Satisfying Few," *The New York Times* (March 14, 1991), p. A1.

298. Eric Briendel, "Racism Is a Two-way Street," *New York Post* (September 7, 1989), p. 31.

299. Dennis Hevesi, "No Violence as 300 March into Bensonhurst Again," *The New York Times* (September 3, 1989), p. 40. Lyle Harris and Joel Siegel, "B'hurst Bluing for Marchers," *New York Daily News* (May 27, 1990).

300. "The Blood on the Brooklyn Bridge," *The New York Times* (September 2, 1989), p. 22.

301. Miguel Garcilazo et al., "The Battle of Brooklyn Bridge," *New York Post* (September 1, 1989), p. 4.

302. Devin Standard, "A Young Black Man Asks: Will I Be Next?" *The New York Times* (September 2, 1989), p. 23.

303. Chris Olert et al., "Black Shoots White Student in Bronx Race Attack," *New York Post* (September 22, 1989), p. 21.

304. Eric Briendel, "Double Standard on Racism," *New York Post* (September 28, 1989), p. 33.

305. Ted Joy, "Danny Gilmore, RIP," *The Quill* (May 1989), pp. 21–27.

306. Mike Mallowe, "Coming Apart," *Philadelphia* (September 1989), p. 162.

307. Mike Barnacle, "A Double Standard for Race Crimes?" *Asbury Park Press* (March 7, 1991), p. A21.

308. Knight-Ridder News, "AWOL Marine in Indiana Admits Seven Racial Killings, Sources Say," *Miami Herald* (February 2, 1991).

309. "3 Blacks Sentenced in '90 Racial Attack," *Chicago Tribune* (May 20, 1992), p. 3.

310. Rex Henderson, "Beating Death of White Raises Racial Tensions," *Tampa Tribune* (May 20, 1990), p. B1.

311. "The Killing Class," *Miami Herald* (February 24, 1991), p. 5J.

312. Donna Gehrke, " 'I Felt Power' While Slaying 6 People, Former Yahweh 'Death Angel' Testifies," *Miami Herald* (January 30, 1992), p. 1A.

313. Sydney Freedberg, "Murder in the Temple of Love?" *Miami Herald* (July 8, 1990), p. 1.

314. Donna Gehrke, "Yahweh, 6 Followers Found Guilty of Conspiracy; Jury Acquits 7 Others," *The Miami Herald* (May 28, 1992), p. 1A.

315. See page 92.

316. Richard Hofstadter and Michael Wallace, eds., *American Violence* (New York: Vintage Books, 1970), pp. 258–69.

317. "What Should Be Done," *U.S. News & World Report* (August 22, 1989), p. 54. See also Department of Justice, *Criminal Victimization in the United States, 1987* (Washington, D.C.: U.S. Government Printing Office, 1989), p. 7.

318. Department of Justice, *Criminal Victimization in the United States, 1987.* Patrick Buchanan, "The 'Real Victims' of Hate Crimes," *New York Post* (March 10, 1990).

319. Gary D. LaFree, "Male Power and Female Victimization: Toward a Theory of Interracial Rape," *American Journal of Sociology*, Vol. 88, No. 2 (September 1982).

320. William Wilbanks, "Frequency and Nature of Interracial Crimes," submitted for publication to *Justice Professional* (November 7, 1990). Data derived from Department of Justice, *Criminal Victimization in the United States, 1987*, p. 53.

321. Andrew Hacker, *Two Nations*, pp. 183, 185.

322. See page 93.

323. "Brooklyn's Wave of 'Bias Crime,' " *New York Post* (November 2, 1991).

324. " 'Wilding Attacks,' " *Orange County (Calif.) Register* (December 11, 1991), p. A3.

325. Peter Noel, "The Perfect White Crime," *Voice* (New York), (January 28, 1992), p. 29.

326. "State: 'Hate Crimes' Hit Whites Hardest," *New York Post* (November 15, 1991), p. 8.

327. "4 Black Youths Accused of Bus Attack on White," *The New York Times* (October 31, 1988), p. A16.

328. Craig Wolff, "10 Teen-Age Girls Held in Upper Broadway Pinprick Attacks," *The New York Times* (November 4, 1989), p. 27.

329. Howard Kurtz, "New York Measures Surge in Bias-Related Crime," *Washington Post* (October 28, 1989), p. A3.

330. Chapin Wright, "Teens Sought in Bias Attack in Subway; Two Arrested," *Newsday* (New York) (October 19, 1989), p. 37.

331. See page 96.

332. Matthew Strozier, "How Gentrification Broke My Nose," *The New York Times* (December 4, 1988).

333. "Justice in Crown Heights," *New York Post* (September 9, 1991), p. 20.

334. "Jew Slain After Fatal Crash," *Newsday* (New York) (August 21, 1991), p. 2ff.

335. Joe Klein, "Deadly Metaphors," *New York* (September 9, 1991).

336. Jimmy Breslin, "It's Not Simply Blacks vs. Jews," *Newsday* (New York) (September 3, 1991), p. 2.

337. "Army of Cops Floods Riot Zone," *New York Post* (August 23, 1991), p. 4ff.

338. "He's the Mayor, Not a Magician," *The New York Times* (August 23, 1991), p. A26.

339. Michael Stone, "What Really Happened in Central Park," *New York* (August 14, 1989), p. 30ff.

340. Alex Jones, "Most Papers Won't Name the Jogger," *The New York Times* (June 13, 1990), p. B3.

341. "Rape Victims' Right to Privacy," *New York Post* (July 21, 1990), p. 12.

342. William A. Tatum, "Jogger Trial: The Lynching Attempt That Must Not Succeed," *Amsterdam News* (New York) (August 11, 1990), p. 12. "The Jogger Trial: A Legal Lynching to Haunt Us," *Amsterdam News* (New York) (August 25, 1990), p. 12.

343. Amy Pagnozzi, "Idiots Who Jeer Jogger Merit Only Contempt," *New York Post* (July 23, 1990), p. 4.

344. "The Governor Joins the Anti-Apartheid Struggle," *City Sun* (July 18–24, 1990), p. 30.

345. Jim Nolan et al., "Jeering Spectators Add Insult to Her Injuries," *New York Post* (July 17, 1990), p. 4. Mike McAlary, "Racism Comes in Many Shades," *New York Daily News* (July 18, 1990), p. 4.

346. "Disorder in Court," *New York Post* (December 15, 1990), p. 24.

347. Mike McAlary, "Courtroom Chaos a Living, Breathing Sculpture of Hate," *New York Post* (December 12, 1990), p. 8.

348. Chris Oliver et al., "Courtroom Mob Scene Spills into the Street," *New York Post* (December 12, 1990), p. 8.

349. Jim Nolan, "Judge Bares Death Threats During Trial," *New York Post* (January 10, 1991), p. 2.

350. Ronald Sullivan, "Police Said to Ignore Warnings on Jogger Suspect," *The New York*

Times (July 31, 1990), p. B3. Ray Kerrison, "Trial was Turned into a Circus," *New York Post* (August 20, 1990), p. 4.

351. "After the Jogger Trial," *New York Post* (August 23, 1990), p. 24.

352. Carol Taylor, "The Jogger Case: Notes From a Courtroom," *Amsterdam News* (New York) (June 30,1990), p.14.   353. Michel Marriott, "Needle Exchange Angers Many Minorities," *The New York Times* (November 7, 1988), p. B1 [emphasis added].

354. Scott McConnell, "Haitian Repatriation: The Silence This Time," *New York Post* (February 8, 1992).

355. Robert Staples, "Black Male Genocide: A Final Solution to the Race Problem in America," *The Black Scholar* (May/June 1987).

356. Ossie Davis, "Challenge for the Year 2000," *The Nation* (July 24, 1989), p. 146.

357. Gerald Horne, "Black Hopes in the U.S. and South Africa," *The New York Times* (March 25, 1990).

358. Felicia Lee, "Black Men: Are They Imperiled?" *The New York Times* (June 26, 1990), p. B3.

359. "Activist Malcolm X Lives on as Blacks Yearn for 'Clarity,' " *San Jose Mercury News* (April 19, 1992), p. 12A.

360. David Horowitz, "The Radical Left and the New Racism," *New Dimensions* (December 1990), p. 36.

361. See page 103.

362. Jack White, "Genocide Mumbo Jumbo," *Time* (January 22, 1990), p. 20. Howard Kurtz, "Drug Scourge Is Conspiracy by Whites, Some Blacks Say," *Washington Post* (December 29, 1989), p. A1. Michael Isikoff, "Crack Trade Is Selma's New Struggle," *The New York Times* (November 21, 1989), p. A1. Gregory Huskisson, "MSU Conference on Black Males Offers Insights, Paths to Improvement," *Detroit Free Press* (April 30, 1989), p. 9A. Arch Puddington, "The Question of Black Leadership," *Commentary* (January 1991), p. 24.

363. Arlene Levinson, "Black Living in Fear: Are They Paranoid or Justly Concerned?" *Houston Chronicle* (February 16, 1992), p. 10A.

364. "Bill Cosby's AIDS Conspiracy," *New York Post* (December 4, 1991), p. 29.

365. Jason DeParle, "Talk of Government Being Out to Get Blacks Falls on More Attentive Ears," *The New York Times* (October 29, 1990), p. B7.

366. Arlene Levinson, "Black Living in Fear: Are They Paranoid or Justly Concerned?" *Houston Chronicle* (February 16, 1992), p. 10A.

367. Alex Freedman, "Rumor Turns Fantasy into Bad Dream," *The Wall Street Journal* (May 10, 1991), p. B1.

368. Chino Wilson, "African Americans Should Not Trust 'Devilish' White People," *The Daily Collegian* (Penn State University) (January 28, 1992).

369. "Unnatural Causes Claim Lives of More Children," *The Wall Street Journal* (February 13, 1989), p. B1.

370. David Boaz, "Yellow Peril Reinfects America," *The Wall Street Journal* (April 7, 1989).

371. Yuji Ichioka, *The Issei: The World of the First-Generation Japanese Immigrants 1885–1924* (New York: The Free Press, 1988), p. 211ff.

372. Lutton, *The Myth of Open Borders*, p. 25.

373. David Boaz, "Yellow Peril Reinfects America," *The Wall Street Journal* (April 7, 1989).

374. William Petersen, "Chinese-Americans and Japanese-Americans" in Thomas Sowell, ed., *Essays and Data on American Ethnic Groups* (The Urban Institute, 1978), p. 63.

375. Lutton, *The Myth of Open Borders*, pp. 26–42.

376. Thomas Sowell, *The Economics and Politics of Race* (New York: William Morrow & Company, 1983), p. 187.

377. Wilson and Herrnstein, *Crime and Human Nature*, p. 473.

378. Lutton, *The Myth of Open Borders*, p. 30.

379. Petersen, "Chinese-Americans and Japanese-Americans," p. 78.

380. Williams, *The State Against Blacks,* p. 6.

381. James D. Phelan, writing in *The Annals of the American Academy of Political Science* (January 1921), quoted in Lutton, *The Myth of Open Borders,* p. 33.

382. Petersen, "Chinese-Americans and Japanese-Americans," p. 84.

383. Sowell, *The Economics and Politics of Race,* p. 187.

384. Calvin Sims, "Seeking Cash and Silent Victims, New York Thieves Prey on Asians," *The New York Times* (October 7, 1990), p. A1. Katherine Foran, "Decoy Cops Protecting Asian Riders," *Newsday* (New York) (August 16, 1990), p. 3.

385. David Treadwell, "Hard Road for Black Businesses," *Los Angeles Times* (September 20, 1991), p. A1.

386. Daniel Lazare, "Black Neighborhoods' Self-Defeating War Against Koreans," *The Wall Street Journal* (October 26, 1988), p. A22.

387. Felicia Lee, "Brooklyn Blacks and Koreans Forge Pact," *The New York Times* (December 21, 1988), p. B1.

388. "Scapegoating New York's Koreans," *New York Post* (January 25, 1990).

389. M. A. Farber, "Black-Korean Who-Pushed-Whom Festers," *The New York Times* (May 7, 1990), p. B1.

390. Jonathan Rieder, "Trouble in Store," *The New Republic* (July 2, 1980), p. 17.

391. "New York Wakes Up to a Civil Rights Emergency," *New York Post* (May 9, 1990), p. 22.

392. Todd Purdum, "Angry Dinkins Defends Role in Race Cases," *The New York Times* (May 9, 1990), p. B1. Todd Purdum, "Dinkins Asks for Racial Unity and Offers to Mediate Boycott," *The New York Times* (May 12, 1990), p. A1.

393. David E. Pitt, "WLIB Owner Warns Against Racist Remarks," *The New York Times* (May 17, 1990). Mark Mooney, "Sutton: I'd Shut WLIB Over Criticism of Dave," *New York Post* (May 17, 1990), p. 2.

394. Arnold H. Lubasch, "Korean Stores Under Boycott Win in Court," *The New York Times* (September 18, 1990), p. A1.

395. Don Terry, "Diplomacy Fails to End Store Boycott in Flatbush," *The New York Times* (July 16, 1990), p. B1.

396. Sam Roberts, "Which Mayor Knows Best on the Boycott?" *The New York Times* (July 30, 1990), p. B1.

397. Robert McFadden, "Blacks Attack 3 Vietnamese; One Hurt Badly," *The New York Times* (May 14, 1990), p. A1. Peg Tyre and Beth Holland, "Battered and Shocked," *Newsday* (New York) (May 14, 1990), p. 5.

398. "Sonny Carson, Koreans, and Racism," *The New York Times* (May 8, 1990). "The Race-Baiters Exposed," *New York Post* (June 4, 1990).

399. "Big Lie in Flatbush," *New York Post* (June 11, 1990), p. 18.

400. Joseph Berger, "Teacher Who Broke Boycott Seeks a Transfer," *The New York Times* (May 18, 1990), p. B2. George Curry, "For Teacher, Lesson Has a Personal Cost," *Chicago Tribune* (May 18, 1990). Chris Oliver, "Boycott-Busting Teacher Gets New Job," *New York Post* (June 1, 1990).

401. Merle English, "Innis Hits Dinkins, Offers Aid to Grocers," *Newsday* (New York) (June 2, 1990), p. 4.

402. "The Boycott Report: Worse Than Useless," *New York Daily News* (September 2, 1990). "The Mayor's Boycott Report: Rewarding the Racists," *New York Post* (September 5, 1990), p. 18.

403. Felicia Lee, "Panel's Boycott Report Called Biased," *The New York Times* (November 8, 1990). Mark Mooney, "City Council Rips Dinkins Panel's Probe of Boycott," *New York Post* (November 8, 1990).

404. "City Hall Heeds the Law," *New York Post* (September 20, 1990), p. 16. Merle English, "Boycotted Store Restocks," *Newsday* (New York) (September 21, 1990), p. 3.

405. David Gonzalez, "Bombs Found on Store Roof in Brooklyn," *The New York Times* (September 24, 1990), p. B1.

406. Owen Fitzgerald, "Mayor Crosses Line," *New York Daily News* (September 22, 1990), p. 3.

407. David Gonzalez, "8 Arrested in Boycott of Brooklyn Store," *The New York Times* (September 25, 1990), p. 34.

408. Sheryl McCarthy, "When Boycotts Were for Just Causes," *Newsday* (New York) (February 4, 1991), p. 11.

409. "Defeat for Anti-Korean Bigotry," *New York Post* (February 4, 1991).

410. Paul Schwartzman, "Korean Deli Owner Gives Up," *New York Post* (May 28, 1991).

411. "Asian Merchants Find Ghettos Full of Peril," *U.S. News & World Report* (November 24, 1986), p. 30.

412. Amy Rosenberg, "Hoagie Shop, Site of Protest, Is Fire-Bombed," *Philadelphia Inquirer* (July 26, 1990).

413. Daniel Lazare, "Black Neighborhoods' Self-Defeating War Against Koreans," *The Wall Street Journal* (October 26, 1988), p. A22.

414. L. A. Chung, "Tensions Divide Blacks, Asians," *San Francisco Chronicle* (May 4, 1992), p. 1.

415. Seth Mydans, "Two Views of Protest at Korean Shop," *The New York Times* (December 24, 1991).

416. Seth Mydans, "Korean's Shooting of Black Girl Focuses Attention on Frictions," *The New York Times* (October 6, 1991).

417. Eric Briendel, "Rap Star to Koreans: 'We'll Burn Your Stores,'" *New York Post* (December 5, 1991), p. 29.

418. Jon Pareles, "Should Ice Cube's Voice be Chilled?" *The New York Times* (December 9, 1991), p. 30. Rick Mitchell, "Power of Hate," *Houston Chronicle* (February 11, 1992), p. 1D.

419. Jeff Pelline, "Lasting Blow to L.A. Neighborhoods," *San Francisco Chronicle* (May 2, 1992), p. 1.

420. Steven Chin, "Innocence Lost: L.A.'s Koreans Fight to Be Heard," *San Francisco Examiner* (May 9, 1992), p. 1.

421. Associated Press, "Korean Leaders Are Alarmed at Violence in Los Angeles," *Oakland Tribune* (May 3, 1992), p. B1.

422. "Warning! Koreans Are Leaving," *New York Post* (October 1, 1991).

423. Marie Lee, "We Koreans Need an Al Sharpton," *The New York Times* (December 12, 1991).

424. "Challenging Blacks to Become Producers in the Marketplace," *Issues & Views* (New York) (Summer, 1989), p. 12.

425. Carter A. Wilson, "Affirmative Action Defended," *The Black Scholar* (May/June 1986), p. 19.

426. See page 124.

427. See page 125.

428. National Research Council, *A Common Destiny*, p. 227.

429. National Research Council, *A Common Destiny*, pp. 64ff, 101, 241.

430. Lester A. Sobel, *Quotas and Affirmative Action* (New York: Facts On File, 1980), p. 2.

431. Edward Snow, "The Grove City Horror Show," *Chronicles* (November 1988), p. 51.

432. See page 127.

433. John H. Bunzel, "Congress Must Take Lead on Civil Rights," *San Jose Mercury News* (July 23, 1989), p. 1C.

434. Clint Bolick, *Changing Course* (New Brunswick, N.J.: Transaction Books, 1988), p. 55.

435. Bolick, *Changing Course*, p. 57.

436. Terry Eastland and William J. Bennett, *Counting by Race*, p. 128ff. Quoted in Bolick, *Changing Course*, p. 56ff.

437. Benjamin Hooks, " 'Self-Help' Just Won't Do It All," *Los Angeles Times* (July 10, 1990), p. B7.

438. Sonia Nazario, "Many Minorities Feel Torn by Experience of Affirmative Action," *The Wall Street Journal* (June 27, 1989), p. A1.

439. Bolick, *Changing Course,* p. 69.

440. Frank A. Lynch, *Invisible Victims* (New York: Praeger Publishers, 1989), p. 102ff.

441. Ralph King, "Judge Bars Race as Sole Factor in Promotions," *The Wall Street Journal* (June 10, 1991), p. B5A.

442. David Pitt, "Despite Revisions, Few Blacks Passed Police Sergeant Test," *The New York Times* (January 13, 1989), p. 1.

443. Lawrence H. Fuchs, *The American Kaleidoscope* (Hanover, N.H.: University Press of New England, 1990), p. 451.

444. Richard Steier, "Fire Exam Too Hard? Guess Again!" *New York Post* (April 15, 1992), p. 3.

445. "You Can't Fight Fire with Quotas," *New York Post* (April 17, 1992).

446. Eric Hanson, "Fire-Fighters See Red as Scores on Promotion Exam Changed," *Houston Chronicle* (October 3, 1991).

447. Fuchs, *The American Kaleidoscope,* p. 452.

448. Andrew Hacker, "The Myths of Racial Division," *The New Republic* (March 23, 1992), p. 21.

449. Hacker, *Two Nations,* p. 113.

450. Lynch, *Invisible Victims,* p. 29ff.

451. U.S. Office of Personnel Management, "Administrative Careers with America," (Qualification Information Statement QI-W, February 1990), p. 3.

452. Judith Havemann, "Revised at Behest of Minorities, New Civil Service Exams Ready," *Los Angeles Times* (April 22, 1990). Robert G. Holland, *Chronicles* (March 1991), p. 9.

453. Joseph Berger, "Plan for Schools on Minority Hiring," *The New York Times* (February 16, 1990), p. A1.

454. Joseph Berger, "Pessimism in Air as Schools Try Affirmative Action," *The New York Times* (February 27, 1990), p. B1.

455. Robert Detlefsen, *Civil Rights Under Reagan* (San Francisco: ICS Press, 1991), p. 74.

456. Clint Bolick, *Changing Course* (New Brunswick, N.J.: Transaction Books, 1988), pp. 73, 74.

457. John Ellement and Peggy Hernandez, "Minority Hiring Review Ordered," *Boston Globe* (September 30, 1988), p. 1.

458. Charles McCoy, "Taking Advantage," *The Wall Street Journal* (February 12, 1991), p. 1A.

459. Angelo Figueroa, "Firefighter Ethnicity a Hot Issue," *San Francisco Chronicle* (December 2, 1990), p. A1.

460. Walter E. Williams, "Lying About Race Becoming Common Because of Quotas," *Gazette Telegraph* (Colorado Springs) (January 25, 1991).

461. Paul Seabury, "HEW and the Universities," *Commentary* (February 1972), p. 44.

462. Neal Devins, "The Civil Rights Commission Backslides," *The Wall Street Journal* (October 19, 1990).

463. Bolick, *Changing Course,* p. 68.

464. Michael Levin, *Feminism and Freedom* (New Brunswick, N.J.: Transaction Books, 1987), p. 108.

465. William O. Douglas, *The Court Years 1939–1975* (New York: Random House, 1980), p. 149.

466. Robert Detlefsen, *Civil Rights Under Reagan* (San Francisco: ICS Press, 1991), p. 141ff.

467. "Wronging Rights," *National Review* (July 23, 1990), p. 14.

468. Barry R. Gross, ed., *Reverse Discrimination* (Buffalo: Prometheus Books, 1977), p. 19.

469. Lester A. Sobel, *Quotas and Affirmative Action* (New York: Facts On File, 1980), p. 167.

470. Linda Greenhouse, "Court Bars Plan Set Up to Provide Jobs to Minorities," *The New York Times* (January 24, 1989), p. 1.

471. "A Setback for Set-Asides," *The Wall Street Journal* (January 25, 1989), p. A20.

472. Linda Greenhouse, "Court Bars Plan," p. 1.

473. Michael deCourcy Hinds, "Minority Business Set Back Sharply by Courts' Rulings," *The New York Times* (December 23, 1991), p. A1.

474. Dorothy Gaiter, "Minority-Owned Business's Surge of '80s Is Threatened," *The Wall Street Journal* (February 27, 1991).

475. Michelle L. Singletary, "How to Profit in the Post-Crosson Era," *Black Enterprise* (February 1990), p. 180.

476. Vern Smith, "A Second Look at Set-Asides," *Newsweek* (July 1, 1991), p. 44.

477. Abigail Thernstrom, "Permaffirm Action," *The New Republic* (July 31, 1989), p. 17.

478. Mark Mooney, "Dinkins Moves to Prove Koch Bias on Contracts," *New York Post* (October 15, 1990), p. 14.

479. See page 140.

480. Calvin Sims, "Dinkins Plan Gives Minority Concerns More in Contracts," *The New York Times* (February 11, 1992), p. A1. "New York Mayor Plans to Increase Contracts Given to Minorities," *The Wall Street Journal* (February 11, 1992), p. A18.

481. Thomas Keans, "Agnos to Order More Contracts for Minorities," *San Francisco Chronicle* (October 12, 1990), p. A5.

482. Hinds, "Minority Business Set Back," p. A1.

483. Smith, "A Second Look," p. 44.

484. See page 142.

485. Detlefsen, *Civil Rights Under Reagan,* p. 34ff.

486. Quoted in Detlefsen, *Civil Rights Under Reagan,* p. 183.

487. Linda Gottfredson, "Hiring Quotas Exist, but Employers Won't Tell," *The New York Times* (August 1, 1990). Ed Koch, "Rights Bill Gets It All Wrong," *New York Post* (April 12, 1991), p. 2.

488. See, e.g., "High Court Ruling Makes It Harder to Prove Job Bias," *San Francisco Chronicle* (June 6, 1989), p. 1.

489. See, e.g., Aaron Epstein, "High Court Deals Blow to Affirmative Action," *San Jose Mercury News* (June 13, 1989), p. 1A.

490. Robert Pear, " '89 High Court Ruling Spurs New Civil Rights Suits," *The New York Times* (October 15, 1990), p. A1.

491. "Nonpracticing Preachers," *New York Post* (September 13, 1989), p. 26.

492. Stephen Wermiel, "Justices Affirm Interpretation of Rights Law," *The Wall Street Journal* (June 16, 1989), p. A10.

493. James Kilpatrick, "High Court Is Taking the Responsible Course," *Omaha World-Herald* (June 22, 1989).

494. Associated Press, "Black Baptists Told Racism at Its Worst," *Omaha World Herald* (September 8, 1990).

495. "Coyly, the Court Turns 180 Degrees," *The New York Times* (June 12, 1989), p. A18.

496. "Affirmative Action Ain't Broke, so . . . ," *Business Week* (June 26, 1989), p. 170.

497. See page 145.

498. Stephen Chapman, "High Court Isn't Reviving the Confederacy, Curtailing Civil Rights," *Omaha World-Herald* (June 20, 1989), p. 11.

499. "Civil-Rights Exemption," *The Wall Street Journal* (July 25, 1990), p. A12.

500. Paul Gigot, "Good-bye to Civil Rights Without Quotas," *The Wall Street Journal* (July 20, 1990), p. A12. Paul Barrett, "President Vetoes Job Bias Legislation; Democratic Proponents Assail the Move," *The Wall Street Journal* (October 23, 1990). Steven Holmes,

"On Job Rights Bill, a Vow to Try Again," *The New York Times* (October 26, 1990), p. A25.
"No Longer the Party of Lincoln," *The Economist* (October 27, 1990), p. 34.

501. Timothy Noah and Albert Karr, "What New Civil Rights Law Will Mean," *The Wall Street Journal* (November 4, 1991), p. B1. Paul Gewirtz, "Fine Print," *The New Republic* (November 18, 1991), p. 10.

502. Reuters, "Coors Hit by Lawsuit Alleging Prejudice," *Orange County* (Calif.) *Register* (November 26, 1991), p. 1.

503. Timothy Noah and Albert Karr, "What New Civil Rights Law Will Mean," *The Wall Street Journal* (November 4, 1991), p. B1.

504. L. Gordon Crovitz, "Bush's Quota Bill: (Dubious) Politics Trumps Legal Principle," *The Wall Street Journal* (October 30, 1991), p. A17.

505. "Legislators Pushed to Live by Own Laws," *Insight* (March 25, 1991), p. 23.

506. "Sue Them, Not Us," *The Wall Street Journal* (November 8, 1991), p. A14.

507. "Congress's Sweetheart Justice," *The Wall Street Journal* (November 1, 1991), p. A14.

508. Miles Benson, "Government Lax in Hiring Minorities," *San Francisco Chronicle* (December 1, 1991).

509. "The David Duke Bill," *The Wall Street Journal* (October 29, 1991), p. A22.

510. Paul Craig Roberts, "Codifying a Debased Citizenship," *Orange County* (Calif.) *Register* (November 7, 1991).

511. Michael Levin, *Feminism and Freedom* (New Brunswick, N.J.: Transaction Books, 1987), pp. 110–12. Peter Kilborn, "Labor Department Wants to Take on Job Bias in the Executive Suite," *The New York Times* (July 30, 1990), p. A1.

512. "How the Right Thing Went Awry," *Business Week* (July 8, 1991), p. 56.

513. Detlefsen, *Civil Rights Under Reagan*, p. 25.

514. Lynch, *Invisible Victims*, p. 145.

515. "Airline Creates Affirmative Action Program to Settle Job Bias Suit," *The New York Times* (May 12, 1991).

516. Thomas Sowell, " 'Civil Rights' That Can Lead to Civil War," *New York Daily News* (April 24, 1990), p. 30.

517. Timothy Noah, "Many Firms, Wary of Touchy Civil-Rights Issues, Keep Silent as Business Groups Seek Bill's Defeat," *The Wall Street Journal* (June 15, 1990), p. A12.

518. David Drier, " 'Disadvantaged' Contractors' Unfair Advantage," *The Wall Street Journal* (February 21, 1989), p. A20.

519. Ralph Vartabedian, "U.S. Program to Help Minority Firms Plagued by Failures," *Los Angeles Times* (July 7, 1991), p. D1.

520. National Research Council, *A Common Destiny*, p. 256.

521. Vartabedian, "U.S. Program to Help Minority Firms," p. D1.

522. Shanon LaFraniere, "Agents Say FBI Has Adopted Hiring, Promotion Quotas," *Washington Post* (June 17, 1991), p. A1.

523. James Workman, "Gender Norming," *The New Republic* (July 1, 1991), p. 16.

524. "Peace Corps Accused of Being Too White," *Insight* (June 18, 1990), p. 24.

525. United Press International, "National Gallery Starts Minority Internships," *Sunday World-Herald* (Omaha) (August 26, 1990), p. 8G.

526. David J. Fox, "Disney Sets Up Minority Program," *Los Angeles Times* (September 27, 1990).

527. Howard Kurtz, "*Inquirer*'s 'Quotas' Divide Staff," *Washington Post* (February 26, 1991).

528. Alex Jones, "Editors Report Gains in 1990 in Minority Hiring," *The New York Times* (April 12, 1991), p. A14.

529. "The Press Is Offering Minority Scholarships," *Asbury Park Press* (February 16, 1992), p. C5.

530. "Private Profit, Public Gain," special supplement to *The Atlantic* (September 1990), p. 21.

531. Dow Jones Newspaper Fund, *Journalism Career Guide for Minorities* (1989).

532. "Newspapers Court Minority Students," *Pittsburgh Post-Gazette* (November 2, 1990), p. 6.

533. Peter Kilborn, "A Company Recasts Itself to Erase Bias on the Job," *The New York Times* (October 4, 1990), p. 1.

534. Joan Rigdon, "PepsiCo's KFC Scouts for Blacks and Women for Its Top Echelons," *The Wall Street Journal* (November 13, 1991), p. 1.

535. Hector Cantu, "7-Eleven Competes for Minority Market," *Hispanic Business* (March 1992), p. 8.

536. Jonathan Tilove, "Recruiting Minorities by the Numbers Nothing New," *Grand Rapids Press* (June 9, 1991), p. F1.

537. Claudia Deutsch, "Listening to Women and Blacks," *The New York Times* (December 1, 1991), p. 25.

538. Joan Rigdon, "PepsiCo's KFC Scouts for Blacks and Women for Its Top Echelons," *The Wall Street Journal* (November 13, 1991), p. 1.

539. Jonathan Tilove, "Many Major Corporations Committed to Affirmative Action," *Grand Rapids Press* (August 4, 1991), p. D7.

540. Jonathan Tilove, "Recruiting Minorities by the Numbers Nothing New," *Grand Rapids Press* (June 9, 1991), p. F1.

541. Rigdon, "PepsiCo's KFC Scouts for Blacks and Women," p. 1.

542. Alan Farnham, "Holding Firm on Affirmative Action," *Fortune* (March 13, 1989), p. 88.

543. Brent Bowers, "Black Boss, White Business," *The Wall Street Journal* (April 3, 1992), p. R7.

544. Nadine Brozan, "Job Fair Is Bleak Portrait of Economic Mood," *The New York Times* (November 13, 1990), p. B1.

545. "Minority Grads Remain in Demand Despite Slump," *The Wall Street Journal* (April 18, 1991).

546. "Helping Minorities with 'Wall Analysis,'" *The Wall Street Journal* (December 12, 1990), p. B1.

547. Jonathan Tilove, "Many Major Corporations Committed to Affirmative Action," *Grand Rapids Press* (August 4, 1991), p. D7.

548. Steven Holmes, "Affirmative Action Plans Are Now Part of the Normal Corporate Way of Life," *The New York Times* (January 22, 1991), p. A20.

549. Detlefsen, *Civil Rights Under Reagan,* p. 151ff.

550. Robert G. Holland, "Dirty Secrets," *Chronicles* (February 1992), p. 44.

551. "Race-Norming," *The Wall Street Journal* (April 8, 1991), p. A18.

552. "The Dirty Iceberg," *National Review* (September 3, 1990), p. 36.

553. Peter A. Brown, "Normin' Stormin'," *The New Republic* (April 29, 1991), p. 12ff.

554. Robert G. Holland, "Big Brother's Test Scores," *National Review* (September 3, 1990), p. 35. Walter E. Williams, "Official Racism Is Still Racism," *New York City Paper* (July 24, 1990). *Washington Post,* "End of the Road Near for Job Aptitude Test," *Sunday World-Herald* (Omaha) (August 5, 1990), "Research Council Endorses Skewing of Aptitude Scores," *The Wall Street Journal* (May 24, 1989), p. A2. Robert G. Holland, "Testscam," *Reason* (January 1991), p. 48.

555. Timothy Noah, "Agency Declines to Ban Use of Test with Disparities," *The Wall Street Journal* (December 16, 1991), p. A16.

556. E. F. Wonderlic & Associates, *The Wonderlic Personnel Test* (Northfield, Ill., 1976), p. 3.

557. Holland, "Dirty Secrets," p. 44.

558. "Adjusted Scoring Now Illegal: To Test or Not to Test Is Now the Question," *HR Manager's Legal Reporter* (March 1992), p. 2.

559. Michael Taylor, "AC Transit Aide Suspended for Biased Remarks," *San Francisco Chronicle* (May 12, 1990), p. A7.

560. "Seeing Through Black Eyes," *Newsweek* (March 7, 1988), p. 26.

561. Amy Stevens, "Anti-Discrimination Training Haunts Employer in Bias Suit," *The Wall Street Journal* (July 31, 1991), p. B1.

562. Marcus Mabry et al., "Past Tokenism," *Newsweek* (May 14, 1990), p. 37ff.

563. "Race in the Workplace," *Business Week* (July 8, 1991), p. 58.

564. John Wagner, "Black Papers Are Fighting for Survival," *The Wall Street Journal* (October 4, 1990), p. B1.

565. "A Hard Climb in a Downturn," *Business Week* (July 8, 1991), p. 58.

566. "Trade Fair Hopes Crowds Go Better with Coke," *The Wall Street Journal* (May 24, 1991).

567. Mindy Fetterman, "Dreams Fail as Auto Sales Falter," *USA Today* (March 14, 1990), p. B1. Krystal Miller and Jacqueline Mitchell, "Car Sales Slump May Hit Minority Dealers Hardest," *The Wall Street Journal* (February 13, 1991), p. B1.

568. Elizabeth Fowler, "Univex Chief Expands Role on Minorities," *The New York Times* (August 8, 1988), p. 25.

569. "How Affirmative Action Really Works," *The Wall Street Journal* (May 15, 1991), p. A14.

570. Christopher Williams, "Big Business Reaches Out to Minority Suppliers," *The New York Times* (November 12, 1989).

571. Michelle L. Singletary, "How to Profit in the Post-Crosson Era," *Black Enterprise* (February 1990), p. 180.

572. "Private Profit, Public Gain," p. 8.

573. Williams, "Big Business Reaches Out."

574. Ray Kerrison, "NYNEX Rings in New Year Ominously," *New York Post* (January 2, 1991), p. 4.

575. "Public Services Found More Efficient if Private Companies Compete," *The New York Times* (April 26, 1988), p. 34.

576. Morton Kondracke, "The Two Black Americas," *The New Republic* (February 6, 1989), p. 18.

577. Kilborn, "Labor Department Wants to Take on Job Bias," p. A1.

578. Ed Lane, "Mobile's New Black Police Leaders Play Historic Roles," *Dallas Morning News* (January 21, 1990), p. 10A.

579. "Public Services Found More Efficient," p. 34.

580. Robert Brustein, "As the Globe Turns," *The New Republic* (February 18, 1991), p. 53.

581. Charles Krauthammer, "The Tribalization of America," *Washington Post* (August 6, 1990).

582. Diane Lewis, "15 Agencies Win Grants to Foster Diversity," *Boston Globe* (July 20, 1990), p. 13.

583. Robert Brustein, "As The Globe Turns," *The New Republic* (February 18, 1991), p. 53.

584. Paul Seabury, "HEW and the Universities," *Commentary* (February 1972), p. 39.

585. Seabury, "HEW and the Universities," p. 42.

586. Stephen Barnett, "Get Back," *The New Republic* (February 18, 1991), pp. 24, 26.

587. Abigail Thernstrom, "On the Scarcity of Black Professors," *Commentary* (July 1990), p. 22.

588. Abigail Thernstrom, "Permaffirm Action," *The New Republic* (July 31, 1989), p. 17.

589. "Yale Trying to Recruit Minority Faculty," *Omaha World-Herald* (February 11, 1990).

590. "Racism, Cynicism, Musical Chairs," *The Economist* (June 25, 1988), p. 30.

591. "Racism, Cynicism, Musical Chairs," p. 33. John Bunzel, "Minority Faculty Hiring," *The American Scholar* (Winter 1990), p. 46.

592. Don Wycliff, "Science Careers Are Attracting Few Blacks," *The New York Times* (June 8, 1990), p. 1.

593. "Black Ph.D.s Increase by 13%," *San Jose Mercury News* (May 4, 1992), p. 7A.
594. John Bunzel, "Minority Faculty Hiring," *The American Scholar* (Winter 1990), p. 46.
595. "Racism, Cynicism, Musical Chairs," p. 33.
596. Thernstrom, "On the Scarcity of Black Professors," p. 23.
597. John Kennedy, "The Law School Tenure Line," *Boston Globe* (April 27, 1990), p. 1.
598. Dinesh D'Souza, "Illiberal Education," *The Atlantic* (March 1991), p. 62.
599. D'Souza, "Illiberal Education," p. 70.
600. John H. Bunzel, "Exclusive Opportunities," *The American Enterprise* (March/April 1990), pp. 3–5.
601. "How Affirmative Action Really Works," *The Wall Street Journal* (May 15, 1991), p. A14.
602. Thomas Sowell, *The Economics and Politics of Race* (New York: William Morrow & Company, 1983), p. 197.
603. See page 169.
604. Abigail Thernstrom, "On the Scarcity of Black Professors," *Commentary* (July 1990), p. 24ff.
605. "Girls Shorted on Scholarships, Test Critics Say," *Omaha World-Herald* (April 13, 1988).
606. Lee Daniels, "Groups Charge Bias in Merit Scholarship Testing," *The New York Times* (June 29, 1988), p. B6.
607. Gary Putka, "Scores on College Entrance Tests Fall, Adding to Concern About U.S. Schools," *The Wall Street Journal* (September 12, 1989), p. A5.
608. John Leo, "Stop Blaming the Tests," *U.S. News & World Report* (March 20, 1989), p. 80.
609. Hacker, *Two Nations,* p. 143.
610. Donald Stewart, "Thinking the Unthinkable," *Vital Speeches of the Day* (May 1, 1989), p. 447.
611. Hacker, *Two Nations,* p. 107.
612. D'Souza, "Illiberal Education," p. 54.
613. John Bunzel, "The University's Pseudo-Egalitarianism," *The Wall Street Journal* (July 12, 1991), p. A10.
614. See page 171.
615. Thomas Sowell, "The New Racism on Campus," *Fortune* (February 13, 1989), p. 115ff.
616. Levin, *Feminism and Freedom,* p. 119. Charles Murray, "The Coming of Custodial Democracy," *Commentary* (September 1988), p. 24.
617. Walter Williams, "Campus Racism," *National Review* (May 5, 1989), p. 37.
618. "Report Points Way to Pluralism," *Palo Alto* (Calif.) *Weekly* (June 7, 1989), p. 17.
619. Stephen Goode, "On the Outs Over Who Gets In," *Insight* (October 9, 1989), p. 9.
620. Ira Heyman, " 'Ethnic Diversity' at UC Berkeley," *San Francisco Chronicle* (June 16, 1990).
621. Diane Curtis, "Fewer Blacks Entered UC Berkeley in '90," *San Francisco Chronicle* (November 28, 1990).
622. IRS Publication 557, *Tax-Exempt Status for Your Organization* (rev. Oct. 1988; still being distributed, and in effect in 1992), p. 12.
623. Associated Press, "Minorities Deserving of Financial Aid, Study Says," *Gazette Telegraph* (Colorado Springs) (June 22, 1991).
624. Nick Anderson, "Minority Enrollment Edges Up at Stanford," *San Jose Mercury News* (June 23, 1990), p. 2B.
625. "Free Graduate School for Minority Students," *The New York Times* (March 21, 1990), p. B5.
626. Don Wycliff, "Science Careers Are Attracting Few Blacks," *The New York Times* (June 8, 1990), p. 1.
627. "Yale Trying to Recruit Minority Faculty."

628. Michel Marriott, "A Wide Range of Help for Minority Students Who Try Engineering," *The New York Times* (March 6, 1991), p. B8.

629. Peter Scarlet, "Program Helps Minorities and Women Finish School, Pursue High-Tech Jobs," *Salt Lake Tribune* (April 21, 1991), p. B8.

630. Susan Chira, "Efforts to Reshape Teaching Focus on Finding New Talent," *The New York Times* (August 28, 1990), p. A1.

631. "Minority Update," *The Chronicle of Higher Education* (June 27, 1990), p. A32.

632. Kathleen Teltsch, "Grant Seeks to Attract Minorities to Teaching," *The New York Times* (September 23, 1990).

633. Mark Lowery, "Life and Death of a Hero," *Newsday* (New York) (February 22, 1990), p. 8.

634. Thernstrom, "Permaffirm Action," p. 18.

635. Thomas Sowell, "No Bias, Please: Scholarship Rule Favors Equality," *The Wall Street Journal* (December 17, 1990).

636. Carl T. Rowan, "Scholarship Flap Shows a Determination to Keep the Underclass Down," *New York Daily News* (December 21, 1990).

637. Rowland Evans and Robert Novak, "Can Scholarships Be Reserved for Blacks Any More Than for Whites?" *New York Post* (December 19, 1990).

638. Karen de Witt, "Ruling Highlights a Rift Among Blacks," *The New York Times* (December 17, 1990). Thomas Sowell, "No Bias, Please." Scholarship Rule Favors Equality," *The Wall Street Journal* (December 17, 1990). Karen de Witt, "U.S. Eases College Aid Stand, but Not All the Way," (*The New York Times*) (December 19, 1990), p. A1. Anthony DePalma, "Educators Report Great Confusion on Minority Aid," *The New York Times* (December 20, 1990), p. A1. Karen De Witt, "Limits Proposed for Race-Based Scholarships," *The New York Times* (December 5, 1991), p. A26.

639. Milo Geyelin, "Court Rejects Scholarship Aid for Blacks Only," *The Wall Street Journal* (February 5, 1992), p. B1.

640. "Tuition at Campus Is Free for All Black Freshmen," *The New York Times* (March 9, 1990), p. A12.

641. Anthony DePalma, "Theory and Practice Are at Odds in Proposal on Minority Scholarships," *The New York Times* (December 7, 1991), p. 10L.

642. "More Colleges Give Minority Scholarships," *USA Today* (December 26, 1990).

643. Todd Ackerman, "Texas A&M Study Calls for Boost in Minority Recruiting," *Houston Chronicle* (May 16, 1992).

644. Felicia Lee, "Minorities at Baruch Charge Neglect Despite Ethnic Mix," *The New York Times* (April 21, 1990), p. 1.

645. "Lamar Alexander and the Diversity Police," *New York Post* (December 2, 1991).

646. James Guyot, " 'Diversity' by Dictation?" *Newsday* (New York) (May 30, 1990), p. 52.

647. "A Nobel for Baruch," *New York Post* (October 18, 1990), p. 24.

648. Lee, "Minorities at Baruch Charge Neglect," p. 1.

649. Courtney Leatherman, "2 of 6 Regional Accrediting Agencies Take Steps to Prod Colleges on Racial, Ethnic Diversity," *Chronicle of Higher Education* (August 15, 1990), p. 1.

650. "The Accreditation Wars," *The Wall Street Journal* (April 23, 1991), p. A22.

651. Jim Sleeper, "The Policemen of Diversity," *Washington Post* (June 30, 1991), p. C1.

652. Allan Bloom, *The Closing of the American Mind* (New York: Simon & Schuster, 1987), p. 95.

653. For a frank discussion of this problem, see Shelby Steele, "The Recoloring of Campus Life," *Harper's* (February 1989), p. 47ff.

654. George F. Will, "The Stab of Racial Doubt," *Newsweek* (September 24, 1990), p. 86.

655. Steele, "The Recoloring of Campus Life," p. 52.

656. Steele, "The Recoloring of Campus Life," p. 51.

657. Donald Werner, "College Admissions: Shaky Ethics," *The New York Times* (1988), no page or date.

658. Vincent Sarich, "Making Racism Official at Cal," *California Monthly* (September 1990), p. 17ff.

659. James Gibney, "The Berkeley Squeeze," *The New Republic* (April 11, 1988), pp. 15–17. Ernest Pasour, "Affirmative Action: A Counterproductive Policy," *The Freeman* (January 1989), p. 30.

660. Susan Chira, "U.S. to Look at Admissions at Berkeley Law School," *The New York Times* (April 7, 1990), p. 8. Vincent Sarich, Department of Anthropology, U.C. Berkeley, "The Institutionalization of Racism at the University of California at Berkeley," p. 3, unpublished.

661. Sarich, "Making Racism Official at Cal," p. 17ff.

662. Renee Koury, "Affirmative Action on Campus in Trouble," *San Jose Mercury News* (February 17, 1991), p. 1A.

663. Thomas and Mary Edsall, "Race," *The Atlantic* (May 1991), p. 73.

664. Stephen Chapman, "A Law School Uproar Raises Unpleasant Facts About Race," *Chicago Tribune* (April 21, 1991).

665. Lino Graglia, "Law School Admissions Policies Are Unequal" (letter), *The New York Times* (May 3, 1991).

666. Stephen Chapman, "A Law School Uproar."

667. " 'Racism' in the Courts," *New York Post* (June 25, 1991), p. 40.

668. Stephen Labaton, "Law Review's Anti-Bias Program Revives Dispute," *The New York Times* (May 3, 1989), p. A10. R. T. Gould, "Writers Must Be Chosen for Talent, Not Race," *Daily Illini* (University of Illinois) (April 30, 1990), p. 21.

669. Dean Congbalay, "Whites No Longer in Cal's Majority," *San Jose Mercury News* (August 30, 1988), p. B1.

670. Fred Siegel, "The Cult of Multiculturalism," *The New Republic* (February 18, 1991), p. 38.

671. Mike Wowk, "MSU Student Suspended Over Racial Cartoon," *Detroit News* (May 3, 1990).

672. Stephen L. Carter, "Racial Preferences? So What?" *The Wall Street Journal* (September 13, 1989), p. A20.

673. "S&L Cave-In Brings Minority Opportunities," *The Wall Street Journal* (May 1, 1990), p. B2.

674. Stephen Labaton, "Few Minority Companies Get Contracts in Savings Bailout," *The New York Times* (June 4, 1991), p. A1.

675. Michael Robinson, "Activists Oppose First Interstate-Allied Merger," *American Banker* (August 13, 1987), p. 15.

676. Richard Schmitt, "Public Service or Blackmail? Banks Pressed to Finance Local Projects," *The Wall Street Journal* (September 10, 1987), p. 35.

677. James Bates, "B of A Policy on Minority Loans to Be Changed," *Los Angeles Times* (October 12, 1991), p. D1.

678. Sarah Bartlett, "Big Banks Discriminate in Mortgages," *The New York Times* (December 11, 1991), p. B4.

679. Williams, *The State Against Blacks,* p. 30 [emphasis in the original].

680. Eric Felton, "Pay Up or Else," *Insight* (May 20, 1991), p. 13.

681. "Invidious Distinction," *The New Republic* (February 5, 1990), p. 4. "Making It Clear," *The Economist* (January 28, 1989), p. 21.

682. Linda Greenhouse, "F.C.C. Tilt to Minorities Weighed by High Court," *The New York Times* (March 29, 1990), p. A16.

683. Hilary Stout, "Education Agency Set to Crack Down on Loan Defaults," *The Wall Street Journal* (May 3, 1991), p. B5C.

684. Jeffrey Tucker, "EZ Living," *Chronicles* (June 1991), p. 47.

685. Eugene Carlson, "Impact of Zones for Enterprise Is Ambiguous," *The Wall Street Journal* (April 1, 1991), p. B1.

686. See page 187.

687. See page 187.

688. Carl Cannon, "California Nominated to Test GOP Strategies for Wooing Minorities," *San Jose Mercury News* (April 29, 1989), p. 1A.

689. James A. White, "Minorities and Women Gain a Bigger Role in Money Management," *The Wall Street Journal* (March 13, 1991), p. 1.

690. Dyan Machan, "Who's Minding the Funds?" *Forbes* (April 1, 1991), p. 102.

691. Steve Hemmerick, "Minorities Statute Hits 4 Managers," *Pensions and Investments* (April 1, 1991), p. 1.

692. Tim W. Ferguson, "Pension-Fund Partiality: Managing to Spread the Wealth?" *The Wall Street Journal* (April 30, 1991), p. A25.

693. H. Jane Lehman, "Judge Allows 'Affirmative Marketing' Based on Race," *Washington Post* (December 31, 1988).

694. Isabel Wilkerson, "One City's 30-Year Crusade for Integration," *The New York Times* (December 30, 1991), p. A1.

695. William Celis 3d, "District Finds Way to End Segregation and Restore Neighborhood Schools," *The New York Times* (September 4, 1991).

696. "Plan to Market Homes," *The Wall Street Journal* (July 3, 1992), p. B3.

697. J. Linn Allen, "Suit Aims at Housing Ads with Only White Models," *Chicago Tribune* (June 21, 1991), p. 1.

698. Jerry Morgan, "Co-Op Sanctioned for Ads Without Blacks," *Newsday* (New York) (November 21, 1991).

699. Robin Pogrebin, "Suit Against Times: A Model Dilemma," *New York Observer* (February 11, 1991), p. 1.

700. Detlefsen, *Civil Rights Under Reagan*, p. 163.

701. Elizabeth McCaughey, "Perverting the Voting Rights Act," *The Wall Street Journal* (October 25, 1989), p. A18.

702. Roberto Suro, "In Redistricting, New Rules and New Prizes," *The New York Times* (May 5, 1990). Charles Lane, "Ghetto Chic," *The New Republic* (August 12, 1991), p. 14.

703. "America's Group Areas," *The Wall Street Journal* (June 12, 1991), p. A12.

704. "Remapping Rulings Favor Minorities," *San Francisco Chronicle* (January 8, 1991), p. A2.

705. James Madison "Federalist Paper No. 10," *The Federalist Papers* (New York: New American Library of World Literature, 1961), p. 82ff.

706. Peter Applebome, " '65 Rights Act Now a Tool for Whites," *The New York Times* (August 8, 1989).

707. "America's Group Areas," *The Wall Street Journal* (June 12, 1991), p. A12.

708. "Racial Gerrymandering," *The Wall Street Journal* (July 29, 1991).

709. Sam Roberts, "Now It's the Law, but New Charter Still Riles Koch," *The New York Times* (April 23, 1990), p. B1.

710. Sylvia Moreno, "New Voice for the Mosaic," *Newsday* (New York) (June 19, 1990), p. 8.

711. William Glaberson, "Old Feuds Stall New City Council as Deadline Nears," *The New York Times* (April 28, 1991), p. A1. "Polarizing the Council," *New York Post* (May 1, 1991). Sam Roberts, "In Some Council Contests, It's Still Us Against Them," *The New York Times* (September 2, 1991), p. 21.

712. "The Redistricting Game," *New York Post* (July 27, 1991), p. 12.

713. "Black Judgeships Offered," *Houston Chronicle* (February 20, 1991).

714. Isabel Wilkerson, "Discordant Notes in Detroit: Music and Affirmative Action," *The New York Times* (March 5, 1989), p. 1.

715. County of Harris (Texas), Department of Personnel, *Resource Newsletter* (January 1992).

716. "City Rule Discriminated Against Blacks," *HR Manager's Legal Reporter* (November 1991), p. 8.

717. Daniel Goleman, "Psychologists Find Ways to Break Racism's Hold," *The New York Times* (September 5, 1989).

718. Philip Shabecoff, "Environmental Groups Told They Are Racists in Hiring," *The New York Times* (February 1, 1990), p. A20.

719. "Minorities Sought," *San Jose Mercury News* (May 9, 1990), p. 1E.

720. Phil McCombs, "Men's Movement Stalks the Wild Side," *Washington Post* (February 3, 1991).

721. Llewellyn Rockwell, *Chronicles* (February 1991), p. 7.

722. Bell, "Bias, Probability, and Prison Populations," p. 18.

723. Lynch, *Invisible Victims*, p. 26.

724. National Research Council, *A Common Destiny*, p. 134 (from a poll taken in 1979–80) and 117.

725. Jeffrey Schmalz, "Racial Tension Spreads in Miami on Second Night after Fatal Shooting," *The New York Times* (January 18, 1989), p. 1. Jeffrey Schmalz, "Miami Mayor Apologizes to Police for Actions at Scene of Disorder," *The New York Times* (January 19, 1989), p. 1. "An Immigration Policy That's Fair to All," *Business Week* (February 6, 1989), p. 114.

726. Jeffrey Schmalz, "Dreams and Despair Collide as Miami Searches for Itself," *The New York Times* (January 23, 1989), p. A1.

727. Jeffrey Schmalz, "Miami's New Ethnic Conflict: Haitians vs. American Blacks," *The New York Times* (February 19, 1989), p. A1.

728. Kenneth S. Tollett, "For Mandela, South Africa Comes First," *The New York Times* (July 25, 1990).

729. Todd Ackerman, "Indians Claim UT Program Evades Them," *Houston Chronicle* (February 24, 1992), p. 9A.

730. William Schmidt, "Private Gifts to Public Schools Bring Questions of Fairness," *The New York Times* (December 27, 1988), p. A1.

731. Michel Marriott, "A New Road to Learning: Teaching the Whole Child," *The New York Times* (June 13, 1990), p. A1.

732. "Racial Ultimatum at Harvard Law," *New York Daily News* (May 2, 1990), p. 24. Fox Butterfield, "At Rally, Jackson Assails Harvard Law School," *The New York Times* (May 10, 1990), p. A14.

733. Carl Rowan, " 'Merit' Is a White Code Word for Maintaining Privilege," *New York Post* (May 24, 1990), p. 29.

734. "A Class Sends Message to Harvard Law School," *The New York Times* (November 21, 1990).

735. Fox Butterfield, "Professor Continues Law School Protest," *The New York Times* (February 28, 1992).

736. Jennifer Toth, "College Affirmative Action: How Serious Is the Backlash?" *Los Angeles Times* (May 16, 1991), p. A5.

737. Renee Koury, "Bid for Minority Hiring," *San Jose Mercury News* (April 5, 1991), p. 1B.

738. Stephen Chapman, "A Law School Uproar Raises Unpleasant Facts About Race," *Chicago Tribune* (April 21, 1991).

739. Diane Curcio, "Essex College Board Chairman Resigns, Charging 'Reverse Racism,' " *Star-Ledger* (Newark) (February 5, 1991), p. 27.

740. Peter Moses, "City Probes Shakedown Attempt on Woody," *New York Post* (December 11, 1991), p. 3. Timothy McDarrah, "Shakedown Sequel: Filmmakers Hire Guards," *New York Post* (December 13, 1991), p. 3.

741. Anthony DePalma, "Boycott Over Visit of Mandela Lives On," *The New York Times* (July 13, 1991), p. 6.

742. United Press International, *Omaha World-Herald* (September 20, 1990), p. 10.

743. Isabel Wilkerson, "Call for Black Militia Stuns Milwaukee," *The New York Times* (April 6, 1990), p. A12. Robbie Morganfield, "An Ultimatum in Milwaukee," *Detroit News* (April 29, 1990), p. 1B.

744. Associated Press, "Rebel Alderman Issues Chilling Threat," *Grand Rapids Press* (January 16, 1992), p. A10.

745. Sobel, *Quotas and Affirmative Action,* pp. 9, 10.

746. Ralph Scott, "Mandated School Busing and Student Learning," *Mankind Quarterly* (Fall 1986), p. 45.

747. Thomas Sowell, *Civil Rights: Rhetoric or Reality?* (New York: William Morrow and Company, 1984), p. 69.

748. Sobel, *Quotas and Affirmative Action,* p. 99.

749. Bolick, *Changing Course,* p. 108.

750. Bob Sipchen, "Tracing the Politics of Racial Liberalism," *Los Angeles Times* (April 25, 1991), p. E17.

751. Bolick, *Changing Course* (New Brunswick, N.J.: Transaction Books, 1988), p. 62.

752. "How Are the Schools?" *The Wall Street Journal* (March 31, 1989), p. R30.

753. Jonathan Tilove, "School Busing Ideals Stall After Hard Climb to Nowhere," *Grand Rapids Press* (January 12, 1992), p. 4A.

754. Allan Gold, "Boston Schools Set to Overhaul Busing Policies," *The New York Times* (December 28, 1988), p. B6.

755. Jonathan Tilove, "School Busing Ideals Stall After Hard Climb to Nowhere," *Grand Rapids Press* (January 12, 1992), p. 4A.

756. "Units to Be Reserved for Blacks," *Vero Beach* (Fla.) *Press-Journal* (June 8, 1990).

757. James Kilpatrick, "Mad Hatter Would Feel at Home in Kansas City," *Omaha World-Herald* (August 18, 1989).

758. "Judge George III," *The Wall Street Journal* (April 23, 1990), p. A14.

759. "Federal Judges Shouldn't be Taxmen," *The Wall Street Journal* (April 23, 1990), p. A14. "Judge George III," *The Wall Street Journal* (April 23, 1990), p. A14. "Court-Ordered Taxation," *Washington Post* (April 20, 1990), p. A26.

760. O. Uribe, *The Effects of School Desegregation on the Academic Achievement of Black Students,* National Institute of Education (September 1983), cited in Ralph Scott, "Sex and Race Achievement Profiles in a Desegregated High School in the Deep South," *Mankind Quarterly* (Spring 1985), p. 291.

761. Ralph Scott, "Desegregatory Effects in Charlotte-Mecklenburg County Schools," *Mankind Quarterly* (Fall/Winter 1984), p. 61ff.

762. "Separate and Equal," *The Atlantic* (September 1991), p. 24.

763. Arthur R. Jensen, "Spearman's g and the Problem of Educational Equality," *Oxford Review of Education,* Vol. 17, No. 2 (1991), p. 178.

764. Ralph Scott, "Education and Ethnicity: The U.S. Experiment in School Integration," (Washington, D.C.: The Council for Social and Economic Studies [undated]), p. 114. Reprint of Ralph Scott, " 'Push-Through' Educational Programs: Threat to Academic Integrity and the Nation's Economic Productivity," *The Journal of Social, Political, and Economic Studies* (Summer 1987).

765. Bolick, *Changing Course,* p. 106.

766. Charlotte Allen, "Busing's Comback," *The American Spectator* (January 1991), p. 27.

767. See page 207.

768. Linda Greenhouse, "Justices Rule Mandatory Busing May Go, Even if Races Stay Apart," *The New York Times* (January 6, 1991), p. A1. David Savage, "Time to End Desegregation Court Orders, Justices Rule," *Los Angeles Times* (January 16, 1991), p. A1. Amy Wells, "Asking What Schools Have Done, or Can Do, to Help Desegregation," *The New York Times* (January 16, 1991), p. B6.

769. Michele Norris, "P.G. Sued Over Teacher Transfers," *Washington Post* (January 24, 1989), p. 1.

770. Aleta Watson, "Minority Teachers Sought," *San Jose Mercury News* (December 31, 1988), p. 1.

771. Joseph Berger, "Pessimism in Air as Schools Try Affirmative Action," *The New York Times* (February 27, 1990), p. B1.

772. See page 208.

773. Jensen, "Spearman's *g* and the Problem of Educational Equality," p. 180.

774. Joseph Berger, "Pessimism in Air as Schools Try Affirmative Action," *The New York Times* (February 27, 1990), p. B1.

775. Thomas Sowell, "Buzzwords Mask Real Ills of Society," New York *Daily News* (July 27, 1990).

776. Joseph Berger, "Pessimism in Air," p. B1. Abigail Thernstrom, "Beyond the Pale," *The New Republic* (December 16, 1991), p. 22.

777. "Boston School-Bias Suit on Hiring is Reopened," *The New York Times* (April 30, 1991).

778. Joseph Berger, "Pessimism in Air," p. B1.

779. "Black University Fights Desegregation Order," *The New York Times* (August 6, 1989), p. 23.

780. Frances Marcus, "After 19 Years, Louisiana Still Seeks a Way to Mix Races at Its Colleges," *The New York Times* (December 27, 1988), p. A11.

781. Art Pine, "Riots Renew Debate on Anti-Poverty Efforts," *Los Angeles Times* (May 5, 1992), p. 1.

782. Thomas Sowell, "Affirmative Action Reconsidered" in Barry R. Gross, ed., *Reverse Discrimination* (Buffalo: Prometheus Books, 1977), p. 129 [emphasis in the original].

783. Thomas Sowell, " 'Affirmative Action': A Worldwide Disaster," *Commentary* (December 1989), p. 33.

784. Shelby Steele, "A Negative Vote on Affirmative Action," *The New York Times Magazine* (May 13, 1990), p. 49.

785. "Civil Rights and Wrongs," *The Wall Street Journal* (July 19, 1990).

786. Linda Lichter, "Who Speaks for Black America?" *Public Opinion* (August/September 1985), p. 42.

787. Sonia Nazario, "Many Minorities Feel Torn by Experience of Affirmative Action," *The Wall Street Journal* (June 27, 1989), p. A10. Associated Press, "Minority Police Hiring Stirs Anger in Denver," *The New York Times* (October 9, 1990), p. A16.

788. Brent Bowers, "Black Boss, White Business," *The Wall Street Journal* (April 3, 1992), p. R7.

789. William Raspberry, "The Civil Rights Movement Is Over," *Washington Post* (February 25, 1987), p. A23.

790. Robert Pear, "Civil Rights Agency Splits in Debate on Narrowing Definition of Equality," *The New York Times* (October 14, 1985), p. A17.

791. Linda Wright and Daniel Glick, "Farrakhan's Mission," *Newsweek* (March 19, 1990), p. 25.

792. Bolick, *Changing Course,* p. 35.

793. Joseph Sobran, "Howard Beach," *National Review* (March 27, 1987), p. 29.

794. Robert Detlefsen, *Civil Rights Under Reagan,* p. 17.

795. Raspberry, "The Civil Rights Movement Is Over," p. A23.

796. Cited in Paul Seabury, "HEW and the Universities," *Commentary* (February 1972), p. 42ff.

797. See page 218.

798. "Liberal Arts," *Chronicles* (September 1989), p. 32 [emphasis added].

799. Anne Wortham, *The Other Side of Racism* (Columbus: Ohio State University Press, 1981), p. 193.

800. Dorothy Rabinowitz, "Biased Panel Serves Up History with a Twist," *The Wall Street Journal* (June 27, 1991), p. A14.

801. "A Tenuous Bond from 9 to 5," *Newsweek* (March 7, 1988), p. 24.

802. Paul M. Barrett, "Justices Reject Board 'Hate Crime' Law as Violation of Free-Speech Guarantee," *The Wall Street Journal* (June 23, 1992), p. A22.

803. "Michel Apologizes for Observation," *The New York Times* (November 17, 1988), p. A11.

804. Floyd Flake, "Michel's Amos 'n' Andy Slur," *The New York Times* (November 21, 1988), p. A15.

805. Jim Nolan, "Hynes Boots Aide over Race Remark," *New York Post* (May 23, 1990), p. 12.

806. Ed Koch, "It's Been a Rotten Year for the Apple," *New York Post* (January 4, 1991), p. 2.

807. Richard Steier, "Latinos Outraged over Remarks by NAACP Big," *New York Post* (October 4, 1990), p. 7. Andrew Kirtzman, "Racism Retort," *New York Daily News* (October 4, 1990), p. 7.

808. David Seifman, "OTB Boss Backs Freeze—Then Hikes Salaries," *New York Post* (December 18, 1990). David Seifman, "Dukes: Minorities Deserve Pay Hikes," *New York Post* (December 19, 1990).

809. Mike Royko, "Bad-Word Dictionary Is Missing Something," *Omaha World-Herald* (June 5, 1990).

810. "Ugh! Oops," *New Republic* (February 18, 1991), p. 39.

811. "Blond Banter," *Chronicles* (February 1992), p. 28.

812. Wortham, *The Other Side of Racism*, p. 191.

813. John Taylor, "Don't Blame Me," *New York* (June 3, 1991), p. 34.

814. National Research Council, *A Common Destiny*, p. 134.

815. "What We Say, What We Think," *U.S. News & World Report* (February 1, 1988), p. 28.

816. Michael Janofsky, "U.S. Sprinters in Fast Lane," *The New York Times* (March 18, 1988).

817. Carlton Putnam, *Race and Reason* (Washington, D.C.: Public Affairs Press, 1961), p. 62.

818. Carlton Putnam, *Race and Reality* (Washington, D.C.: Public Affairs Press, 1967, p. 135ff.

819. "Policy at Gannett Seeks More Minority Voices in Newspapers," *The New York Times* (November 27, 1988), p. A16.

820. David Shaw, "Newspapers Struggling to Raise Minority Coverage," *Los Angeles Times* (December 12, 1990), p. 1.

821. William Robbins, "Armed, Sophisticated, and Violent, Two Drug Gangs Blanket Nation," *The New York Times* (November 25, 1988), p. A1.

822. Drummond Ayres, "Washington Finds Drug War Is Hardest at Home," *The New York Times* (December 9, 1988), p. A11.

823. Bill Gordon, "Crack's Incredible Cost to S.F.," *San Francisco Chronicle* (February 21, 1989), pp. 1, 12, 13.

824. Don Feder, "Blacks Again Are the Victims of Years of Racial Demagogy," *Orange County* (Calif.) *Register* (May 3, 1992), p. K1. "How the Defense Dissected the Tape," *Newsweek* (May 11, 1992), p. 36.

825. Linda Deutsch, "Jury Believed Police Had Right to Use Plenty of Force," *Orange County* (Calif.) *Register* (April 30, 1992), p. A4. Sheryl Stolberg, "Jurors Tell of Angry, Bitter Deliberations," *Los Angeles Times* (May 8, 1992), p. A3.

826. Greg Meyer, "We Must Have a Way to Safely Take a Suspect Down," *San Jose Mercury News* (May 3, 1992), p. 1.

827. Murray Rothbard, "Rockwell vs. Rodney and the Libertarian World," *Rothbard Rockwell Report* (July 1991), p. 4. Henry Weinstein, "White Says Jury Was the Worst Possible," *Los Angeles Times* (May 8, 1992), p. A3.

828. "How the Defense Dissected the Tape," *Newsweek* (May 11, 1992), p. 36.

829. One of the best early summaries of the trial testimony is "The Rodney King Trial: What the Jury Heard," *Washington Inquirer* (May 22, 1992), p. 4.

830. Associated Press, "King Passenger Claims He Was Beaten," *Las Vegas Review-Journal* (May 5, 1992), p. 5A.

831. Richard Stevenson, "Los Angeles Chief Taunted at Hearing," *The New York Times* (March 15, 1991). Associated Press, "Black Officers Association Denies Departmental Racism," *San Jose Mercury News* (March 31, 1991), p. 4B. Weinstein, "White Says Jury Was the Worst Possible," p. A3.

832. Paul Lieberman, "Jurors Tell of Their Fear and Disbelief," *San Francisco Chronicle* (May 1, 1992), p. 1.

833. Associated Press, "Members: Race No Factor in Verdict," *Orange County (Calif.) Register* (May 1, 1992), p. A11.

834. Richard Serrano, "Cops in Beating Acquitted on 10 of 11 Counts," *San Francisco Chronicle* (April 30, 1992), p. A1.

835. Sheryl Stolberg, "Jurors Tell of Angry, Bitter Deliberations," *Los Angeles Times* (May 8, 1992), p. A3.

836. "The Toll," *Los Angeles Times* (May 7, 1992), p. A6.

837. "Violence Continues Across U.S., Troops Called Out in Vegas," *San Francisco Chronicle* (May 2, 1991), p. A9.

838. "Rescued Truck Driver Is Recovering," *San Francisco Chronicle* (May 4, 1992), p. A6.

839. " 'We're on Your Side,' Victim Told Attackers," *San Jose Mercury News* (May 4, 1992), p. 9A.

840. "Orinda Man's Fatal Decision: Trying to Protect His Shop," *San Jose Mercury News* (May 4, 1992), p. 9A.

841. Tom Mathews et al., "The Siege of L.A.," *Newsweek* (May 11, 1992), p. 34.

842. Yasmin Anwar, "Beating Victims Wrong Color, Wrong Place," *Oakland Tribune* (May 3, 1992), p. 1. Ann O'Neill, "Racial Tension Seen in Attacks," *San Jose Mercury News* (May 6, 1992), p. B1. "Violence Continues Across U.S., Troops Called Out in Vegas," p. A9.

843. Juan Williams, "Being Black, Being Fair," *Washington Post* (July 16, 1989), p. B1.

844. Quoted in Michael Levin, *Feminism and Freedom* (New Brunswick: Transaction Books, 1987), p. 159, no reference cited [emphasis added].

845. Stephen Farber, "Minority Villains Are Touchy Network Topic," *The New York Times* (March 1, 1986), p. 50.

846. James McPherson, "The Glory Story," *The New Republic* (January 8 and 15, 1990), p. 22ff. "Clouds of Glory," *The Economist* (January 20, 1990), p. 103.

847. "Actors Switched in 'Bonfire,' " *Washington Post* (April 20, 1990), p. C7.

848. Lorrin Anderson, "The Way it Was?" *Chronicles* (September 1991), p. 53.

849. Lorrin Anderson, "Race, Lies, and Videotape," *National Review* (January 22, 1990), p. 40.

850. Wayne King, "Fact vs. Fiction in Mississippi," *The New York Times* (December 4, 1988), p. H15.

851. Robert Cauthorn, "Cinema Apartheid," *Arizona Daily Star* (July 15, 1990), p. D1.

852. William Schneider, "An Insider's View of the Election," *The Atlantic* (July 1988), p. 36.

853. Linda Lichter and Robert Lichter, *Prime Time Crime* (Washington, D.C.: The Media Institute, 1983), p. 23.

854. Don Kowet, "Prime Time Watchers See Society Through a Distorted Screen," *Insight* (July 1, 1991), p. 36.

855. Clifford May, "Jackson Urges Voters' Support for Dinkins Bid," *The New York Times* (September 4, 1989), p. 30.

856. Henry Gates, "TV's Black World Turns—but Stays Unreal," *The New York Times* (November 12, 1989), p. H1.

857. "Miles Davis Can't Shake Boyhood Racial Abuse," *Jet* (March 25, 1985), p. 61.

858. Karen Bates, " 'They've Gotta Have Us,' " *The New York Times Magazine* (July 14, 1991), p. 15.

859. "In Dekline," *The Economist* (February 24, 1990), p. 26.

860. Theodore Pappas, "A Doctor in Spite of Himself," *Chronicles* (January 1991), p. 25ff. Theodore Pappas, "Cultural Revolutions," *Chronicles* (April 1991), p. 6.

861. Gerald Early, "Malcolm X: The Prince of Faces," *Los Angeles Times Book Review* (September 8, 1991), p. 3.

862. *Report of the National Advisory Commission on Civil Disorders,* pp. 223, 228.

863. Associated Press, "Black Caucus Flexes Its Muscles," *Washington Times* (September 15, 1989).

864. Associated Press, "100 Groups Form Coalition to Help Blacks," *The New York Times* (August 20, 1990).

865. Associated Press, "Winner Is . . . Miss Illinois," *San Jose Mercury News* (September 9, 1990), p. 4A.

866. National Research Council, *A Common Destiny,* p. 188ff.

867. James Barron, "Black-Hispanic Alumni Unit Approved by Baruch College," *The New York Times* (April 25, 1990), p. B5. "Minority Grads, College Settle Fight," *Newsday* (New York) (April 25, 1990), p. 29.

868. See page 239.

869. Lynch, *Invisible Victims,* p. 19.

870. See page 240.

871. Joseph Berger, "Campus Racial Strains Show 2 Perspectives on Inequality," *The New York Times* (May 22, 1989), p. 1.

872. "An Organization for White Rights Prompts Protests," *The New York Times* (April 8, 1990), p. 41.

873. Robin Wilson, "New White-Student Unions on Some Campuses are Sparking Outrage and Worry," *Chronicle of Higher Education* (April 18, 1990), p. A1.

874. Stephen Goode, "Efforts to Deal with Diversity Can Go Astray," *Insight* (September 10, 1990), p. 15.

875. Carol Ness, "Majority Turning into a Minority," *San Francisco Examiner* (April 4, 1991), p. A4.

876. Jack Foley, " 'European' Students Urged to Form Clubs," *San Jose Mercury News* (February 13, 1992), p. 3B.

877. Ralph Viguda, "A Troubled Time to Be a White Male," *Seattle Post-Intelligencer* (May 12, 1991), p. A9.

878. "Much Ado About the Wrong Thing," *The Economist* (November 9, 1991), p. 25.

879. "White Fire Fighter Gets Job, Pay in Bias Case," *Chicago Tribune* (June 28, 1991).

880. Associated Press, "Whites to Organize Against Phone Company Promotions," *The New York Times* (February 26, 1990), p. B9.

881. "What's in a Name?" *Houston Chronicle* (February 7, 1992).

882. Lynch, *Invisible Victims,* p. 86ff.

883. Frederick R. Lynch, "Race Unconsciousness and the White Male," *Society* (January/February 1992), p. 35.

884. Robert S. Boyd, "Panel Hopes to Remove Racial Tactics in '92 Elections," *San Jose Mercury News* (May 4, 1991), p. 5A. John Bare, "Panel Urges Stop to Campaign Racism," *San Jose Mercury News* (April 6, 1991), p. 4A.

885. Peter Applebome, "Louisiana Tally Is Seen as a Sign of Voter Unrest" (October 8, 1990), p. A1. Tyler Bridges, "Duke of Demagogy Rides a Populist Horse," *The Wall Street Journal* (October 9, 1990). "A Portrait of Louisiana's Voters," *The New York Times* (November 18, 1991), p. B6.

886. Wilson, "New White-Student Unions on Some Campuses," p. A1.

887. "Black and White: A Newsweek Poll," *Newsweek* (March 7, 1988), p. 23.

888. Ronald Smothers, "Mississippi's New Chief Fought Race-Based Plans," *The New York Times* (November 11, 1991).

889. Gregory Patterson, "Black Middle Class Debates Merits of Cities and Suburbs," *The Wall Street Journal* (August 6, 1991), p. B1.

890. Sam Fulwood, "The Rage of the Black Middle Class," *Los Angeles Times* (November 3, 1991), p. 22.

891. Asra Nomani, "Steeped in Tradition, 'Step Dance' United Blacks on Campus," *The Wall Street Journal* (July 10, 1989).

892. Bill Maxwell, "To Black Frats: Grow Up," *The New York Times* (May 11, 1991), p. L23.

893. Janice Simpson, "Tidings of Black Pride and Joy," *Time* (December 23, 1991), p. 81. Merle English, "Kwanzaa Holiday Expo: Commemorating Culture," *Newsday* (New York) (December 13, 1991), p. 23.

894. Yumi Wilson, " 'Unforgettable' Night of Honors for Natalie Cole," *San Francisco Examiner* (January 12, 1992), p. D7.

895. "George C. Fraser, a Voice for African-Americans," *Continental Profiles* (May 1991), p. 26.

896. David Streitfield, "Tapping a Market," *Book World* (August 19, 1990), p. 15.

897. *Publishers Weekly* (January 20, 1992), *passim.*

898. Fred Barnes, "The Minority Minority," *The New Republic* (September 30, 1991), p. 18.

899. John Taylor, "Don't Blame Me," *New York* (June 3, 1991), p. 34.

900. Lena Williams, "In a 90s Quest for Black Identity, Intense Doubts and Disagreement," *The New York Times* (November 30, 1991), p. 1.

901. Paul Gigot, "Potomac Watch," *The Wall Street Journal* (July 19, 1991).

902. Julius Lester, "What Price Unity?" *Voice* (September 17, 1991), p. 39.

903. Lena Williams, "In a 90s Quest for Black Identity," p. 1.

904. Reported in Richard Cohen, "Academic Bondage," *New York* (May 5, 1991), p. 11.

905. R. W. Apple, "Jackson Sees a 'Character Flaw' in Clinton's Remarks on Racism," *The New York Times* (June 19, 1992), p. A1. Reed Irvine & Joseph Goulden, "NBC's Gumbel: "Killing Whites' in Context," *Washington Inquirer* (June 19, 1992), p. 5.

906. Andy Logan, "Around City Hall," *The New Yorker* (March 2, 1992), p. 81.

907. Joyce Ladner, "Bring Back the Orphanages," *Washington Post* (October 29, 1989), p. B1.

908. See page 250.

909. "Court Sets Terms for Whites Adopting Black," *The New York Times* (August 10, 1990), p. A13.

910. Mona Charen, "The New Racism in Adoptions," *Newsday* (New York) (January 8, 1991).

911. Kathy Dobie, "Nobody's Child," *Village Voice* (August 8, 1989), p. 18ff.

912. Mona Charen, "The New Racism in Adoptions," *Newsday* (New York) (January 8, 1991).

913. See page 251.

914. Kathleen Teltsch, "Blacks' Charities Struggle to Meet Cosby Challenge," *The New York Times* (January 15, 1989), p. A1.

915. Linda Greenhouse, "Supreme Court to Review Record on Bias in Mississippi Colleges," *The New York Times* (April 16, 1991), p. A19.

916. David Nicholson, "Why Howard University Exploded Last Week," *Washington Post* (March 12, 1989), p. D1. Drummond Ayres, "House Panel Warns Howard U. About Spending," *The New York Times* (September 3, 1989), p. 24.

917. Anthony DePalma, "Finding Some Shortcomings, Panel Calls for Major Changes at Howard," *The New York Times* (November 28, 1990), p. B9.

918. See, e.g., Anthony DePalma, "Separate Ethnic Worlds Grow on Campus," *The New York Times* (May 18, 1991), p. 1.

919. Stephen Goode, "On the Outs Over Who Gets in," *Insight* (October 9, 1989), p. 13.

920. Richard Bernstein, "Black and White on Campus: Learning Tolerance, Not Love, and Separately," *The New York Times* (May 26, 1988).

921. "Blacks Form Graduation Panel of Their Own," *The New York Times* (February 17, 1991).

922. Carol Jouzaitis, "Some Students Steering Clear of School Melting Pot," *Chicago Tribune* (May 12, 1991).

923. Dinesh D'Souza, "The Visigoths in Tweed," *Forbes* (April 1, 1991), p. 84.

924. Shelby Steele, "The Recoloring of Campus Life," *Harper's* (February 1989), p. 55.

925. Allan Bloom, *The Closing of the American Mind* (New York: Simon & Schuster, 1987), p. 96.

926. Bloom, *The Closing of the American Mind*, p. 96ff.

927. Gary Seay, " 'By Popular Demand' " (letter), *The New York Times* (June 23, 1991).

928. Thomas Sowell, "Campuses Grant Free Speech Only to Ideologically Correct," *San Jose Mercury News* (July 24, 1989), Sec. B.

929. William A. Henry, "Upside Down in the Groves of Academe," *Time* (October 22, 1991), p. 67.

930. David Savage, "Forbidden Words on Campus," *Los Angeles Times* (February 12, 1991).

931. "The Mystery of Black Anti-Semitism," *New York Post* (June 3, 1991), p. 24.

932. "Anti-Semites at Columbia," *New York Post* (January 26, 1991), p. 16.

933. "Take Care," *The Economist* (February 10, 1990), p. 20.

934. Steve France, "Hate Goes to College," *ABA Journal* (July 1990), p. 44.

935. Jay Matthews, "IQ-Test Ban Debate Takes on New 'Twist,' " *San Jose Mercury News* (July 12, 1987), p. C1.

936. "Inventive Incentive?" *Harper's Magazine* (July 1990), p. 26.

937. Associated Press, "Bush's Backing of All-Male Schools Is Criticized," *The New York Times* (September 11, 1991). Todd Purdum, "Dinkins Backs School Geared to Minorities," *The New York Times* (March 9, 1991), p. 25. Dirk Johnson, "Milwaukee Creating 2 Schools Just for Black Boys," *The New York Times* (September 30, 1990), p. 1. Rob Polner, "Blacks-Only School in Works," *New York Post* (November 6, 1990), p. 22.

938. Andrea Peyser, "New 'Black Male' HS Would Admit Other Races and Females," *New York Post* (March 19, 1991). Amy Harmon, "300 Rally in Support of All-Male Schools," *Los Angeles Times* (August 22, 1991).

939. Isabel Wilkerson, "To Save Its Men, Detroit Plans Boys-Only Schools," *The New York Times* (August 14, 1991), p. A1.

940. Harmon, "300 Rally."

941. Hilary Stout, "ACLU, NAACP, and NOW all Give Poor Marks to Plans to Help Inner-City Black Male Students," *The Wall Street Journal* (September 10, 1991), p. A22.

942. Suzanne Daley, "Inspirational Black History Draws Academic Fire," *The New York Times* (October 10, 1990), p. 1.

943. Wilkerson, "To Save Its Men," p. A1.

944. Joseph Berger, "Proposal Outlines Features of Separatist-School Plan," *The New York Times* (January 22, 1991), p. B3.

945. Andrew Sullivan, "Racism 101," *The New Republic* (November 26, 1990), p. 18ff.

946. John Leo, "A Fringe History of the World," *U.S. News & World Report* (November 12, 1990), p. 25.

947. "A is for Ashanti, B is for Black," *Newsweek* (September 23, 1991).

948. Michael Ottey, "Black Schools Promote Afrocentric Education," *Asbury Park Press* (New Jersey) (November 4, 1990), p. A1.

949. Sara Rimer, "Do Black and White Children Learn the Same Way?" *The New York Times* (June 24, 1988), p. B1.

950. Joseph Berger, "What Do They Mean by 'Black Learning Style'?" *The New York Times* (July 6, 1988).

951. "Special Education for Blacks Requested," *Insight* (March 12, 1990), p. 60.

952. Marcia Farr Whiteman, ed., *Reactions to Ann Arbor: Vernacular Black English and Education* (Arlington, Va.: Center for Applied Linguistics, 1980), p. 10.

953. Eleanor Wilson Orr, *Twice as Less* (New York: W. W. Norton & Company, 1987), p. 185ff.

954. Lisa Rossetti, " 'Black English' Teacher Hired," *California Review of Berkeley* (November 1989).

955. "N.Y. Addiction Theory," *Washington Post* (March 18, 1989), p. A4.

956. "SUNY-Funded 'Study' Paints Jews as Racist," *New York Post* (March 11, 1991), p. 21.

957. "Emissary Declares Ramses' Race Is a Dead Issue: He's Egyptian," *Chicago Tribune* (March 19, 1989), p. 16.

958. National Research Council, *A Common Destiny*, p. 199.

959. "Black Boycott Targets Revlon," *San Jose Mercury News* (December 21, 1986), p. 2C.

960. Alix Freedman, "Heilman, Under Pressure, Scuttles PowerMaster Malt," *The Wall Street Journal* (July 5, 1991), p. B1.

961. Gretchen Morgenson, " 'Where Can I Buy Some?,' " *Forbes* (June 24, 1991), p. 82.

962. "When Games Turn Nasty," *Newsweek* (August 27, 1990), p. 44. Mike Royko, "PUSH Didn't Exactly Shove," *Omaha World-Herald* (October 4, 1990).

963. Laurie Grossman, "After Demographic Shift, Atlanta Mall Restyles Itself as Black Shopping Center," *The Wall Street Journal* (February 26, 1992), p. B1.

964. *U.S. News & World Report* (November 16, 1987), p. 41.

965. Dirk Johnson, "Jackson's Refusal to Back Daley Angers Some in Party," *The New York Times* (March 6, 1989), p. A12.

966. David Greising, "That's His Honor, not Hizzoner," *Business Week* (May 20, 1991), p. 41.

967. Audrey Edwards and Craig Polite, *Children of the Dream* (New York: Doubleday, 1992), p. 14.

968. Fred Barnes, "Skin Deep," *The New Republic* (April 10, 1989), p. 10ff.

969. Susan Howard, "Not the Retiring Type," Part II *Newsday* (New York) (March 12, 1990), p. 8.

970. Earl Caldwell, "In City, It Was Race Within a Race," New York *Daily News* (September 13, 1989), p. 43.

971. D. D. Guttenplan, "Whites Join Blacks for Dinkins," *New York Newsday* (September 13, 1989), p. 3. "Sources of Support," *Newsday* (New York) (November 8, 1989), p. 5.

972. John F. Davis, "Playing Pigmentation Politics," *Village Voice* (September 12, 1989), p. 32.

973. Ken Auletta, "Mayoral Flight's Ready for Takeoff, and I'm Getting on with Dinkins," *New York Daily News* (October 29, 1989), p. 37.

974. Mark Mooney, "Ex-Dinkins Organizer Boasts He's 'Antiwhite,' " *New York Post* (October 21, 1989), p. 4.

975. Martin Mayer, "Sonny Carson Isn't the News," *Newsday* (New York) (June 14, 1990), p. 68.

976. Sam Roberts, "First Black Mayor," *The New York Times* (November 8, 1989), p. A1.

977. Michael Oreskes, "Black Virginian Close to a Historic Triumph," *The New York Times* (November 8, 1989), p. A1.

978. David Shribman and James Perry, "Black Moderates Win at Polls by Targeting Once-Elusive Whites," *The Wall Street Journal* (November 9, 1989), p. A1.

979. Marilyn Millow and Myron Waldman, "White Vote Backed Helms," *Newsday* (New York) (November 8, 1990). Michael Kinsley, "What's Really Fair," *Time* (November 19, 1990), p. 124.

980. Donald Baer, "The Race in Black and White," *U.S. News & World Report* (July 23, 1990), p. 29.

981. Larry Tye, "In South, Ballot Box Inequality Lingers On," *Boston Globe* (July 23, 1990), p. 1.
982. Richard Morin and Dan Balz, "Shifting Racial Climate," *Washington Post* (October 25, 1989), p. A1.
983. Juan Williams, "Alex Williams and the Crossover Strategy," *Washington Post Magazine* (February 12, 1989), p. 21.
984. Barone and Gregg, "The Inward Turn of Black Americans," *U.S. News & World Report* (May 8, 1989), p. 33.
985. Tye, "In South, Ballot Box Inequality Lingers On," p. 1.
986. Hacker, *Two Nations,* p. 208.
987. Robin Toner, "Real-Life Politics in Deep South," *The New York Times* (March 30, 1989), p. A10.
988. William Robbins, "Old Outpost of Slavery Joins Era of Black Mayor," *The New York Times* (March 28, 1991), p. A20.
989. See page 267.
990. Dorothy Gaiter, "Against the Grain," *The Wall Street Journal* (July 3, 1991), p. 1.
991. Paul Ruffins, "Interracial Coalitions," *Atlantic Monthly* (June 1990), p. 34.
992. Juan Williams, "Alex Williams and the Crossover Strategy," p. 20.
993. See, e.g., Michael Winerip, "A Crusader Sees Only One Issue in Yonkers: Race," *The New York Times* (August 30, 1988), p. B1.
994. Walter E. Williams, *The State Against Blacks* (New York: McGraw-Hill, 1982), p. 12; refers to *The New York Times* (July 24, 1970), p. 27.
995. Williams, *The State Against Blacks,* p. 13.
996. Herbert London, *Chronicles* (May 1987), p. 8.
997. "Cardinal Suspends Black Priest After Breakaway Church Service," *San Jose Mercury News* (July 5, 1989), p. 7A.
998. *San Jose Mercury News* (July 17, 1989).
999. Elizabeth Kastor, "Artist Expected Portrait to Draw Angry Reaction," *Washington Post* (December 1, 1989), p. B1. Alexis Moore, "Provocative Painting of Jackson Attacked," *San Jose Mercury News* (December 1, 1989), p. 10A.
1000. Jacob Neusner, "People Who Put Color Ahead of Art," *The New York Times* (August 31, 1988).
1001. Charles Krauthammer, "American Drifting Toward 'Tribalism,'" *New York Daily News* (August 5, 1990), p. 37.
1002. Esther Iverem, "Racial Remarks Force Recall of State Manual," *The New York Times* (May 4, 1987), p. B3. "Manual: All Whites Racist," *Omaha World-Herald* (May 4, 1987).
1003. Ze'ev Chafets, "The Tragedy of Detroit," *The New York Times Magazine* (July 29, 1990), p. 50.
1004. Danyel Smith, "Harry Allen: Hip Hop's Intellectual Assassin," *SF Weekly* (February 13, 1991), p. 1.
1005. Thomas W. Hazlett, "Racism, Pro and Con," *Reason* (August–September 1990), p. 58.
1006. Maria Newman, "Avoiding Confrontations in Wake of Racial Attack," *The New York Times* (January 13, 1992), p. B3. Peter Moses, "Cops Guard Schools Amid Race-Attack Jitters," *New York Post* (January 10, 1992). Mitch Gelman, "State Urges Bias Crime Crackdown," *Newsday* (New York) (January 14, 1992).
1007. Scott McConnell, "When the Crime Is White on Black . . . ," *New York Post* (January 11, 1992).
1008. Michele Parente, "Bias Rape in Brooklyn," *Newsday* (New York) (January 15, 1992), p. 3. Chapin Wright, "2 More Incidents in Brooklyn," *Newsday* (New York) (January 20, 1992), p. 5. Curtis Rist, "Hate Strikes Back," *Newsday* (New York) (January 9, 1992), p. 3.

1009. Don Broderick, "Cops: 'Bias Attack Victim' Admits Hoax," *New York Post* (January 18, 1992), p. 2.

1010. Maria Newman, "Police Puzzled by Lack of Leads in Bias Attacks on Black Youths," *The New York Times* (February 6, 1992). Peter Moses, "2 Sides Clash Over Bias Puzzle," *New York Post* (February 7, 1992), p. 10. "The Bronx Bias Investigation," *New York Post* (February 7, 1992), p. 22.

1011. "City Hall's Curious Silence," *New York Post* (February 26, 1992). Scott McConnell, "Double Standard," *New York Post* (February 29, 1992).

1012. Charles Silberman, *Criminal Violence, Criminal Justice* (New York: Random House, 1978), p. 118.

1013. Silberman, *Criminal Violence, Criminal Justice*, p. 153.

1014. Eldridge Cleaver, *Soul on Ice* (New York: McGraw-Hill, 1968), p. 14.

1015. Cleaver, *Soul on Ice*, p. 14ff.

1016. Silberman, *Criminal Violence, Criminal Justice*, p. 389.

1017. Silberman, *Criminal Violence, Criminal Justice*, p. 389.

1018. Leo Carroll, "Race, Ethnicity, and the Social Order of the Prison" in *The Pains of Imprisonment*, ed. Johnson and Toch, (Beverly Hills: Sage Publications, 1982), pp. 192ff.

1019. William Wilbanks, *The Myth of a Racist Criminal Justice System* (Monterey, Calif.: Brooks/Cole Publishing Company, 1987), p. 135ff.

1020. Daniel Lockwood, "Reducing Prison Sexual Violence" in *The Pains of Imprisonment*, ed. Johnson and Toch, (Beverly Hills, Calif.: Sage Publications, 1982), p. 261.

1021. Carroll, "Race, Ethnicity, and the Social Order of the Prison," p. 193.

1022. "Blacks Less Free Under Blacks: Tutu," *Washington Times* (March 27, 1990).

1023. "Africa's Heart of Darkness," *The Economist* (August 27, 1988), p. 29. "After the Killing," *The Economist* (September 3, 1988), p. 41. Jane Perlez, "The Bloody Hills of Burundi," *The New York Times Magazine* (November 6, 1988), p. 90ff.

1024. Patrick Buchanan, "Losing Touch with Reality," *New York Post* (October 31, 1990), p. 27.

1025. Leo Carroll, "Race, Ethnicity, and the Social Order of the Prison," p. 192.

1026. Thomas Sowell, *Civil Rights: Rhetoric or Reality?* (New York: William Morrow & Company, 1984), p. 108.

1027. Press conference at a meeting of blacks in government, broadcast on C-SPAN (August 16, 1989).

1028. T. E. Lawrence, *Seven Pillars of Wisdom* (New York: Dell, 1926), p. 28.

1029. Rita Kramer, "Bullhorn, Bat, and Burgeoning Broadsides," *The Wall Street Journal* (March 29, 1989), p. A14.

1030. William Raspberry, "The Civil Rights Movement Is Over," *Washington Post* (February 25, 1987), p. A23.

1031. Walter Williams, "Race, Scholarship, and Affirmative Action," *National Review* (May 5, 1989), p. 38.

1032. Shelby Steele, "I'm Black, You're White, Who's Innocent?" *Harper's* (June 1988), p. 51.

1033. Steele, "I'm Black, You're White," p. 51.

1034. Glen Loury, "Black Dignity and the Common Good," *First Things* (June–July, 1990), p. 19.

1035. Roy Innis, "Dr. King's Legacy Betrayed," *New York Post* (January 8, 1992).

1036. Glenn Loury, "Thomas's Black Foes Fear His Leadership," *Newsday* (New York) (August 1, 1991), p. 99. J. Anthony Lukas, "Why I Can't 'Bork' Clarence Thomas," *The Wall Street Journal* (September 5, 1991), p. A15. Paul Gigot, "The Real Reason the Black Caucus Opposes Thomas," *The Wall Street Journal* (July 9, 1991).

1037. Tony Brown, "Becoming a Republican," *The Wall Street Journal* (August 5, 1991).

1038. Carolyn Lochhead, "In Poverty's Hard Clutch, Little Chance for Escape," *Insight* (April 3, 1989), p. 8.

1039. See page 288.

1040. Morton Kondracke, "The Two Black Americas," *The New Republic* (February 6, 1989), p. 17.

1041. Bloom and Bennett, "Future Shock," *The New Republic* (June 19, 1989), p. 18.

1042. William Ryan, *Blaming the Victim* (New York: Vintage Books, 1971), p. 247ff.

1043. See page 290.

1044. See page 290.

1045. See page 291.

1046. "What's Really Squeezing the Middle Class?" *The Wall Street Journal* (July 26, 1989), p. A12.

1047. Susan Chira, "Educators Ask if All-Girl Schools . . . ," *The New York Times* (October 23, 1991), p. B5.

1048. LyNell Hancock, "Ujamaa Means Controversy," *Village Voice* (November 6, 1990), p. 14.

1049. Rene Sanchez, "D.C. Dropouts Quit Earlier, Study Finds," *Washington Post* (January 12, 1989), p. A1.

1050. Kathleen Sylvester, "Dropouts: Education's Early Warning System," *San Francisco Chronicle* (April 12, 1992), p. B7.

1051. Mike Mallowe, "Coming Apart," *Philadelphia Magazine* (September 1989), p. 160.

1052. John Hood, "Money Isn't Everything," *The Wall Street Journal* (February 9, 1990), p. A10. Edwin West, "Restoring Family Autonomy in Education," *Chronicles* (October 1990), p. 17.

1053. Don Feder, "Schools Have Flunked Out," *Orange County* (Calif.) *Register* (September 9, 1991), p. B9.

1054. "Pick Your Number," *The Economist* (February 17, 1990), p. 27.

1055. See page 293.

1056. Bolick, *Changing Course*, p. 106. Associated Press, "School Costs Up but Not Grades, Report Laments," *Omaha World-Herald* (August 24, 1989), p. 16. "Willingly to School," *The Economist* (October 7, 1989), p. 25.

1057. Gary Putka, "Education Reformers Have New Respect for Catholic Schools," *The Wall Street Journal* (March 28, 1991), p. 1.

1058. James S. Coleman et al., *Equality of Educational Opportunity* (1966), p. 325. Cited in Allen J. Matusow, *The Unraveling of America* (New York: Harper & Row, 1984), p. 224ff.

1059. Hood, "Education: Money Isn't Everything," p. A10.

1060. National Research Council, *A Common Destiny,* p. 372.

1061. Seth Mydans, "Academic Success Seen as Selling Out, Study on Blacks Says," *The New York Times* (April 25, 1990).

1062. Linda Stewart, "Some Black Students Bear a Burden by Being Smart," *Detroit Free Press* (September 24, 1991), p. 1A.

1063. Christopher Jencks, "Deadly Neighborhoods," *The New Republic* (June 13, 1988), p. 28.

1064. Cheryl Laird, "Teenage Moms," *Houston Chronicle* (January 8, 1992), p. 1D.

1065. "The American Dream, the American Nightmare," *The Economist* (October 7, 1989), p. 19.

1066. Paul Richter, "Beneath the Bitterness Over Race," *Los Angeles Times* (August 13, 1991), p. A1.

1067. Mortimer Zuckerman, "Mentioning the Unmentionable," *U.S. News & World Report* (June 4, 1990), p. 82.

1068. Robert Woodson, "We Need to Examine the Side Effects of the Civil Rights Movement," *Issues & Views* (Fall 1991), p. 4.

1069. M. A. Farber, "A Growing Foster-Care Program Is Fraught with Ills," *The New York Times* (November 22, 1990), p. B1.

1070. National Research Council, *A Common Destiny,* pp. 412, 544.

1071. Charlotte Allen, "Teenage Birth's New Conceptions," *Insight* (April 30, 1990), pp. 9, 11.

1072. Felicity Barringer, "After Long Decline, Teen Births Are Up," *The New York Times* (August 17, 1990), p. A14.

1073. "Families," *The Economist* (May 26, 1990), p. 113.

1074. Leonard Silk, "Now, to Figure Why the Poor Get Poorer," *The New York Times* (December 19, 1988), p. E1.

1075. National Research Council, *A Common Destiny,* p. 523.

1076. Bloom and Bennett, "Future Shock," p. 18.

1077. Sheryl McCarthy, "Condom Sense Spoken by Students Themselves," *Newsday* (New York) (December 10, 1990), p. 6.

1078. "Rising Childhood Poverty Tied to Living Patterns," *The Wall Street Journal* (July 26, 1991), p. B1.

1079. Charlotte Low Allen, "Teenage Birth's New Conceptions," *Insight* (April 30, 1990), p. 11.

1080. Nicholas Eberstadt, "America's Infant Mortality Problem: Parents," *The Wall Street Journal* (January 20, 1992).

1081. Thomas Sowell, "Parental Attitudes, Not Federal Money, Make the Difference in Child Care," *New York Post* (January 17, 1992).

1082. Daniel Goleman, "Sad Legacy of Abuse: The Search for Remedies," *The New York Times* (January 14, 1989), p. B7.

1083. Bryce Christensen, *Chronicles* (May 1989), p. 9.

1084. Karl Zinsmeister, "Growing Up Scared," *The Atlantic* (June 1990), p. 52.

1085. Elaine Kamarck, "Fatherless Families: A Violent Link," *Los Angeles Times* (May 7, 1992), p. B7.

1086. Isabel Wilkerson, "Marriage Lets 8 Couples Reclaim Their Lives," *The New York Times* (November 14, 1988), p. A1.

1087. Bill McAllister, "To Be Young, Male, and Black," *Washington Post* (December 28, 1989), p. A1.

1088. Ronald Smothers, "Loss of Mail Jolts Tenants into Action," *The New York Times* (January 3, 1989), p. A12.

1089. Jane Gross, "Collapse of Inner-City Families Creates America's New Orphans," *The New York Times* (March 29, 1992), p. 1A.

1090. Jane Gross, "Grandmothers Bear a Burden Sired by Drugs," *The New York Times* (April 9, 1989), p. A1.

1091. Gross, "Grandmothers Bear a Burden," p. A1.

1092. Richard Stengel, "The Underclass: Breaking the Cycle," *Time* (October 10, 1988), p. 41.

1093. David Savage, "1 of 4 Young Black Men Are in Jail or on Parole, Study Says," *San Francisco Chronicle* (February 27, 1990), p. A1.

1094. Joel Brenner, "Area Businesses Tap New Source to Solve Severe Labor Shortage," *Washington Post* (September 9, 1989), p. A1. David Whitman and Dorian Friedman, "The Surprising News About the Underclass," *U.S. News & World Report* (December 25, 1989), p. 76. "When Companies Steer Schools," *The Economist* (January 13, 1990), p. 15.

1095. *The Economist* (January 18, 1992), p. 68.

1096. Elizabeth Wright, "Click! I Get It!" *Issues & Views* (Fall 1989), p. 10.

1097. Christopher Jencks, "Deadly Neighborhoods," *The New Republic* (June 13, 1988), p. 26.

1098. "What to Do?," *The Economist* (October 19, 1991), p. 29.

1099. A. E. Hippler, *Hunter's Point: A Black Ghetto* (New York: Basic Books, 1974), cited in J. Wilson and R. Herrnstein, *Crime and Human Nature* (New York: Simon & Schuster, 1985), pp. 304, 335.

1100. Ehrenberg and Marcus, "Minimum Wages and Teenagers' Enrollment and Employment Outcomes," *Journal of Human Resources* (Winter 1982), pp. 39–58, cited in Charles Murray, *Losing Ground* (New York: Basic Books, 1984), p. 290.

1101. Charles Murray, "Underclass," *Sunday Times Magazine* (London) (November 26, 1989), p. 26.
1102. "What's Really Squeezing the Middle Class?" *The Wall Street Journal* (July 26, 1989), p. A12.
1103. Charles Murray, "Here's the Bad News on the Underclass," *The Wall Street Journal* (March 8, 1990).
1104. Andrew Hacker, *Two Nations*, p. 90ff.
1105. Lawrence M. Mead, *Beyond Entitlement* (New York: The Free Press, 1986), p. 204.
1106. See page 302.
1107. Charles Murray, *Losing Ground* (New York: Basic Books, 1984), p. 165.
1108. William Tucker, *Vigilante: The Backlash Against Crime in America* (Briarcliff Manor, N.Y.: Stein & Day, 1985), p. 315.
1109. Lawrence Mead, *Beyond Entitlement* (New York: The Free Press, 1986), p. 29.
1110. Jason DeParle, "Why Marginal Changes Don't Rescue the Welfare System," *The New York Times* (March 1, 1992), p. 3.
1111. Dorothy Gaiter, "Programs to Get Jobs for Poor Lift Earnings but Don't End Much Poverty," *The Wall Street Journal* (July 24, 1991), p. A12.
1112. Jason DeParle, "Why Marginal Changes Don't Rescue the Welfare System," *The New York Times* (March 1, 1992), p. 3.
1113. Jason DeParle, "To Moynihan, Welfare Dependency Signals New Ill," *The New York Times* (December 9, 1991).
1114. Gaiter, "Programs to Get Jobs for Poor," p. A12.
1115. Richard Paddoc, "Workfare Plan Falls Short as Relief Rolls Lengthen," *Los Angeles Times* (March 5, 1991), p. A3.
1116. Debra Saunders, "Welfare Reform, California Style," *The Wall Street Journal* (February 25, 1992).
1117. Pete Hamill, "City's Welfare Mess Unique in History," *New York Post* (September 19, 1991), p. 5.
1118. Spencer Rich, "The Underclass: Beyond Just Poor," *Washington Post* (June 26, 1989), p. A9.
1119. National Research Council, *A Common Destiny*, p. 290ff.
1120. Karl Zinsmeister, "Growing Up Scared," *The Atlantic* (June 1990), p. 52.
1121. National Research Council, *A Common Destiny*, p. 214.
1122. "Black and White: A Newsweek Poll," *Newsweek* (March 7, 1988), p. 23.
1123. "Pregnant Teens Respond to Adoption Counseling," *The Wall Street Journal* (May 17, 1991), p. B1.
1124. "Teen Pregnancies Called Sensible," *Omaha World-Herald* (February 22, 1990).
1125. See page 305.
1126. Murray, *Losing Ground*, p. 223.
1127. Carolyn Lochhead, "The Radical Era's Legacy: A Class Snared in Penury," *Insight* (April 3, 1989), p. 16.
1128. Lois Romano, "The Long, Long Journey of James Meredith," *Washington Post* (November 3, 1989), p. C1.
1129. Martin Tolchin, "Reducing Welfare Rolls and Adding Self-Esteem in Oklahoma," *The New York Times* (November 19, 1988), p. A6.
1130. Joanne Jacobs, "How GAIN/JOBS Works—or Doesn't," *San Jose Mercury News* (December 7, 1989), p. 9B.
1131. Mead, *Beyond Entitlement*, p. 136. See also National Research Council, *A Common Destiny*, p. 291.
1132. Richard Paddock, "Workfare Plan Falls Short as Relief Rolls Lengthen," *Los Angeles Times* (March 5, 1991), p. A3.
1133. "Wisconsin Families Lose Welfare Money When Teens Cut School," *Washington Post* (December 12, 1989), p. 5A.
1134. "On Welfare and Truants," *The New York Times* (March 21, 1990), p. B5.

1135. Murray, *Losing Ground,* p. 235.

1136. "Crack," *The New York Times* (May 28, 1989), p. E14.

1137. Gina Kolata, "Experts Finding New Hope on Treating Crack Addicts," *The New York Times* (August 24, 1989), p. A1.

1138. Wilson and DiIulio, "Crackdown," *The New Republic* (July 10, 1989), p. 21.

1139. "The Kickback from Cocaine," *The Economist* (July 21, 1990), p. 40.

1140. Gina Kolata, "In Cities, Poor Families Are Dying of Crack," *The New York Times* (August 11, 1989), p. A1.

1141. James Tobin, "A Lust for Power Lures Girls to Gangs," *Detroit News* (June 16, 1991), p. 1C.

1142. Felicia Lee, "For Gold Earrings and Protection, More Girls Take Road to Violence," *The New York Times* (November 25, 1991), p. A1.

1143. Jan Hoffman, "Locking Up Mommy," *New York Daily News Magazine* (May 13, 1990), p. 11.

1144. Eloise Salholz et al., "Women in Jail: Unequal Justice," *Newsweek* (June 4, 1990), p. 38.

1145. Michael Massing, "Why Bennett Is Losing," *The New York Times Magazine* (September 23, 1990), p. 43.

1146. Bill Gordon, "Crack's Incredible Cost to S.F.," *San Francisco Chronicle* (February 21, 1989), p. A12.

1147. Gordon, "Crack's Incredible Cost to S.F.," p. A12.

1148. Charles Krauthammer, "Children of Cocaine," *The Washington Post* (July 30, 1989), p. C7.

1149. Clara Hemphill, "A Tormented Cry," *Newsday* (New York) (September 28, 1990), p. 6.

1150. Suzanne Daley, "Born on Crack and Coping with Kindergarten," *The New York Times* (February 7, 1991), p. 1.

1151. Timothy Egan, "Chief Judge Says Crack May Overwhelm Courts," *The New York Times* (December 3, 1990), p. B3.

1152. Susan Chira, "Crack Babies Turn 5, and Schools Brace," *The New York Times* (May 25, 1990), p. A1.

1153. Dennis Walcott, "His Foster Kids Play Blindman's Buff," *Newsday* (New York) (November 8, 1989), p. 73.

1154. "Caring for the Children," *Newsday* (New York) (October 3, 1990), p. 26.

1155. "Stats Show Decline in Crack Use," *New York Post* (October 11, 1990), p. 25.

1156. Cathy Trost, "Babies of Crack Users Crowd Hospitals, Break Everybody's Heart," *The Wall Street Journal* (July 18, 1989), p. 1. "Crack," *The New York Times* (May 28, 1989), p. E14. Gordon, "Crack's Incredible Cost to S.F.," p. A12. George E. Curry, "Crack Abuse Turning Women to Prostitution," *Chicago Tribune* (April 28, 1989), p. 6. "Who Pays the Bills?" *The Economist* (March 18, 1989), p. 27. "Crack Babies," *The Economist* (April 1, 1989), p. 29.

1157. "The AIDS Plague Spreads," *The Economist* (July 15, 1989), p. 23.

1158. Michael Isikoff, "Crack Holds Many Inner-City Women in Its Grip," *Washington Post* (August 20, 1989), p. A18.

1159. Alexander Reid, "Rate of Illness from Sex Rises in Teenagers," *Boston Globe* (April 11, 1990), p. 1.

1160. "Blacks' Syphilis Rate Up Sharply," *The New York Times* (May 17, 1991), p. A19.

1161. "Blacks' Syphilis Rate Up Sharply," p. A19.

1162. Jim Merlini, "Panel: Sex Disease Fight Takes Funds," *Ledger Enquirer* (Columbus, Ga.) (July 19, 1990), p. D2.

1163. William Blair, "New York Sees a Surge in Syphilis and Will Start Testing All Babies," *The New York Times* (December 5, 1989), p. B2.

1164. Jack Kresnak, "Syphilis Reaches Epidemic Level," *Detroit Free Press* (July 15, 1991), p. A1.

1165. "The AIDS Plague Spreads," *The Economist* (July 15, 1989), p. 23. George E. Curry, "Crack Abuse Turning Women to Prostitution," *Chicago Tribune* (April 28, 1989), p. 6. John Bunzel, "AIDS Risks in Black and White," *The Wall Street Journal* (December 17, 1991).

1166. George Esper, "AIDS Shortening Women's Lives," *Los Angeles Times* (February 10, 1991), p. A20.

1167. "Health Picture Rosy for Whites, Grim for Blacks," *Chicago Tribune* (March 23, 1990). "AIDS Now No. 1 Killer of Young Black Women in New York," *New York Post* (July 11, 1990), p. 19.

1168. Frank Reeves, "State Newborns to Get AIDS Test," *Post-Gazette* (Pittsburgh) (November 23, 1990), p. 1.

1169. United Press International, "AIDS Cases in U.S. Now Top 200,000," *New York Post* (January 17, 1992).

1170. Clarence Page, "Deathly Silence," *The New Republic* (December 1991), p. 15.

1171. "Let the Tumbrils Roll," *The Economist* (April 1, 1989), p. 20.

1172. Mitch Gelman, "Transit Cops' Bosses Turned Thefts into 'Lost Property,'" *Newsday* (New York) (November 20, 1989), p. 5.

1173. "The American Dream, the American Nightmare," *The Economist* (October 7, 1989), p. 19.

1174. "Washington Leads in Homicides," *Orange County (Calif.) Register* (January 2, 1992), p. A4.

1175. Elizabeth Rosenthal, "U.S. Is by Far the Homicide Capital of the Industrialized Nations," *The New York Times* (June 27, 1990), p. A10.

1176. Seth Mydans, "Homicide Rate Up for Young Blacks," *The New York Times* (December 7, 1990), p. 1.

1177. Scott Martelle, "State Leads Nation in Black Homicide Rate," *Detroit News* (June 27, 1990), p. 1A.

1178. Associated Press, "Guns Take Ever-Higher Toll Among Young Blacks," *The New York Times* (March 17, 1991), p. 31.

1179. Hilary Stout, "Life Expectancy of U.S. Blacks Declined in 1988," *The Wall Street Journal* (April 9, 1991), p. B1. "AIDS, Homicides Increase Gap in Black, White Life Expectancy," *Detroit News* (January 8, 1992), p. 3A.

1180. "Violent Crimes Increase by 5.5% for 1988, Establishing a Record," *The New York Times* (August 13, 1989), p. 22.

1181. "Uncivil Wars," *The Economist* (October 7, 1989), p. 38.

1182. Lynne Duke, "Spending for Cocaine Here May Rival That for Food," *Washington Post* (July 19, 1989), p. A14.

1183. "Crack," *The New York Times* (May 28, 1989), p. E14.

1184. Drummond Ayers, "Rewards Offered in Campaign to Stem Murders in the Capital," *The New York Times* (August 12, 1989), p. 8.

1185. Paul Barrett, "Killing of 15-Year-Old Is Part of Escalation of Murder by Juveniles," *The Wall Street Journal* (March 25, 1991), p. 1.

1186. Warren T. Brookes, "Christmas, Fatherhood, and America's Murder Plague," *New York City Tribune* (December 28, 1990), p. 9.

1187. "Washington Leads in Homicides," *Orange County (Calif.) Register* (January 2, 1992), p. A4.

1188. Bill Steigerwald, "Where a Rising Murder Rate Is No Big Thing," *Los Angeles Times* (January 14, 1992).

1189. "The War at Home: How to Battle Crime," *Newsweek* (March 25, 1991), p. 35.

1190. Jason DeParle, "42% of Young Black Males Go Through Capital's Courts," *The New York Times* (April 18, 1992), p. A1.

1191. Bob Herbert, "The Fear of Violence Is Coring the Big Apple," *New York Daily News* (July 1, 1990).

1192. Don Terry, "Project Tenants See Island of Safety Washing Away," *The New York Times* (February 4, 1991), p. A1.

1193. Russell Ben-Ali, "Murders Down in '91," *Newsday* (New York) (January 3, 1992).

1194. Scott Bowles and David Grant, "Detroit Homicides Surge in 1991," *Detroit News* (January 1, 1992), p. 1A.

1195. "Getting Worse More Slowly," *The Economist* (January 4, 1992), p. 21.

1196. Associated Press, "Chicago's New 'Bloodbath' Makes '20s Look Tame," *Detroit News* (September 1, 1991), p. 9A.

1197. "Washington Leads in Homicides," p. A4.

1198. Pat Prince, "Crime-Safe Urban Design Is Proposed for St. Paul," *Star Tribune* (Minneapolis) (December 21, 1991), p. 5B.

1199. "Getting Worse More Slowly," *The Economist* (January 4, 1992), p. 21.

1200. John Tierny, "In New York, It's Not Easy Being Green," *San Jose Mercury News* (May 25, 1990), p. 2A.

1201. Blanka Eckstein, "Through a Glass Darkly," *Newsday* (New York) (October 29, 1990), p. 46.

1202. Calvin Sims, "15 More Areas in Subways to Be Closed," *The New York Times* (March 29, 1991), p. B1.

1203. "Down the Toilet," *The Wall Street Journal* (July 22, 1991), p. A8.

1204. See page 316.

1205. Sam Roberts, "Even the Nuns Have to Carry Mugger Money," *The New York Times* (December 21, 1989), p. B1.

1206. Stephanie Strom, "Ministers in Poor Areas Arming Against Crime," *The New York Times* (April 23, 1990), p. B1.

1207. Jane Gross, "Bystander Deaths Reshape City Lives," *The New York Times* (August 12, 1990), p. 18.

1208. Associated Press, "Police Scrutinize Store Owner Who's Killed 5 in Self-Defense," *San Jose Mercury News* (February 23, 1992), p. 8B.

1209. Carl Goldfarb, "Wynwood Firm Rises from Ashes," *Miami Herald* (June 4, 1991), p. 1B.

1210. Rogers Worthington, "Violent Society Blamed for 'Crimes of Fashion,' " *San Jose Mercury News* (January 26, 1992), p. 4A.

1211. "No Room at the Prisons," *The Economist* (August 1, 1987), p. 30. Ellen Joan Pollock and Milo Geyelin, "U.S. Incarceration Rate Highest," *The Wall Street Journal* (January 7, 1991), p. B5.

1212. Jay Edward Simkin, "Control Criminals, Not Guns," *The Wall Street Journal* (March 25, 1991), p. A10.

1213. Rex Smith, "New York's Prison Boom," *Newsday* (New York) (October 8, 1990), p. 14.

1214. Roberto Suro, "As Inmates Are Freed, Houston Feels Insecure," *The New York Times* (October 1, 1990), p. A16.

1215. "Justice System Floundering in Philadelphia," *Omaha World-Herald* (August 16, 1990).

1216. Stephen Labaton, "Glutted Probation System Puts Communities in Peril," *The New York Times* (June 19, 1990), p. A1.

1217. Associated Press, "Capital Led the Nation in '88 Justice Spending," *The New York Times* (July 16, 1990), p. A11.

1218. Gene Koretz, ". . . But There's No Mistake About Exploding Jail Costs," *Business Week* (March 18, 1991), p. 20.

1219. Tom Kando, "L.A. Debate—Police Are Also Victims," *The Wall Street Journal* (March 19, 1991), p. A24.

1220. Dean Chang, "U.S. Funds for Cops?" *The New York Times* (September 17, 1990), p. 3.

1221. See page 319.

1222. Isabel Wilkerson, " 'Crack House' Fire: Justice or Vigilantism?" *The New York Times* (October 22, 1988), p. A1.

1223. Alan Gathright, "Critically Needed Backup Falls to the Moonlighters," *San Jose Mercury News* (July 10, 1989), p. 1A.

1224. Jeffrey Schmalz, "Trial Forces Miami to Confront Its Legacy of Racial Tensions," *The New York Times* (November 13, 1989), p. A1.

1225. Jeffrey Schmalz, "Fearful and Angry Floridians Erect Street Barriers to Crime," *The New York Times* (December 6, 1988), p. 1.

1226. Karl Zinsmeister, "Growing Up Scared," *The Atlantic* (June 1990), p. 51.

1227. Anastasia Toufexis, "Our Violent Kids," *Time* (June 12, 1989), p. 16.

1228. Felicia Lee, "New York City's Schools See Crime Rising in Lower Grades," *The New York Times* (April 24, 1990), p. A1.

1229. John Kifner, "How to Stop Dis from Escalating into Bif and Bam," *The New York Times* (June 2, 1990).

1230. Wilson and Herrnstein, *Crime and Human Nature,* p. 425.

1231. Carolyn Lochhead, "The Radical Era's Legacy: A Class Snared in Penury," *Insight* (April 3, 1989), p. 16.

1232. Kando, "L.A. Debate," p. A24.

1233. "Where Crime Breeds," *The Economist* (August 1, 1987), p. 30.

1234. Susan Watson, "Homicide Reaps City's Young," *Detroit News* (October 6, 1990), p. 1A.

1235. Michael Abramowitz, "Homicide Top Killer of D.C. Children," *Washington Post* (March 1, 1989), p. B1.

1236. Associated Press, "22,244 Youths Fatally Injured in '86, CDC Says," *Arizona Daily Star* (July 7, 1990), p. 14A.

1237. Michael Dorgan, "Assault Rifles Rip Flesh, Hospital Budgets," *San Jose Mercury News* (January 23, 1989), p. 1.

1238. Mike Royko, "Army Should Go Beyond L.A. with Its Docs," *Omaha World-Herald* (November 9, 1989).

1239. Jesse Katz, "Hospitals Caught in Crossfire," *Los Angeles Times* (November 4, 1991), p. A1.

1240. Tamar Lewin, "Gunshots Cost Hospitals $429 Million, Study Says," *The New York Times* (November 29, 1988), p. A8. "Who Pays the Bill," *The Economist* (March 18, 1989), p. 27.

1241. See page 322.

1242. David Gergen, "Drugs and White America," *U.S. News & World Report* (September 18, 1989), p. 79.

1243. Jane Gross, "Emergency Room: A Crack Nightmare," *The New York Times* (August 6, 1989), p. A1.

1244. Richard Price, "Gangs Are Overrunning L.A.," *Detroit News* (December 26, 1990), p. 7B.

1245. Mark Thompson, "L.A.'s Black Poor Demand Law and Order," *The Wall Street Journal* (May 23, 1989).

1246. Associated Press, "Medical Emergencies for Addicts Are Said to Have Dropped by 20%," *The New York Times* (May 15, 1990), p. A20.

1247. "Good-bye, Cocaine," *The Economist* (September 8, 1990), p. 28.

1248. David Anderson, "The Crack Leap in Washington," *The New York Times* (May 9, 1990), p. A30.

1249. "Stats Show Decline in Crack Use," *Newsday* (New York) (October 11, 1990), p. 25.

1250. "Hello, Heroin," *The Economist* (September 8, 1990), p. 33.

1251. Felicia Lee, "Can A Change in Rules Alter Young Lives?," *The New York Times* (March 11, 1990), p. E22.

1252. Krystal Miller, "School Dress Codes Aim to Discourage Clothing Robberies," *The Wall Street Journal* (April 5, 1990), p. A1.

1253. Karl Zinsmeister, "Growing Up Scared," *The Atlantic* (June 1990), p. 61.

1254. Associated Press, "N.Y. School Kids Get Police Escort," *Mainichi Daily News* (Tokyo) (May 10, 1990), p. 4.

1255. Robert McFadden, "In Debate Over Security in Schools, System's Diversity Keeps Solutions Elusive," *The New York Times* (March 2, 1992), p. B3.

1256. Karl Zinsmeister, "Growing Up Scared," *The Atlantic* (June 1990), p. 65.

1257. Chapin Wright, "Dinkins Tackles School Violence," *Newsday* (New York) (March 12, 1992), p. 4.

1258. Jospeh Berger, "Ferocity of Youth Violence Is Up, a School Official Says," *The New York Times* (November 11, 1989), p. L31.

1259. Jackson Toby, "To Get Rid of Guns in Schools, Get Rid of Some Students," *The Wall Street Journal* (March 3, 1992), p. A14. N. R. Kleinfield, "Where a Youth Program Maintains a Burial Fund," *The New York Times* (February 27, 1992), p. B2.

1260. Mark Mooney, "Pol's Son Runs for His Life," *The New York Post* (September 11, 1990), p. 4.

1261. Stuart Marques, "Sex, Drugs Near P.S. 76 in Queens," *New York Daily News* (October 23, 1990). Paul La Rosa, "Prison of Fear," *New York Daily News* (October 14, 1990), p. 3.

1262. Paul La Rosa, "Garden of Evil," New York *Daily News* (October 7, 1990), p. 3.

1263. Joelle Attinger, "The Decline of New York," *Time* (September 17, 1990), p. 39.

1264. Don Broderick, "Tot, 3, Packs Loaded Gun to Nursery School," *New York Post* (December 6, 1990), p. 3.

1265. Seth Mydans, "Bullets as Well as Blackboards: Children Learn Lessons of 90s," *The New York Times* (June 16, 1991), p. 14.

1266. Seth Mydans, "On Guard Against Gangs at a Los Angeles School," *The New York Times* (November 19, 1989), p. A1.

1267. Seth Mydans, "Bullets as Well as Blackboards," p. 14.

1268. Anemona Hartocollis, "School Violence Felt Nationwide," *Newsday* (New York) (February 28, 1992), p. 27.

1269. "Crime Draws Some of the Lines in Blueprints for Schools," *New York Times* (March 6, 1991), p. B8.

1270. Ann V. Bollinger, "TB Alert: No One Is Safe," *New York Post* (October 15, 1990), p. 4. "Keeping TB Under Control," *New York Post* (October 22, 1990), p. 16.

1271. Jean Latz Griffin, "TB Makes a Deadly Comeback," *Chicago Tribune* (February 20, 1992), p. 4.

1272. Chris Spolar, "D.C.'s Problems Spill into Libraries' Hushed Realm," *Washington Post* (June 8, 1989), p. A1.

1273. Dan Holly, "I-395 to Remain Half-Lit," *Miami Herald* (February 2, 1992), p. 1B.

1274. Elijah Anderson, "Neighborhood Effects on Teenage Pregnancy" in Christopher Jencks and Paul Peterson, eds., *The Urban Underclass* (Washington, D.C.: The Brookings Institution, 1991), pp. 375–98.

1275. Carolyn Lochhead, "Poor Neighborhoods Fall to a Widening Decay," *Insight* (April 3, 1989), p. 11.

1276. Mortimer Zuckerman, "Mentioning the Unmentionable," *U.S. New & World Report* (June 4, 1990), p. 82.

1277. "The Toni Award," *The New Republic* (June 19, 1989), p. 9.

1278. Art Pine, "Riots Renew Debate on Antipoverty Efforts," *Los Angeles Times* (May 5, 1992), p. 1.

1279. "More Spending on the Poor," *The Wall Street Journal* (May 8, 1992), p. A8.

1280. William Bennett, "The Moral Origins of the Urban Crisis," *The Wall Street Journal* (May 8, 1992), p. A8.

1281. See page 332.

1282. Arthur Jensen, "Spearsman's g and the Problem of Educational Equality," *Oxford Review of Education*, Vol. 17, No. 2 (1991), p. 174ff.

1283. Barbara Kantrowitz, "A Head Start Does Not Last," *Newsweek* (January 27, 1992), p. 44.

1284. Joseph Berger, "Dropout Plans Not Working, Study Finds," *The New York Times* (May 15, 1990), p. B1.

1285. Joseph Berger, "Costly Special Classes Serve Many with Minimal Needs," *The New York Times* (April 30, 1991), p. A1.

1286. Charles Murray, "The Coming of Custodial Democracy," *Commentary* (September 1988), p. 24.

1287. Irving Kristol, "Cries of 'Racism' Cow Crime Fighters," *The Wall Street Journal* (February 28, 1989).

1288. William Rusher, "Ambush in the Drug War," *Washington Post* (May 19, 1989), p. F3.

1289. "Delaware Bill Would Restore Whipping Post," *The New York Times* (January 29, 1989).

1290. Mike Royko, "Advice to Women Out at Night: Carry a Gun," *San Jose Mercury News* (November 9, 1989), p. 7B.

1291. Gordon Crovitz, "A Chief Justice Makes the Case for Vigilantism," *The Wall Street Journal* (December 12, 1990), p. A17.

1292. Ed Foster-Simeon, "Parents of Misdoers Can Get the Hoosegow," *Washington Times* (August 1989), p. E1. Karen Diegmueller, "Punishing Parents for Actions of their Wayward Children," *Insight* (October 16, 1989), p. 18.

1293. Kenneth Bacon, "Many Educators View Involved Parents as Key to Children's Success in School," *The Wall Street Journal* (July 31, 1990), p. B1.

1294. Ray Kerrison, "Time Mag Portrays Our City as Hell," *New York Post* (September 12, 1990), p. 4.

1295. "School Study Assails New York Failure Rate," *The New York Times* (July 24, 1990), p. B4.

1296. William Tucker, *Vigilante*, p. 170.

1297. Lawrence Auster, "The Regents' Round Table," *National Review* (December 8, 1989), p. 18ff.

1298. Carol Innerst, "New York School Reports Assails Western Culture," *Washington Times* (January 2, 1990), p. A1.

1299. Albert Shanker, "Incentives for Attendance," *The Wall Street Journal* (April 8, 1990), p. E8.

1300. Suzanne Alexander, "For Some Students, the Value of Learning Is Measured in Pizzas and Parking Passes," *The Wall Street Journal* (January 29, 1992), p. B1.

1301. Mary Jane McKay, "Paying Parents to Help," *The New York Times*, Education Section (November 4, 1990), p. 12.

1302. Deborah L. Cohen, "Milwaukee School to Pay Parents for Attending Workshops," *Education Week* (October 31, 1990), p. 5.

1303. "A Pecuniary Payoff for Prenatal Care," *Insight* (February 26, 1990), p. 57.

1304. Harmeet Singh, "To Lower Infant Mortality Rate, Get Mothers Off Drugs," *The Wall Street Journal* (May 1, 1990), p. A18.

1305. Nicholas Eberstadt, "America's Infant Mortality Problem: Parents," *The Wall Street Journal* (January 20, 1992).

1306. "Compassionate Prenatal Care," *Boston Globe* (July 20, 1990), p. 10.

1307. Noel Perrin, "Paying Kids Not to Get Pregnant," *Washington Post* (July 8, 1990).

1308. Eugene Meyer, "Rural Official's Idea for Discouraging Teen Births: Cash," *Washington Post* (May 3, 1990), p. C1.

1309. Spencer Rich, "The Underclass: Beyond Just Poor," *Washington Post* (June 26, 1989), p. A9.

1310. "College Reaching Out to Serve Its Neighbors," *The New York Times* (January 7, 1990), p. 35.

1311. Karl Zinsmeister, "Growing Up Scared," *The Atlantic* (June 1990), p. 54.

1312. "Is Sterilization the Answer?" *Newsweek* (August 8, 1988), p. 59.

1313. Karen Diegmueller, "Punishing Parents for Actions of Their Wayward Children," *Insight* (October 16, 1989), p. 19.

1314. Douglas Besharov, "Crack Babies: The Worst Threat Is Mom Herself," *Washington Post* (August 6, 1989), p. B1.

1315. Isabel Wilkerson, "Women Cleared After Drug Use in Pregnancy," *The New York Times* (April 3, 1991), p. A15.

1316. Jane Gross, "Grandmothers Bear a Burden Sired by Drugs," *The New York Times* (April 9, 1989), p. A1.

1317. See page 342.

1318. "Where Your Welfare Dollars Go," *The Council Reporter* (St. Louis, Mo.), Vol. 6, No. 1, p. 3.

1319. Donald G. McNeil, "Challenging Dinkins Over the Homeless," *The New York Times* (February 2, 1992), Sec. 4, p. 18.

1320. "Sparing a Dime," *The Economist* (August 19, 1991), p. 24.

1321. William Galston, "Home Alone," *The New Republic* (December 2, 1991), p. 43.

1322. See page 348.

1323. Johns Hopkins University, "Population Reports," Series K, No. 3, (March–April 1987). "The Five-Year Contraceptive," *American Health* (September 1989), p. 17. Andrew Purvis, "A Pill That Gets Under the Skin," *Time* (December 24, 1990), p. 66.

1324. See page 349.

1325. Tamar Lewin, "A Plan to Pay Welfare Mothers for Birth Control," *The New York Times* (February 9, 1991), p. 9.

1326. See page 349.

1327. See page 351.

1328. Lee Rainwater and William Yancey, *The Moynihan Report and the Politics of Controversy* (Cambridge, Mass.: The M.I.T. Press, 1967), p. 55 and *passim.*

1329. Alex Jones, "An Editorial Stirs a Newsroom Feud," *The New York Times* (December 21, 1990).

1330. Margie Fienberg, "3 P.M. Bell Sparks Subway Hell on Wheels," *New York Post* (November 2, 1989), p. 4.

1331. Ze'ev Chafets, *Devil's Night: And Other True Tales of Detroit* (New York: Random House, 1990), p. 4.

1332. See page 352.

1333. Gina Kolata, "In Cities, Poor Families Are Dying of Crack," *The New York Times* (August 11, 1989), p. A1.

1334. Margaret Trimer, "Theater Shootings Mirror Film's Action," *Detroit Free Press* (November 20, 1989), p. A1.

1335. Audrey Edwards and Craig Polite, *Children of the Dream* (New York: Doubleday, 1992), pp. 241, 273.

1336. See, e.g., Playthell Benjamin, "The Attitude Is the Message," *Village Voice* (August 15, 1989), p. 23ff.

1337. Quoted in Clarence Page, "Sending the Right Signals to Students," *Los Angeles Times* (December 18, 1990).

1338. Alexis de Tocqueville, *Democracy in America,* trans. George Lawrence (Garden City, N.Y.: Doubleday, 1966), pp. 357–61.

1339. James McPherson, "Slavery and Race," *Perspectives in American History,* Vol. III (Cambridge, Mass.: Harvard University Press, 1969), p. 470.

Index

DATE DUE

Demco, Inc. 38-293